ISBN 978-1-396-45465-3
PIBN 11252191

THE
BIBLE IN WALES

Cardiff, Wales. Free libraries.

A Study in the History of the Welsh
People, with an Introductory Address
and a Bibliography.

LONDON:

HENRY SOTHERAN & CO.,
140 Strand & 130 Piccadilly.

1906.

SIX HUNDRED COPIES PRINTED FOR
THE LIBRARIES COMMITTEE OF THE CARDIFF CORPORATION
AT REES' ELECTRIC PRINTING WORKS,
PLYMOUTH STREET, CARDIFF,
SEPTEMBER, 1906.

PREFACE.

FOR the centenary year of the British and Foreign Bible Society, 1904, the Committee of the Cardiff Public Libraries decided to bring together for exhibition in the Reference Library as many editions as could be procured of the Scriptures in Welsh, or in other languages if printed in Wales. The proposal was enthusiastically approved, and loans from public and private collections were liberally offered, with the result that almost every edition of the Scriptures coming within the scope of the exhibition was obtained. The exhibition was open from March 1st to September 30th, 1904, and was visited by a large number of people.

A desire to permanently record the knowledge thus acquired led to the preparation of this volume. It was found that while the editions up to 1800 had been frequently described (not always accurately), yet no account had been given of the issues of the nineteenth century. The work of collecting and verifying the information proved a lengthier task than was anticipated, and delayed the completion of the work.

It should be noted that the Bibliography was printed first, although it appears last in the volume. In a few cases fuller information has led to the modification or the discarding of some of the notes in the Bibliography. When, therefore, there is a divergence between the facts as stated in the historical essay and in the Bibliography, the former represents the revised position.

So many willing helpers have contributed to the production of this work that it is impossible to enumerate all. I am grateful, and assure them that I am fully sensible of the fact that without their help this book could not have existed. To Sir John Williams, Bart.; Mr. J. H. Davies, M.A., of Cwrtmawr; Mr. Henry Blackwell, of New York; Mr. H. F. Moule, M.A., Librarian of the British and Foreign Bible Society's Library; and the Rev. Thomas Shankland, Welsh Librarian of Bangor University College, my thanks are especially due for valuable help continuously given, and to the Cardiff Libraries Committee for the generous way in which they have encouraged every step. The materials for the Bibliography were collated and arranged by Mr. James Ifano Jones, Chief Assistant in the Reference Library. I am responsible for the historical survey.

I am fully aware that in this attempt to bring into order the Bibliography of the Welsh Bible there are omissions and possibly errors. A note of any additions or corrections will at all times be welcome.

THE CENTRAL LIBRARY,   JOHN BALLINGER.
    CARDIFF,

12th September, 1906.

CONTENTS.

List of Illustrations.

EXPLANATORY NOTES.

Every *recorded* edition down to 1900 appears in the Bibliography.
The *date* stands before each entry.

The *title* in all early editions is given *verbatim et literatim*. Where no title was accessible, the substance of such title is given within square brackets. Any words in a " Description " printed in italics stand for a literal transcript.

In the line following the title are given the *printer* (or *publisher*), the *place*, and the *date*, unless these have been already supplied in the title. When they are not found anywhere in the book itself, but ascertained from other ·sources, they are enclosed within square brackets. When they are conjectural, a query-mark is added.

The letters, 𝕭.𝕷., commencing the next line, indicate that the book is printed in *black-letter*—" English," or " Gothic " type.

The same line contains the *size-mark*—f°, 4°, 8°, etc., standing for *folio*, *quarto*, *octavo*, etc.—with the number of pages to the forme or sheet enclosed within round brackets. (Size-marks are often used inaccurately). Also, the dimensions of the *printed page* and of the *leaf* are given both in millimeters and inches, subject, in the case of the latter, to binder's cutting.

In the *description* of certain editions, "preliminary" leaves (or pages) mean all those which precede the actual text. A full register of signatures is given, together with the total number of leaves (or pages) in the book whenever the leaves (or pages) are not numbered. When they are, in ordinary editions, the signatures are not given. Unless the contrary is stated, A—Z indicates the normal signature-alphabet of 23 letters—A B C D E F G H I (or J) K L M N O P Q R S T V (or U) X Y Z. The recto of a leaf is indicated by *a*, the verso by *b*. In ordinary editions only such details are given as suffice for identification.

With the exception of the respective versions of William Myddeltori, Edward Kyffin and Edmund Prys, metrical versions of the Psalms have not been recorded as editions of the Scripture. But the following pages show how often Prys's version occurs bound up with copies of the Bible or New Testament.

The number that closes an entry is that assigned to the edition in the Bibliography for purposes of reference.

Dutxe

...ght worshippfull my humble remembred ew. I am glad ...
your late recouerye & present health w... I befeeche ...
... to continue to his glorye & ye good of ... countri ...
royce mee not a litle when I understood ... your w... ...
as inquifitive whether ye pfalmes are translated ...
... tounge or not I fent you by your man ...
... them y are printed hee had finished fome fiftye ...
... hee dyed this tyme feuen yeares in ye tyme of y ...
... he departed this worlde in his custodye when ...
... ye co ... I left your proberbs ye pfalmes and ...
... tree ... of me pertymes with other good thin ...
... ittishe tounge wch weare all lost and gone by ...
... I could neuer heare nor learne where an ...
... beftowed I often enqyred but could not lea ...
... and by whofe meanes they weare confaighe ...
... heare not of any that are about ye pfalmes fone ou ...
... who promifed them longe agone fit as yet ho ...
... his pmis nor I expecland of mo ...
... heere bookes woorthy your realmge g prefent ...
... worshippe with a litle treatis written by a greate ...
... fecretarye to y late Philipp of Spayne ...
... Brittania his laft edition with ye mappes of a ...
... lately printed and bounde in follio & thus humbly ...
... defiringe ye lorde to guide & protect ...
... tuous ladye and all your religious and well ...
... with all bleffinges externall in this prefe ...
... in y other to come with all bleffinges ...
... houfe in cloth foyer in London: Iune y ...

... my ladye to beftowe
... deinge of my litle booke

... our worshippes m ...
... feruice readye
... Tho Galesbur

Tho. X Salesbury
to —
Sir John Wynn, Knight,
Gwydir.

X Editor of Capt. Middle-
ton's Metrical Version
of the Psalms, printed
1603.

To the right worll. Sr:
John Gwynne knight
att his house in
Gwydir these
Deliver

Rhann o Psalmau Dafydd
Brophwyd, iw canu ar ol y
dôn arferedig yn Eglwys
Legr. Simon Stafford ai
printiodd dros Thomas
Salesbury yn Llundain,
1603.

Mr. Preston's Coll^n. M.S. Vol. 41.

ADDRESS

BY

SIR JOHN WILLIAMS, BART.,

At the opening of the Exhibition of Printed Scriptures in Welsh in the Cardiff Reference Library, 1st March, 1904.

WE are here to-day to open this Exhibition of Welsh Bibles, in which are to be found examples of almost every edition of the Sacred Volume published between the year 1567, when Salesbury's Testament Newydd was first issued, and the year 1900. It is an exhibition the like of which has never been seen before. We owe it to the energy and organising power of the genius of this Library—John Ballinger.

It would be out of place for me to make a long speech, but it would not be inappropriate to the occasion were I to make some reference to the efforts made in the past to supply the Welsh people with the Scriptures in their own language, as well as to the special event which has given rise to this exhibition.

The first Welsh Bible was published in the year 1588. For many years before that time William Salesbury had been engaged in translating portions of it, especially parts of the New Testament ; for in the year 1551, nearly forty years before the first appearance of the Welsh Bible, he published a book called "Kynniver llith a ban," which consists of the Epistles and the Gospels as they are found in the Book of Common Prayer. Before this time—the year 1551—the only portions of the Scriptures which had appeared in print in the Welsh language were the Lord's Prayer, the Ten Commandments, and two or three verses from the New Testament, which are to be found in " Yny lhyvyr hwnn " by Sir John Prys, published in the year 1546—five years before the appearance of Salesbury's " Kynniver llith a ban." It is clear that Salesbury was engaged in translating the New Testament, or those portions of it which are in the Book of Common Prayer, some time before the year 1551. He completed the work, and published the New Testament in Welsh for the first time in the year 1567. Nine years before this Mary had died, and Elizabeth became Queen. Being of the Reformed Church, and mindful of the spiritual needs of her subjects in Wales, it was enacted by her Parliament in the fifth year of her reign (1563) that the Bible should be translated into Welsh, under the supervision of the four Welsh Bishops and the Bishop of Hereford : and that a copy of it should be placed in every Cathedral, Collegiate, and Parish Church, and Chapel of Ease throughout Wales, by the first day of March, 1566, under a penalty of forty pounds in case of failure, to be levied on each of the said Bishops. Unfortunately, the Bishops, with one exception—whose name should be ever kept in remembrance, Richard Davies, Bishop of St. David's—proved themselves to be passive resisters, whether by reason of conscientious objection, incompetence, indifference, or other cause, I leave to the historian of the period to discover. The Act was not obeyed. The consequence of this disobedience was that the Welsh were without a Bible for 25 years after the enactment

b

of Elizabeth, and 22 years after every Church and Chapel of Ease in the Principality should by law have been in possession of the Sacred Book.

As I have already said, Salesbury had been engaged for many years upon a translation of the New Testament and had completed it in 1566, for it was published in the following year. As far as is known, no steps had been hitherto taken to translate the whole of the Scriptures into Welsh; but about this time, or perhaps a few years later, William Morgan, Vicar of Llanrhaiadr Mochnant (a parish among the hills of Denbighshire), began upon the task. This parish seems to have an inspiring atmosphere, for Wales is indebted to others of its incumbents for valuable services rendered to Welsh literature, but to none of them in the same degree as it is to William Morgan. It does not appear that William Morgan undertook the great work in consequence of the Act of Parliament, nor of commands from the Queen, nor of the prayers of the Bishops, but rather that he was impelled to it by a deep sense of the needs of his countrymen. After having overcome many difficulties —money and other, he published his translation of the whole of the Old Testament and Apocrypha, together with an improved version of Salesbury's New Testament, in the year 1588. The number of copies printed is uncertain. It has been estimated at 500, and also at 1,000. The larger number would be sufficient to supply every Church in the Principality with a copy.

Thirty-two years elapsed before the second edition appeared in 1620. This was the work of Bishop Parry, and is our Authorised Version. Of this edition it is probable that 1,000 copies were printed. Both Morgan and Parry's Bibles were large volumes, suitable for Churches, and up to this time no Bibles suitable for the home or for the pocket had been printed. Ten years more had to pass away, and the people—the laity—had to become alive to the religious needs of the country before such a boon was obtained. In the year 1630 two Welshmen resident in London, Sir Thomas Middleton and Rowland Heylin, published an edition (believed to be about 1,500 copies) of a small Bible, at the price of five shillings. This is Vicar Prichard's "Beibl bach." After the publication of this, the "Beibl bach," seventeen years elapsed before any part of the Scriptures was again published, when, in the year 1647, Vavasor Powel and Walter Cradoc issued 1,000 copies of the New Testament. This was the first New Testament suitable for the pocket, and one of the first fruits of the experience of the "Itinerant Preacher." This edition was published when the war between King Charles and the Parliament was drawing to its final stages, and we consequently miss the name of the King's Printer on the title-page. The fact that the right of publishing the Scriptures was invested in the King's Printers alone had until this period, and for a long time after the Restoration, added to the difficulty of printing and publishing Welsh Bibles; and this difficulty was not entirely overcome until towards the end of the eighteenth century. Before the year 1654—the early part of the Commonwealth—on the most favourable estimate, only 3,500 Bibles and 1,000 New Testaments in addition to that of Salesbury, had been published. This meant about one Bible to every 70 of the inhabitants. In the year 1653 Oliver Cromwell became Lord Protector, and during the first year of his sway 6,000 copies of the Bible, known as "Beibl Cromwel," were issued by Vavasor Powel and Walter Cradoc. It is said that Cromwell contributed towards the cost of this edition. Whether this be a fact or not, it is clear from other circumstances that the Protector was mindful of the religious affairs of the Principality.

From this time on, the Scriptures were published at shorter intervals, and in greater numbers. In 1672 Stephen Hughes, the "Apostle of Carmarthenshire," published an edition of 2,000 Testaments, and six years afterwards another of 8,000 Bibles and 1,000 New Testaments; and in another eleven years a third of 10,000 copies of the Bible. In this great work he was assisted by Archbishop Tillotson, Thomas Gouge, Bishop Thomas, Calamy, and others. Here we see the first indication of co-operation in the work of supplying Bibles for Wales, and the suggestion of a Society for printing and distributing religious literature.

Parting with Stephen Hughes, we welcome another patriot—Moses Williams, to whom we owe an incalculable debt, not only for the literature which he supplied to, but also for that which he preserved for Wales. He issued two editions of the Bible, together numbering 15,000 copies. These were followed by two editions, each 15,000 copies, by Richard Morris—a member of a family of whose services to Welsh literature the inhabitants of the country have a keen if not a sufficient appreciation. The four editions—those of Moses Williams and those of Richard Morris—were published by the Society for Promoting Christian Knowledge.

One more edition, that of John Evans, of Portsmouth, consisting of 20,000 copies, appeared before it was discovered how to publish Bibles without infringing upon the rights of the King's Printers. This discovery was made and put in practice by Peter Williams in 1770, when he published " Y Beibl Sanctaidd, gyd a Nodau a Sylwiadau ar bob Pennod." The "Nodau a Sylwiadau" formed a protection for him from any attacks on the part of the King's Printers of greater efficacy than mail would have been to him in warfare: Peter Williams and his Bible became as popular in Wales and as necessary to the family as Vicar Prichard and his "Canwyll" had been, for about 38 editions of the work have been published.

In 1790 Peter Williams and David Jones issued the Bible of John Canne in Welsh. This passed through several editions.

Now we come to the period at which the B. & F. Bible Society was founded, the centenary of which this exhibition is designed to celebrate—a Society which during the 100 years of its existence has done more than any other, and perhaps than all other agencies which preceded it, to spread a knowledge of the Bible, not only in Wales and the United Kingdom, but throughout the whole world.

I cannot speak of all that this Society has accomplished, but I should like to refer to its origin and to that apparently trifling episode which gave the impulse to form it—the desire of Mari Jones for a Welsh Bible.

Mari Jones was a poor Welsh maid, living at the foot of Cader Idris, near Dolgelly, who had some knowledge of the Bible, which made her desirous of possessing a Bible of her own. The nearest copy of it was at a house two miles distant from her little home, and there was no copy on sale nearer than Bala—25 miles away; and it was by no means certain that a copy could be obtained there. This tells us how scarce Welsh Bibles were even at that comparatively recent period. Having saved a little money to pay for the book, she started one morning for Bala, and walked the 25 miles with bare feet. The following morning she called upon Thomas Charles, of whom alone Bibles could be bought. To her dismay, Mr. Charles told her that all the copies which he had received were sold or bespoken. This caused the child the deepest sorrow ; her grief was distressing, her appeals pitiable, so much so that Thomas Charles, unable to resist her entreaties, spared her one of the copies already promised. The little maid's face beamed again; she dried her tears, and started on her return journey with an inexpressible joy. Interesting as her story is, we will not pursue it further.

The journey of the bare-footed maid to Bala is the cause of our meeting here to-day, for it was that journey that impelled Thomas Charles to propose to the Council of the Religious Tract Society to form a Society to supply Wales with Bibles, whereupon Joseph Hughes said, " If a Society for Wales, why not a Society for the whole Kingdom and for the whole world?" And the British and Foreign Bible Society was established. The name of Mari Jones is written on that rôle of heroines whereon are the names of the little Hebrew maid, and the widow whose all was two half-farthings. Mari Jones is the presiding genius here to-day. I almost hear her whisper, " Beibl i bawb o bobl y byd."

I have touched upon some points in the history of the Welsh Bible, but there is another story which appeals to us in a very touching manner, and that is the story of individual volumes in the show cases.

What would the Librarian not give for the New Testament which Salesbury kept for his own use at Caedu ? or the Bible which Bishop Morgan used in his study at Llandaff ? What a priceless volume would be the copy of the " Beibl bach," which Vicar Prichard carried with him on his preaching tours, with notes in it telling the story of itself and its owner ! What valuable copies would those be which were the daily companions of Stephen Hughes, Daniel Rowlands, Howell Harris, and especially that little volume which was the inspiration of William Williams's ever-living hymns ! But, although none of these volumes are here, there are a few whose story should not be lost. The Bible of Moses Williams is here—that grand patriot when Welsh patriotism was not so fashionable as it is to-day, fired by the example of the old Hebrew to preserve the literature of his race. Here is the pocket Bible of Richard Morris—a copy of " Beibl Cromwel " with his notes, presumably for the edition of the Bible which he published. Here is also the working Bible of that great preacher, John Jones, Talysarn. Here is " Beibl Mari Jones," the volume she bought of Mr. Charles on her epoch-making visit to Bala in 1800.

We cannot help regretting the paucity of the histories of individual volumes, as well as the scarcity of certain Welsh books. How is it that so few of the books—the personal possessions of the men I have referred to—cannot be found now ? How have they disappeared or become so scarce ? I used to think that it was the result of carelessness and neglect, and perhaps of consignment to the flames; and this is doubtless true in some degree, but it is not the whole truth. Some months ago I took a parcel of books to the binder. They had seen better days, and wanted a new suit. They did not look very respectable, and I attributed their condition to neglect and abuse ; but my eyes were opened to the cause of it by the binder, who expressed his admiration for the use which had been made of them, adding that he rarely saw English books which showed signs of having done such service. Their condition was not the result of neglect and illtreatment, as I had supposed, but of the attention which they had commanded, and the service which they had rendered. I felt proud of my ragged company as well as of my country-men.

What will be the future of the individuals forming this exhibition ? What will become of these rare volumes which Mr. Ballinger has brought together ? They will be dispersed in a few months. Will they ever be brought together again ? Of what use will they be in the future ? What service will they do for Wales ? Or will they pass in to the .rooms of the auctioneer for the purpose of mere exchange, and be dispersed the world over ? ˙Many of them have come here from private libraries, and it is often the fate of such libraries to end their existence in the auction-room. Should this happen to any of the libraries from which exhibits have been kindly lent for this exhibition, I trust that there will be found Welshmen patriotic enough to secure and preserve them for their country. Others again are from public libraries, or at least libraries which are in a sense the property of the nation, and are not likely to come under the hammer ; while others again, although they belong to private owners, will be deposited in public libraries, and so assured to Wales. It is of the greatest importance that these relics of the past shall be secured for the nation, because of the light which they throw upon the mental and religious history and upon the language of the Principality. I sincerely hope that this exhibition will not only arouse greater interest in the Society whose centenary it is designed to celebrate, but that it will also kindle a love for our literature in the past, which will at all cost ensure its preservation for future ages.

QUEEN ELIZABETH'S PATENT, 1563, TO WILLIAM SALESBURY AND JOHN WALEY FOR THE EXCLUSIVE PRINTING OF THE SCRIPTURES IN WELSH FOR SEVEN YEARS.

From the MS. in the British Museum.

THE BIBLE IN WALES.

CHAPTER I.

THE EARLY TRANSLATIONS.

Early translations of portions of Scripture into Welsh—The movement for translating the Prayer Book and the Bible—The Prayer Book and the New Testament of 1567—The whole Bible of 1588.

To understand rightly the history and character of the Welsh people, it is essential to study their religious history, because religion has influenced Welsh life and thought more than anything else, and no people, during the last three hundred years, has clung more closely to the Bible than the Welsh.

An account of the circulation of the Bible in Wales must therefore throw considerable light upon the progress of civilisation in Wales ; and it was to contribute to a knowledge of the forces which have made the Welsh people what they are to-day that the proposal to hold an exhibition of the Scriptures in Welsh was first put forward. A desire to place on record in a permanent form the knowledge so gained led to the preparation of this volume.

Many attempts have been made from time to time to tell the story of the Welsh Bible. Some deal only with the sixteenth and seventeenth centuries, while none carry the story much beyond 1800. The first of these attempts was made by Moses Williams, Vicar of Devynnock, and the manuscript of it is now preserved amongst the Shirburn MSS. belonging to Sir John Williams, Bart. Moses Williams's account does not appear to have been printed during his lifetime, but it formed the basis of Dr. Thomas Llewelyn's " Account of the British or Welsh versions and editions of the Bible," London, 1768. Dr. Llewelyn wrongly ascribes the MS. from which he gleaned all his facts to Richard Morris, who transcribed the MS. of Moses Williams, adding notes of his own. The transcript is in the British Museum (Add. MSS. 14952).

In Wales it is quite a common thing to find in cottages three, four, or more Bibles. Quartos and folios of the late eighteenth and early nineteenth centuries are to be found in nearly every Welsh household, often several different issues. These are not merely kept for show, but bear marks of having been read regularly for generations. The quarto Bibles of Peter Williams are the most used of any; the folios of Peter Williams, Samuel Clark, and others, are not so much used.

The question what translations of the Scriptures into Welsh existed prior to those recorded in the Bibliography which forms a later section of this work, is one which does not come within our scope. We propose to confine ourselves to the printed Welsh Scriptures. The existence of Welsh translations in MS. before the appearance of the first New Testament in 1567 has been dealt with by Archdeacon Thomas in his invaluable book on " The Life and Work of Bishop Davies and William Salesbury," Oswestry, 1902.

The earliest known printed Welsh Scriptures before 1567 consist of the Lord's Prayer, the Ten Commandments, and three verses from the New Testament in "Yny lhyvyr hwnn," the earliest known printed Welsh book, edited by Sir John Prys (or Price), and brought out in 1546. Five years later, 1551, William Salesbury brought out the lectionary, "Kynniver llith a ban," containing the Gospels and Epistles for each Sunday and holy-day throughout the year. These two books are of native origin, and indicate the beginning of the movement which culminated in the complete Bible being translated into Welsh.

In 1555 appeared Conrad Gesner's "Mithridates. De Differentiis lingvarvm tvm vetervm, etc.," which gives, among examples of the different languages, the Lord's Prayer as an example of Welsh. The translation is not that printed by Sir John Prys in "Yny lhyvyr hwnn," but an older version, given to Gesner by John Bale, sometime Bishop of Ossory, to whom the "Mithridates" is dedicated. Gesner's work was printed at Zurich, and is the first example known of Welsh being printed outside London. In the same year Gesner printed a sheet (14½" x 13¼") containing the Lord's Prayer in twenty-three languages, Welsh being one. The sheet is dated "Septimo Calendas Septembris" (*i.e.*, Aug. 26), 1555. There is a copy in the University Library, Cambridge. The Welsh version is the same as appears in the "Mithridates" with some press errors corrected. The following is a copy :—

Eyn taad rhwn wyt yn y nefoedd, santeiddier yr henw tau. Deued y dyrnas dau: Gwneler dy wollys, ar y ddayar megis ag yn y nefi. Eyn bara beunyddawl dyro inni heddiw. A maddeu ynny eyn deledion: megis ag i maddeuw in deledwyr ninau. Ag na thowys ni in brofedigaeth, namyn gwared ni rhag drwg. Amen.

The book was re-issued in 1610 with the same version of the Lord's Prayer, and in addition the first five verses of Genesis i. from the Bible of 1588.

In 1561 a Diocesan Council held at St. Asaph ordered that, after the Epistle and Gospel had been read in English, they should be read also in Welsh.* At the same council an order was made for the Catechism in Welsh to be read in each church every Sunday. No copy of the Catechism in Welsh of so early a date is known; it is one of the lost books of Wales, like the "Litany" printed in 1562. The reading of the Epistles and Gospels in Welsh stirred up a longing for the whole Bible in the native tongue, and petitions were prepared and sent to those in authority expressing that longing. A rough draft of a petition to the Bishops of the Welsh Dioceses forms part of the Gwysaney Manuscript.† This petition urges that "it may please your good lordships to wyll and require and com'aund the learned men to traducte the boke of the Lordes Testament into the vulgare walsh tong so by sooch meanes as well the p'achers themselfes as also the multitude of them may be the‡ . . . . together in dew knowledge of their Lordes good wyll."

William Salesbury was the active spirit voicing the earnest desire of his fellow-countrymen to hear the Word of God read in their native language. In the preface to "Oll Synnwyr pen Kembero" he suggests that his countrymen should petition the King's Majesty and His Council that the Scriptures might be translated into Welsh for the sake of those who were not and were never likely to be able to learn English. The efforts put forward by William Salesbury were supported

*Archdeacon Thomas's "Davies and Salesbury," p. 72.
† *Ibid.*, p. 3.
‡ Original defective.

by many eminent men, some of whom had been his contemporaries at Oxford, while others were neighbours in Denbighshire and other parts of North Wales. It is a fact worth notice that in the sixteenth century North Wales, and especially Denbighshire, was the cradle of many of the men who made a mark upon the literary history of Wales. Amongst these friends of Salesbury was Richard Davies, afterwards Bishop of St. Asaph, and later of St. David's. By reason of his position, it is probable that the Bishop was the leader in securing the passing of the Act for the translation of the Prayer Book and the Bible into the Welsh tongue. His zeal for the welfare of his fellow-countrymen was shown in various ways. While Bishop of St. Asaph he was a near neighbour of Salesbury, and also of Gruffydd Hiraethog, Humphrey Lhuyd of Denbigh, William Myddelton (the translator of the Psalms), and several other men of note living within the area. In exile during the reign of Mary, Richard Davies resided at Geneva, in an atmosphere of Biblical translation; and after his return he was one of the Committee appointed to translate the Bishops' Bible. It is not difficult to believe that it was during his brief tenure of the Bishopric of St. Asaph that the plan for the translation into Welsh of the Scriptures and the Prayer Book was agreed upon. The Act V. Elizabeth, chapter 28 (1563) was the outcome. In the same year a patent was granted to "William Salisbury and John Waley" for the sole printing in the Welsh tongue for seven years, of the Bible, the Book of Common Prayer, and the Homilies. (See illustration.)

The translation of the Prayer Book was undertaken by Richard Davies, by this time Bishop of St. David's, and the New Testament by William Salesbury, with the assistance of the Bishop and of Thomas Huet, Precentor of St. David's. Davies and Salesbury worked together, the latter spending much of his time at the Bishop's Palace, Abergwili. The fruit of their labours appeared in 1567. The Prayer Book was issued first, followed later in the same year by the New Testament. The former was re-issued in 1586. Of the 1567 Prayer Book only three copies are recorded—one in the Swansea Public Library, one with Sir John Williams, Bart., and one in private hands. Each copy lacks the titlepage. The detailed description given in the Bibliography is the result of a collation of the three copies. This Prayer Book contains the first printed translation, and, so far as is known, the first translation made into Welsh of all the Psalms. The Epistles and Gospels are not translated from the English Prayer Book, nor are they those of the "Llith a Ban" and of the 1567 New Testament. It would appear that the Bishop, while working with Salesbury on the New Testament, followed his own plan for the translations in the Prayer Book. The use of some words was called in question, and in the 1586 Prayer Book appears "An Explanation of certaine wordes, being quarrelled withall, by some, for that in this translation they be otherwise written, then either the unlettered people or some parts of the countrie sounde, or speake them."

The New Testament of 1567 was undertaken by William Salesbury at the request of the five Bishops (Hereford being included with the four Welsh Dioceses). The Bishop of St. David's (Richard Davies) translated I. Timothy, Hebrews, James, and I. and II. Peter; while the Book of Revelation was done by Thomas Huet, Precentor of St. David's. All the other books were translated by Salesbury, who supplied the notes, alternative readings, and explanatory words in the margins, and the "Argument," taken from the Geneva Bible, prefixed to each book. Salesbury also wrote the dedication to Queen Elizabeth, in English, and an address in Welsh "At yr oll Cembru," in which he writes of Bishop

Davies as " Menevia's second St. David.' The Bishop also wrote an " Epistol at y Cembru," which is printed after the dedication to Elizabeth, and in which he reviews the history of the Church in Wales, and the degradation which followed upon the destruction of the old Welsh books of history and Scripture after the coming of the Normans. He looks forward with hopefulness to the time when the whole of the Scriptures could be read in the Welsh tongue. When this was written the Bishop expected the Old Testament to be translated and printed with the same expedition as the Prayer Book and the New Testament. In his expectation he was disappointed. After working together earnestly and amicably for years, Salesbury and Davies are said to have had a difference about " the general sense and etymology of one word,"[*] which put an end to their friendship. The work on the Old Testament upon which they had entered was never finished, and twenty-one years elapsed between the appearance of the New Testament and that of the whole Bible, which came from quite another source. Bishop Davies had died seven years before, in 1581.

The first issue of the New Testament is a small thick quarto of 426 leaves (852 pages). The title and preliminary matter occupy 24 leaves, the text folios 1 to 401, the last two leaves of the text being unnumbered; the colophon follows on the recto of folio 402, also unnumbered. Some copies contain 4 leaves of corrections, explanations, rules, etc., at the end of the volume. Charles Ashton states[†] that he saw one copy with the colophon on the back of the title ; this, however, requires verification. The title and the Almanack are printed in red and black. A curious woodcut appears on the title in illustration of the text John iii. 19, " This is the condemnation that light is come into the world, and men loved darkness rather than light." For the translation, the text chiefly followed was Beza's edition of 1556, and to a lesser extent the two Stephanic editions of 1550 and 1551, while reference was often made to the Vulgate, the Latin text of Erasmus, Beza's two versions of 1557 and 1560, together with Beza's Annotations on his text, 1565.[‡]

It is not the purpose of this work to enter into any philological or literary details; but some reference may here be made to the difficulties which beset the path of the early translators into Welsh. The Welsh spoken in North Wales differed considerably from that spoken in South Wales, as in a lesser degree it does to-day, and there was no standard that the translators could adopt. Further, the printed literature was scanty and comprised a very much smaller vocabulary than was required for large works such as the Prayer Book and the New Testament. The translators had therefore to compile vocabularies for their own use ; and it is not to be wondered at that criticism was forthcoming of many of the words used and the meanings attached to them. The four leaves of corrections subsequently issued by Salesbury deal not only with the printer's errors, but also explain and defend the use of words in the preliminary addresses by Bishop Davies and by Salesbury, as well as in the text. The books were set by compositors who did not understand a word of Welsh; and having regard to all the circumstances, the existence of printers' errors and of a difference of opinion as to the words used, is not surprising.

The issue of the whole Bible in 1588 superseded the New Testament of Salesbury. The second translator was more successful

---

* Sir John Wynn's " History of the Gwydir Family."

† " Bywyd ac Amserau yr Esgob Morgan," p. 76.

‡ The Rev. Dr. T. C. Edwards, Trans. Liverpool Welsh Nat. Soc.

Testament
Newydd ein Arglwydd
JESV CHRIST.

Gwedy ei dynnu, yd y gadei yꝛ ancyfia=
ith, 'air yn ei gylpdd oꝛ Groec a'r Llatin, gan
newidio ffurf llythyꝛen y gairiae-dodi. Eb law hyny
y mae pop gair a dybitwyt y bot yn andeallns,
ai o ran llediaith y 'wlat, ai o ancynefin-
der y debnydd, wedy ei noti ai eg-
lurhau ar 'ledemyl y tu da-
len gydꝛychiol.

bot golauni ir byt, a' charu o ddynion y tywyllwch

Matheu xⅢ.f.
Gwertbwch a veddwch o rudd
(Ll'yma'r Man lle mae'r modd
Ac mewn banangen vy bydd)
I gaely Perl goel bap wedd.

TITLEPAGE OF FIRST WELSH TESTAMENT, 1567.

in producing a smooth and easily understood book. This, however, does not destroy the fact that the earlier translators by their labours prepared the way, and rendered inestimable services to their countrymen. It is not known how many copies of the Testament were printed. About fifty copies are recorded, and there are probably others which have not come to light. It is a much treasured volume. Many of the copies are in public institutions or kept as heirlooms, reducing the copies which may change hands down to a small number. There is a copy in the ancient library of Hereford Cathedral, chained to the bookcase with the original chain fitted with a swivel in the last link to facilitate the handling of the book. This is the only instance of a copy being chained. The Bishop of Hereford was joined with the four Welsh bishops in the translation act of 1563.

A reprint of the 1567 New Testament was projected in 1819 by Mr. Robert Saunderson, printer, of Bala, but only one part of 48 pages appeared. (See No. 71). It was, however, reprinted in 1850 under the direction of the Rev. Isaac Jones, at the press of James Rees, of Carnarvon. (See No. 188). The publisher was Robert Griffith, of Carnarvon.

The translation of the complete Bible including the Apocrypha was the work of William Morgan, D.D., Vicar of Llanrhaiadr-ym-Mochnant, afterwards Bishop of Llandaff and later of St. Asaph. Morgan was a good Greek and Hebrew scholar, and commenced to translate the Five Books of Moses. A complaint was made against him to the Bishop of St. Asaph (William Hughes). The nature of the complaint is unknown; whatever it was, it met with no encouragement from the Bishop, and was in consequence laid before the Archbishop of Canterbury (John Whitgift), before whom Morgan had to appear at Lambeth. The Vicar and the Archbishop had been together at Cambridge, where Morgan was one of Whitgift's pupils. The result of the meeting of the master and his pupil cannot be better described than in the words of Archdeacon Thomas:—" Whitgift, on learning what Morgan was about, and having satisfied himself as to his scholarship and ability, made him his chaplain, and persuaded him to go on and complete the whole Bible, himself generously undertaking to discharge all costs, and promising him hospitality at Lambeth when the work was ready for the press. The complaint against him having thus been providentially over-ruled for good, Dr. Morgan returned to Llanrhaiadr and braced himself afresh for the great task before him."*

In his work he had the assistance of the most eminent divines and linguists among his countrymen, namely, William Hughes, Bishop of St. Asaph; Hugh Bellot, Bishop of Bangor; Dr. Gabriel Goodman, Dean of Westminster; Dr. David Powel, Vicar of Ruabon; Edmund Prys, Archdeacon of Merioneth; Dr. John Davies, Rector of Mallwyd; and Richard Vaughan, Provost of St. John's Hospital, Lutterworth, Leicestershire, afterwards Bishop successively of Bangor, Chester, and London. By the loan of books and critical examination of his work, these able men did much to encourage him. Dr. Goodman not only lent counsel and advice, but also gave Morgan a home in London for a year while the work was passing through the press. This hospitality had been proffered by the Archbishop, but the difficulty of constantly crossing back and fore over the Thames between Lambeth and London made the generous offer of the Dean of Westminster more acceptable.

* " Davies and Salesbury," pp. 119-120.

Dr. Gabriel Goodman was a native of Ruthin, and the founder of the Grammar School there. He, like Bishop Richard Davies, had been one of the translators of the Bishops' Bible.

A copy of the Welsh Bible was presented by Morgan to the Library of Westminster Abbey, where it is still preserved. An inscription on the titlepage is believed to be in the handwriting of Dr. Jaspar Gryffydd of Ruthin. At the end are two pages of errata printed in roman and italic types. These two pages have been reprinted in Archdeacon Thomas's " Davies and Salesbury," pp. 139-140, and reproduced in facsimile in Professor Powel's facsimile of the 1588 edition of the Psalms. (See No. 371).

There is no information as to when the translation of the Bible was begun by Morgan. If he commenced after he was appointed Vicar of Llanrhaiadr in 1578, the work of translating occupied less than nine years, while the printing took about a year. The reference in the dedication to the defeat of the Spanish Armada (28 July, 1588,) shows that the printing was then not completed, while the date in the copy presented to Westminster Abbey (Nov., 1588,) fixes the time when the work was finished.

The book is a small folio printed in Black Letter, containing 561 leaves, or 1,122 pages. The Apocrypha is included. The text is divided into chapters and verses, with contents at the head of each chapter. The Psalms are divided up as they are to be sung in the daily services of the Church, the days of the month being indicated in the headlines, and the Psalms for morning and evening service by sidenotes. The title is printed in black and red, enclosed in a woodcut border used by the deputies of Christopher Barker for English Bibles of that time. The Royal Arms at the top of the border has for supporters a lion and a dragon, the latter adopted by the Tudor sovereigns. The New Testament has a separate title enclosed in the same border, but printed in black only. Each book is commenced with a large decorated initial letter. Some of the books also have decorated head- and tail-pieces in the form of panels across the page. The number of copies printed is not recorded. The Act of Parliament stipulated that a copy should be supplied to every Parish Church in the Principality, to " remain in such convenient places within the said Churches, that such as understand them may resort at all convenient times to read and peruse the same : and also that such as do not understand the said language [*i.e.*, English] may by conferring both Tongues together, the sooner attain to the knowledge of the English Tongue." In view of the fact that there were at least 800 parishes in Wales, it seems probable that somewhere between 800 and 1,000 copies were printed. Very few complete copies remain. The number recorded perfect and imperfect is about 50.

The question has often been raised whether Morgan did the whole work of translation himself, and from what texts—English, Greek, or Hebrew. Mention has already been made of the names of eminent Welsh scholars from whom Morgan acknowledges that he received help. Mr. Herbert Vaughan has pointed out* that Morgan's task was far less difficult of performance than the work undertaken by Davies and Salesbury twenty years before. Not only did he enter into the labours of these two pioneers, but on all hands he received sympathy and help, financial and literary.

---

* " The Translators of the Welsh Bible," in the *Church Quarterly Review,* vol. lx. 46 (1905).

Inserted in the Llanstephan MS. of Moses Williams already referred to is a letter from Richard Morris dealing with the sources of Morgan's translation. This letter, not having been printed before, is given here:—

" SIR,

" The following remarks (among others of less consequence) have occurred to me in the progress I have already made in collating and correcting of orthography of the Welsh Bible, which I submit to your consideration, and beg the favour of your sentiments thereon. Y cŷn a gerddo a yrir says the old proverb—so your kind communicative temper and former favours to me emboldens me to be again thus troublesome.

" There are some persons of great learning who insist that the Welsh translation of the Scriptures is not done from the original Hebrew and Greek but from the English ; sure I am that whatsoever ye book speaks ye contrary, besides ye manifest differences in the phraseology, the very sense differ in many places which I have particularly noted, and I believe the prefaces to these antient editions you have by you, confute this reflection upon the ability of our countrymen. Dr. Davies in the preface to his grammar declares that himself was assisting in both translations of the folio Bible,—that of Bp. Morgan in 1588 and of Bp. Parry in 1620; There were also concerned in the former Dr. David Powel and Archdeacon Pryse &c. persons whose great skill in the original languages no one ever denied to call in question; and can any one imagine *they* should copy Translation which ye English themselves allow to abound in errors ? an absurdity of the first magnitude ! The marginal notes and references indeed prove to have been taken from the English Bible, but I would be proud of your opinion upon ye whole matter, for which [I] will make bold to call in a few days. I am, with great respect, Sir, Your most obliged hble servant

" RICHD. MORRIS.

" Lovel Court
" Paternoster Row
" 14 May 1745."

Folio 2 contains numerous examples to prove the contentions in the letter, which is addressed

" To
" WILLIAM JONES, ESQ.,
" in Beaufort Buildings,
" Strand."

For the New Testament Morgan had the translation of 1567 to work upon, which he did with so much success that the rugged Welsh of Salesbury was transmuted by Morgan into a smooth and easy literary gem. How far otherwise he entered into the labours of his predecessors is a matter which rests upon a somewhat spiteful observation made by Sir John Wynn of Gwydir :* " He had the benefit and help of Bishop Davies's and William Salesbury's work, who had done a great part thereof: yet he carried the name of all." Morgan does justice to Bishop Davies " of pious memory, who above all men has deserved well of our church." Salesbury, however, has received less than his due at Morgan's hands. Sir John Wynn is not without prejudice where Morgan is concerned, an unfortunate quarrel between the twain embittering the Bishop's later years. There are three letters of Morgan's surviving, all relating to the substance of the quarrel.† Sir John Wynn, keen to enrich himself and his family by leases of Church property, found the Bishop a stumbling block in the way of his plans.

With regard to the texts from which Morgan worked, Archdeacon Thomas says:—" We cannot say whether he followed one particular Version of the Old Testament, but he appears from internal evidence

* " History of the Gwydir Family," p. 96. .

† The letters are printed in Yorke's " Royal Tribes of Wales " (Appendix), and were reproduced in facsimile at the cost of Mr. John Cory, D.L., in 1905. Two of the original letters are in the Library of St. Asaph Cathedral, and the other is in the Cardiff Public Library.

to have had before him not only a Hebrew Text, but also the Latin Vulgate and the English Geneva Bible, and to have been guided in many instances by the Latin translation brought out by Paganinus in 1521." Morgan was a good scholar. He took his degree of Bachelor of Divinity and was appointed Vicar of Llanrhaiadr in the same year; and five years later he received the full degree of Doctor of Divinity. The Archbishop inquired as to his qualifications for the work of translation by asking, "Are you as conversant with the Welsh language as you are with the Hebrew and Greek?" The reply was, "I hope, my Lord Archbishop, that you will allow me to assure your Grace that I understand my mother-tongue better than any other language." Clearly Morgan was thoroughly well qualified for the work. That his success was great in spite of the errors which escaped, is evidenced by the story that the late Bishop Thirlwall of St. David's, a member of the last English Revision Committee, never decided finally on the correct rendering of a verse without consulting the Welsh Bible.* Morgan's Bible anticipates many of the changes introduced into the English Bible at the last revision.

---

* Hughes's "Life and Times of Bishop William Morgan," p. 131.

Cradwriaeth   Pen. j.

LLYFR CYNTAF
MOSES, YR HWN A ELWIR
GENESIS.

PENNOD. I.

SECOND ISSUE.

Cradwriaeth   Pen. j.

LLYFER CYNTAF
MOSES, YR HWN A ELWIR
GENESIS.

PENNOD. I.

FIRST ISSUE.

Welsh Bible, 1630.   Part of first page of two issues to show variations.

CHAPTER II.

THE PSALTER.

Morgan's Psalms—Kyffin's Psalms—Myddelton's Psalms—Prys's Psalms.

MORGAN'S version of the Psalms as in the Bible of 1588 was published in the same year in a small quarto for use in the daily services.

The version of the Psalms in the Prayer Books of 1567 and 1586 was not popular; and in the third issue of the Prayer Book in 1599, Morgan's translation was substituted. Parry's revised version of the Psalms appeared in the Prayer Book of 1621. Copies of Morgan's 1588 edition of the Psalms are rare. It was, however, in 1896, reproduced in facsimile, with an introduction by Professor Powel.

The translation of the Psalms in a metrical form for use in the services of the Church, occupied the attention of at least four Welshmen after the completion of the Bible. Maurice Kyffin, in the preface to his Welsh translation of Jewel's "Apology," 1594 or 1595, lamented his inability, owing to lack of leisure, to make such a translation. He may, however, have been the moving spirit which prompted Edward Kyffin, who was probably his brother, to undertake a task which he also left incomplete. Only Psalms i.—xiii. 5 appeared in the small volume issued in 1603 (No. 8a) by Thomas Salisbury, who in the same year was likewise responsible for the publication of Myddelton's metrical version (No. 8). Mrs. Alan Gough, of Gelliwig, Carnarvonshire, is the owner of a letter written by Thomas Salisbury to Sir John Wynn of Gwydir, which throws some light upon obscure points. A facsimile of the letter and its indorsement is given. The following is the text of it:—*

"Right worshippfull my humble dutye remembred etc: I am glad to heare of your late recouerye & present health wch I beeseche ye lorde still to continue to his glorye and ye good of our countrey itt reioyced mee not a litle when I understood yt your worshippe was inquisitive whether ye psalmes are translated into our vulgar tounge or not I sent you by your man a coppy of them yt are printed hee had finished some fiftye of them before hee dyed this tyme seuen yeares in ye tyme of ye greate sickness he departed this worlde in his custodye (when I came into ye co-[untrey] I left your proverbs ye psalmes and many good trea[tyses] of mr Perkynnes wth other good thinges in ye brittishe tounge wch weare all lost and gone by his untymly death I coulde never heare nor learne where any of them weare bestowed I often enquyred but could not learne of any howe and by whose meanes they weare convaighed away I heare not of any that are about ye psalmes save only Archdeac. Price who promised them longe agone but as yet hath not accomplishd his promise nor ye expectacion of many havinge not any newe bookes worthy your readinge I presumde to present your worshippe wth a litle treatis written by a greate statesman somtyme secrettarye to ye late Philipp of Spayne, mr Camdens Brittania his last edition wth ye mappes of all ye shiers [is] latly printed and bounde in follio thus humbly takeinge leave desyreinge yc lord to guide & protect [your] worshippe your v[e]rtuous ladye and all your religious and well nurturd issue wth all blessinges externall in this present life and in ye other to come wth all blessinges spirituall from my house in cloth fayer in London : June ye 22.

"Sr I pray my ladye to bestowe
"ye readeinge of my litle booke "Your worshippes in all
"Copied by P.W. 1795. "service readye
  "Tho: Salusburye."

* The letter is kept in a copy of Myddelton's Psalms, 1603, which has led to the supposition that it is the book alluded to. The facts, however, as given in the letter, do not fit Myddelton, and they do fit Kyffin. The words, "Copied by P.W.," refer to Peter Bayley Williams, the son of Peter Williams the commentator. The letter is printed in the *Cambro-Briton*, Vol. I., 1820, with an inaccurate footnote.

The book sent was Kyffin's Psalms, as appears from the title quoted
on the indorsement, and also from the statement that he had translated
about fifty of the Psalms before he died.   The year in which the letter
is written is not given; but the reference to the great sickness suggests
that Kyffin died in 1603, the year of the outbreak of plague in London.
This would make the date of the letter 1610, which is confirmed by the
reference to Camden's " Britannia," with the maps, issued in that year.
It will be seen from the letter that Kyffin's death occurred in London.
Salisbury may have fled into the country to escape the plague.   Edward
Kyffin was the administrator of the estate of Maurice Kyffin in 1599,
and in it described as " Preacher."

   The "Dictionary of National Biography," following Williams's
"Eminent Welshmen," makes Maurice Kyffin the son of Richard Kyffin
of Glasgoed, in the parish of Llansilin, Denbighshire.   This, however,
is not correct, as Mr. W. P. Williams, of Cae'r Onnen, Bangor, is able
to show.   The fact brought out by Salisbury's letter that Edward Kyffin
died in London early in the 17th century confirms Mr. W. P. Williams's
conclusions.

   It is curious that while writing about the unfinished translation of
Kyffin, and the, as yet, unfulfilled promise of Archdeacon Prys, no
reference is made to the translation by Captain Myddelton, because
Salisbury published this in the same year.

   William Myddelton was the third son of Richard Myddelton,
Governor of Denbigh Castle, and combined the practice of poetry with
an officer's life in the navy.   It was he that brought to the Lord High
Admiral, Sir Thomas Howard, news of the great Spanish fleet prepared
for his destruction in 1591, and thus enabled him to escape the trap
laid for him.   Myddelton finished his translation of the Psalms on January
24, 1595, in the West Indies.   It is the first metrical version of the
Psalms printed in Welsh; but being in the strict Welsh metres, on
which Myddelton was an authority, it did not become popular.   There
were three issues, with the preliminary matter varying in each, the text
being the same in all.   They are fully described under No. 8.   A
reprint was issued in 1827.

   The letter of Salisbury quoted above refers in a desponding tone
to the projected translation by Archdeacon Prys.   If the date of the
letter has been correctly inferred as 1610, Salisbury may well have been
despondent.   He had "promised them longe agone, but as yet hath
not accomplishd his promise nor ye expectacion of many."   The
"expectacion" was not fulfilled for another eleven years, because Prys's
Psalms first appeared in the Prayer Book of 1621.   Prys died in 1624.

   A skilful composer in the strict Welsh metres, and an active
participant in the bardic controversies of his day, Prys, in translating
the Psalms, deliberately rejected the stereotyped forms in which Welsh
poetry had hitherto appeared, in order to adapt them to congregational
singing.   His success was complete, and in striking contrast to
Myddelton's failure.   Prys's Psalms were reprinted in Bibles and Prayer
Books, and sung throughout the Principality for more than two centuries;
and even to-day several of them are in constant use.   Some chants are
also given in the first and immediately subsequent editions, and there
is usually a separate title.

   In addition to Prys's Psalms, the Prayer Book of 1621 contains the
version of the Psalms from the Bible of 1620.   The two versions
continued to appear together down to the early years of the 19th
century.

RHANN O
PSALMAE DAFYDD
BROPHWYD I VV CA-
nu ar ôl y dôn arferedig yn
Eglwys Loegr.

Simon Stafford a'i printiodd
yn LLunden dros T. S.
1603.

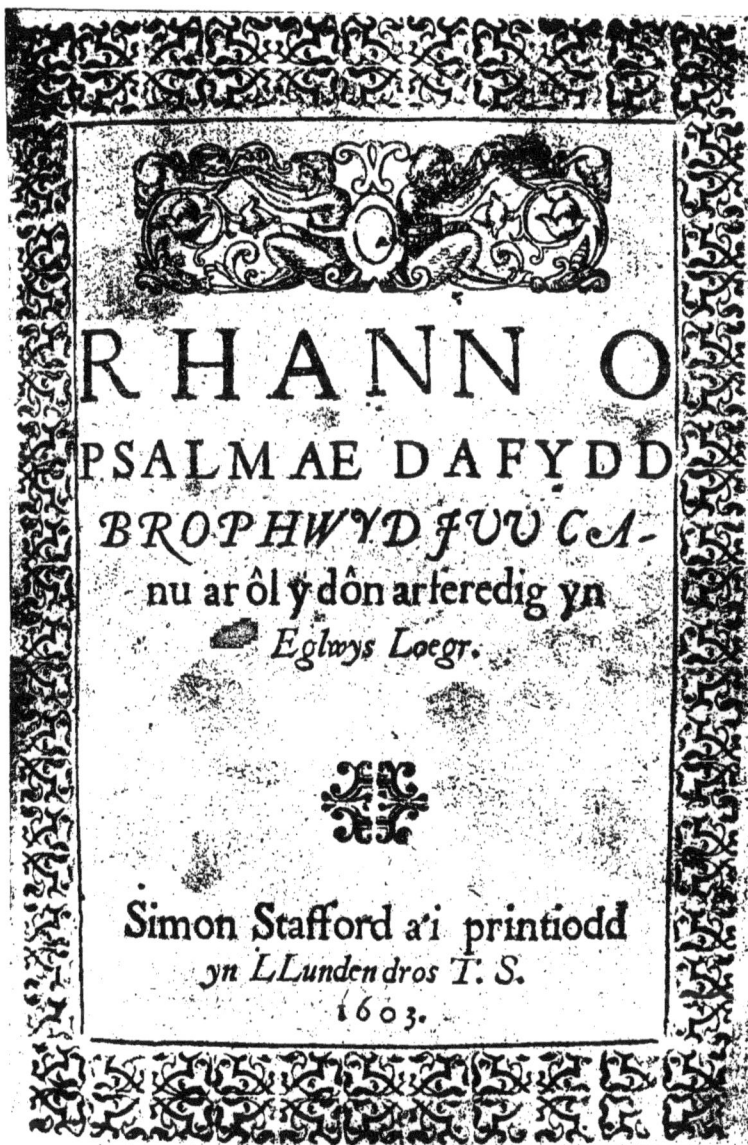

TITLE PAGE, KYFFIN'S PSALMS, 1603.

A PAGE OF TEXT, KYFFIN'S PSALMS, 1603.

CHAPTER III.

THE REVISED BIBLE.

Bishop Parry's Bible—The " Beibl Bach"—Financial help by London Welshmen—The 1641 N.T. an error—The 1647 N.T.—The Cromwell Bible—Rarity of the Commonwealth issues—The lost N.T. of 1654.

THE revised English Bible issued in 1611 prepared the way for a revision of the Welsh Bible. This was undertaken by Richard Parry, Morgan's successor at St. Asaph, with the help of Dr. John Davies of Mallwyd. The Hebraisms of Morgan were rejected by Parry, whose endeavour seems to have been to follow the English version of 1611. That this was an error, the revision of the English in the nineteenth century proves. It has already been said that Morgan's Bible antici-pated many of the improved renderings introduced into the English Bible at the last revision. Bishop Parry's Bible deprived the Welsh people of some of the advantages of Morgan's scholarship. Bishop Parry's revision was issued in a magnificent folio in 1620. The title is set within an elaborate engraved border, of the same design as is found in English folio Bibles of the period. The rose and thistle, symbolising the union of the crowns of England and Scotland under James I., are prominent in the design. In some of the head-pieces throughout the volume the harp for Ireland and the Prince of Wales's plume for Wales are introduced. This Bible was supplied to all the Churches in Wales. In many of the Churches it still remains, occasionally carefully treasured, but in some instances sadly neglected. Many copies have found their way into private hands, slightly defective for the most part, the first title with other leaves at the beginning and end being generally missing. It is still the authorised Welsh Bible, though its orthography has been interfered with, as will appear in due course. Many omissions and mistakes occur. Four folio pages of corrections appeared either from the hand of Charles Edwards, author of " Hanes y Ffydd," or from that of Dr. George Griffith, Bishop of St. Asaph.* Moses Williams says of this, " 1672. About this time there was printed a sheet in f° entitled *Some Omissions and Mistakes in the British Translation and Edition of the Bible appointed to be had and read in Churches in Wales, to be supplied and rectified.* Some say 'twas by *Charles Edwardes* the Author of a Book call'd *Hanes y Ffydd."* (Llanstephan MS.) There are two copies of the corrections in the British Museum, and one of them has, in a hand apparently contemporary, the following note :—" Sd by Bp Griffith of St. A." A later note, however, points out that Bishop Griffith of St. Asaph died in 1666. This conflict of evidence as to the authorship and the date led to the two copies, acquired at different times, being catalogued as if they were different issues of the corrections; and they are described as if they were two issues in the printed catalogue of the British Museum. They are two copies of the same four pages. Stephen Hughes in the preface to " Gwaith Mr. Rees Prichard," 1672, says that the corrections were printed by " some well-wisher of our country," and that copies were on sale with Mr. Goff at Carmarthen.

---

* Bishop Griffith had, in 1640, brought the question of a new edition of the Welsh Bible before Convocation.

d

The following note (in Welsh) appears on the errata sheet printed by Morgan for the 1588 Bible:—

"True it is, and often has it been seen (the dear Welshman) that no work is made perfect at once. Do not thou wonder, then, if errors escaped in the great and difficult and painful work of translating the Bible into Welsh: as twice as many escaped in other famous and belauded Bibles. And in the New Testament of this [Bible] there is more blundering than in all the other part. How and why that happened, thou shalt soon know (through God), when that Testament is printed, with less errors, and in a smaller size and at a lower price. If thou shalt see other errors, for the sake of God, and the country, and thine own soul, inform the translator thereof, so that the next printing be as pure as he wishes it to be and endeavours to make it, and as thou also oughtest to wish and do."

From this it appears that Bishop Morgan had designed to print the New Testament in a small volume at a low price, so that it might find a place in the homes of the people. His excellent project, for what reason is unknown, was never carried out. The last years of his life were embittered by the hostility towards him displayed by Sir John Wynn, who resented the Bishop's opposition to Wynn's attempts to enrich himself by leases of Church property. Morgan's own circumstances were not free from embarrassment. There is a note of sadness in the letter to Sir John Wynn which we reproduce: "I rest, your sickly neighbour." This was a few months before his death.

Thomas Salisbury, in a note prefixed to Myddelton's Psalms, 1603, says that the New Testament prepared by Morgan is ready for the press. This is the last heard of it. The disturbance of business in consequence of the plague may have had something to do with the disappearance of the manuscript, as it had with the loss of "many other good treatises in the British tongue," lost through the untimely death of Edward Kyffin, to which Salisbury makes such pathetic reference in the letter already quoted.

It was not until the year 1630 that a Welsh Bible for the people was available. It owed its existence to Rowland Heylin, an Alderman of London, who was descended from an ancient family of Pentreheylin, in the parish of Llandysilio, Montgomeryshire, and Sir Thomas Myddelton, the brother of William Myddelton, the translator of the Psalms. These two were the active promoters. Whether they were helped by others, or bore the charges themselves, is uncertain. Moses Williams, in the Llanstephan MS. already cited, says that in 1630 the Bible "was reprinted in 8° at London, at the expense chiefly of Sir Thomas Middleton of Chirk Castle, and Rowland Heylin Alderman of London." Griffith Jones ("Welch Piety," 1742, p. 12,) says : "Certain citizens and mercers of London (I can find the names but of two of them, viz. Sir Thomas Middleton and Rowland Heylin) moved with compassion towards the poor in Wales, procured at great expence an impression of the Welch Bible in octavo ; which proved to be of great service to revive religion among them." Strype, on the other hand, gives all the credit to Heylin alone:—"Alderman Heylin being sprung from Wales, charitably and nobly at his own cost and charges, in the beginning of King Charles's reign, caused the Welsh Bible to be printed in a more portable bulk, being only printed in a large volume before for the use of churches. He also caused the book called 'The practice of piety' to be printed in Welsh for the use of the Welsh people : and a Welsh or British Dictionary to be made and published for the help of those that were minded to understand that ancient language." (Strype's continuation of Stow's "Survey of London," 1720, vol. 2b., p. 142). This is clearly giving too much credit to Heylin, because the corrector of the press, in his preface to the 1630 Bible, says, "And here thou must acknowledge

FACSIMILE LETTER OF WILLIAM MORGAN, BISHOP OF ST. ASAPH, TRANSLATOR OF THE BIBLE INTO WELSH.

The original letter is in the Cardiff Public Library.

gratefully the great care and cost of certain pious and honourable citizens and merchants of London, (among whom chiefly and especially are Sr. Thomas Middleton, an honourable knight, and Rowland Heylin, two aldermen of the same city.")*

Beyond this it is impossible to get except by guessing, of which there has already been far too much amongst writers on this and other Welsh subjects. The statement, for instance, that the sum contributed by the promoters was a thousand pounds appears to be merely a guess; and if the number of copies printed was one thousand five hundred (another guess), it is manifestly wrong. The guess as to the number originated with Dr. Thomas Rees: "We are not informed how many copies of this first people's edition of the Welsh Bible were printed. It is supposed that they did not exceed 1,500—less than two copies for every parish."† Until some definite evidence can be produced, the thousand pounds contribution and the 1,500 copies printed cannot be accepted.

Moses Williams describes the 1630 Bible as follows :—"This edition has the Book of Common Prayer in short (or as the printers term it, a service) annexed to it, with the Psalms in prose (which was needless, seeing they are divided into portions in the body of the Bible) as also Archdeacon Pryse's version thereof in meter, with musical notes to sing them by. The Welsh preface bespeaks the Curator of the press to be a native of Duffryn Clwyd, at least to have lived a considerable time somewhere in that neighbourhood."

The Epistles and Gospels are not reprinted in the Prayer Book prefixed to the Bible. Under each collect is given the passages fixed for that day, and in the New Testament the passages are marked with [   ] at the beginning and end, and in the margins by a ⁀⁀ for the beginning of the passage and a ⁀⁀ for the end.

Moses Williams's suggestion that the proofs were corrected by some one from the Vale of Clwyd agrees well with another suggestion, that the editor was Robert Lloyd, Vicar of Chirk, one of the active Welsh literary men of the period: he translated and printed in 1629 a sermon on " Repentance " by Arthur Dent, and in the following year Dent's " Plain Pathway to Heaven." Lloyd dates the preface of the latter from his room at Foster Lane in London, Sep. 20, 1629. The year 1630 also saw the issue of Lewis Bayly's " Practice of Piety " in Welsh, translated by Rowland Vaughan, who speaks of Lloyd in the preface as " the learned Clergyman and my dear teacher." The passage from Strype already quoted connects Rowland Heylin with the Welsh edition of " The Practice of Piety." In the same year a small tract (14 pp.) called " Car-wr y Cymru " was issued from the same press as the " Plain Pathway " of 1630. This also was probably brought out by Robert Lloyd. Again, Dr. John Davies, of Mallwyd, was in London about 1630—2, bringing out his dictionary and " Llyfr y Resolusion," both printed in 1632. This appears from his preface to the latter book. The facts as now set out suggest that Myddelton, Heylin, and other London Welshmen, supplied the funds for printing the Bible and other books to be circulated in Wales, the literary side of the movement being in the hands of Robert Lloyd, Rowland Vaughan, and others. Lloyd was in London in September, 1629, and probably Vaughan was also there about the printing of " The Practice of Piety." Seeing that the Bible was passing through the press at the same time, and possibly

* The original is in Welsh.
† " History of Protestant Nonconformity in Wales," 2nd ed'n, 1883, p. 14.

at the instance of the same promoters, it requires no stretch of imagination to believe that one or both of these men also supervised the printing of the Bible.

The scarce book, " Car-wr y Cymru," 1631, contains an address in English " To all the Worthy and True-hearted Well-willers and furtherers of the Spiritual weale of Wales, who have put their helping hands and *hearts to that late necessary* and worthy worke of Setting forth the Bible in Welsh, in a small volume, The Author of this Welsh treatise, wisheth Wisdome's Gift (as a gracious Recompence of Reward from the Lord) viz.: Length of daies, riches and honor; with Eternall life which *is the gift of God through* Iesus Christ our Lord, Amen." (Rowlands's " Cambrian Bibliography," p. 112). This confirms the theory that Myddelton and Heylin were leaders of a London movement for supporting those who had at heart the religious advancement of Wales. There must have been some one or more behind inspiring and directing.

The Bible of 1630 is a small thick octavo, containing 1,118 pages of rather small print. The Prayer Book at the beginning, and Prys's Psalms at the end, have each a separate title, the former in the same woodcut border as is used for the title of the Bible and the New Testament. The title of the Psalms is enclosed in a narrow decorated border. Copies were sold at 5s. each; and its appearance was hailed by Rhys Prichard, Vicar of Llandovery, in the following stanza :—

> " Mae'r bibl bach yn awr yn gysson,
> Yn iaith dy fam iw gael er coron,
> Gwerth dy grys cyn bod heb hwnnw,
> Mae'n well nâ thref dy dâd i'th gadw."[*]

There is a copy extant with a different woodcut device at the head of Genesis, and many variations in the first eighty pages. The illustrations of the first page of the two issues will convey a better idea of the difference than any amount of description. Misprints in the first are corrected in the second, and words added by the translator, printed in italics in the first, are in the second in roman type enclosed in brackets. Copies of the second issue are not rare; but they are generally imperfect. A few years ago it was frequently to be bought for a trifle; but the volume is now more prized by owners of it.

Rowlands records in "The Cambrian Bibliography" under the year 1641, a New Testament on the authority of the Rev. William Thomas, of Bwlchnewydd, Carmarthenshire. Inquiries leave no doubt that this is an error, and that Mr. Thomas mis-read the date. The details correspond with the New Testament of 1741 (No. 21).

The next period in the history of the Bible in Wales is of peculiar interest. It covers the time of the Civil War and the Commonwealth, and the rise of Nonconformity. Names well known to Welsh people —Vavasor Powel, Walter Cradoc, Charles Edwards, and Stephen Hughes—flit across the page, only to elude all attempts to unravel the mystery of Wales and Welshmen during those eventful years from the outbreak of the great Civil War (1642) to the Restoration (1660). Between those dates three editions of the Scriptures in Welsh appeared—a New Testament in 1647, a complete Bible in 1654, and

---

[*] "Gwaith Mr. Rees Prichard," 1672, p. 8. Literally rendered into English, the stanza reads thus :—

> The little Bible is now commonly
> In thy mother's tongue to be had for a crown ;
> Sell thy shirt ere thou lackest that:
> 'Tis better than thy father's home to preserve thee.

another New Testament in the same year. The New Testament of 1647 is referred to before its appearance: "And now again I hear Mr. Cradock is procuring the New Testament to be printed in Welsh in a little volume, whereby it may grow more portable and more common" (John Lewis's "Contemplations upon these Times," 1646). There were two issues of the New Testament, both bearing the date 1647, the second having some of the mistakes corrected, though many remain. Stephen Hughes, some years later, referred to it as having hundreds of errors ("Gwaith Mr. Rees Prichard," 1672). This was the first time for any Scriptures to be printed in Welsh at the instance of the Nonconformists.

In a sermon before the House of Commons, July 21, 1646, Cradoc said, "And what if you should spend one single thought upon poore contemptible Wales? its little indeed, and as little respected, yet time was the enemy made no small use and advantage of it, how inconsiderable soever wee deem it; oh let not poore Wales continue sighing, famishing, mourning and bleeding, while you have your daies of Feasting, rejoycing, Thanksgiving and praysing God. Oh how loath I am to mention it to you? is it not a sad case that in thirteene Counties there should not be above thirteene conscientious Ministers who in these times expressed themselves firmly and constantly faithfull to the Parliament, and formerly preached profitably in the Welch Language twice every Lord's Day?" ("The Saints Fulness of Joy," 1646, p. 34.)

The same ideas were expressed by Vavasor Powel in the preface to his catechism, "The Scripture's Concord," issued in the same year (1646):—"Having finished this little Catechism in English, it is translated into Welsh for my dear and soul-hungering countrymen, who have not to my knowledge any, excepting one (if one), of this nature, nay, far worse, have not of godly, able Welsh ministers, one for a county, nor one Welsh Bible for five hundred families; although in some parts, where the Gospel came, they far and near pressed into it night and day, by violence took it, and through tribulations were followers of it. They are not so soulful but they will prize the least crumb herein, and the rather because it is only the Scripture which they diligently learn and examine. Couldest thou hear their groans for Bibles and teachers, and see their grace and growth without them, thou wouldest by thy prayers, purse, persuasions, and power, endeavour to supply them forthwith. If thou readest no farther, yet remember Wales' spiritual wants."[*]

The scarcity of Welsh Bibles is constantly referred to in the literature of the seventeenth and eighteenth centuries. That eagerness to possess the Bible which characterised the Welsh people in the eighteenth century was not a distinguishing feature in 1649, as the following extract shows:—"For in many places, people are so ignorant of the Word of God and so carelesse of knowing it, that among 20 families there can scarce one Welsh Bible be found and as for the English Bible, in the family where any is; it is but uselesse in respect of the generalitie of those which know nothing and understand nothing in that tongue."[†]

Contemporary allusions point to Walter Cradoc as the chief agent in having the New Testament of 1647 printed. How many copies were printed, or at what price they were sold, cannot be traced. The number has been stated in one place as 1,000, and in another as 3,000. These

* Quoted in Dr. Rees's "Nonconformity in Wales," 2nd ed'n, pp. 68—69.

† "Sail y Grefydd Gristnogawl," 1649, quoted by Mr. J. H. Davies in the Transactions of the Liverpool Welsh Nat. Soc., 1897—8, p. 67.

are only guesses. Vavasor Powel says, "In a few years time a great part of a former Impression of the Welsh-Bible, was bought up, and afterwards two Editions more, one of the New-Testament, and another of the whole Bible, and of these two I believe are sold off, at least between 5 and 6000." ("The Bird in the Cage," 2nd ed'n, 1662.)

The Bible of 1654 is sometimes called by the Welsh "Beibl Cromwel." Of the supposed tradition, that Cromwell himself contributed to the cost of its production, there is no evidence. Moses Williams says, "The Old and New Testament and the Singing Psalms were printed at London (I suppose by the Dissenters) in the same volume [size] with that of anno 1630 but the character is somewhat larger in the face, and far more beautiful to the eye, tho' of a closer body, as will easily appear by comparing of them together." (Llanstephan MS.) The text follows the 1630 Bible, the Prayer Book and the Apocrypha being omitted. Prys's Psalms are at the end in some copies. The letter J as used in modern speech appears in this Bible. The ɪ form of the letter I had been used in the Bibles of 1588 and 1620 in accordance with the usage of the time, ɪ being used for the initial letter of a word, and I in the middle of a word. The use of ɪ for the consonantal sound, and of I for the vocalic sound, gradually became fixed, and it is interesting to find the change definitely accepted in 1654. In 1630 I is used throughout, and in the 1647 New Testament both forms are used indifferently for initials, Ioseph and Joseph occurring on the same page in Luke iii.

The number of copies printed is stated by Charles Edwards ("Hanes y Ffydd," 1671, p. 152) to be 6,000. This does not agree with the statement of Vavasor Powel already quoted, which gives the sale of the 1647 Testament and the 1654 Bible as "at least between 5 and 6000." The price of the Bible was six shillings, and in 1671 about fifty copies remained unsold with a Mr. Owen, a stationer, in London. ("Gwaith Mr. Rees Prichard," 1672.)

Copies of the 1647 New Testament and the 1654 Bible are rare. Fewer copies of both are recorded than of any preceding edition. Why? It is not easy to answer. Were it not for the testimony of Vavasor Powel, that between "5 and 6,000 copies" were sold, it might be supposed that, owing to the difficulties of the time, the machinery for distributing the copies in Wales failed to act—that a large stock remained on hand in London, and perished in the Great Fire of 1666. It may be that, after the Restoration, the Royalist proclivities of the Welsh people led them to put away the books associated with the Commonwealth period. This, however, does not seem a probable explanation. There is nothing either in the text or the format of the books to which exception could be taken by the most sturdy Royalist. The survival of so many copies of the "Beibl bach," distributed throughout the length and breadth of Wales, supports the supposition that for some reason the next two books were not widely circulated in the homes of the people. The matter is incapable of solution on the evidence available, and must, for the present at any rate, remain a subject of speculation. It may be remarked here that the scarcity of the Welsh Prayer Books prior to the 1664 edition is due to the opposition to a liturgy which prevailed during the Commonwealth.

There is a perfect copy of the 1654 Bible in the chained library of All Saints' Church, Hereford. This library was bequeathed in 1715 by William Brewster, M.D.

Scarce as are the two editions of the Scriptures just referred to, they have to give place in rarity to the New Testament of 1654 mentioned by Charles Edwards: "And as God gave seed to the sower, he multiplied the loaves to the eaters, and there were again printed six thousand Welsh Bibles in small type, and they became as cheap as English Bibles. And for the sake of old people, and those having weak sight, large numbers of the New Testament in Welsh were printed separately in larger type. Thus was Welsh writing made plain upon tables that he may run that readeth it."[*] ("Hanes y Ffydd," 1671, p. 152.) No copy of this Testament is known to Welsh bibliographers of the present day. It is described in the *Revue Celtique*, vol. I., p. 377, by the late Chancellor Silvan Evans, who obviously had a copy before him when he wrote the description. It agrees with the Testament of 1647 so closely as to suggest that it is a reprint or a re-issue with a new title-page, with Prys's Psalms added. The points of resemblance may be thus stated :—

		1647.	1654.
Printer	... ...	Matthew Symmons.	M. S.
Size ...	... ...	12mo	12mo.
No. of pages (text)	...	820	820.

The only points of difference—the date and the addition of the Psalms—do not affect the theory, while the size of the type used for the 1647 Testament is so much larger than that used in the Bible of 1654, as to fully meet the description given by Charles Edwards. The Bible of 1654 was printed by James Flesher, while the New Testament was from the printing office of M.S., almost certainly the initials of Matthew Symmons, the printer of the 1647 Testament. That the type of the Testament was kept standing is shown by the fact that there was a second issue with many of the mistakes corrected. The 1654 issue may have been a third printing, or the unsold copies of the second issue with a new title, and the Psalms added. If it was simply a using up of the unsold sheets, then some of the copies extant without titlepages may have had the 1654 title. The question can only be settled by the discovery of a 1654 N.T. with a titlepage, or of a second N.T. similar to the 1647 issue with Prys's Psalms at the end.

[*] The original is in Welsh.

CHAPTER IV.

BIBLES FOR THE PEOPLE.

Stephen Hughes's New Testament—Beginnings of a literary and religious movement—The Bible of 1677-8—Thomas Gouge and his coadjutors—The Bible of 1689-90—The third folio Bible (1690).

BEFORE the end of the Commonwealth a part of the poems of Rhys Prichard was brought out, with a preface signed " H.M.," conjectured to be Henry Maurice, an Independent minister. A further part was issued in 1670, with a preface by Stephen Hughes, who also brought out the four parts of "Canwyll y Cymru" in 1672. The introductory matter to these editions of Rhys Prichard's poems contain many references to the circulation of the Scriptures and other religious books in Welsh; these are practically the only contemporary sources giving an account of the work which was being carried on.* Stephen Hughes states in one preface that the printing of the poems led to multitudes learning to read Welsh, who afterwards bought Testaments and Bibles. And he adds, "As to the Welsh Bible, it will be long before it will be printed, unless some monied men lay out a thousand pounds towards printing it ; the booksellers in London say, we will not lay out our money on this work, because an impression of 6000 Welsh Bibles will take twenty years, or fourteen years to sell, (while we are selling about 30,000 English Bibles every year), and we, who live by our crafts, cannot wait so long without our money back." ("Y Drydedd Ran o waith Mr. Rees Prichard," etc., 1670.)

Two years later, in 1672, the New Testament was published with the Psalter at the beginning and Prys's Psalms at the end. Stephen Hughes was the chief promoter of this edition, with the assistance of William Thomas, Bishop of St. David's (formerly Dean of Worcester), some other Churchmen, and many of the Independents and Presbyterians. The names of Hugh Edwards of Llangadoc, David Thomas of Margam, Samuel Jones of Brynllywarch, and William Lloyd of St. Petrox, are mentioned as having taken part in the enterprise. Thomas Gouge has also been mentioned in connection with this edition; but he is not referred to by Stephen Hughes, though they were known to each other at this time.

The type of this Testament is much larger than in the two editions of the people's Bible, and must have been a boon to old people. Many of the errors of former editions were also corrected. Stephen Hughes was very urgent about the need for another edition of the whole Bible in a better type and at a lower price than the former editions. The passionate desire of godly men to bring the Bible and other Christian literature within the reach of the Welsh people in their own tongue, which began with Myddelton and Heylin, still burned, and so spread as to ultimately result in kindling an equally passionate desire on the part of the people themselves to possess the Scriptures. Up to

---

* For an account of the different editions of the poems of Rhys Prichard, see *Y Cymmrodor*, vol. xiii., pp. 1—75.

this time the people's desire had only been feeble. The seed sown, however, produced abundant fruit later.   There were stirrings of a literary movement in Wales about this time induced by religious awakening following a period of toleration.   Stephen Hughes, Charles Edwards, and others, were the leaders of Welsh origin, while later Thomas Gouge came to organise the workers and to supply the financial support which was lacking.   As an illustration of the earnestness of men anxious to promote the religious welfare of Wales, and of the difficulties they had to overcome, the following passages from Stephen Hughes's address to ministers prefixed to "Gwaith Mr. Rees Prichard," 1672, are here literally translated :—

" And the country, Reverend Sirs, is beholden to you the others, [Bishop Thomas of Worcester having been specially acknowledged for his support in bringing out the third part of the Vicar's work] for the help you (among other estimable gentlemen and ministers) gave me in the work of printing the New Testament, and the Psalms, and Mr. Perkins's Catechism, (which is shortly to come to the country) so that the Welsh people that lack English, might have in their own tongue instruction in the matters of their eternal salvation.

.   .   .   .

" Having had already a proof of your love towards our country, I hope   .   .   . that you will be pleased to take in good part that I entreat you to do your best to have the whole Welsh Bible again printed.

" For although the Testaments be sent to the country to supply the present lack of the Word of God in print that is there,   .   .   .   it were a sore pity to let people be without the whole of it.   .   .   .

" Many in our country have a desire to buy Welsh Bibles as well as Welsh Testaments, as the Welsh dealers know quite well, from the frequent enquiries which have been made for them in their shops for some years, where they are not to be had for money.

" There are not left here but about fifty of them, and those so dear that workmen, and servants, especially poor shepherds, cannot reach them: because they must pay more in the country than is paid here for them.

.   .   .   .

" These people cannot make any use at all of the English Bible, neither can thousands of heads of families in Wales, because the language is strange unto them.

.   .   .   .

" As all this is quite known to you, may it please you, Reverend Sirs, as the whole of the honourable Bishops of our Country (in all probability) do not know the need of the people in this thing, either because the common people do not show them their need in this matter ;   or else because the ministers do not consider as they ought to do the condition of the people, or make it known to the Bishops; may it please you, for that reason, to lay the thing before the Bishops of Wales; and to entreat them, as if for your life, to have the whole Welsh Bible printed again.

" Firstly, to cause to be printed the Bible on good paper, and to give six months' notice to prepare the paper, and to cause new type to be cast expressly (especially the type proper to our language more than to any other language, such as d, y, w, ŵ, ŷ, â, ê, î, ô, û,) of the same kind as those* with which the metrical Psalms bound with the Testament are printed; because some aged people, though they use spectacles, cannot read a small-type Bible; and unless type be expressly cast, it will be necessary to let pass (as we had to in several places in the Testament, and Psalms, &c., for the want of type) *pob* and *bod* instead of pôb, and bôd, *ir*, and *ar*, and *dyn*, instead of i'r, a'r, dŷn, am and an, instead of a'm, a'n, &c.

" Next, that the whole be not impaired, as some Welsh books have been impaired, may it please you to entreat the Bishops to send four men learned, careful, conscientious, and skilled in the language, to attend the press, and who will undertake as in the presence of God to correct the sheets while printing, reading them two together twice, and the other two twice again.

.   .   .   .

" And so that the errors in the print be fewer, it were better to give the Church Bible as copy, rather than the small Bible; because the compositors would read that better than the other.

* This letter is called the Brevier letter and is that wherewith Fields excellent Cambridg Bible is done in. [This sidenote is in English.]

. " And though three thousand Bibles might serve our country for ten years : yet if it be desired to issue them cheap [or cheaply, or at a cheap price], so that the poor as well as the rich may buy them, six thousand must be printed (oh ! that ten thousand might be printed) the more that are printed the cheaper they will be: because when the press has been made ready to print one thousand, it is possible with a little more trouble, and less than half the cost, to print the second thousand, and so on.

" It is not to be expected that the booksellers in London will lay out their money for printing the Welsh Bible, as they do for printing the English Bible; because they get their money in with a great profit from the English Bible in a few years: but if they printed our Bibles, that is a large number of them, so that they should be cheap; they would not have their money in until after ten, yea, fifteen or more years. And therefore, say they, it is more profitable for us to lay out our money on interest than on Welsh Bibles that lie so many years in our shops ere they be all sold. Thus it may be expected that they would almost give their eyes out of their heads rather than give a thousand or fifteen hundred pounds to reprint our Bible. And indeed I cannot hear that they ever printed it at their own cost. It is at the cost of gentlemen from the country that the work has been hitherto done: and unless it be again done at the cost of such [men], there is no probability that a Welsh Bible will ever come to Wales, while Wales is Wales. . . . .

" Sir Thomas Middleton, more than anybody else, showed first this mercy towards our country, that is, to be at the cost of printing the Bible as a small book, for the benefit of the common people: (though it existed before as a large book in the Churches).

" Now, if six thousand Bibles be printed in the type with which the Cambridge Bible was printed, they will cost about fifteen hundred pounds: if in the small type, about a thousand pounds. It were easy for the Bishops, by laying out some of their own money, to get the remainder, by entreating them in the matter, from the Lords, Knights, Gentlemen and Ministers, and Merchants of Wales, promising them the value of their money in the books, to be sold throughout the land, by those appointed by them to do so for them, so that they may have their money again.

" I hope that you, the Reverend Dr. Thomas have not forgotten what you promised here in London within these two years; namely, that you would be ready to help this good work of printing the Welsh Bible."

This appeal resulted in the issue of an edition of the Bible in 1677-78, copies of which occur in various forms. A full copy contains, in addition to the Old and New Testaments, the Prayer Book, the Apocrypha, and Prys's Psalms. In some the Prayer Book is omitted, and in others the Apocrypha. The errors of former editions were corrected by the sheet of corrections issued a few years before, and already described under the 1620 Bible. Stephen Hughes, with the assistance of Thomas Gouge, was the editor and the chief promoter. Gouge had been led by reading the life of Joseph Alleine to pursue Alleine's design of devoting his life to the spread of the Gospel in Wales. He was 63 years of age when, in 1672, this call came to him; and for the remaining nine years of his life he pursued it consistently and earnestly. The circulation of religious books in the Welsh language was an important part of his plan. " The Whole Duty of Man " translated and published in 1672, " The Practice of Piety " in 1675, some of his own works, the Church Catechism, and many other books, were printed and circulated either at the expense of Gouge or with funds which he collected for the purpose. The frequency with which copies of the books issued through his agency still occur in all parts of Wales, shows the thoroughness and the liberality with which they were bestowed.

The printing and paper of the 1677-78 edition are better than those of the 1630 and 1654 editions. The number of copies printed has been put at 8,000, one thousand being said to have been given away gratuitously, while the others were sold for four shillings a copy bound in calf, with clasps.*

* So in Tillotson's sermon on the death of Gouge. Some copies in contemporary binding never had clasps.

A copy of this Bible, preserved among the heirlooms of the Duke of Bedford at Woburn Abbey, contains an inscription that throws some light upon the way in which the thousand copies for free distribution were provided.   The following is a copy of the inscription* :—

For the Right Honble   Earle of Bedford, Knt of yᵉ noble order of
    the Garter

In thankfull acknowledgement of his bounty to Wales in contributing towards yᵉ charge of printing the thousand Bibles in the British language, wᶜʰ are to be freely given to poore Families, and of teaching many hundreds of poore children to read, and write

> Jo. Tillotson
> Edw: Stillingfleet
> Benj. Whichcot
> John Meriton
> Tho. Gouge
> Benjamin Calamy
> Thomas Firmin
> John du Bois

William Russell, fifth Earl and first Duke of Bedford, was born in 1613, and died in 1700.   He played an important part in the affairs of the seventeenth century.

All the names,† except that of John Du Bois, attached to the inscription are well known.   John Tillotson, Canon of St. Paul's, was afterwards Archbishop of Canterbury; Edward Stillingfleet, Master of the Temple, became afterwards Bishop of Worcester ; Benjamin Whichcote, Vicar of St. Lawrence Jewry, was one of the Cambridge Platonists and an eminent divine and philanthropist; John Meriton, Rector of St. Michael's, Cornhill, remained at his post during the plague of 1665, and was very active in uniting and rebuilding Churches after the fire of 1666; Benjamin Calamy, Incumbent of St. Mary Aldermanbury, was afterwards Vicar of St. Lawrence Jewry and Prebendary of St. Paul's ; Thomas Firmin was a friend of Tillotson's, a London merchant and philanthropist, whose efforts to ameliorate the condition of the poor are well known ; he was also a friend of Thomas Gouge; and his biographer claims that Firmin was a seconder of Gouge in his scheme for publishing the Welsh Bible and other books.   Referring to Tillotson's sermon on the death of Gouge, the biographer of Firmin says,

" That great Preacher has given us an account of Mr Gouge's Religious Charity in printing divers good books, in the Welsh and English tongues, to be given to those that were poor, and sold to such as could buy them; the chief of these Prints and the most expensive was an edition of the *Bible* and *Liturgie* in the Welsh tongue; no fewer than eight thousand copies of this work were printed together.   One cannot question that Mr. Firmin contributed to, and procured divers sums for this excellent undertaking of his friend; tho' all is attributed to Mr Gouge, who was chief in that great and good work.   After Mr Gouge's death I find the sum of £419. 9s given to buy a number of those Bibles, whereof Dr Tillotson (then Dean of St. Paul's) gave £50, Mr Morrice £67, other persons the rest, but there was in the receipts £26. 13. to balance the disbursement, and that I judge was Mr Firmin's money."‡

This may be allowed without in any way detracting from the value of Gouge's work.   He came at the opportune moment, and welded together the forces working for the good of Wales.   Gouge knew

* Printed with some inaccuracies in Rowlands's " Cambrian Bibliography." The copy here given is an exact transcript kindly supplied by Mr. Pickering, Librarian to the Duke of Bedford.

† Mr. Shankland gives a longer list of persons interested in the work.   See *Seren Gomer*, 1903, p. 101.

‡ " The Life of Mr Thomas Firmin, late citizen of London, written by his most intimate acquaintance," 1698.

Stephen Hughes and, possibly, Charles Edwards, before 1672. By his influence, Tillotson, Firmin, and other powerful friends, were enlisted in the work. The society promoted by Gouge was the culminating point of a movement not confined to Wales: he was the means of inspiring the Irish people to move for an Irish Bible; and educational institutions similar to those which he introduced into Wales were started in Germany and in New England.

This impression of the Bible was sold off in a few years. The demand increased, because so many people had been taught to read in the schools established through the efforts of Thomas Gouge. Eight hundred, sometimes a thousand, poor children were educated in these schools each year; and in several places as many more were taught in schools established by people desirous of extending the good work of Gouge's schools. In the "Life and Writings of the Rev. James Owen" (London, 1709,) is quoted a sheet giving a return of a year's work, entitled, "An account of what hath been done in Wales this last year from Midsummer 1674 to Lady Day 1675, in pursuance of the above-said trust, upon the encouragement of divers worthy persons, to this Pious and Charitable Design." Among the things enumerated are, thirty-two Welsh Bibles, all that could be had in Wales or London, bought and distributed in several families; and 240 New Testaments in Welsh, to be given away to poor people that could read Welsh. The success of Gouge as an organiser is referred to by Tillotson, who knew him well, and was himself a liberal contributor to the Bible fund. Speaking of the designs for teaching the children to read and for supplying the Bible and other books in Welsh to adults, Tillotson says,

"And in both these designs, through the blessing of God upon his unwearied endeavours, he found very great success. For by the large and bountiful contributions which, chiefly by his industry and prudent application, were obtained from charitable persons of all ranks and conditions, from the nobility and gentry of Wales, and the neighbouring counties, and several of that quality in and about London; from divers of the right reverend bishops, and of the clergy; and from that perpetual fountain of charity the City of London, led on and encouraged by the most bountiful example of the right honourable the Lord Mayor and the Court of Aldermen; to all which he constantly added two-thirds of his own estate, which, as I have been credibly informed, was two hundred pounds a year; I say, by all these together, there were every year eight hundred, sometimes a thousand poor children educated, as I said before; and by this example, several of the most considerable towns of Wales were excited to bring up, at their own charge, the like number of poor children, in the like manner, and under his inspection and care."[*]

Griffith Jones, of Llanddowror, also writes in similar terms of the assistance given to Gouge's work. ("Welch Piety," 1741-2, pp. 13-14).

Thomas Gouge died in 1681. The work went on under the guidance of Stephen Hughes, who put in hand another edition of the Bible. He did not, however, live to see it through the press. After Hughes's death in 1688, the labour devolved upon David Jones, of Llandyssilio, who was largely assisted by Lord Wharton and other contributors.[†] The fourth Baron Wharton (1613-1696) was a strong and liberal supporter of the Puritans. By a deed made in 1662, he settled some of his lands near Healaugh, Yorkshire, upon trustees, the income to be used for supplying 1,050 Bibles and as many Catechisms yearly to as many poor children residing in the counties in which his estates lay—Buckingham, York, Westmoreland, and Cumberland—as had learnt by heart seven specified Psalms. This scheme remained in

---

[*] Tillotson's sermon at the funeral of Thomas Gouge.
[†] Calamy, "Account of Ejected Ministers," 1713, vol. II., p. 720.

operation a few years ago, and probably still goes on. Lord Wharton had some connection with Wales, his daughter Mary having married first, in 1673, William Thomas, of Wenvoe Castle, near Cardiff, and secondly, in 1678, Sir Charles Kemeys, of Cefn Mably, near Cardiff.

According to Calamy's account of David Jones, he distributed 10,000 copies of this Bible in Wales. Moses Williams,* of Devynnock, on the other hand accuses David Jones of abusing the confidence of those who subscribed generously by leaving out the Prayer Book Service and the Apocrypha, printing " only the two Testaments and the singing Psalms, and those too so. very incorrect and imperfect, that some even of his own persuasion have complained thereof. The volume indeed was the same with the former impression, as were also the types, except that, they had been constantly used in the interim in printing English, which is the chief reason this is so very illegible. The paper may be well supposed to be the cheapest he could lay his hands on. What number he printed I never could learn, but it must have been very considerable, since 'tis notorious that for binding some of them he gave the Bookbinders what quantity they required of perfect books at the same rate as if they had been waste paper." (Llanstephan MS.) Moses Williams is wrong in blaming David Jones for the omission of the Prayer Book and Apocrypha. Stephen Hughes, of whom Moses Williams writes that he " was eminent for rather more. than answering the expectations of his subscribers " (Llanstephan MS.), had planned the omissions. In his prefatory letter to the first Welsh issue of the " Pilgrim's Progress," in 1688, Hughes says,

"If the Bible in Welsh is to be printed again some of you will.have to be satisfied to receive it although it will only contain the O. and N.T.'s and the singing psalms bound together because thus many of them may be printed so that the Bibles will be cheaper for the poor people. And as for the Service book together with the Psalms for reading and the Psalms in Verse they may be had in Welsh bound together with those who sell the books of Mr Thomas Jones in Wales."†

The Prayer Book referred to was printed for Thomas Jones in London, 1687. The omission of the Apocrypha was clearly part of Hughes's project, the aim being to reduce the cost in order that the Bibles might be sold at a moderate price. The complaint about the quality of the paper disappears for the same reason. There remains the charge of waste and the imperfections of the press. David Jones may not have possessed the qualities of a good proofreader. There must have been some reason for the bitter feeling displayed by Moses Williams, who was born in David Jones's lifetime, and appears to have been a fair-minded and tolerant man, as well as a scholar.

The third folio Bible for use in Churches was issued in 1690 from the University Press, Oxford. This was the first time for the Scriptures in Welsh to be printed out of London. The first English Bible printed at Oxford is dated 1674. The folio of 1690 is known as Bishop Lloyd's Bible, William Lloyd, Bishop of St. Asaph and afterwards of Worcester, being the chief promoter of its publication. The editor and corrector of the press was the Rev. Pierce Lewis, of Llanvihangel Tre'r Beirdd, Anglesey, who, for his superior skill in his mother-tongue and his care of this work, was styled by his contemporaries of Jesus College " The Welsh Rabbi."

The volume is a handsome folio, printed with a fine Roman type, and contains " Bishop Lloyd's Chronology " and Scattergood's references

---

* It should be noted that Moses Williams was in his turn attacked on the ground of his omissions and corrections.

† The original is in Welsh.

in the margin. The chronology ascribed to Lloyd is a reproduction of the dates (reckoned Anno Mundi) which had already appeared in certain Oxford printed English Bibles beginning with 1679. Lloyd may have been the compiler of the chronology. He was a student of the subject, and is supposed to have prepared the revised Biblical chronology, giving dates B.C. and A.D., which first appeared in the London folio of 1701, and has been reproduced in most editions of King James's version down to the present day. This chronology has been inserted without any authority in English Bibles for nearly two centuries. It is based on Archbishop Ussher's " Annales Veteris et Novi Testamenti," 1650-4.*

Mistakes which had escaped in former Welsh Bibles are corrected in this, "and a great many of the mutable consonants in the beginning of proper names are varied, or left out, as the idiom of the Welsh tongue requires. Some words indeed are erroneously spell'd according to the vulgar pronunciation in North Wales, such as gonest and gonestrwydd for onest and onestrwydd; gaiaf for gauaf, cynhaiaf for ·cynhauaf, Daiar for Dacar or Dayar, &c."†

---

* Catalogue of editions of Holy Scripture in the library of the B. & F.B.S., 1903, vol. I., p. 248.

† Moses Williams. Llanstephan MS.

The Bible of 1717-18—Moses Williams's Account—Re-issue 'of the Bible in 1727—Richard Morris and the Bibles of 1746 and 1752—Other S.P.C.K editions.

THE Welsh Bible of 1717-18 was brought out through the Society for Promoting Christian Knowledge,, which had been established in 1698. The society had for one of its best supporters Sir John Philipps, Bart., of Picton Castle, Pembrokeshire, and many other influential Welsh subscribers. The needs of the Welsh people received a considerable share of attention throughout the eighteenth century. In 1713 the society issued a circular containing proposals, and inviting subscriptions, for printing the Bible in Welsh. This circular was sent out at the instance of Moses Williams, Vicar of Devynnock, and other correspondents in Wales. Copies were to be sold to subscribers at 4s. 6d. each book in quires, and 5s. 6d. bound in calf; subscribers to pay down 2s. 6d. for each copy, and the balance on delivery.* Moses Williams solicited subscriptions in Wales, and was also the editor of this edition, which is known as " Beibl Moses Wiliams." The supporters of Moses Williams in the enterprise included Sir John Philipps of Picton Castle, Griffith Jones of Llanddowror, John Vaughan of Derllys (father of Madam Bevan), the four Welsh bishops, the Bishops of Hereford and Worcester (William Lloyd), and many members of the S.P.C.K. resident in Wales. Ten thousand copies were printed by John Baskett, the king's printer, who had asserted his sole right to the printing of the Bible. The first sheet was finished and produced to the society by November, 1715, and the printing of the complete work finished by May, 1718. From a minute in the society's books, it would appear that only four thousand copies of the two maps were printed for insertion in the Bible. Six thousand copies, therefore, must have been issued without the maps. The maps were given, the first by J. Jones, and the second by Richard Mostyn. The printer had stipulated that about half the edition should be subscribed for before the printing commenced : the 4,000 maps may have been inserted in the subscribers' copies. The occurrence of the maps in copies with the 1717 titles implies that they were added to the first copies issued. The minutes of the society show that no copies were put into circulation before May, 1718.

Copies occur in several forms, and with varying dates, partly due to the variation of the contents to suit different classes, and partly to the reprinting of the general title and portions of the Old Testament. A full copy of the first issue consists of the Old Testament, the Apocrypha, the New Testament, a Scripture index (" Mynegai'r Beibl Cyssegrlan "), and Prys's Psalms. Copies were issued for Noncon-

---

* Mr. Shankland has made an exhaustive and invaluable study of the work of the S.P.C.K. in printing and circulating Welsh books ; and he prints extracts from the minutes and correspondence of the Society. ("Diwygwyr Cymru" in *Seren Gomer*, Jan., 1904.)

formists without the Apocrypha and the Scripture index, while to meet the claims of members of the Church of England copies were issued in 1718 with the Prayer Book preceding the Old Testament. In this issue the dates are P.B., 1718; O.T., 1718; N.T., 1717; Prys's Psalms, 1717. The two maps are (1) Palestine, (2) The Journeyings of the Apostles. This edition in all its forms represented a total of 10,000 copies. About 1,000 copies were distributed gratuitously. ("Welch Piety," Sept., 1741—Sept., 1742). The Prayer Book and the Scripture index occur separately.

The following account (Llanstephan MS.) of this edition was written four years after publication, by the editor, Moses Williams :—

"Anno 1718. About four years agoe the Society at London for Promoting Christian Knowledge having received Advice from some of their Correspondents in Wales that a new Impression of the Bible in 8° for the use of the common People was very much wanted, after mature Deliberation agread to make that of Anno 1677-78, their Specimen, & to print Proposals for Subscription, to carry on the Work. I spent a whole year in Wales on this Errand, and another at London while the Founders were getting ready the Letter, & have been two more in the Press, before I could finish it. As to an Account of this Edition, 'tis printed by that of Oxon 1690, compared with that of Lond. 1677-78. Some Thousands of suppletive Words that are put into the Text to make out the Sense, & had hitherto been printed in Roman Characters, are distinguished in this by being in Italick; & others that were erroneously printed in Italick, are here in Roman, as being in the Original. In proper Names the Hebrew Letter Y is always expressed by S, and not promiscuously by S and Z as in the former Impressions. The mutable Initials are every where varied or left out according to Grammar, excepting a few Words that begin with C, as Cæsar, Cyrene, &c. which being commonly pronounced Sesar, Syrene in Imitation of the English, I have left to the Reader's Choice as formerly.* To the End of it is added Mr. Nichols's Chronological Index, translated from the English by S. Williams Rector of Llan Gynllo in Cardiganshire. There are also in it two Maps, the one of the Travels of the Apostles, and the other of the Land of Canaan : the Plate of the first was given by Richard Mostyn of Penbedw in Denbighshire Esquire, & that of the second by the Reverend Mr. Jones Vicar of Llanamddy frwys in Carmarthenshire, and the Expence of Paper and Press-work was borne by the aforementioned Society. This Edition has also a Service to it, with the Acts of Uniformity, the Offices for Consecrating & Ordering of Bishops Priests & Deacons, the xxxix Articles, the Canons, Mr. Archdeacon Pryse's Version of the Psalms in Meter, the Hymns, & some Family Devotions. Mr. Lewis Thomas, who was the Contriver of printing the Singing Psalms &c. in that small Character at Oxon, printed off the first Sheet thereof without or rather contrary to my Directions, & that is the Reason Pryse's Letter is left out, & the Index of the Psalms & that of the Hymns put asunder in that preposterous manner.

"I am sensible, tho' I have put to my best Endeavours to make this Edition of the Bible & Common Prayer, &c. compleat & correct, 'tis no more without Defects & Errata's than other's generally are ;-if it has but as few, I am content. My circumstances would not allow me to keep Coadjutors to assist me in the revising it. 'Tis highly probable therefore that a curious Reader may discover several mistakes, in this as well as in the former Editions, and no Doubt may be able to make material Amendments to it in all its Parts, by diligently comparing them with their Originals. For my own Part I shal look into it yet more narrowly from time to time-& rectifie what I find or think amiss in it. And I should be very glad if my Countrymen would communicate to me their Observations upon it, that I might either justifie what they may think amiss, or else own the mistake & minute it in an interleav'd Copy to be examined and consider'd of by proper Judges, before it be put to the Press whenever another Impression is on foot."

*All Speeches or Sentences begin with a Capital, the better to distinguish them.

Instead of x I have substituted Cs throughout, as being the oldest & the best way of expressing that sound.

In most compound Words I have omitted the Hyphens, e:g. Godinebwr Bethel, for Godineb wr, Beth-El, &c.

In the Margin against the Contents of the Chapters in the O. Testament are notes shewing at wt Time or Times such Chapters are read; whereby the Reader may also see what Chapters are never read in the Church. These are omitted in the New T. because 'tis so often read throughout in the Year, excepting the Apocalypse, whereof some few Chapters only are read.

The Service at the Healing, being not used in England at present, is therefore left out.

Memdum to print E.P.'s Letter at ye Bottom, vi Ed. 1630.

f

In less than ten years the S.P.C.K. found it necessary to re-issue the Welsh Bible; and, accordingly, in 1727 a fresh edition was brought out. The number of copies printed of this issue has been variously estimated at from 5,000 ("Y Gwyddoniadur Cymreig," vol. I., p. 639,) to 20,000 (Rees's "Nonconformity in Wales.") William Roberts ("Nefydd") estimated the number at 10,000 ("Seren Gomer," 1855, p. 433). Griffith Jones bought above 2,000 copies, some of which were given and some sold to pay for the teaching of others to read. In addition, the Protestant Dissenters of London sent out of their funds and charities some hundreds to be distributed by their ministers. ("Welch Piety," 1741-1742, p. 15.) The omission of the marginal references in this edition made it less useful and acceptable to the Welsh people, who had been used to those advantages in all former Bibles. ("Welch Piety," 1741-1742, p. 15.) The contents before each chapter are also omitted. The Scripture Chronology, Table of degrees of men, and Table of Jewish time, following the New Testament, are omitted. A list of Hebrew names and words, with their equivalents in Welsh, as found in the margins of the complete Bible of 1717-18, is inserted. In other respects it is a reprint of the former edition, with some revision of the orthography, including the Service, the Apocrypha, and Prys's Psalms. The object of the omissions was economy, to enable the copies to be sold at a low price, four shillings. Some copies have the date, 1728, to Prys's Psalms, and others omit the Prayer Book, as in the former edition.

The third S.P.C.K. edition of the Bible was issued in 1746, from the Cambridge University Press. The editor was Richard Morris, an official in the Navy Office, and a brother of Lewis Morris of Anglesey. This Bible is known as "Beibl Rhisiart Morys." Griffith Jones was the chief promoter of its publication. He printed in 1741 "An address to the charitable and well-disposed in behalf of the poor in the Principality of Wales," wherein he states that two charitable gentlewomen have, of their own accord, freely offered thirty guineas, and two other very worthy persons propose to give one hundred pounds each, towards helping the poor to the Word of God in their native tongue. He appeals for further contributions towards supplying the poor " with Welch Bibles, Common Prayer Books, and Catechisms."

It was in December, 1743, that the S.P.C.K., in response to urgent representations, agreed to proceed with the printing of another edition of the Welsh Bible, to consist of 15,000 copies, and towards which liberal contributions had been made through the Rev. Griffith Jones and also direct to the society. This edition is a thick demy octavo volume, printed in double columns with small roman type. The contents of the chapters are given, and also marginal references fuller and more numerous than in any previous edition. Most copies have two maps ; but some have three. The price was four shillings and sixpence. The sale of this edition was rapid. By means of the Circulating Charity Schools, a large number of people had been taught to read, and these were eager to possess the Scriptures. They were, however, very poor; many were in want; and nearly all lived upon the barest necessaries of life. To pay four shillings and sixpence even for the Bible was to most of them a matter of impossibility, as Griffith Jones explains in " Welch Piety,"—his annual accounts of the Charity Schools. Many copies were distributed gratis by the aid of funds subscribed for the purpose, in response to Griffith Jones's appeals. A Baptist minister, the Rev. Joseph Stennett, D.D., of Lincoln's Inn Fields, London, also gave some hundreds of copies to the Baptists in Wales, eighty of which

were distributed in Glamorgan and Monmouthshire. (Joshua Thomas's
" Hanes y Bedyddwyr," 1778, p. 56.)

The 15,000 copies of the 1746 edition were insufficient to meet the
demand, and the S.P.C.K., " from a compassionate and Christian
regard to their wants put in the press another edition of the Bible,
consisting of the same number of copies, as likewise of five thousand New
Testaments, and as many Common Prayer Books in the same language."
Griffith Jones writes in October, 1749 (" Welch Piety," 1748-9, pp.
17-18),

> " The great Cry and most incessant Application that is now every where in these
> Parts for Welch Bibles, which yet are distributed among them with all convenient
> Dispatch, shews, that the Number of Welch Readers is of late Years greatly increased
> among us. They might indeed have cried all their Life for Bibles, without the least
> Hope of being supplied, but for the abundant Donations of very numerous Benefactors,
> and the charitable Assistance of the Society for Promoting Christian Knowledge. The
> Demand for Bibles is so extraordinary now, as the Society informs you in their last
> Year's Account, that this Impression, large as it is, (not less than Fifteen Thousand
> Copies) will fall exceedingly short of it; for which Reason the said Society have it
> already in their Thoughts, in tender Compassion to the Poor, to print again, as soon as
> possible, another Edition of the Bible, with an additional Number of New Testaments,
> and Common Prayer Books in the Welch Language. It is our humble Duty both to
> pray God to prosper them, and do what in us lies, to convey to our latest Posterity a
> most grateful Remembrance of what these worthy Gentlemen are doing, and also
> what other charitable Friends have done formerly, toward promoting the Welfare of
> their poor Countrymen. We are also very greatly and inexpressibly obliged to all the
> Promoters of our Welch Schools. For the Bible itself can be but of little Use to the
> Poor, if by the Charity of good People they are not taught to read it."

The second issue of " Beibl Rhisiart Morys " appeared in 1752,
making 30,000 Bibles and 5,000 New Testaments supplied by the
S.P.C.K. in six years, at a cost of about £6,000. The 1752 issue is of
the same size, form, and contents, as that of 1746; but it was printed
from new type. The following letter, copied by the Rev. Thomas
Shankland from the society's records, shows how the books were distributed in Wales :—

> " A Letter sent to the Society's Members, concerning the dispersing of the Welsh
>   Bibles.
> " Sir,
>   " The Society for promoting Christian Knowledge having at length happily
> finished, by the blessing of God, and the joint contributions of worthy benefactors, a
> second impression of 15,000 Welch Bibles and Common Prayer Books, besides a
> separate Edition of 5000 New Testaments, and as many Common Prayer Books for
> the benefit of schools and servants, are considering how, and through whose hands,
> they may order such distribution of them, as will diffuse the good they hope to do
> thereby throughout the whole Principality of Wales. The Society have reason to
> believe from the letters and accounts that have been received, that even this second
> impression (large as it is) will fall short of the extraordinary and universal demand
> that is made for it; and therefore they think themselves concerned, not only to prevent
> abuses of every kind in the distribution, but also to take what care they can that it be
> dispersed most prudently, usefully, and extensively, and with a particular regard to the
> families of the poor. To which end they are come to this resolution, That they will
> have, without respect of persons, a due regard not only to the Extent of each Diocese,
> but likewise to the number and circumstances of its Welch inhabitants. Accordingly,
> I have it in Command from the Society to desire their own members, and of everyone
> else that shall be any-wise intrusted with such a distribution that they will do it in the
> most prudent and faithful a manner, distinguishing each parish, nay each family, if
> it may be, wherein they distribute the books; and being careful, that though they have
> not the plenty they could wish, there may be still no such scarcity, but that each single
> family may be benefited, without doing a prejudice to the others, who may stand in
> equal need of the same blessing, and are known to be no less willing to use it
> religiously: It being both the intention and the desire of the Society, to supply all
> their wants, at least in such equal proportions as the impression will allow of. I am
> farther to acquaint you, that the Society are come to a determination to send only
> *one half* of the number of Bibles allotted to each member at present; and that they
> require certificates how these have been disposed of, as also remittances for the said
> packets, before they will give orders for a second Distribution. The Society hope,

that the Distributors will be content to receive the Bible in such proportions, under this assurance, that they will be equally dealt with in their several packets, till the whole number the Society have alloted to each of them be compleated and sent.

"The Price of each Bible with a Common Prayer Book will be no more, bound together, than three shillings and sixpence; of a New Testament and Common Prayer Book bound together Two Shillings: of the Prayer-Book alone one Shilling and Sixpence; carriage included: so that whatsoever the distributors shall pay on this account, will be deducted out of their remittances for packets, which they are desired to make with dispatch. I have nothing more to add, but that the Society do, in the strongest terms, desire it of their members and others who may be concerned in the distribution of the Bibles &c. that they will guard most diligently and carefully against their being sold at a higher Price than the Society have set upon them, or or [*sic*] falling into the hands of such as would make merchandice of the Word of God.

"I am, Sirs
"Your very humble Servant
"T. Broughton
"Secretary.

"Bartlet's-Buildings
"April 2. 1754"

There was no further issue of the Welsh Bible until the year 1769. The edition of 1752 was not sold out ten years later, for some copies contain an "Hyfforddiadau" bearing the date 1762, which has given rise to a supposition that the Bible was reprinted in that year. Reference to the titles of the Old and New Testaments will show that copies of the 1752 Bible were made up with the "Hyfforddiadau" of 1762.

For the issue of 1769 the S.P.C.K. called in the Rev. John Evans, M.A., of Portsmouth, as editor; and he, to the great annoyance of Richard Morris and other Welsh scholars, reverted to the orthography of the 1690 Bible. It consists simply of the Old and New Testaments, with notes and references in footnotes, and is printed from a good clear type in a thick demy octavo volume containing 2,308 pages. The reversion to the older orthography was a mistake, and may account for the slow sale. The minutes of the society show that after the 1799 edition had been sold out in the spring of 1800, there still remained between three and four hundred copies of the 1769 edition in the society's store; and it was agreed to offer these at 2s. 9d. each to members who had failed to secure as many copies of the new edition as they had applied for.

It was with a view to increasing the number of copies of this edition that the Rev. Thomas Llewelyn, LL.D., published his "Account of the British or Welsh versions of the Bible," 1768. The number printed was increased to 20,000. Six years after publication, Mr. Sporton, a London merchant, gave 500 copies to the Congregationalists through the hands of the Rev. Benjamin Evans, of Llanuwchllyn, afterwards of Trewen, Newcastle Emlyn. The Book Society for Promoting Religious Knowledge among the Poor, founded 1750, was one of the chief agencies in distributing copies of this edition to the Nonconformists in South Wales. Dr. Thomas Llewelyn became a member of this Society in 1768, and co-operated in the scheme for distribution. One thousand copies were purchased by the society. Eight copies were sent to every minister in the six counties of South Wales, and four to each minister of Welsh congregations in Monmouthshire. The society had intended to distribute Bibles also in North Wales; but finding that Dr. Daniel Williams's Trustees were willing to undertake the distribution and expense for North Wales, it was agreed that a portion of the 1,000 copies should be assigned to them. Mrs. Marlow, of Leominster, purchased 120 copies from the Book Society, and presented them to the Baptists for use in the chapel services.

The S.P.C.K. did not again reprint the Welsh Bible for thirty years; and then, in 1799, reverted to the orthography of the 1752 edition, but, as subsequently transpired in the controversy over the 1809 Bible, errors were allowed to escape in the printing. Ten thousand copies of the whole Bible were printed, and 2,000 of the New Testament. The Bishops of Bangor and of St. Asaph, according to the report of the Society, urged the importance of another edition, and persuaded the Society to undertake it. Behind the bishops, however, was the Rev. Thomas Jones, of Creaton, who had been working hard for some time to procure a further supply of Welsh Bibles, and had even drawn up a scheme for a Society specially to undertake the work. He discussed the subject in correspondence with the Rev. Thomas Charles.* He was one of those earnest and pious workers who took an active part in founding the British and Foreign Bible Society. This 1799 Bible was the edition sold by the Rev. Thomas Charles to Mary Jones, the Welsh maid whose pathetic appeal for a copy of the Bible is said to have led to the organisation of the Bible Society. The story of Mary Jones and her Bible has touched the hearts of the people as much as any incident of modern times. The copy bought by her is now preserved in the library of the Bible Society, and was lent, after considerable pressure, for the Bible Exhibition in the Cardiff Library in 1904. Immediately the fact that it was in the exhibition became known, a constant stream of people from all parts came to see it. To many of them the rare and beautiful treasures in the collection went for nothing : they came just to look at Mary Jones's Bible.

Altogether, the S.P.C.K. issued between 1718 and 1900 nearly sixty editions of the Scriptures in Welsh, including a folio Bible for Churches, and diglott New Testaments in Welsh and English. Special donations were made for the first five editions of the S.P.C.K.; but subsequent issues appear to have been undertaken from the general funds of the Society, the copies being sold at one half the prime cost of the sheets, nothing being charged for the binding. Thus the 1799 Bible was sold bound for 2s. 9d. The binding cost the society 2s. per copy; so that the society contributed 4s. 9d. on every copy. Each New Testament cost for printing 1s., and for binding 1s. 4d.; but it was sold at 6d. The total charge on the society's funds for the 1799 edition, after accounting for all receipts, was £2,568 6s. 8d. The whole edition was sold out in six months. The Rev. Griffith Jones makes frequent references in "Welch Piety" to the Welsh people's debt of gratitude to the S.P.C.K. The work of the society for nearly 200 years, in providing the Scriptures for the Welsh people in their own language, is beyond praise.

The Bibles used in Churches are usually supplied by the S.P.C.K. Folio editions for this purpose were issued in 1789 and 1852. The stereotype plates of the last named are kept at the Clarendon Press, and used when a new issue is called for. The folio Bible has, in many Churches, been abandoned in favour of a large quarto issued by the S.P.C.K. in 1859 from the same plates as the quarto Bible issued by the British and Foreign Bible Society in 1841. The 1841 Bible, or a reprint of it, is to be found on the pulpit of nearly every Welsh chapel. In many lists of Welsh Bibles a folio edition, 1799, appears, following an entry in Rowlands's "Cambrian Bibliography." All efforts to trace a folio of this date have failed. It seems quite certain that the large demy octavo volume of that year has been wrongly called a folio. Mr. Charles Ashton records a folio Bible under the date 1801 ; but all inquiry for a copy has been fruitless.

* "Memoir of the Rev. Thomas Jones," by John Owen, 1851, pp. 198-200.

CHAPTER VI.

LOCAL EFFORTS TO SUPPLY THE SCRIPTURES.

Unauthorised printing—Peter Williams's Bible—The Trevecca Pocket Bible—Other locally printed Bibles and Testaments.

A NEW TESTAMENT dated 1741 opens a new chapter in the history of the Bible in Wales. It is the first of a long and highly successful series of local efforts to supply the needs of the people. Hitherto, the printing and circulation of the Bible in Welsh had been controlled in London, and all the issues had the imprimatur of the authorised printers. As early as 1687 the Welsh Prayer Book was printed for Thomas Jones, then of London, but later of Shrewsbury, whether by arrangement with the authorised printers or not cannot be ascertained. This was the starting point. Thomas Jones re-issued the Prayer Book in 1700, 1708, and 1712—in each case from Shrewsbury. Throughout the eighteenth century the printers of Shrewsbury, Wrexham, and Chester, did a considerable trade in Welsh books, and the Prayer Book was one of their staple products. The authorised printers of the Bible were, however, stringent in asserting their rights, as the S.P.C.K. found when planning their first issue of the Welsh Bible. It·is, therefore, a point of considerable interest that the first encroachments upon these rights,—the Welsh New Testaments of 1741, 1756, and 1779—appeared with no printer's name or place of printing. That these three issues of the New Testament were unauthorised, the concealment of the printers' names clearly implies. There is no evidence of any consequences. It is quite likely that the facts never came to the knowledge of the authorised printers, the sale of the books being confined to Wales, and quite out of the regular line of the publishing trade as carried on in London. Even if the authorised printers were aware of what was going on, it is difficult to imagine that they could lay claim to material damage, for, as has been shown, they never undertook any issue of the Scriptures in Welsh without guarantees and subsidies. Local printers, on the other hand, put their money in a trade venture ; but it is doubtful whether they found it a profitable undertaking. At any rate, they were the first people who offered the Scriptures to the Welsh people in the ordinary way of trade.

Thomas Durston, the well-known printer at Shrewsbury, was the printer of the New Testament of 1741, a handy-sized volume, with fairly large clear type, printed in double columns, and neatly bound in calf. The Royal Arms printed on the titlepage gives the book an appearance of that authority which in reality it lacked. The text is that of the S.P.C.K. edition of 1727.

The New Testament of 1756, although it has the name of neither printer nor place, was almost certainly printed at Shrewsbury by John Eddowes. It is a crown octavo, printed with a large clear type in double columns, and follows the orthography of the later editions of the S.P.C.K., 1746 or 1752.

It will be noted that Durston and Eddowes each issued only one edition of the New Testament. They could hardly have found it a profitable undertaking to compete with the New Testaments issued by the S.P.C.K.: and from an advertisement of ʃ. Eddowes in a book issued by him in 1783 ("Amryw Salmau a Hymnau Profiadol, . . . Gan ʃ. Griffith," etc.), it would appear that he was offering to his customers the S.P.C.K. Testament.

The third New Testament in the unauthorised group, also without name of printer or place, was printed and published by John Ross at Carmarthen. Dr. Thomas Llewelyn, author of the "Account of the British or Welsh versions of the Bible," 1768, is said to have "prevailed with Mr Ross. . . . to undertake the publication of a good pocket edition of the Welsh New Testament, which proved very useful."* Dr. Llewelyn criticised the neglect of the authorised printers in not providing an adequate supply of Bibles in Welsh, and felt that the failure of the patent-holders to supply the needs of the Welsh people justified the issue of unauthorised editions: "I would make no objection to any thing, provided the country be duly supplied,"† he says; and although the words are not used in the sense of sanctioning infringement of the patentees' rights, they show that the right of the people to the Bible was the paramount idea. It is not certain what part Dr. Llewelyn took in connection with the 1779 New Testament—whether he merely instigated it, as the extract given above says, or took a more active share, as tradition asserts. It is a smaller volume as regards the size of the page, but thicker, than the Shrewsbury New Testaments, and the lines are across the page instead of in two columns. The chapter-contents are omitted.

The insufficient supply of Welsh Bibles from English sources, which had led to the clandestine printing of the New Testament, was the cause of a remarkable movement to meet the difficulty, initiated by the Rev. Peter Williams, and imitated by others. It is not too much to describe the work of Peter Williams as remarkable, seeing that it was the means, directly or indirectly, of taking the Bible into nearly every Welsh household, while in the hearts of the Welsh people the Bibles containing his notes occupy a place enjoyed by no other edition. The movement is remarkable, too, for the fact that its strength is still unexpended. From 1770—the date of the first issue—down to 1900, thirty-eight issues have been made in one form and another. The last issue was in 1895, by a firm at Porth, in the Rhondda Valley (No. 369), who in the course of eight years disposed of over 8,000 copies handsomely bound at £2 5s. each.

The right of the two Universities to the sole printing of the Bible did not, so it was discovered, extend to editions with notes and comments, these being, under copyright law, the property of the commentator. Peter Williams, by adding at the end of each chapter a note summarising and explaining the text, not only obtained the benefit of copyright, but also supplied the comment which enabled the Welsh people to better understand the Scriptures. So acceptable were these notes, that in the Welsh mind their authority became hardly less than the text itself. In one other important point Peter Williams was able to meet the special need of the people. By printing the Bible in a large clear type, and issuing it in periodical parts at one shilling each, he brought a useful family Bible practically within the reach of the poorest people.

* Richards's "Welsh Nonconformists' Memorial," 1820, p. 285.
† "Account of British . . . Versions," 1768, p. 66.

He commenced preparing the commentary in the year 1766, taking as his model the Bible with observations by Mr. Ostervald. A prospectus was issued in 1766, and the publication extended over nearly four years,—1767-1770. The Old and New Testaments, with Prys's Psalms, were comprised in fifteen parts, of which 8,600 copies were printed. The Apocrypha was printed last, in a smaller number, the purchase being at the subscriber's option. It is for this reason that copies occur with and without the Apocrypha.

The printing was done by John Ross, of Carmarthen, a Scotchman who taught himself the Welsh language, and who became an extensive printer and publisher of Welsh books. His career extended over an unusually long time: the earliest appearance of his imprint is 1763, and it occurs as late as 1807. He was also the printer of two other issues of Peter Williams's Bible,—those of 1779-81 and 1797-6.

Before the issue of this Bible, no systematic commentary in Welsh on the whole Bible had appeared. The New Testament had been summarised and, to some extent, explained by Christmas Samuel, of Panteg, in "Golwg ar Destament Newydd," 1728, and the Gospels harmonised and expounded by the Rev. John Evans, the editor of the 1769 Bible, in "Cyssondeb y Pedair Efengyl," 1765. To Peter Williams, however, belongs the credit of being the first Welsh commentator on the whole Bible, as well as the first to cause the Welsh Bible to be printed in Wales.

Peter Williams died in 1796. Edition after edition of his Bible appeared after his death, at first mainly from Welsh presses,—Chester, Carmarthen, Merthyr Tydfil, Carnarvon, and Swansea. With two exceptions, the local presses adhered to the quarto form. In 1823-25 this Bible appeared for the first time with a London imprint, a massive folio, which form the London editions retained until 1868, when a quarto size, larger than the Welsh printed quartos, was adopted by Blackie and Son. The difference in size is of some importance. The smaller quarto editions show nearly always signs of constant use, while the folios and large quartos appear to have been kept as show-books, comparatively little used. The introduction of plates into the London editions may have helped to sell the books, but for family reading the old plain quartos have retained popularity against all others.

In connection with the issue of 1828-30 by J. L. Brigstocke, Carmarthen, a sheet was printed containing a scheme for the formation of " Bible Clubs," the members to contribute two shillings and two pence per month for a year. When sufficient money was in the hands of the treasurer to pay for a Bible, the members drew lots, and the holder of the winning number had to give security to complete the payments, after which the Bible was handed over. One other rule was enacted : if a member had to leave the neighbourhood before the end of the year, the value of the subscriptions paid had to be taken in other books. Apparently no money would be returned ; and it is not clear what happened if a member who had drawn a Bible in the lottery removed before the payments were completed. Of course, there was the guarantee.

Twenty years after the publication of his family Bible, Peter Williams was associated with David Jones, a Baptist minister of Pontypool, in the publication of a pocket Bible. The marginal notes and references made by John Canne for an English Bible first printed at Amsterdam in 1647, were translated into Welsh, and added to the text. The printing was done at Trevecca, at the printing press belonging to

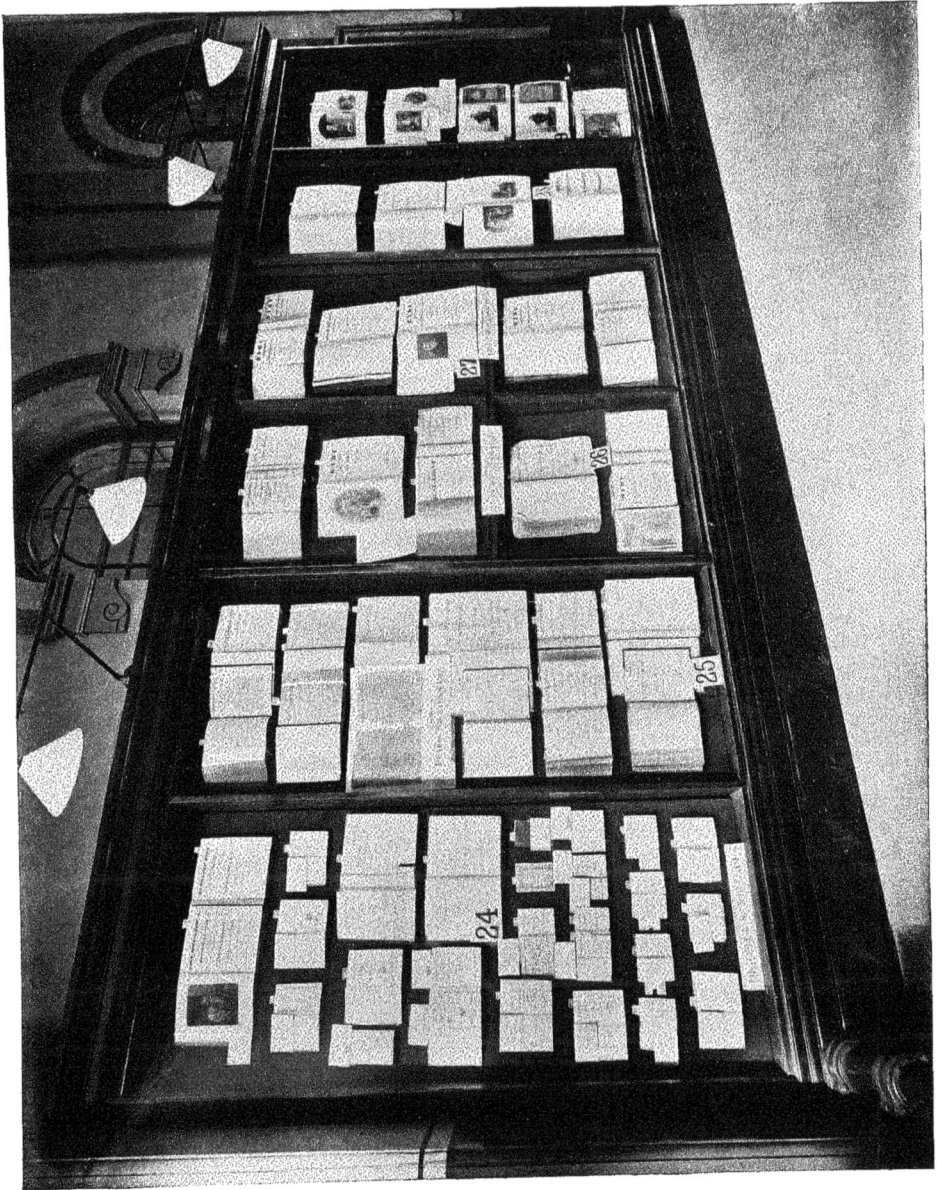

SHOW CASE IN THE WELSH BIBLE EXHIBITION CONTAINING DIGLOTT EDITIONS

the community founded by Howell Harris.* The type used—diamond—is very small. Four thousand copies were printed, and bound in full calf, for sale at six shillings each, and a number were also sold in parts at one shilling per part. The total number printed is believed to have been 6,000. The prospectus announcing the Bible is dated 1786, the issue in parts commenced in 1788, and the printing was completed in 1791. These varying dates have led to some confusion; but they all relate to the same book. Copies of the New Testament occur separately. The exact relations of Peter Williams and David Jones to this Bible are uncertain; but in letters to his son, now in the Cwrtmawr collection, Peter Williams continually refers to his work in correcting the proofs.

The publication is said to have resulted in a loss of £600, which troubled the closing years of David Jones and his wife,† and swept away all the profits made by Peter Williams on his great Bible.‡ The loss may have been partly owing to the very small size of the type used, making the book difficult to read save for people with unusually good sight. The type was specially obtained by the Trevecca press for this work, which added to the expense. The main cause of the loss, however, may have been due to the withdrawal of support by the Calvinistic Methodist Association. The proposal to print a pocket Bible was encouraged by the Baptist and Calvinistic Methodist Associations, notice of the intention being disseminated in the Circular Letters of the Baptist Association in 1787 and 1788; and it is likely that similar notice of the proposal was given at the meetings of the Calvinistic Methodists.

Peter Williams had been charged by the Calvinistic Methodists with heresy for some comments in the first chapter of the Gospel of St. John in his family Bible. In the Bible of 1790 the received translation was altered in a few verses, with the view, as was alleged, of supporting the supposed heresy. The discovery that in a Bible encouraged by the Association, and issued from a Methodist printing-press, the heresy as to the nature of the Trinity was repeated in what they considered to be an aggravated form, led to the expulsion of Peter Williams from the Calvinistic Methodist ministry. The financial loss already referred to was a natural consequence. Though formally condemned by the Association, and refused re-admission, Peter Williams retained the sympathy of the people of his own time, his opponents being of a younger generation. The great preacher, Daniel Rowland, of Llangeitho, stood by his friend ; and it was not until after the death of Daniel Rowland that the expulsion took place. An elegy on Peter Williams was printed at the Trevecca press immediately after his death.

" Beibl John Cann " was reprinted at Carmarthen in 1812, the New Testament being again issued from Carmarthen in 1823, followed by the Old Testament in 1826. Copies occur with these two issues bound together—1826-1823. The variations of the text introduced into

---

* For an account of the Trevecca Press, see " The Library," July, 1905.

† The Rev. J. Spinther James, M.A., D.Litt., refers to the 1790 Bible in " Hanes y Bedyddwyr." He supplements in a letter the information there given as follows :—" David Jones's widow, Hannah Jones of Dolgoch, who was a farmer and maltster before she married David Jones, was, soon after his death, 1792, on account of ' dyled y Beibl Bach,' made a bankrupt. According to my information, she spent the remainder of her life at Newcastle-Emlyn, receiving parish relief. She was alive in 1837-39, and is mentioned by David Jones in his ' Hanes y Bedyddwyr' (1839) as being in need."

‡ " The English Works of . . . Eliezer Williams," 1840, p. clxxxv.

the 1790 edition were corrected to the accepted readings in the Carmarthen reprints. They were also corrected for the Bible printed at Carmarthen in 1796 containing the marginal references of John Canne, and the notes of William Romaine. The offending passage in the family Bible was printed as originally written in the first four editions. In the fifth (John Evans, Carmarthen, 1807,) it was altered, presumably by David Humphreys, the son-in-law of Peter Williams; and the alteration was retained in all the editions issued by John Evans. It was also adopted by Lewis Evan Jones, who issued four editions from his press at Carnarvon. The printers of the first London issue (1823-25) state in the prospectus that they have printed Peter Williams's notes as he wrote them, and this is the course followed invariably except by the two printers named. This general statement is made with the reservation that six editions have not been checked on this point.

The publication of the Bible in numbers, introduced into Wales by Peter Williams, was found to meet the special circumstances of the poorer people. An English Bible, bearing the date 1779, and the imprint of John Ross, Carmarthen, appears also to have been issued in numbers. The volume contains "Arguments prefixed to the different books, and moral and theological observations at the end of each chapter, composed by the pious and Reverend Mr. Ostervald, Professor of Divinity, and one of the Ministers of the Reformed Church at Neufchatel." The Ostervald notes were "translated at the desire of and recommended by the Society for Propagating Religious Knowledge." Copies of the Bible with these notes occur with different imprints, namely, London, Edinburgh, Southampton, Carlisle, Newcastle-upon-Tyne, Carmarthen, and possibly others. In no case does the imprint occur on the body of the book, being always on the titlepage only. It looks as if the work had been printed at some centre, and localised for distribution with a special titlepage ; but this is not borne out by an inspection of the books, the issue from each centre being different in type and, to some extent, in contents. The explanation may be that some society promoted and encouraged the printing of this Bible for circulation among the poor at a very low price. Efforts to obtain evidence of this have not been successful. Nor is it clear whether the "Society for Propagating Religious Knowledge" is the same as the Society for Promoting Christian Knowledge. The Old and New Testaments were issued from Carmarthen in 107 numbers of four leaves each ; the Apocrypha, which is not in all copies, being issued after the New Testament, though bound up in its proper sequence in the volume. The signatures of the Apocrypha in the 1779 issue do not fit in with those of the Old and New Testaments. In the second Carmarthen issue of 1789 the signatures of the Apocrypha are different ; there is a new general title, and a list of subscribers is omitted. In all other respects the sheets of 1779 and 1789 are the same.* The third issue from Carmarthen in 1807 is exactly the same as that of 1789, except for a new general title with a slight alteration in the imprint, namely : " Printed by John Ross, M,DCCC,VII, For Hobday and Ryder, Albion-House, Birmingham." In the three issues the N.T. title is dated 1779. The list of subscribers in the first issue contains just over eight hundred names. After twenty-eight years the "remainder" of the first English Bible, with the imprint of a Welsh printer, was sold off to a firm in England.

---

* The British Museum copy of the 1789 issue is extensively illustrated with engravings and maps.

There is one other instance of an English Bible being printed in Wales, and it is represented by only two known copies. The story of its production is somewhat peculiar. In 1839 an edition of the Rev. Joseph Harris's diglott Bible, in parallel columns, was printed at Swansea by Benjamin Hull, who formulated a plan of re-making the English portion of the text, and issuing it as an English Bible with the title, "The Christian's New Evangelical and Self-Interpreting Family Bible." The diglott edition does not contain the Apocrypha, but the English edition does, the imprint of a London firm being found on it. The explanation is simple : to save expense, the publisher purchased the requisite number of copies of sheets containing the Apocrypha from a firm in London. The style and type of the Aprocrypha differ distinctly from the rest of the book.

With the printing of the Trevecca Bible of 1790 commenced a series of locally printed Bibles and Testaments, with brief notes, introduced to evade the rights of the authorised printers. In some instances, only one or two notes are inserted, and these so brief as to leave no doubt as to the reason for their introduction.

The 1790 Bible with the notes of Canne, and the 1796 Bible with the notes of Romaine, the second having been printed at Carmarthen, may have been the means of stirring up another Carmarthen printer, John Evans, to publish editions of the Scriptures. Altogether eleven issues bear his imprint between the years 1801 and 1822. His first venture was a Bible issued in thirteen sixpenny parts, the first appearing in 1800 and the last in 1802, the titlepage bearing the latter date. It is a thick demy octavo, printed in double columns, with the marginal notes of Dr. John Brown, of Haddington. It contains also tables of the miracles and parables, and Isaac Watts's rhymed version of the Psalms translated by David Jones, of Caio. Some copies do not contain the Psalms. The advertisements of John Daniel and John Evans show that there was keen rivalry between them as printers and publishers, and the issue of a Bible by John Evans in 1802 appears to have been resented by John Daniel, who still held a stock of the 1796 Bible. On the appearance of the first part of Evans's Bible in 1800, John Daniel proceeded to advertise his stock of the 1796 Bible as if it were a new edition at a much reduced price.

John Evans brought out four editions of Peter Williams's Bible—1807, 1811, 1822-21, and 1830-29; and he also published four editions of the New Testament—the first in 1801, for John Richards; the second in 1802, for Titus Lewis, a Baptist minister, of Carmarthen; the third in 1811, with a few phrases from Peter Williams's commentary; and the fourth in 1822—a re-issue of Titus Lewis's edition.

A New Testament with a short comment at the foot of two of the pages was printed at Merthyr in 1808, by William Williams, a well-known printer. Another New Testament bearing the Merthyr imprint appeared in 1822, from the press of the Rev. John Jenkins, of Hengoed. This Testament also has the brief notes. This press became well-known in connection with the commentary of Jenkins, of which more hereafter. It was started April 21st, 1819, by John Jenkins and Thomas Williams "Gwilym Morganwg." Williams retired from the joint ownership before the end of the same year, the press continuing in the name of Jenkins alone. In 1827 he removed the press to Maesycwmmwr, and in 1831 to Cardiff.

The multiplication of copies of the Scriptures at very low prices after the establishment of the British and Foreign Bible Society rendered the local printing of the text of the Scriptures unnecessary and unprofitable ; but as late as the year 1845, there was a tiny New Testament with a few very short footnotes printed at Wrexham. It is described in the Bibliography (No. 171a) from the only recorded copy, now in the Cardiff Library.

CHAPTER VII.

THE GROWTH OF COMMENTARIES.

Commentaries of native origin—Translated commentaries—Development of local printing—Ministerial presses—The system of publishing in numbers.

THE success of Peter Williams's Bibles caused considerable activity in the publication of works in numbers, and also led to different religious bodies providing Bibles with suitable commentaries for their adherents. In compiling the Bibliography of the Welsh Bible, it was found necessary, in order to keep the work within reasonable limits, to adopt a rule excluding all editions with comments interspersed with the text. Hence, some " Esboniadau " are excluded which are almost as much a requisite in some households as the Bible of Peter Williams in others. Some of these were original works, while others were translations.

The earliest of the translations was that by the Rev. John Evans, M.A., of Francis Gastrel's " Christian Institutes," which appeared in Welsh in 1773, as " Y Deddfau Cristianogol," from the press of John Ross, of Carmarthen. The " Christian Institutes " is a collection out of the writings of the Old and New Testaments delivered in the words of Scripture. The translator was the author of " Cyssondeb y Pedair Efengyl," 1765, and editor of the 1769 edition of the Bible (No. 25).

Another translation was by the Rev. Richard Jones, Curate of Ruthin, who, between 1801 and 1807, published Dr. Adam Clarke's paraphrase of the four Gospels, with notes by other English commentators. This work appeared in four volumes—one on each Gospel, the first from the press of W. Minshull, of Chester, in 1801 ; the second and third from the press of W. Collister Jones, of Chester, in 1802 and 1804, respectively ; and the fourth from the press of Broster and Son, of Chester, in 1807.

The translation of the commentary of John Guyse on the New Testament, was done into Welsh by the Rev. William Thomas, of Bala. The first part of this was printed at Machynlleth in 1803, and the last at Merthyr in 1815. This work is a curiosity on account of the number of times the translator changed his printer, returning more than once to the same office. The stages of its printing are : Machynlleth, Bala, Machynlleth, Trevecca, Bala, Carmarthen, Bala, Merthyr Tydfil. William Thomas published some small books, mostly printed at the Trevecca Press ; he complained of the trouble he had with the printers there in connection with the publication of Guyse's commentary, as the parts were never ready to time. He is said to have bought the paper himself, and sent it to the printers. He would send his son from Bala to Trevecca on horseback, to get the parts and convey them to the distributors about the country. Sometimes the son had to wait about for weeks for the printers to finish a part. The translator died in 1809, before the completion of the work, and the last eight parts were seen through the press by the Rev. Ebenezer Jones, of Pontypool. The delays in bringing out the work wearied the subscribers, who at first numbered 1,800, but who, before the end, had declined to 800, resulting in a loss of £300. Very few complete copies now exist.

An unhappy fate also overtook the Welsh issue of the Bible with commentary by the Rev. Thomas Coke, LL.D., who was born at Brecon, and who himself arranged for the translation and printing. His relations with the translators and printers were not happy ; and the work, which took from 1806 to 1813 to print, was not very successful. It is in three volumes, quarto. The first two volumes were translated by Thomas Roberts, Wesleyan preacher of Bonwm, near Corwen ; the third volume from Matthew to the end of the Epistles by John Hughes, Wesleyan minister, of Brecon, author of "Horæ Britannicæ," 1818-19 ; and the remainder by Timothy Davis, of Evesham, a Unitarian minister, son of David Davis, Castell Hywel.

The printer of the first portion, J. Hemingway, Chester, became bankrupt when the O.T. was finished, and delay occurred in publishing the N.T., which was commenced by London printers; but so many mistakes were made that John Hughes threw up the work, which was later transferred to a Carmarthen printer, with Timothy Davis as translator. ("Yr Eurgrawn Wesleyaidd," 1849, pp. 163-165, 193-194.)

By 1810 the first volume of the Rev. Dr. John Gill's commentary on the New Testament had appeared from the press of John Evans, of Carmarthen, translated by Christmas Evans, Titus Lewis, and Joseph Harris "Gomer"; but about 1818, owing to lack of subscribers and irregular payments for the parts issued, the second volume was left unfinished after 15 parts, comprising Acts—I. Cor. v. 9, had been issued. The first volume consisted of 28 parts, sold at 1s. each, or £1 12s. bound. In a note in "Seren Gomer" for Apr. 8, 1818, the editor says that not much less than £50 was owing for parts in Carnarvonshire alone, while in another note in "Seren Gomer" for Sept. 8, 1819, the editor reports that the publisher, John Evans, complains that the support is inadequate to carry on the work, but that if 300 pledged themselves to take it, he would proceed without delay. The required number of subscribers was not secured, as may be inferred from the preface of the publisher of the second edition, which appeared in shilling parts between 1849 and 1854. Its size is imperial octavo, and it is still found bound in two volumes in many a Welsh Baptist home and library. The printer and publisher of the second edition was the Rev. William Owen, of Cardiff, who adopted the first translation as far as it had proceeded, and finished the remainder himself. In his preface he says that at the commencement of the work he had 700 subscribers, but that before the end they had dwindled to 500. He complains also that he had lost "several scores of pounds at the hands of unfaithful subscribers and distributors." Copies of this work are still being sold by a bookseller at Cwmavon, Glamorgan.

The commentary of the Rev. Samuel Clark was translated by John Humphreys, a Calvinistic Methodist minister, of Caerwys, Flint-shire. It was issued in sixty-two parts, title dated 1813, and is usually found strongly bound in leather, sometimes with the large-headed brass nails so much used by the Welsh binders of the late eighteenth and early nineteenth centuries, in imitation of the brass bosses of an earlier time. Copies of Peter Williams's Bibles often have these brass nails, and they were no doubt serviceable in preventing the wearing of the leather by rubbing on tables or desks.

The commentary on the New Testament by the Rev. George Lewis, D.D., of Llanuwchllyn, the publication of which commenced in 1802, went on for twenty-seven years before it was completed in seven octavo volumes. The name of Edward Davies, Lewis's son-in-law, appears as co-editor on volumes V.—VII. Volume I. was printed at Chester by W.,.C. Jones, the other six volumes at Wrexham by John Painter. Dr. Lewis died in 1822.

The commentary accompanying the Bible of David Davies, Congregational minister, of Swansea, was of native origin. It was printed at Carmarthen, being issued in forty parts at one shilling each, and the titlepage is dated 1815. The work was completed by another David Davies, Congregational minister, of. Pantteg, Carmarthenshire, who wrote the notes to the Book of Revelation. At the end is bound up with a separate title, dated 1817, Isaac Watts's metrical version of the Psalms, done into Welsh by David Jones, of Caio. It is a quarto volume of 1,358 pages ; and as a family Bible was much used in the first half of the nineteenth century.

The Bible, with commentary by the Rev. John Jenkins, known as " Jenkins Hengoed," was one of the most popular, especially with the Baptists, though the work was also accepted as a sound authority by Calvinists of all denominations. Jenkins commenced life as a collier, became a Baptist minister, and prepared a commentary on the whole Bible fuller than the commentary of Peter Williams. This Bible, with commentary interspersed with the text, was printed at Jenkins's own press, and sold in parts. To his ministerial labours Jenkins added those of author, printer, publisher, and bookseller. His stipend was small, and it is a remarkable achievement for a man of small income to have produced the three bulky quarto volumes containing his commentary, and to have carried the work through without loss. His reputation as a theologian contributed to his success, and helped him to secure subscribers from all over Wales. Following the practice which even yet survives in Wales, he went on preaching tours for the purpose of selling his book to the chapel members up and down the country.

When the Old Testament was completed (April, 1828,) he printed a note complaining that many subscriptions were in arrear, and prompt payment is asked for, as even when all the money owing had been paid, the book would barely cover its expenses. The work was completed in 88 parts, sold for one shilling each. The publication of the parts extended over about ten years. On completion, the three volumes were offered at four guineas for ready money, or four pounds eight shillings with a year's credit and adequate security. Jenkins died June 5, 1853.

Matthew Henry's commentary up to Joshua ii. was translated into Welsh by John Llwyd, of Penybryn, Dolgelly, and published by Richard Jones of the same town.* The first part appeared May. 1, 1820. Like the earlier venture of John Evans, of Carmarthen, in connection with Dr. Gill's commentary, it appears that, after the issue of 17 parts at 1s. each, the publication came to an end for lack of support. Part 17 included the titlepage and preliminary matter. The wrapper of parts 5 and 6, issued as a double part, contains a notice that, unless the work is better patronised and payments made more promptly, it would have to be discontinued.

This failure was followed by a successful attempt on the part of the Rev. Evan Griffiths, Congregational minister, of Swansea. He commenced the publication of a Welsh version of Matthew Henry in 1828,

---

* John Llwyd's name alone appears on the title as translator; but in an advertise-ment of the first part, on the wrapper of " Seren Gomer," May, 1820, the work is described as translated without abbreviation under the editorship and care of the Rev. Simon Lloyd, M.A., of Bala, and the Rev. Michael Jones, of Llanuwchllyn.

using John Llwyd's translation as far as it went, and enlisting helpers to carry it on. By far the greater part was translated by Evan Griffiths himself, who also superintended the whole work, together with the publication and distribution of the parts, and ultimately the printing at a press which he established at Swansea. With the publication of the fourth volume in 1835, the work was brought to a successful conclusion.

John Wesley's commentary on the New Testament was first translated into Welsh and published in 1825. The translators were the Revs. Hugh Hughes and John Williams 2nd, Wesleyan ministers. It was issued in twenty shilling parts. Another translation was made by Rowland Hughes, Wesleyan minister, and published in a small 8vo. volume in 1850.

In 1828 a Welsh version of John Calvin's commentary on the Psalms was printed and published at Brecon, in a quarto volume of 530 pages.

Burkitt's " Help and Guide to the New Testament " was translated into Welsh by the Rev. Josiah Thomas Jones, Congregational minister. He, like so many other preachers, set up a printing-press of his own, at which he printed his translation, which is dated 1835.

The commentary of James Hughes " Iago Trichrug," a compilation translated from several English commentators, was of considerable authority amongst the Calvinistic Methodists. The New Testament was published first, in 1835, the four volumes dealing with the Old Testament appearing at intervals from 1848 to 1843. The New Testament was re-issued in 1846 and 1860.

The Bible commentary and critical notes of Dr. Adam Clarke were translated by the Rev. John Jones " Idrisyn," and printed at Llanidloes, in six volumes, between 1837 and 1845, under the title, " Yr Esboniad Berniadol." The translator afterwards made a commentary of his own, " Y Deonglydd Berniadol," in five volumes, printed at Llanidloes in 1852. Eight editions of this commentary have appeared and eighty thousand copies of it are said to have been sold in Wales and America. The author was up to the year 1853 a printer at Llanidloes, and a Wesleyan local preacher. In that year he joined the Church of England, and at his death in 1887 was Vicar of Llandyssiliogogo.

The commentary of Owen Jones " Meudwy Môn," in three volumes, printed at Mold in 1838-40-42, was chiefly used by the Calvinistic Methodists.

The Rev. Thomas Scott's commentary on the Prophets, translated by Thomas Jones, of Amlwch, printed and published at Carnarvon in 1840, is a quarto volume of 675 pages.

The notes on the New Testament of Albert Barnes were translated by Dr. Thomas Rees, of Swansea, and four volumes were printed at Llanelly, 1846-50; but owing to irregularity in the issue of the parts, and a consequent failure of regular support from the subscribers, the work was suspended before completion. It was afterwards brought out by Mr. Thomas Gee, of Denbigh, complete in six volumes.

The Rev. Evan Evans " Ieuan Glan Geirionydd " was the editor of an illustrated Bible with commentary and notes, brought out in three volumes in 1844-47-50, and comprising the Old Testament only. This Bible is illustrated largely with woodcuts. Mr. Hugh Jones " Erfyl " and others assisted in its production.

In 1861 Messrs. Hughes and Son, of Wrexham, issued the first part of Dr. John Kitto's commentary on the New Testament, translated and added to by the Rev. Owen Thomas, D.D., of Liverpool. Its size is octavo, and it is sold bound complete in two volumes, the titlepages dated respectively 1862 and 1885. This, like the Bible of Ieuan Glan Geirionydd, is called "Y Beibl Darluniadol" (= The Pictorial Bible). The Rev. John Hughes, Calvinistic Methodist minister, of Liverpool, had proceeded with the translation as far as Matthew xv., when owing to his death, August 8, 1860, Dr. Owen Thomas was engaged to continue the work.

Amongst other commentators were the Rev. Robert Ellis "Cynddelw," a Baptist minister whose commentary on the New Testament in several volumes was issued in parts between 1855 and 1875, when he died leaving the work incomplete; the Rev. Thomas Lewis of Risca, afterwards of Newport, whose commentary for the family, "Esboniad y Teulu," first issued in 1871, has recently been republished at Carmarthen; and the Rev. T. Roberts "Scorpion," author of "Y Testament Daearyddol," and "Esboniad Cyflawn ar y Testament Newydd," in two volumes, Dolgelly, 1880-85.

Several Calvinistic Methodist ministers were engaged in preparing the popular "Testament yr Ysgol Sabbathol," in two volumes, published first in 1866-71, and kept regularly in print. It is chiefly used by teachers in the Calvinistic Methodist Sunday Schools.

It is impossible to do more than thus briefly enumerate some of the commentaries used by the Welsh people in the study of the Bible. The number of such works is so large, that any effort to treat of them would involve departure from the main theme of this history. There are, however, two small books which ought to be mentioned: they are "Y Testament Daearyddol" and "Y Testament Cyfeirnodawl." These are the pocket reference books on the New Testament; and devout Welshmen and Welshwomen still carry the one or the other in the pocket for ready reference, especially on Sundays.

h

CHAPTER VIII.

Through Controversy to Peace.

Foundation of the Bible Society—Proposed revision of the orthography —The first Welsh issues of the new Society—The authorised text of 1808—Mr. Charles's Bible, 1814—Ioan Tegid's attempts at a revised orthography.

THE British and Foreign Bible Society, founded on the 7th of March, 1804, owes its origin mainly to the dearth of Welsh Bibles and the difficulty of procuring a further supply. Appeals made to the Society for Promoting Christian Knowledge, hitherto the principal source, met with very little encouragement. From 1769 the Society did nothing beyond printing a folio Welsh Bible for churches until the edition of 1799 was put in hand. The number of copies determined upon for the 1799 issue, — 10,000 Bibles and an extra 2,000 New Testaments,—was quite insufficient to meet the demand. The revivals had brought many converts to religion, who, unable to obtain Bibles for themselves, visited the houses of more fortunate neighbours for the purpose of reading the Word of God. The worn condition of Welsh Bibles in circulation at this time bear out the reports of the constant use made of them. The minds of earnest men were much exercised how to overcome the dearth of Welsh Bibles. The Rev. Thomas Jones, of Creaton, Northamptonshire, who had held curacies on the Welsh Borders, and whose sympathies were with the Welsh people, seems to have conceived the idea of some such Society as afterwards took shape at the hands of Thomas Charles and others. In the "Memoir of Thomas Jones," by John Owen (London, 1851,) the following account of his relation to the Bible Society drawn up by himself in 1833 is printed :—

"It is now generally allowed, that the British and Foreign Bible Society had its cradle in Wales . . . Two things alone can be mentioned as the occasion of this society,—the great dearth of Bibles and Testaments in the Principality of Wales,—and the failure of the Christian Knowledge Society to supply that country with sufficient numbers.

"On visiting South Wales in the year 1791, I found that there was a loud and general cry for Bibles among the lower classes, when none were to be had for money. On my return to England I established a correspondence with some of the clergy in South Wales, and with my friend, Mr. Charles, in North Wales, in order to gain information as to the extent of want of Bibles in the Principality." Then Mr. Jones describes the steps he had taken to prevail on the Christian Knowledge Society to publish a large edition of Welsh Bibles. Through the intervention of his Bishop, Dr. Madan, he succeeded, and the Society printed ten thousand copies, which came out of the press in 1799. The whole edition was sold in a very short time, and was not found to have been half sufficient to supply the want. An earnest and repeated application was made for another edition, but it was met with a repeated denial.

"In this failure," says Mr. Jones, "as to the old Society, may be seen the seed of the new Bible Society. Had the Committee of the Society granted the supply Wales called for, it is probable a new Society would not have been established to this day."

Having thus completely failed with the old Society, Mr. Jones attempted to devise means to get Bibles by subscriptions in the Principality ; he sent his plan to Mr. Charles.

" He and others," he says, " approved of it, and without loss of time endeavoured to act upon it : but owing to scarcity of money in that part of the kingdom, no great progress was made. Mr. Charles, at his usual time of the year went to serve at Spa-field Chapel : and while in town he made known to his friends there the great dearth of Bibles in Wales, and how he had failed to obtain any more from the old Society. The case was taken into consideration ; and, I believe, the first that acted in the affair was that excellent man, the late Rev. Joseph Hughes. So the new Society was soon formed ; and may it continue to bless mankind till time shall be no more."

The distinct parts which these originators of the Society have acted, were these:— Mr. Jones repeatedly tried the old Society and failed ; he then proposed to form a new Society in Wales, and that failed ;—Mr. Charles, his partner in these struggles, while in London, unburdened his mind to a company of friends, detailed what had been done, and proposed to form a Society for the purpose in London :—Mr. Hughes, one of the company, said, " If for Wales, why not for England, and for the whole world ! "

Thus commenced the British and Foreign Bible Society; which has done wonders already, and is destined, we hope, to do still greater wonders.

The Rev. Thomas Charles, of Bala, whose evangelistic labours up and down the country made him fully acquainted with the difficulties, was much concerned, and constantly introduced the subject into his letters and conversations. It was at a committee meeting of the Religious Tract Society held in a Counting-House in Lower Thames Street, London, on the 7th December, 1802, that Mr. Charles put the question, " How a large and cheap edition of the Bible could be had in Welsh, and how, if possible, a permanent repository of Bibles could be procured, that there might be no more scarcity of them amongst the poor Welsh." During the discussion which followed, the Rev. Joseph Hughes, a Baptist Minister, of Battersea, made the suggestion which contained the germ of the future Society in these words, " Surely a Society might be formed for the purpose ; and if for Wales, why not for the Kingdom ; why not for the whole world ? "

From the discussion thus incidentally initiated sprang the British and Foreign Bible Society. The story of the Society, its founders, and its operations, has often been told. The work which it has done in circulating the Scriptures amongst the Welsh people more than realises the dream of Thomas Charles of " a permanent repository of Bibles, that there might be no more scarcity of them."

The Bible Society went straight to the hearts of the Welsh people; and during the first year a fund of nearly £1,900 was subscribed towards the funds by the Principality, mainly through the exertions of Mr. Charles and Dr. Warren, Bishop of Bangor. In the first report of the Society are printed extracts from a letter written by a clergyman in North Wales, Feb. 22, 1805, which are as follows :—

" There are none of our poor people willing to live and die without contributing their mites towards forwarding so glorious a design. Their zeal and eagerness in the good cause, surpasses every thing I have ever before witnessed.

" On several occasions we have been obliged to check their liberality, and take half what they offered, and what we thought they ought to give. In very many instances, servants have given one-third of their wages for the year.

" In one instance a poor servant-maid put down one guinea on the plate, being one-third of her wages : that it might not be perceived what she put down, she covered the guinea with a halfpenny. One little boy had with much trouble reared a brood of chickens ; when the collection came to be made, he sold them all, and gave every farthing he got for them towards it ; and this was his whole stock, and all the living that he had. Innumerable instances of a similar nature might be mentioned. Great joy prevails universally at the thought that poor heathens are likely soon to be in possession of a Bible ; and you will never hear a prayer put up without a petition for the Bible Society and heathen nations."

The same spirit has been manifested by Welshmen ever since. The Annual Reports of the Society frequently refer to the consistent support received from Wales. A Welsh auxiliary of the Society, formed in

London in 1814-1815, contributed £450 to the funds. As soon as the Welsh found their way in any numbers to the United States, they there formed themselves into auxiliaries, and contributed to the funds of the American Bible Society, as will appear later. Measures were at once taken to obtain a large supply of the Scriptures in Welsh. The objects of the Society were greatly assisted by the introduction of stereotype printing, which had just been discovered, and adopted by the University Press at Cambridge. On the 3rd day of September, 1804, it was decided to order 20,000 Welsh Bibles and 5,000 Testaments from the Cambridge Press, the Rev. Thomas Charles being appointed to prepare the copy for the press. With the sanction of the Syndics of the University Press, it was decided to print from the Bible of 1799, revised by Mr. Charles.

Unfortunately, Mr. Charles did not confine himself to correcting the rather numerous errors in the 1799 edition. He proposed to revise the orthography in accordance with the scheme of Dr. William Owen-Pughe and others who at the time were endeavouring to get their views on Welsh orthography accepted. On this, and on another occasion, did the zeal of the advocates of language reform outrun discretion. To alter the orthography of the received text of the Bible was a proceeding not to be countenanced, however eminent the authority proposing it, and when the nature of the changes intended leaked out, a controversy arose which lasted for many years.

The opening shot was fired by the Rev. John Roberts, Vicar of Tremeirchion, curator of the press for the 1799 Bible. In a letter to the Secretary of the S.P.C.K., Mr. Roberts stated that improper alterations in the orthography of the Welsh version were being made by Mr. Charles. The Secretary of the S.P.C.K. sent extracts from Mr. Roberts's letter to the Bishop of London, who brought the subject before the President of the Bible Society. A sub-committee was at once appointed to consider the matter, and the sub-committee referred the question of the proposed changes to the Rev. Walter Davies " Gwallter Mechain." Ultimately, it was found that, by the Act of Uniformity, the sanction of the four Welsh Bishops and the Bishop of Hereford was necessary before any changes could be introduced ; and steps were taken to comply with the law in this respect.

The proceedings are fully set out in a pamphlet by the Rev. William Dealtry : " A Vindication of the British and Foreign Bible Society," etc., London, 1810. This was in reply to charges brought against the Bible Society in more than one pamphlet, the Welsh Bible forming the groundwork of the attack. It should be noted that the Society was in no way to blame. Immediately the facts were disclosed, steps were taken to arrive at a correct decision ; and the Society is entirely free from any suspicion of a desire to alter the received text. Some friends of the S.P.C.K. unwisely tried to use the incident to damage the new Society. In calling attention to the danger of unauthorised alterations, the S.P.C.K. and its supporters were absolutely in the right. Subsequent events, however, disclosed a want of cordiality towards the Bible Society on the part of some supporters of the S.P.C.K. ; and the Society which had received coldly all suggestions for the new edition of the Welsh Bible, realising, too late, that a mistake had been made, hurried forward a new edition, following the text of 1746. For the sake of uniformity, the Bible Society agreed to follow the same text ; but found later that the S.P.C.K. had altered its decision, and was following the 1752 text. A letter addressed to the S.P.C.K. on the subject elicited a reply which was not candid. Altogether, the behaviour of the S.P.C.K. at this period, and for some years before, was not what its best friends could have desired. The Bible Society, more wisely counselled, overcame the obstruction of the older Society without loss of dignity, and waxed stronger for the fierce light thrown upon its proceedings. By agreeing to follow the same text as the S.P.C.K., the new Society removed any possible ground for criticism. It is not necessary to discuss further the technical merits of the controversy, beyond stating that, while the 1799 Bible had many inaccuracies, the changes proposed by Mr. Charles were not restricted to a correction of misprints, and never received the approval of Welsh scholars. It was fortunate that the British and Foreign Bible Society was saved from putting forth a Bible which would have been unpopular with the Welsh people.

The issue of the Society's Welsh Scriptures was retarded by the controversy. It was not until July, 1806, that the New Testament was put into circulation. There are three issues dated in this year, distinguishable by the imprint,—the first, "Argraffedig gan Ioan Smith . . . Mai 6, 1806"; the second, "Argraffedig gan Richard Watts . . . Mai 6, 1806"; and the third with the same imprint as the second, but with the date on the last leaf altered to "Mai 7." The three issues make up 10,000 copies, sold at one shilling each. The Rev. John Owen* quotes from "*The Christian Observer*" for July, 1810, the following account of the manner in which these Testaments were received, given on the authority of an "eye-witness":—

"When the arrival of the cart was announced, which carried the first sacred load, the Welsh peasants went out in crowds to meet it; welcomed it as the Israelites did the ark of old; drew it into the town; and eagerly bore off every copy, as rapidly as they could be dispersed. The young people were to be seen consuming the whole night in reading it. Laborers carried it with them to the field, that they might enjoy it during the intervals of their labor, and lose no opportunity of becoming acquainted with its sacred truths."

The whole Bible was printed and published for the Society in the following year, 1807, copies of the New Testament being also issued separately. 20,000 copies of the Bible were printed, the proofs being read by Dr. William Owen-Pughe. Some copies had been worked off before it was discovered that a whole chapter (Judges viii.) had been omitted. Before the omission was discovered 2,750 copies had been bound and sent out. These were rectified by cancelling two pages (189-190) and inserting four (189, 190, 189*, and 190*); but some copies were not traced, and such of these as survive still lack the eighth chapter of Judges. In the un-issued copies sheet H (pages 169-190) was reprinted, the contents at the head of each chapter being abridged, which enabled the printers to bring in the missing chapter. This was not the only disaster due to the eagerness of the promoters to get the work completed. In Psalm cv. verse 36 is omitted, the text of verse 33 being repeated in its place, and a portion of verse 4 of Jeremiah xxxv. is omitted. Corrections were issued for these errors, but not inserted in all copies. The mistakes were detected by the Rev. Thomas Charles.†

Meanwhile the S.P.C.K. were making arrangements for a new edition of the Bible. Having regard to the controversy over the text, the Welsh Bishops took steps to have the whole Bible carefully collated by a committee of three persons. The Rev. Walter Davies "Gwallter Mechain" was one of the three. The names of the other two do not

---

* "History of the Origin and First Ten Years of the Bible Society," 1816, vol. I., p. 263.

† These facts have been kindly supplied by the Rev. D. E. Jenkins, of Denbigh, who is engaged upon a biography of Thomas Charles, in which the subject will be more fully treated.

appear to be on record ; but it is likely that the Rev. David Hughes, Rector of Llanfyllin, who afterwards corrected the press, was one, and the Rev. Francis Owen, then of Christ Church, Oxford, afterwards Rector of Efenechtyd, may have been the other. The text of the 1752 edition was collated by this committee with Parry's Bible, 1620, and the folio of 1690. The result is thus given in the Bishop's certificate prefixed to the edition :—

> "From this collation, it appears, that some emendations in the orthography were made in the edition of 1690, commonly called Bishop Lloyd's, which have been generally approved ; and that it has been important only to correct some errors, chiefly of the press, in later copies of the Bible, and to restore the orthography of proper names after the text published in the year 1620."

The certificate is signed by the four Welsh Bishops and the Bishop of Hereford, who approve the text as required by the Act of Uniformity, 14 Caroli II., Ch. IV., Sect. 27. This became the authorised text of the Welsh Bible, and has been adhered to ever since. It was adopted by the Bible Society with certain very slight modifications in the edition of 1814. The following letter, written by the Rev. Walter Davies to " Tegid " in 1825, is valuable as coming from one of the committee which collated the text :—

> " You begin with four questions—
>
> " I. Whether I approve of Mr. Hughes's Bible ?
>
> " I am at a loss to know what edition you intend to designate by this appellation. If you mean the edition printed at Oxford in 1799, I cannot recommend it as a pattern for future editions . . . .
>
> " But if you give the name of Hughes to the Oxford edition of 1809, I must beg leave to change my opinion. In this edition, the errors of 1799 are avoided, as the edition of 1752 was followed. I was one out of three deputed to read over the edition of 1752, for the purpose of correcting inaccuracies in orthography and punctuation. I was an advocate for uniformity in general ; but I was outvoted in almost every instance. The word *meistraid*, for instance, I wanted to be printed so altogether ; but my friends saw no deformity in *meistryd, meistred, meistreid*—sometimes one, sometimes the other, 'for the sake of variety,' said they. In one verse of 1752 I observed *uniawn* and *union* : I proposed uniformity ; but it was negatived. Bishop Parry, in 1620, has *diffaethwch* uniformly throughout ; Bishop Lloyd, in 1690, has *diffaithwch* and *diffeithwch* ; the editions of 1717, 1746, 1789, follow *diffeithwch* altogether. I succeeded in proposing the restoration of Bishop Parry's *diffaethwch* ; as I wished *di-ffaeth* to represent *barren, sterile ;*—as a distinction from *di-ffaith*, a word in common use for *base, vile, &c.* However, in the stereotyped 12mo editions of the Bible Society, I find *diffaith* again adopted, excepting in *Job* xxxviii., 27, where ' *tir diffaeth* ' occurs.
>
> " You now see that I disapprove of the edition of 1799, upon good grounds, but that in a great measure I approve of that of 1809, though it be a specimen of the old orthography.
>
> " Your question II. is; How do I approve of Mr. Charles's edition of 1814 ?
>
> " I approve of it equally with that of 1809, though there may be some variations in literal orthography between them. Mr. Charles, owing to a compromised understanding between the two Societies, was under considerable restrictions in the preparation of this edition. I remember well the alterations he intended for an edition in 1814, [*sic* 1804] and which caused some unpleasant discussions at the time. Mr. Charles, in 1814, adopted more of the ' *suaviter in modo*,' and in my opinion can scarcely give offence to the most rigid advocates of the old orthography.
>
> . " Your question III. may be soon answered, by saying that the Welsh people are in general partial to *Marginal References*, and they are very useful. But I am of opinion that they have not been revised since the middle of the last century. They should be correct and without inappropriate references ; otherwise they would be worse than blank margins. A correct edition of such a Bible would be very desirable for the Principality."

As the letter just quoted shows, the Bible Society adopted the text of the 1809 Bible, with some slight modifications in the orthography made by the Rev. Thomas Charles. To put its intentions beyond doubt, the Society, in 1810, amended the wording of its first rule—"The designation of the Society shall be the British and Foreign Bible Society, of which the sole object shall be, to encourage a wider circulation of the Holy Scriptures. The only copies in the languages of the United Kingdom to be circulated by the Society, shall be the Authorized Version, without note or comment." As altered, the latter part of the rule reads, "to encourage a wider circulation of the Holy Scriptures without note or comment : the only copies in the languages of the United Kingdom to be circulated by the Society shall be the Authorized Version."

The Bible of 1814 was prepared by the Bible Society in response to a generally expressed desire for a larger type. It was printed from stereotype plates, and reprinted again and again. As the 1809 issue became the standard for the S.P.C.K. editions, so the 1814 has been adhered to by the Bible Society. Attempts to rake the dead ashes of the controversy met with scant success ; and when next a difficulty arose over alterations to the text, there is a marked absence of suspicion and bitterness towards both Societies.

Another attempt to introduce a revised orthography, this time of the New Testament only, was made by the Rev. John Jones " Ioan Tegid," who was employed to supervise the printing of the Welsh and English New Testament of 1826. The Bible Society, having inquired what text was to be followed, received a reply from the printer that " he believes Mr. Jones, as corrector of the press, intends to use the text of Mr. Hughes (1809) to print from, and to read by that which was corrected by Mr. Charles, of Bala" (1814). This was satisfactory to the Bible Society, and an order was given for 2,000 copies, which were duly delivered. It was not until after the publication of the New Testament of 1828, also supervised by "Ioan Tegid," that the Bible Society heard of the objections to the 1826 diglott. The S.P.C.K., on the other hand, refused to accept the copies of the 1826 issue, for which its committee had contracted. The matter appears to have remained in abeyance until the issue of the 1828 New Testament. This edition, as soon as it became known, met with strenuous opposition, especially from members of the Church of England. The Rev. W. Bruce Knight, then Chancellor, afterwards Dean, of Llandaff, vigorously assailed the changes. His objections are fully set out in two pamphlets,* and may be summed up in his own words —he was unwilling to allow "private opinion, private criticism, private interpretation, and individual caprice," to be exercised on the text of the Scriptures, and adds, "Of the consequences of such conduct I think it unnecessary to dwell."

The changes introduced were brought before the Bible Society and the S.P.C.K. Memorials from the clergy of the Dioceses of Llandaff and Bangor were sent to the S.P.C.K., objecting to the changes introduced. Objections came also from other quarters ; and the two Societies formally repudiated the action of " Ioan Tegid," and refused to take any copies.

That " Ioan Tegid " was perfectly honest in his intentions there can be no doubt ; his mistake was in taking upon himself the responsibility of introducing alterations without proper authority and sanction being obtained. In a letter to the Bishop of Oxford (Dr. Lloyd) he says, " I wish it to be understood, that when I undertook upon me to conduct the

---

*(1) "Remarks, historical and philological, on the Welsh language," Cardiff, 1830; (2) " A Critical Review of the Rev. J. Jones's reply to the Rev. W. Bruce Knight's Remarks on Welsh Orthography," Cardiff, 1831.

Testament through the press, that [*sic*] I was influenced by no other motive than that of presenting to my country a correct and genuine copy." In another letter dated March 31st, 1829, he says, "The Testament has already gone through four editions. The first edition which appeared early last spring consisted of 2,000 copies, the other three of 5,000 each ; and I can assure your Lordship, that there is a great demand for it in the country, and that it is greatly approved of by the rising generation. I am willing to stand or fall by the reception my Testament will have in Wales ; let this decide in favour of, or against the orthography."*

A movement was subsequently made by Dr. William Carey, Bishop of St. Asaph, who proposed to submit to a small committee, consisting of the Rev. Henry Parry (Llanasa), the Rev. Rowland Williams (Meivod), and the Rev. Walter Davies "Gwallter Mechain," the proof sheets of a new edition of the New Testament, with such alterations as " Ioan Tegid " thought were necessary to secure a faithful edition which would be favourably received throughout the Principality. It was intended to submit the sheets also to similar committees in the other dioceses. The proposal was not, however, carried into effect.

---

* The figures of editions here given, while accurate as regards the total number printed, cannot be relied upon as to the numbers of each issue, if more than one actually was made. The Bible Society ordered 5,000 before the book went to press, and cancelled the order after it was printed. These letters and others are printed in " Gwaith Gwallter Mechain," Vol. III., Carmarthen, 1868.

CHAPTER IX.

PEACE AND PLENTY.

The work of the Bible Society—The Naval and Military Bible Society— The American Welsh editions—Diglott editions—Modern translations into Welsh—Welsh Scriptures for the Blind—Conclusion.

AFTER the controversies mentioned in the last chapter, all parties accepted the two standard texts, 1809 and 1814. There are shades of difference in orthography; but the two are so nearly alike that no further objections to either have disturbed the peace for nearly seventy years.

It has already been stated that between 1718 and 1900 the S.P.C.K. issued nearly sixty editions of the Scriptures: more than fifty of these belong to the nineteenth century. From its foundation to the year 1900, the Bible Society has issued at least 208 dated editions, not counting the embossed Scriptures for the blind, which will be dealt with later, and omitting undated editions, of which there have been many, and which it has been impossible to collate, as they are stereotype reprints and no account of them is available. The dated editions of the Bible Society, so far as they are recorded, may be summarised thus :—

Editions of the whole Bible, 1807-1900		...		100
„ „	N.T.,	„		87
„ „	Diglott N.T.,	„		11
„ „	Single books	„		10

It must be borne in mind that this table only includes such editions as are recorded in the Bibliography. It is known that there are others of which particulars have not been obtained.

The early issues of the Bible Society are somewhat rare. They may be easily recognised by following closely the description given in the Bibliography. The date, May 6, 1807, on the final page of the Bibles printed at Cambridge was retained for several years. Many people have been misled by this into believing they possessed one of the first issues, an error which would be corrected by a reference to the title of the Old or the New Testament.

The association of the Bible Society with the Cambridge University Press for the printing of Welsh Bibles was continued from 1806 up to 1814. In that year the first Welsh Bible for the Society was printed in London. No Welsh Scriptures were printed in London between 1769 and 1814.

The Bible Society did not issue a Welsh Bible printed at Oxford until 1824. The S.P.C.K. issued an edition printed at Cambridge in 1826, but did not revert to London until 1847. These dates, except perhaps the last, are important, as they indicate the wearing away of the difficulties which had prevented the full utilisation of the forces of the two societies. The scanty means of a large proportion of the Welsh people made it necessary to fix the prices as low as possible if the design of the Society to bring the Scriptures within the reach of the poorest was to be effective. The price of the 1806 New Testament was tenpence in cloth, one shilling in sheep, and eighteenpence in calf, and of the Bible of 1807 three shillings and threepence in calf. In 1852 the whole Bible was issued at tenpence, the N.T. having been put on sale at fourpence two years earlier. This fourpenny Testament had a very extensive sale. The Sunday School Testament (a 16mo issued first in 1859 at fourpence bound in leather) has also sold very largely, and is still used in Sunday Schools, having been frequently reprinted. An earlier issue (crown 8vo, 1835,) is stamped on the cover "For use in Sunday Schools exclusively." In 1865 the N.T. was published at twopence, and in 1885 at one penny, each being constantly reprinted as necessary. The issue of single books of the Bible in small pocket volumes, sold for a penny each, began in 1862 with the Gospel of St. John. Six other books, at least, have been issued in this form.

Besides these cheaper issues, the Society has provided from time to time large-type editions for the benefit of people with defective sight, and also more expensive editions. Reference has already been made (p. 41) to the quarto edition first issued in 1841 for use in places of worship. This is the first Welsh Bible issued by the Society with marginal notes and references. A small (crown 8vo) Bible issued in the same year has also the marginal notes and references, and from this time Bibles with references were continually printed for the Society.

The Jubilee of the Bible Society was celebrated in 1853, and copies sold in that year have stamped on the covers "Blwyddyn y Jubili 1853." This occurs on editions issued before 1853, and on at least one dated 1854. A history of the Society in Welsh was published at this time, written by the late Rev. Thomas Phillips, D.D., of Hereford, the Welsh Agent of the British and Foreign Bible Society. The book is entitled, " Llyfr y Jubili," and was printed by Gee and Son, Denbigh, in 1854.

A Welsh Bible was issued by the Society in 1897 in honour of the Diamond Jubilee of Queen Victoria. The copies are stamped on the cover "Er Coffhad am Drigain Mlynedd o Deyrnasiad V.R. 1837—1897." It was illustrated with eight maps and sold at prices ranging from one to three shillings according to the binding, or without the maps at elevenpence.

The Welsh Bible that belonged to Mary Jones came in 1877 into the possession of Robert Oliver Rees, of Dolgelly, the author of " Mary Jones and her Bible," who, in the same year, presented it to the library of the Welsh Calvinistic Methodist College at Bala. In 1880, the Principal, the late Rev. Dr. Lewis Edwards, presented it to the Bible Society.

In 1840 an edition of the N.T. in Welsh was printed by the Bible Society for the Naval and Military Bible Society (founded in 1780) for the supply of Scriptures to the men in the two services. The copies are stamped on the covers " Naval and Military Bible Society." The Society took some copies of the 1845 Bible, and obtained other supplies of Welsh Scriptures from time to time, and in 1787 supplied twenty-five copies to enable a clergyman in Wales to meet the scarcity of Bibles in his parish.* A printed slip on a copy of the 1845 edition of the Bible (No. 169) gives the price to sailors as 8d.

The American Bible Society was founded in 1816, but did not make any provision for printing the Scriptures in Welsh until 1854, in which

* Owen's " History of the Origin . . . of the Bible Society," vol. I., p. 3.

year a New Testament, Welsh and English in parallel columns, was published by the Society. Probably, the demand for Welsh Scriptures in America before 1854 was limited, and such as could be supplied by importing Welsh Bibles and Testaments from London. The flow of Welsh settlers into America, and their tendency to form groups in particular districts, which enabled them to hold divine service in their native language, would increase the demand. The Welsh settlers proceeded to form Bible Societies almost as soon as they arrived, the contributions of the members being forwarded annually to the parent Society in New York.* The Annual Report for 1905 gives a list of forty-three Welsh auxiliaries that contributed to the Society's funds during the year. The largest number of Welsh auxiliaries are in Wisconsin (14), New York State (8), and Minnesota, Iowa, and Ohio (5 each). The other States having Welsh auxiliaries are Vermont, Illinois, Kansas, Missouri, and Nebraska. From 1854 to 1900 at least thirty editions of the Scriptures in Welsh have been issued from New York. The diglott New Testament has been issued nine times, the New Testament, Welsh only, thirteen times, and the whole Bible, Welsh only, eight times. The following list of American editions has been compiled with great difficulty, and is printed here as a basis for further inquiry :—

No in Bibliography.	Date.	Description.
210*a*	1854	N.T. Diglott, 1st edn.
218	1855	N.T. Diglott, 2nd edn.
224	1856	N.T. Diglott, 3rd edn.
232	1858	Bible. 1st edn.
234*a*	1859	Bible. 2nd edn.
237	1859	N.T. 1st edn.
248*a*	1861	N.T. 2nd edn.
258	1863	N.T. 3rd edn.
263*a*	1864	N.T. Diglott, 4th edn.
270*a*	1865	N.T. 4th edn.
282*a*	1867	N.T. 5th edn.
285	1868	Bible. 3rd edn.
285*a*	1868	N.T. Diglott. 5th edn.
287*a*	1869	N.T. 6th edn.
297	1871	N.T. 7th edn.
297*a*	1871	N.T. 8th edn.
297*b*	1871	N.T. Diglott, 6th edn.
300*a*	1872	Bible. 4th edn.
306*a*	1873	N.T. Diglott, 7th edn.
311*a*	1874	N.T. 9th edn.
315*a*	1875	N.T. 10th edn.
338*a*	1881	N.T. Diglott, 8th edn.
340*a*	1882	Bible. 5th edn.
343*a*	1882	N.T. 11th edn.
346*a*	1885	N.T. Diglott, 9th edn.
358	1889	N.T. [12th edn.]
361	1891	Bible. 7th edn.
363	1893	S. Luke.
367	1894	N.T. [13th edn.] 56,000 printed.
380	1900	Bible. [8th edn.] 24,000 printed.

Missing from the above list, Bible, 6th edn., between 1882 and 1891.

* For an account of some of these Societies see "Hanes Cymry Minnesota," 1895, pp. 56—64.

. In the year ending March 31st, 1905, the Society distributed the following Scriptures in Welsh :—

Bibles	509
Testaments	339
Testaments and Psalms ...	64
Testaments (Welsh and English)	593
Gospels	76

The publications kept in stock include the whole Bible in Welsh in seventeen styles, ranging in price from five dollars down to twenty-five cents per copy, Testaments ranging from seventy-five cents down to ten cents, diglott Testaments at twenty-five and thirty-five cents, Testaments with the Psalms fifty-five cents, and the Gospel of St. Luke three cents. This last was issued in 1893, as a souvenir of the Columbian Exposition. In addition to meeting the needs of Welshmen in the United States, the Society provides for the Welsh Colony in Chubut, through its agent at Buenos Aires, who is responsible for the distribution of Welsh Scriptures in Patagonia. In 1904 "the Rev. Esau Evans, a good Welshman of long residence in that region," was started off with a cart containing a good supply of Scriptures in Welsh, Spanish, and Italian. Mr. Evans was still absent on his mission when the report was prepared; but the agent at Buenos Aires states that the Welsh Colony had contributed in the year then expiring three hundred dollars for the work of the Society, the largest sum ever contributed at one time through the Buenos Aires agent.

The British and Foreign Bible Society has also from time to time supplied Scriptures to the Welsh colonists in Patagonia, and the colonists have sent contributions to the funds of the Society in grateful acknowledgment. After the disastrous floods that nearly ruined the colony some years ago, the Committee of the British and Foreign Bible Society very readily replaced the lost and damaged Bibles.

Editions of the Scriptures with Welsh and English in parallel columns date from 1823, when the Rev. Joseph Harris "Gomer" and J. A. Williams brought out the first part of a diglott Bible from their printing-press at Swansea. The work was issued in forty-five parts at one shilling each. The Rev. J. Harris died in 1825, and the work was completed by his partner, the last part being issued in 1827. The sale was very large, there being 1,500 subscribers in Glamorganshire and Monmouthshire alone. It was reprinted in 1839, and twice again *circa* 1850. The New Testament has been very frequently published in this form both in this country and in America. The first diglott N.T. was printed at Denbigh, in 1824, by Thomas Gee (father of the late Thomas Gee), who issued it in six parts at one shilling each, with marginal notes to every verse.

The publication of the N.T. in diglott form obviously met a want, and it was re-issued again and again by the Bible Society from 1826 onwards, by the S.P.C.K. from 1831, and by local printing offices at Carmarthen, Dolgelly, Merthyr, and Llangollen. One of the issues from the last named place is the Gospel of St. Matthew for the use of children, tourists, visitors, etc., price sixpence. Altogether there have been at least twenty-five editions of the New Testament in diglott form printed in Wales, Oxford and London, besides nine printed in New York for the American Bible Society. The following is a table of the editions:—

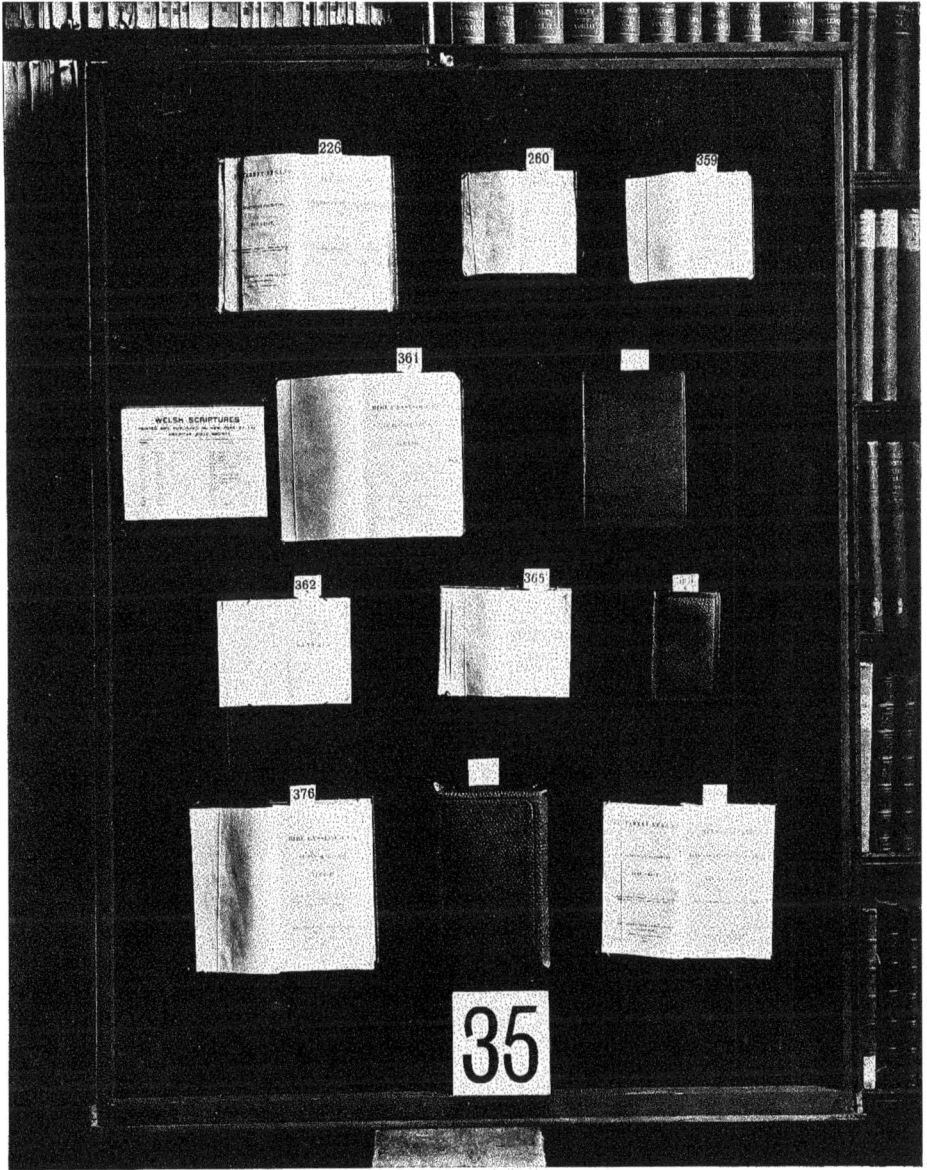

SHOW CASE IN THE WELSH BIBLE EXHIBITION CONTAINING
WELSH SCRIPTURES PRINTED IN NEW YORK.

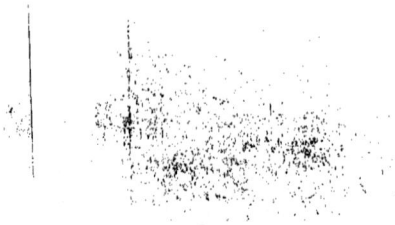

No. in Bibliography.	Date of Publication.	Place of Printing.	Description.
87	1823-27	Swansea	Bible. "Gomer"'s.
92	1824	Denbigh	N.T. 1st N.T. diglott.
98	1826	Oxford	N.T. 1st B. & F. diglott.
99	1826	Carmarthen	N.T. Issued in parts.
103	1827	Dolgelly	N.T. Same as 92.
120	1831	Oxford	N.T. 1st S.P.C.K. diglott.
150	1839	Swansea	Bible. "Gomer"'s.
154	1840	Oxford	N.T. S.P.C.K.
182	1849	Merthyr and Oxford	N.T. "Jones Llangollen"'s.
186	[*Circa* 1850]	Swansea	Bible. "Gomer"'s.
190	1850	Oxford	N.T. S.P.C.K.
202a	1853	London	N.T. B. & F.
203	1853	Llangollen	N.T.
206	1853	Llangollen	Matt. only, for use of visitors.
210a	1854	New York	N.T. American B.S.
211	1854	London	N.T. B. & F.
212	1854	Oxford	N.T. S.P.C.K.
218	1855	New York	N.T. American B.S.
224	1856	New York	N.T. American B.S.
233	1858	London	N.T. B. & F.
244	1860	London	N.T. S.P.C.K.
249	1861	London	N.T. B. & F.
259	1863	London	N.T. B. & F.
263	1864	London	N.T. B. & F.
263a	1864	New York	N.T. American B.S.
285a	1868	New York	N.T. American B.S.
290	1870	London	N.T. B. & F.
297b	1871	New York	N.T. American B.S.
301	1872	London	N.T. B. & F.
306a	1873	New York	N.T. American B.S.
312	1874	London	N.T. B. & F.
322	1876	London	N.T. B. & F.
338a	1881	New York	N.T. American B.S.
346a	1885	New York	N.T. American B.S.
	Undated	London	N.T. B. & F.
	Undated	London	N.T. B. & F.
	Undated	London	N.T. B. & F.

Various efforts have been made during the last hundred years to translate anew portions of the Scriptures into the Welsh language. The first of these was made by John Jones, LL.D., a barrister, who was born at Derwydd, Llandybie, Carmarthenshire, and who wrote a "History of Wales" and other works, none of them of great importance. He published in 1818 a new version of the Four Gospels, translated direct from the Greek into Welsh; but as his knowledge of Welsh was not good, the result was not satisfactory. The New Testament was again translated from the Greek by the Rev. John Williams "Philologos," of Rhosllanerchrugog, a Baptist minister, who used the Welsh word *trochi* (to immerse) instead of the more generally used *bedyddio* (to baptise), and *trochiedydd* (immerser) instead of *bedyddiwr* (baptist). The work was published in 1842 under the title, "Yr Oraclau Bywiol" (The Living Oracles), and it has been reprinted twice (1881 and 1887), under the editorship of the Rev. Dr. Owen Davies, Carnarvon.

The Rev. Thomas Briscoe, sometime Vicar of Holyhead, made new versions direct from the Hebrew into Welsh of the books of Isaiah, Job, Proverbs and Psalms. These were published in three separate volumes at Holywell in the years 1853, 1854 and 1855. He also published in 1894 a translation into Welsh of the New Testament based on the revised English version. The varied readings of the revised

English text had been done into Welsh in 1882 by the Rev. John Ogwen Jones, B.A.; and in 1888 the Rev. Owen Williams, Carnarvon, had published "Testament yr Efrydydd" (The Student's New Testament), containing the alterations in readings and translations adopted in the English revised translation.

The first number of a translation from the Septuagint version of the Old Testament was published at Carmarthen in 1866. This number contains Genesis i.—x. 2. The translator, the Rev. Evan Andrews, B.A., Vicar of Llandefeiliog, Kidwelly, had designed to publish the whole in three volumes, and had translated the five books of Moses, and a portion of the Book of Joshua. He was encouraged by the opinions of some of the leading Welsh scholars; but found that the sale of the first number did not justify him in proceeding. This single number of the Septuagint in Welsh is extremely rare, and a copy had not been found when the Bibliography was printed Through the kindness of the translator's daughter, a copy has now been placed in the Public Library at Cardiff. The following is a description of it :—

Dy. 8° (8); lines across the page, with commentary and footnotes beneath in double columns; wrapper; 184×112 mm., 227×150 mm.

$7\frac{1}{4} \times 4\frac{3}{8}$ in., $8\frac{1}{16} \times 5\frac{7}{8}$ in.; 32 pp.

DESCRIPTION.—Title (on wrapper), not dated; "I'r darllenydd hynaws.," signed " E. A.," *b ;* Gen. i.—x. 2, sigs. 1—4⁴ and *b*, pp. 1—32; testimonials to the work, dated respectively " Oct. 12, 1865," and " Dec. 19th, 1865."

The Song of Solomon was translated literally from the Hebrew, with brief notes, by A. Rhys Thomas.. It was printed at Llanelly in 1870. A new version of the Minor Prophets from the Hebrew, with variant marginal readings from other texts, was made by the Rev. John Davies " Shon Gymro," of Ietwen, Congregational minister at Glandwr, Pembrokeshire, and published at Llandilo in 1881. The Rev. William Edwards, B.A., D.D., Principal of the Pontypool-Cardiff Baptist College, brought out in 1894—8 two volumes of a version of the New Testament from the Greek, with critical notes and introductory chapters. This is the most thorough attempt yet made to re-translate the New Testament. The volumes already issued comprise the Four Gospels and the Acts of the Apostles.

Portions of the Welsh Bible in embossed characters for the use of the blind have been issued from time to time, mainly in Moon's embossed type, the simplified roman letter. Some books, the epistles to the Colossians and Philippians, and the Gospel of St. Mark, are recorded as being embossed in Braille character, and issued by the British and Foreign Blind Association. The reproduction of single copies of any book in the Braille character is easy and not expensive. It is not therefore necessary to prepare and stock books of which only a very limited number are required. Readers of the Braille system can get any part of the Bible from the British and Foreign Blind Association, 33, Cambridge Square, London, W.

The Bible Society first issued embossed Scriptures in Welsh in 1882; and, practically, the whole of the New Testament, and parts of the Old, are now available in the Moon type. The demand for the Scriptures in this form has been small, and the provision of them is an evidence of the Society's earnestness in its great work of supplying the Scriptures to all mankind in the form most acceptable. A list of the volumes is set out at the end of the Bibliography.

Such is the story, imperfectly told, of the Bible in relation to the people of Wales. From the issue of the first Testament in 1567 to the year 1800, thirty-three editions are recorded ; from 1801 to 1900, three-hundred-and-forty-nine, not counting those undated and embossed editions for the blind. It is hardly possible to estimate the numbers of the various issues, and to attempt to arrive at the total copies circulated would be surrounded with almost insurmountable difficulties. It would be better to regard the influence which the Bible has had in moulding the character of the Welsh people, and, judging from the number of editions, among no other small nationality is there evidence of such a demand for the Scriptures.

BIBLIOGRAPHY.

THE BIBLE IN WALES.

BIBLIOGRAPHY.

1 5 4 6. Yny lhyvyr | hwnn ỳ traethir. | Gwyðor kymraeg. | Kalandyr. |
Y gredo, ney bynkeu yr | ffyð gatholig. | Y pader, ney weði yr
arglwyð. | Y deng air deðyf. | Saith Rinweð yr egglwys. | Y.
kampey arveradwy | ar Gwyðieu gochlad- | wy ae keingeu. |
M.D.XLVI.   [*Edward Whitchurch : London.*]

ℬ.ℒ., in black and red ; 8° (16) ; 138 × 85 mm., 173 × 118 mm. ⎱ (leaves cut by
                                   5⅞₆ × 3⅜ in.,   6⅞₆ × 4⅝ in. ⎰   binder).

Contains the Lord's Prayer, the Decalogue, and three verses from the N.T., being
the first known printed portions òf the Bible in Welsh. Edited by Sir John Prys,
Knight, of Brecon (1502-55).   Facsimile reprint issued 1902 (Jarvis and Foster,
Bangor—J. M. Dent and Co., London), edited by John H. Davies, M.A., for the .Guild
of Graduates of the University of Wales. The eighth commandment (*Thou shalt not
steal*) is omitted in the text, but supplied in a list of errata at end of book.·

DESCRIPTION.—Title (in woodcut border, with a monogram, *EWCR*, at the bottom),
    blank, *b* ; Address to the reader, *Kymro yn danvon Annerch at ỳ darlheawdyr*,
    ff. 2-3 (not numbered or signatured) ; Orthographical rules, ff. 3-4 ; Calendar,
    ff. 5-10 (signatured A¹ on *a* of f. 5) ; *Almanak dros ugaint mlyneð*, f. 11, *a ;
    Blwyðyn yr haul*, etc., f. 11, *b ;* Numerals, f. 12 ; Creed, Lord's Prayer, etc., etc.,
    ff. 13-17 (signatured B¹ on *a* of f. 13 and Bⁱⁱⁱ on *a* of f. 14) ; blank, f. 17, *b*.
    Total ff., 17=34 pp.

                                                                    1.

1 5 5 1. Kynniver | llith a ban or yscry | thur lan ac a ðarlleir yr Eccleis
pryd | Commun / y Sulieu a'r Gwilieu | trwy'r vlwyðyn : o Cam- |
bereiciat / W.S. | Tit. ii. | . . . | Rom. i. | . . .
                              Robert Crowley : London.   1551.

ℬ.ℒ.; 8° (8) ; 148 × 114 mm., 191 × 130 mm. ⎱ (leaves cut by binder).
                5⅞ × 4¼ in.,   7½ × 5¼ in. ⎰

Gospels and Epistles as in Pr. Bk. Translated and edited by W[illiam] S[alesbury].
Facsimile of titlepàge in *Transactions of the Honourable Society of Cymmrodorion*
(London, 1899).

DESCRIPTION.—Title ; *Gwae'r Offeirieit byt*, etc. (Taliesin stanza), *b ;* Dedication
    [in Laṭin] of W.S. to the Bishops of St. David's, Llandaff, Bangor, and.Hereford,
    sig. A*i* and *b ;* text, *Dalen i.—Dalen lxxxv.* (leaves numbered *i.—lxxxv.*) ;
    A copy of the Kynges moste gracious priuilege, b ; Colophon, *Imprinted at |
    London by Roberte Crow- | ley for William Sales- | bury dwellynge in | Elye
    rentes in | Holbourne. | Anno Domini. | M.D.L.I. |* , *a ;* blank, *b*.   Total ff.
    (first two and last not numbered), 88=176 pp. Folio xxxviii. wrongly numbered
    xxxvi.

                                                                    2.

1 5 5 5. Mithridates. | De Diffe | rentiis lingva- | rvm tvm vetervm | . . . | Conradi Gesneri | . . . | M.D. LV. | Tigvri excvdebat | Froschovervs.

8° (16) ; 122×650 mm., 149×90 mm.
4⅞×2₁₆⁹ in.,   5⅛×3₁₆⁹ in.

Contains the Lord's Prayer, an older version than that given in No. 1. Printed at Zurich by Froxhover. Reprinted, with the addition in Welsh of Gen. i. 1-5, Zurich, 1610, by Wolphian. The Lord's Prayer in 23 languages, including the Welsh version slightly corrected, was issued from the same office in the same year on a broadside sheet.

DESCRIPTION.—Title ; blank, *b ;* Dedication, sig. A² and *b ;* text, ff. 1-78 ; blank, *b.* The Lord's Prayer in Welsh appears on *b* of f. 13. Total ff., ii.+78=80=160 pp.

3.

1 5 6 7. [The Book of Common Prayer.]

Henry Denham for Humphrey Toy : London. 1567.

𝕭.𝕷 ornamental initials ; foolscap f° (8 and 12) ; 235×151 mm., 288×184 mm.
9¼×5₁₆¹⁸ in.,   11₁₆⁷×7¼ in.

First Welsh edition of Pr. Bk., translated by Richard Davies, D.D., Bishop of St. David's, and William Salesbury. Reprinted 1586.

DESCRIPTION.—(No copy with title known.) Title ; ? blank, *b ; Act am Vnfvrviat,* etc., sigs. ¶ii—¶iiij and *b ; Y Racymadrodd,* sigs. ¶v—¶vi and *b ; Or Ceremoniis,* sig. ¶vii (not numbered) and *b ; Y Tabul ar Kalendar,* etc., sig. ¶viii (not numbered); *Y Tabul am drefn y Psalmeu,* etc., sig. *Y Drefn,* etc., sigs. ✲(i)—✲(iii); *Yr Almanack, b ; Y Gahcl y Pasc,* etc., sig. ✲(iiii) ; list of movable feasts (no headline) and *Bod cadw,* etc., *b ;* calendar (no headline), sigs. ✲(v)—✲(x) and *b* (not numbered) ; text, sigs. A(i)—[F(vi)] and *b ; Dalē* (ff.) i.-cxliii. ; colophon on *b* of f. cxliii., viz. :—*Imprinted at London | by Henry Denham, at the costes and | charges of Humfrey Toy, | 1567. | ¶And are to be solde at his shop at the | sygne of the Helmet in Paules | churchyard. | (*) | ¶Cum priuilegio ad imprimen- | dum solum. | ;* tailpiece ; title of Psalms ; text of Psalms, sigs. Aij—[Oᵛⁱ] and *b ;* ff. ii.-lxxxiiij. ; colophon, *b,* as at end of Pr. Bk. Total ff., 18 (not numbered) + cxliii.+lxxxiiij.=245, or 490 pp.

4.

1 5 6 7. Testament | Newydd ein Arglwydd | Jesv Christ. | Gwedy ei dynnu, yd y gadei yr ancyfia- | ith, 'air yn ei gylydd or Groec a'r Llatin, gan | newidio ffurf llythyreu y gairiae-dodi. Eb law hyny | y mae pop gair a dybiwyt y vot yn andeallus, | ai o ran llediaith y 'wlat, ai o ancynefin- | der y devnydd, wedi ei noti ai eg- | lurhau ar 'ledemyl y tu da- | len gydrychiol. | . . . | Matheu xiii.f. | Gwerthwch a veddwch o vudd | (Llyma'r Man lle mae'r modd | Ac mewn ban amgen ny bydd) | I gael y Perl goel hap wedd. |

Henry Denham for Humphrey Toy : London. 1567.

𝕭.𝕷., black and red ornamental initials, 31 long lines to the full page, with marginal notes ; sm. 4to (16) ; calf ; 157×91 mm., 188×145 mm.
6₁₆³×3₁₆⁹ in.,   7⅜×5₁₆¹¹ in.

First N.T. in Welsh. Edited by William Salesbury, who was also translator except of I. Timothy, Hebrews, James, I. and II. Peter (Richard Davies) and Revelations (Thomas Huet). Marginal notes occur—f. 310, end of II. Thess.—*O Lyuer ccned-* | *leth, &c. yd y | van hyn,* W.S.: | *a'r Epistol iso.* | D.R.D.M. *ci* | *translatodd.* | ; f. 317. beginning of II. Tim. *W.S. yr vn | hwn, a'r ddau | iso | ;* f. 327, beginning of Hebrews, D.R.D.M. *yr | vn hwn at yr | Ebraicit, y | ddau i Petr, | a'r vn i Iaco | ;* f. 344, *b,* beginning of James, *D.R.D.M.;* f. 351, *b,* beginning of I. Peter *D.R.D.M.;* f. 362, *b,* beginning of I. John, *W.S. tri Ioan | ac vn Iudas.* | ; f. 373, beginning of Revelations, *T.H.C.M. a translatoedd oll text yr Apocalypsis yn icith ci wlat.* The initials mean— *W.S.,* William Salesbury ; *D.R.D.M.,* Dr. Richard Davies Mynyw (*i.e.,* St. David's); and *T.H.C.M.,* Thomas Huet Cantor Mynyw (*i.e.,* Precentor of St. Davids.)

Acts xxi. and xxii. to verse 12, and II. Tim. to end of Revelations, divided into verses. All other text not divided into verses. Each book preceded by a summary, *Yr Argvment.*

Re-issued with colophon on *b* of title, and 8 pp. at end containing errata (3 pp.), a reply as to the errors found by certain critics in the epistle of the Bishop of St. David's (2 pp.), explanations, rules, etc. (2 pp.), blank, 1 p.

For reprints, see Nos. 71 and 188.

DESCRIPTION.—Title ; blank, *b; Almanach dros. xxv. o vlynyddeu,* sigs. ₊ii—₊iiii., etc. (ff. 2-8, not numbered); blank, *b;* dedication, *To the most Ver- | tuous and noble Prince Eliza- | beth, by the grace of God, of England, | Fraunce and Ireland Queene, defender of | the Faith, &c.,* signed *William Salesbury,* sigs. a.j.— a.ij. and *b* (ff. 9-10, not numbered) ; address to the Welsh people by Dr. Richard Davies, *Richard can 'rat | Dyw Episcop Menew, yn damu- | no adnewyddiat hcu ffydd catholic a' gol- | launi [sic] Euangel Christ ir Ccmbru oll, yn en- | wedic i bop map encid dyn o vewn | cy Escopawt.,* sigs. a.iii.—c.iii. (ff. 11-23, not numbered); address to the Welsh people by William Salesbury, *At yr oll Cembru | ys ydd yn caru ffydd ei hcu dcidieu y Bri- | tanieit | gynt, b* of sig. c.iii. (unsigned) ; the advice of St. Chrysostom to laymen, etc., in Latin, *D.Io. Chrisost. Archiepiscop. | . . . 405.,* and in Welsh, *Cygor Sanct Ioan Aur-eneu ir | llaicon ai 'rei bydol. ccccv.,* sig. c.iiii. (unsigned, f.24) ; contents, *Gosodiat Llyvræ y Testa- | ment Newydd, a, niuer eu penneu a'r dalenne., b* of sig. ciiii. (unsigned); text, sigs. A.j.—Eee.iij. and *b* (ff. 1-399); table of Epistles and Gospels read in Churches, *Tabul i gahel yr | Epistolæ a'r Euangelon y ddallenir [sic] yn yr | Eglwys trwy'r vlwyddyn.,* sigs. Eee iiij.—Eeev. (ff. 400-401, not numbered); colophon, *Imprinted at Lon | don by Henry Denham, at the | costes and charges of Humfrey | Toy, dwelling in Paules church | yarde, at the signe of the | Helmet. | Cum priuilegio ad imprimen- | dum solum. | Anno. 1567. Octob. 7.,* sig. Eee vi. (unsigned, f. 402, not numbered) ; blank, *b.* Total ff., 24+402=426= 852 pp.

5.

1588. Y Beibl Cys- | segr-lan, sef | yr Hen Desta- | ment, a'r Newydd. | 2. Timoth. 3. 14, 15. | Eithr aros di yn y pethau a ddyscaist, ac a ymddyried- | wyd i ti, gan wybod gan bwy y dyscaist. | Ac i ti er yn fachgen wybod yr scrythur lân, yr hon |·sydd abl i'th wneuthur yn ddoeth i iechydwria | eth, trwy'r ffydd yr hon sydd yng-Hrist Iesu. | Imprinted at London by the Deputies of | Christopher Barker, | Printer to the Queenes most excel- | lent Maiestie. | 1588. |

B.L., ornamental initials, double columns, with marginal references ; foolscap f° (12); stamped calf on oak boards ; 260×135 mm., 323×220 mm.

10 6⁄16 × 5 6⁄16 in., 12 3⁄4 × 8 5⁄8 in.

First complete Bible in Welsh, translated and edited by William Morgan, D.D. The number of copies printed is not known ; but as it was an edition for the churches, and they numbered 800, according to the Bishop's returns made in 1603 (Ed. Owen's Catalogue of MSS. in Brit. Mus., pp. 159-160), the number printed approached 1,000. Dr. Morgan voluntarily undertook the work of translating while Vicar of Llanrhaiadr-ym-Mochnant, and practically bore the cost and responsibility of publishing, although he in his dedication acknowledges "the help of the generosity, authority, and advice," of John Whitgift, Archbishop of Canterbury. He was also encouraged and assisted by William Hughes, D.D., Bishop of St. Asaph; Hugh Bellott, D.D., Bishop of Bangor; Gabriel Goodman, D.D., Dean of Westminster, who befriended him during the year he spent in London reading and revising the proofs ; David Powell, D.D., Vicar of Ruabon, the editor of Humphrey Llwyd's English translation of Caradoc of Llancarfan's *Historie of Cambria,* 1584; Edmund Prys, Archdeacon of Meirioneth, the author of the rhymed version of the Psalms; and Richard Vaughan, who died Bishop of London in 1604. John Davies, D.D., of Mallwyd, also, claims in the preface to his *Antiquæ Lingvæ Britannicæ* (London, 1621), that he had a share in the translation of both this edition and No. 9.

The text, which includes the Apocrypha, is divided into chapters and verses, with contents preceding each chapter. The headlines denote the days of the month (thirty) on which the Psalms are to be sung, and side notes in the text indicate the Psalms for morning and evening service. The copy in the Library of Westminster Abbey contains 2 pp. of errata, printed in Roman and Italic types. This errata has been reprinted in Archdeacon Thomas's *Davies and Salesbury* 1902 (pp. 139-144), and is reproduced in facsimile in No. 371.

DESCRIPTION.—Title, in woodcut border, with the Royal Arms, the supporters being a Lion and a Dragon, the latter introduced as a compliment to the Tudors (the same border used for English Bibles printed by Barker); blank, *b;* dedication in Latin, *Illvstrissimae, | Potentissimae, Sere- | nissimæ qve Principi Eli- | zabethae, Dei gratia, Angliæ, Galliæ, & Hiber- | niæ Reginæ*, etc., sigs. *ij—*iij (ff. 2-3, not numbered); names of promoters, etc., and contents, sig.* [iv] (f. 4, not numbered); calendar, *b* of sig.*v—sig. *vi (*b* of f. 4—f. 5, not numbered); table of chapters to be read in Churches, sig. [vi] (f. 6, not numbered); text (Gen.—Mal.), tailpiece, Royal Arms, with Lion and Dragon Supporters, on f. 351, sigs. A.i.—Nnn.iii. (ff. 1-351); blank, *b;* text (Apocrypha), sigs. Nnn.iiii.—Dddd.iiii and *b* (ff. 352-436); title of N.T., in same woodcut border as general title, *Testament | Newydd ein | Harglwydd Iesv | Grist. | Rom. 1. 16. | Nid cywilydd gennif Efengyl Grist, o | blegit gallu Duw yw hi er iechydwria- | eth i bob vn a'r sydd yn credu. | Anno 1588.* |, sig. Eeee.j. (f. 439); blank, *b;* text (*Mathew—Gweledigaeth Ioan*), sigs. Eeee.ii.—Zzzz viii. (ff. 440-555); table of Epistles and Gospels read in Churches, *b*. Total ff., 6+555=561=1122 pp.

NOTE.—Dr. Morgan revised his version of the N.T. with a view to publishing it in a more correct and cheaper form (see statement in the copy of the Bible presented by him to the Library of Westminster Abbey in token of his gratitude to the Dean and Chapter for their great and continual hospitality during the printing of the work). From the address to the reader prefixed by Thomas Salesbury to No. 8, published the year before Dr. Morgan's death, it is inferred that it was then ready for the press. Why it was not published, and what became of the MS., is not known.

6.

1588. Psalmau | Dafydd o'r vn cy- | fieithiad a'r Beibl | cyffredin. | Iaco. 5. 13. | A oes neb yn esmwyth arno ? | caned Psalmau. | Anno. 1588.

[Deputies of Christopher Barker : London.]

𝕭.𝕷., ornamental initials, 35 long lines to the full page ; 4° (16); calf ;
175×102 mm., 198×147 mm.
6¹⁴⁄₁₆×4 in., 7¹³⁄₁₆×5¹³⁄₁₆ in.

Version of No. 6, corrected, intended for use in the Church service instead of the version in Nos. 4 and 5, for which it was substituted in the next edition of the Pr. Bk., 1599. The days of ·the month (thirty) are indicated in the headlines, and the Ps. for morning and evening service in side notes, as in No. 6. For fac-similé reprint, see No. 371.

DESCRIPTION.—Title, in composite woodcut border; blank, *b;* text, sigs. A.ii.—Liv.; blank, *b*. Total pp., 168 (not numbered).

7.

1603. Psalmæ | y Brenhinol | Brophvvyd Da- | fydh, gwedi i cynghanedhu | mewn mesurau cymreig. | Gann Gapten Wiliam Middelton. | Yn nesaf y gallodh at fedhwl yr | Yspryd glân. | Simon Stafford | a Thomas Salisbury a'i printiodhyn | Llunden. 1603. |

𝕭.𝕷., ornamental initials ; sm. 4° (8) ; calf ; 163×80 mm., 179×134 mm.
6⁶⁄₁₆×3³⁄₁₆ in., 7¹⁄₁₆×5¼ in.

First printed metrical version of the Psalms in Welsh, composed according to the rules of *cynghanncdd* (= assonance) peculiar to Welsh poetry. This version never became popular, and was superseded by that of No. 10. It was reprinted in 1827 (Llanfair-Caereinion, R. Jones). The author was a captain in Queen Elizabeth's navy fighting the Spaniards in the West Indies, where, at Scutum, January 24, 1595-6, the work was finished. He was the third son of Richard Myddelton, governor of Denbigh Castle. The editor was Thomas Salisbury, whose name appears in the imprint ; he was the son of Pierce Salisbury, of Clocaenog, Denbighshire, and was admitted a freeman of the Stationers' Company October 16, 1588. There are copies of 3 variants as to prefatory matter in the British Museum.

DESCRIPTION.—*Variant* A :—Title ; blank, *b ; Mawl-gerdh farwnad i Gapten | William Middelton |*, signed *Edward Kyffin.*, pp. 3-4 ; *Doeded y prydydhion þa fesur | ne fesurau yw hwnn (os medrant) a | dosbarthant ef.* |, signed *Tho Price ai Kant | ag ai gwranta.* |, p. 4 ; *At y Darllcnvdh*, signed *Thomas Salisbury*, p. 5 (numbered at foot) and p. 6 (not numbered) ; *To the Worshipfull M. Tho. Middleton Esquier,* | etc., signed *Thomas Salisbury.*, p. 7 (not numbered) ; blank, *b ; At y pendefigion fritaniaid M. Pierce Gryffydh | or Penrhyn*, *M. Thomas Price, o blas Iolyn | M. Thomas Glynn, a M. Wiliam Glynn o lynn | Lhivon, M. Wiliam Gruffydh o Gaer-arvon, M.* | *Fowlke Lloyd o Ffoks-hal, a M. Edmund | Price o l'cirion.* |, signed *Thomas Salisbury*, p. 9 ; *Mawl-gerdh i'r Awdur.*, signed *Tho. Price.*, p. 10 ; *To the Reader*, signed *Thomas Salisbury*, pp. 11-12 ; text, sigs. A-2q⁴, pp. 1-287 ; *Terfyn.* | *Apud Scutum Insulam occidentalium Indorum | finitum erat hoc opus, vicesimo | quarto Ianuarij, Anno salutis | nostræ. 1595. | Halleluiah.* |, end of p. 287 ; blank, *b.* Total pp., 12+288=300.

Variant B:—Title ; blank, *b ; To the Worshipfull Tho. Middelton Esquier,* | etc., p. 3 ; blank, *b ; I'w anwyl-gariadus wlâd-wr a gwiw | ymgeledhwr ei iaith, Mr. George Rogers: | Thomas Salisbury yn damuno pôb Llwydhi- | ant a llewenydh.* |, signed *Thomas Salisbury.*, pp. 5 (numbered *3* at foot) and 6 ; *To the Reader*, signed *Thomas Salisbury*, pp. 7-8 ; text, as in variant A. Total pp., 8+288=296.

Variant C :—Title ; blank, *b ; To the high and mighty Monarch,* | *James*, etc., signed *Thomas Salisburie.*, pp. 3-4 (not numbered); *To the Reader*, signed *Thomas Salisbury,* ·pp. 5-6 (not numbered) ; text, as in variants A and B. Total pp., 6+288=294.

8.

1603. Rhann o | Psalmae Dafydd | Brophwyd iw ca- | nu ar ôl y dôn arferedig yn | Eglwys Loegr. | Simon Stafford a'i printiodd | yn Llunden dros. T.S. | 1603. |

ℬ.ℒ., with the prose version of No. 6 in Roman type in a·parallel column ; crown 8° (8); 163×128 mm., 187×135 mm.
6⅜×5 1/16 in., 7⅜×5 5/16 in.

A rhymed version of Ps. i.—xiii., and the first attempt in free meters. The author was Edward Kyffin, son of Richard Kyffin, of Glasgoed, Llansilin, Denbighshire, and brother of Maurice Kyffin, the author of *The Blessednes of Brytaine* (1587), and other works. The initials, T.S. in the imprint, stand for Thomas Salisbury, the editor and part-printer of No. 8.

DESCRIPTION.—Title, in ornamental border ; blank, *b ;* preface, *At fyngharedigion wlâd-wyr | y Sawl a gârant Ogoniant yr Arglwydd, | ag ymgeledd ei gwlad- | iaith. | Wrth weled mor ofalus ydiw | ieithyddion eraill am ei gwlad- | iaith*, etc., ending *Yr eiddoch iw orchymyn | yn-Christ Iesu. | Edward Kyffin.* | *ä ē ï õ ū wỳ ỳ | Lle' gwel och y llythrennau ychod | a'r nodau hynn dros ei pennau | rhaid fydd ei llefaru hwynt yn hir*, sigs. A²—A³ ; blank, *b ;* text (Ps. i.—xiii.), sigs. B-D ; ends with Ps. xiii. 5. *Terfyn ar hynn: hyd oni | threfno Duw ₋ Gvmmorth ymhellach,* sigs. E¹—E². Total leaves, 17 (not numbered).

8a.

1620. Y Bibl | Cyssegr-lan, | sef yr Hen Desta- | menta'r | Newydd. |
2. Tim. 3.16. | Yr holl Scrythur sydd wedi ei rhoddi gan | yspryd-
oliaeth Dduw, ac sydd fuddiol i | athrawiaethu, i argyoeddi, i
geryddu, i | hyfforddi mewn cyfiawnder : | 17 Fel y byddo dyn
Duw yn berffaith, we- | di ei berffeithio i bob gweithred dda. |
Printedig | Yn Llundain gan Bonham | Norton a Iohn Bill, |
Printwyr i Ardderchoc- | caf fawrhydi y | Brenhin. | 1620. |

B.L.., ornamental initials, double columns, with marginal notes and references,
large f⁰ (12); stamped calf on oak boards, sometimes with clasps, and large brass
bosses on sides ; 332×205 mm., 385×255 mm.
13¹⁵⁄₁₆×8¹⁄₁₆ in.,   15⅛×10⅜ in.

Revision of No. 6, by Richard Parry, D.D., Bishop of St. Asaph, assisted by John
Davies, D.D., of Mallwyd.   In this version the Hebraisms of No. 6 were in very many
instances rejected for the Anglicisms of the English Authorised Version of 1611.   This
is the version still in use.   The editi n, like that of No. 6, was solely for use in churches.
There were many errors ; and about 1666, and afterwards about 1672, according to
the British Museum Catalogue, either Charles Edwards (the author of *Hanes y Ffydd*,
1st ed'n London, 1666) or R. [*sic* George] Griffith, D.D., Bishop of St. Asaph, prepared
and published a foolscap f⁰ sheet (4 pp.) of errata, entitled *Some | Omissions and
Mistakes | in the | British Translation and Edition of the Bible, ap- | pointed to be
had and read in the Churches | in Wales, to be supplied and rectified.* | The second
issue of this errata is recorded in Rowlands's *Cambrian Bibliography,* p. 200,
with a footnote by the editor (the late Rev. Chancellor D. Silvan Evans), thus :—
"[Moses Williams, *Cofrestr*, rh. 23.]"   Stephen Hughes, in his *Llythyr at rai
Gweinidogion*, etc., preceding the 1672 edition of *Canwyll y Cymru*, says in a
marginal note on *b* of sig. a³ *Y mac'r | sheete iw | chael ar | werth gan | Mr Goff
o | Gaerfyr- | ddyn.*(=The sheet is on sale at Mr. Gough's of Carmarthen); but he
does not mention the name of the publisher, etc. : he only speaks of him as *rhyw
Ewyllysiwr da i'n Gwlâd* (=some well-Wisher to our Country).
The days (thirty) on which the Ps. are to be used are indicated in the headlines,
and the morning and evening service in side notes as in Nos. 6 and 7.

DESCRIPTION.—Title, in the wide woodcut border used for the folio Bibles printed
by Bonham Norton and John Bill, containing emblematic representations of the
Twelve Tribes and the Twelve Apostles ;   blank, *b;* Latin dedication by
Dr. Parry, *Sacrosanctæ | et Individvae Trinitati, | vni Deo optimo maximo,
nominis | Sanctificationem ; Iacobo Dei ciusdem gratiâ Magnæ | Britanniæ,
Franciæ, & Hiberniæ Regi Augustissimo, fœlicitatem | omnem precatur, creatura
humilis, subditus fidelis.* | , sig. *a²* and verso; Dr. Morgan's Latin dedication
to Queen Elizabeth as in No. 6, sigs. *a³*—*a⁴* (unsigned, the headpiece comprising
the Prince of Wales's feathers and two Celtic harps); Dr. Morgan's list of
promoters, etc., as in No. 6, *b;* calendar, sigs. B¹—B⁶ and *b;* ¶*Almanac
tros 33. o flynyddoedd.,* sig. c *; 1 gael y Pasc byth.,* *b;* ¶*Tabl a Chalendar,
yn hyspysu trefn y Psalmau a'r llithiau,* and *Y Drefn pa wedd heb law'r
Psalmau y dosparthwyd bod darllain y rhan arall o'r Scrythur lân,* sig. c² ;
¶*Pennodau neilltuol, ncu briod, iw darllcn yn llithicu cyntaf ar | Foreuol a
Phrydnhawnol weddi, ar y Sulieu trwy'r holl | Flwyddyn, a rhai o'r ail
Llithiau.* | , *b* of sig. c²—sig. c³; *Y Tabl i ddangos pa drefn y darllennir y
Psalmau ar | Foreol a Phrydnhawnol weddi.* | , *b;* table of feast-days, etc.,
sig. c⁴ ; *Henwau a threfn llyfrau,* etc., *b.;* text (Gen.—Mal.), sigs A—Nnn⁶ ;
blank, *b;* text (Apocrypha), sigs. Ooo—Eeee⁵ and *b;* a blank leaf; title of
N.T., in composite woodcut border, containing the Royal Arms, with emblematic
figures in the upper part, and the Lion and Unicorn at the bottom ; on the sides
the initials *I.R.* (Iacobus Rex), each surmounted by a crown, *Testament Newydd
ein | Harglwydd a'n | Hiachawdr | Iesv Crist. | Rhvf. 1. 16.* | *Nid oes arnaf
gywilydd o Efengyl Grist, | oblegid gallu Duw yw hi, er lcchydwriaeth | i bob
vn a'r sydd yn credu. | Printiedig yn Llundain gan Bon- | ham Norton a
Iohn Bil, | Printwyr i Ardderchoccaf fawrhydi | y Brenhin.* | Anno. | 1620. |
blank, *b;* text (Matt.—Rev.), sigs. [A]—[Y³] ; index to Epistles and Gospels, *b.*

1621. Llyfr y Psalmau, Wedi ev | cyfieithv, a'i ǀ cyfansoddi | ar fesvr cerdd, | yn Gymraeg. | Drwy waith | Edmwnd Prys | Archdiacon | Meirionnydd, | (***) | A'i Printio | Yn Llvndain. | 1621. |

Bonham Norton and John Bill : London. 1621.

𝕭.𝕷., double columns, sm. 4° (16); 176×125 mm, 189×146 mm. ⎫ measurements of
6¹⅛×4¹⅛ in., 7⁷⁄₁₆ × 5¾ in. ⎭ title.

First edition of Edmund Prys's rhymed version of the Ps., in free meters, published with the Pr. Bk. (1621). This version became at once popular, and has maintained its popularity up to recent times. The music of several of the tunes is also printed. The 1621 Pr. Bk. also contains the version of the Ps. (with separate title-page) from No. 9. This version, with slight modifications in orthography, has been adopted for the Pr. Bk. down to the present day, the rhymed version of Edmund Prys being usually added as an appendix to Pr. Bks. and Bibles.

DESCRIPTION.—Title, in woodcut border ; blank, *b;* address to the reader, *At y Darlleydd ystyriol.* (in Roman type, with a headpiece comprising the Royal Arms and Supporters, and emblems of the rose and the thistle), sig. A² and *b ; Te Deum.* (and Canticles), with a headpiece, sigs. A³—A² [*sic* A⁴] and *b;* Psalms, sigs. B—I⁷ (ff. 1—63, numbered thus :—1, 2, 3, 4, 7, 6, 7, 8, 9, 10, 11, 12, 13, 14, 15, 16, [17, omitted], 18, 19, 20, 21, 22, [23, omitted], 24, 25, 26, [27, omitted], 28, [29, omitted], 30, 31, 32, 33, 34, 35, 35, 37, 38, 39, 40, 41, 42, 43, 44, 45, 46, 47, 48, 49, 50, 53, 55, 53, 61, 57, 58, 59, 60, 61, 62, 63, 67, 65) ; table of first lines, *b* of sig. I⁷—sig. I⁸ (*b* of f. 63—f. 64, not numbered) ; blank, *b.* Total ff. 4+64=68=136 pp.

N.B.—The pages of the text vary in size.

10.

1630. Y Bibl | Cyssegr-lan, | sef yr Hen | Destament | A'r Newydd. | 2 Tim. 3. 16, 17. | . . . Printiedig | yn Llvndain gan | Robert Barker Printiwr i | Ardderchoccaf fawrhydi y Bre- | nin : a chan Assignes Iohn Bill, | Anno Dom. 1630. |

Cr. 8° (16) ; ornamental initials ; small Roman type ; double columns, with marginal notes and references ; calf ; 153×83 mm., 164×109 mm.
6 x 3¼ in., 6½×4¹⁄₁₆ in.

Reprint of No. 9, and first people's edition, price 5/- This is the Bible referred to by Rhys Prichard, Vicar of Llandovery (1579-1644), in *Canwyll y Cymry—*

> " Mae'r bibl bach yn awr yn gysson,
> Yn iaith dy fam iw gael er coron,
> Gwerth dy grys cyn bod heb hwnnw,
> Mae'n well nâ thre dy dâd i'th gadw."
>
> —*1672 ed'n, p. 8.*

Sir Thomas Middleton and Rowland Heylin, two London Welshmen, contributed a thousand pounds towards the cost of printing and publishing. Generally known as *Beibl Midltwn.* It is not improbable that the Rev. Robert Llwyd, Vicar of Chirk, Denbighshire, corrected the press for this edition. About 1,500 copies were printed. There were two issues of this edition ; the collation of both issues is the same, but the sheets A—E (80 pp.), containing Gen. i.—Lev. xx. 26, differ as follows, viz.:—The first issue has *Llyfer Cyntaf Moses,* etc., as heading to Genesis, but the second ¶*Llyfr Cyntaf Moses,* etc.; the headpiece on the same page (sig. A) is not the same ; and while, in the first issue, words added by the translator are italicized, they appear in the second in square brackets. Very many of the misprints in the first issue are corrected in the second.

B

DESCRIPTION.—Title of Pr. Bk., *Llyfr* | *Gweddt* | *Gyffredin,* | *a gwenido-* | *gaeth Y Sacra-* | *mentav :* | *A Chynneddfau a Ceremoniau* | *eraill yn Eglwys Loegr.* | · *Printiedig yn Llvndain gan* | *Robert Barker Printiwr i* | *Ardderchoccaf fawrhydi y Bre-* | *nin: a chan Assignes Iohn Bill,* | *Anno Dom. 1630.*, in woodcut border, blank, *b;* Text of Pr. Bk., sigs. A²—G² and *b;* title of Bible, in the same woodcut border, sig. G³ (unsigned); blank, *b;* Dr. Parry's Latin dedication to King James I., as in No. 9, sigs. G⁴—G⁵ and *b* (unsigned); Dr. Morgan's Latin dedication to Queen Elizabeth, as in Nos. 6 and 9, sigs. G⁶—G⁷ and *b* (unsigned); an address to the reader, *At y Darlleydd*, probably by the corrector of the press, sigs. G⁸ and *b* (unsigned); names of promoters, etc., as in Nos. 6 and 9, sig. H. (unsigned); ¶*Hemwav a threfn llyfrav,* b; text (Gen.—Mal.), sigs. A—Nn⁵ and *b;* text (Apocrypha), sigs. Nn⁶—Yy⁴; blank, *b;* title of N.T., *Testament* | *Newydd ein* | *Harglwydd* | *a'n Hiachawd-* | *wr Iesv Grist.* | *Rhvf. 1. 16.* | . . . *Printiedig yn Llvndain gan* | *Robert Barker Printiwr i* | *Ardderchoccaf fawrhydi y Bre-* | *nin: a chan Assignes Iohn Bill,* | *Anno Dom. 1630.* | , in the same woodcut border; blank, *b;* text (Matt.—Rev.), Yy⁶—Lll⁷ and *b*—colophon at the end; a blank leaf; title, *Llyfr y Psalmau,* | *Wedi ev* | *cyfieithv, A'i* | *cyfansoddi* | *Ar Fesur Cerdd,* | *yn Gymraeg.* | *Drwy waith* | *Edmwnd Prys* | *Archdiacon* | *Meirionnydd.* | (*₊*) | *A'i Printio* | *Yn Llvndain.* | *1630.* | ; blank, *b;* an address to the reader, ¶*At y Darlleydd Ystyriol,* sig. A² and *b;* *Te Deum,* sig. A3 and *b;* text of Psalms, with music as in No. 10, sigs. A⁴—E.⁷ and *b;* table of first lines, sig. E⁸ and *b.* Total pp. (not numbered), 112+14+570+142+200+80=1118.

11.

1 6 4 7. Testament | Newydd ein | Harglwydd | a'n Hiachawdr | Jesv Grist. | Rhvf. 1.16. | . . . | Printiedig yn Llundain gan | Matthew Symmons yn ymyl y llew | goreurog yn heol Alders- | gat. 1647. |

Sm. 12° (24); Roman type ; lines across the page ; calf, with clasps ;
119×60 mm., 131×74 mm.
4⅝×2⅞ in.,   5⅛×2¹⁶⁄₁₆ in.

This edition was the first by and for Nonconformists, the editors and publishers being Vavasor Powel and Walter Cradoc. John Lewis, of Glasgrug, Abervstwyth, in his *Contemplations upon these times; or, the Parliament explained to Wales, etc.* (London, 1646), says, *And now again I hear Mr. Cradock is procuring the New Testament to be printed in Welsh in a little volume.* No contents precede chapters. 1,000 copies printed. Re-issued in the same year. with printer's errors corrected. Stephen Hughes, in his *Llythyr. at rai Gweinidogion,* etc., preceding the 1672 edition of *Canwyll y Cymru,* speaks of the errors as being *cannoedd* (=hundreds).

DESCRIPTION.—Title ; blank, *b;* text, sigs. A²—Kk¹² (pp. 1-820). Total pp., ii.+820=822.

12.

1 6 5 4 ₌ 5 6. Y Bibl | Cyssegr-lan, | Sef yr Hen | Destament | a'r | Newydd. | 2 Tim. 3. 16, 17. | . . . Printiedig yn Llundain gan James Flesher, aca [*sic*] werthir gan Thomas Brewster, tan lûn y tri Bibl yn | ymmyl Pauls ; yn y Flwyddyn 1654. |

Cr. 8° (16); small Roman type, double columns, with marginal notes and references; calf ; 158×84 mm., 162×109 mm.
6³⁄₁₆×3¼ in.,   6⅜×4¹⁄₁₆ in.

Fourth edition, reprint of Nos. 9 and 11, omitting Pr. Bk. and Apocrypha. Some. times called *Beibl Cromwel,* the Protector, according to tradition, having contributed towards the cost of publishing it. The English *J* as pronounced in *Joseph, Jeremiah,* etc., appears in this edition for the first time, although its form is found in Nos. 6 and 9 ; *e.g., Jsrael, Jsaac,* etc. 6,000 copies printed (see *Y Ffydd Ddi-Ffvant,* Oxford, 1671, by Charles Edwards ; p. 152) were printed, some occurring with Prys's Ps., dated 1656, at the end. What the price of this edition was may be inferred from a marginal note on *b* of sig. A³ of Stephen Hughes's *Llythyr at rai Gweinidogion*, etc., preceding the 1672 edition of *Canwyll y Cymru—Mr. | Owen, a | Stationer | at the | white Hart | in Bread-street in | London, | has about | 50 Welsh Bibles yet | unsould, which the | Dealers | of Wales | would do | well to | send for. | They may | have them | for 6s. a | Book, it | may be 4d. | less if they | buy any | quantity. |* Charles Edwards, in his *Y Ffydd Ddi-Ffvant* (Oxford, 1671), p. 152, says that this Bible was "as cheap as English Bibles" (=*cyn ratted à biblau Saesonaec*).

DESCRIPTION.—Title ; *Henwav a threfn llyfrav, b;* text (Gen.—Mal.), sigs. A²—Nn⁴ ; blank, *b;* title of N.T.; blank, *b;* text (Matt.—Rev.), sigs. [A²]—[M⁸] and *b;* title of Prys's Ps., *Llyfr y | Psalmau, | Wedi Eu Cyfieithu, | A'i Cyfansoddi | ar fesur cerdd, | yn Gymraeg. | Drwy waith | Edmund Prys | Archdiacon Meirionnydd. | Printiedig yn Llundain gan James Flesher, | yn y Flwyddyn 1656. | ;* index to first lines, *b;* text, sigs. A²—D⁸ (pp. 1-60, numbered 1-14, 13-58) ; 1 blank leaf. Total pp., 560+192+62=822.

13.

1654. Testament Newydd ein Harglwydd a'n hiachawdr Jesu Grist. London. Printed by M. S. for John Allen at the Sun-rising in St. Pauls Churchyard. 1654. 12°, pp. 820+134=954.

No copy of this edition is known. Quoted from *Revue Celtique*, vol. I., p. 377, a note says, *It contains the metrical Psalms as well as the New Testament.* Mentioned by Charles Edwards, in *Y Ffydd Ddi-Ffvant* (Oxford, 1671), p. 152, where he says, *Ac fel y | rhoddes Duw hâd ir hauwr, amlhâodd y torthau ir bwyttawyr a phreintwyd eilwaith chwe mîl o Fiblau | Cymraeg a llythyrennau mân, ac aethont cyn rat- | ted a biblau Saesonaec. Ac er mwyn hên bobl, a | rhai fyddent a golugon gwannach, printwyd llaw- | eroedd o'r Testament Newydd yn gymraeg ar eu | pennau eu hunain a llythyrennau brâsach. Felly | gwnawd scrifen gymraeg o ewyllys Duw yn eglur | ar lechau, fel y rhedo yr hwn ai darllenno.* (=And as God gave seed to the sower, he multiplied the loaves to the eaters and there were again printed six thousand Welsh Bibles in small type, and they became as cheap as English Bibles. And for the sake of old people, and those having weak sight, large numbers of the New Testament in Welsh were printed separately in larger type. Thus was Welsh writing made plain upon tables, that he may run that readeth it).

14.

1672. Testament | Newydd | ein | Harglwydd | a'n Hiachawdwr | Jesu Grist. | The New Testament of our Lord | and Saviour Jesus Christ. | Rhvf. 1. 16. | . . . Printiedig yn Llundain gan E. Tyler a R. Holt, | dros Samuel Gellibrand, tan lûn y Bel (at the Ball) | ym Monwent Powls. 1672. |

Cr. 8° (8) ; double columns ; calf ; 154×91 mm., 6⅛×3⅜ in.
101×107 mm., 6⅛×4⅜ in.

Edited by Stephen Hughes, and published with the assistance of Hugh Edwards, of Llangadoc, Carmarthenshire; David Thomas, of Margam; Samuel Jones, of Brynllywarch, Llangynwyd, Glamorganshire; William Lloyd, of St. Petrox, Pembrokeshire; and others, including probably Thomas Gouge, of London, although he is not named like the above by Stephen Hughes in his *Llythyr at rai Gweinidogion*, etc., preceding the 1672 edition of *Canwyll y Cymru.* The association of his name with the publication of this edition is based upon a MS. account by Richard Morris, of the Navy Office, and cited by Thomas Llewellyn, LL.D., of Hengoed, in *An Historical Account | of the | British or Welsh | Versions and Editions | of the | Bible* (London, 1768), p. 50. The type is larger than that of Nos. 11 and 13. There are no contents to chapters, or marginal references. The Testament is preceded by the Ps. as in the Pr. Bk., and followed by Prys's metrical version. 2,000 copies printed.

DESCRIPTION.—General title, *Llyfr y | Psalmau, | ynghyd | â Thestament | Newydd ein Harglwydd a'n | Hiachawdwr Jesu Grist. | The Book of Psalmes in Prose | and Meeter; &c. | Printiedig yn Llundain gan E. Tyler a R. | Holt, ac a werthir gan Samuel Gellibrand, tan | lûn y Bel (at the Ball) ym monwent Powls, a | chan Peter Bodvel yng-Haerlleon, a John Hughes | o Wrecsam, 1672.* | blank, *b;* text of Ps., sigs. a²—m⁴; end of Ps. and list of N.T. books, *b;* title of N.T.; blank, *b;* text (Matt.—Rev.), sigs. A³—Kkk³; blank, *b;* title of Prys's Ps., with the imprint, *Printiedig | Yn Llvndain. 1672.;* blank, *b;* text, sigs. A—L⁴. Total pp. (not numbered), 90+446+90=632.

15.

1677=78. Y Bibl | Cyssegr-lan, | Sef yr Hen | Destament | a'r Newydd. | II. Tim. III. 16, 17. | . . . Printiedig yn Llundain gan John Bill, Christopher Barker, | Tho. Newcomb, a Henry Hills, Printwyr i Ardderchoccaf fawrhydi y | Brenin : ac a werthir gan John Hancock, tan lûn y tri Bibl yn | Popes-Head Alley, yn Cornhill. 1677. |

Dy 8° (16); small Roman type; double columns, with marginal notes and references; calf, with clasps ; 175×89 mm., 183×120 mm.
$$6\tfrac{7}{8}\times 3\tfrac{7}{16} \text{ in.,} \qquad 7\tfrac{3}{16}\times 4\tfrac{3}{4} \text{ in.}$$

Edited by Stephen Hughes, who, assisted by Thomas Gouge, was the prime mover in its publication. A number of copies issued without the Apocrypha and Pr. Bk., and a smaller number of copies without the Apocrypha only.

DESCRIPTION.—Title of Pr. Bk., *Llyfr | Gweddi | Gyffredin, | A | Gweinidogaeth | Y | Sacramentau. | A | Chynneddfau a Ceremoniau | eraill yr | Eglwys, yn ol arfer Eglwys | Loegr. | Printiedig yn Llundain gan John Bill, Christopher Barker, | Thomas Newcomb, a Henry Hills, . . . | 1678.* | ; contents of Pr. Bk., *b ;* preface and text of Pr. Bk., sigs. A²—E⁸; Royal Imprimatur in Welsh, signed *Edw. Nicholas,* with the Royal Arms as headpiece, *b ;* title of Bible, dated 1677 ; *Henwav a threfn Llyfrav,* etc., *b ;* text (Gen.—Mal.), sigs. A²—Pp⁶ ; blank, *b ;* text (Apocrypha), sigs. A—K³ and *b ;* 1 blank leaf ; title of N.T., dated 1678 ; blank, *b ;* text (Matt.—Rev.), sigs. Pp⁸—Eee⁶ and *b ;* title of Prys's Ps., dated 1678; index to first lines, *b ;* text, sigs. Eee⁸—Iii⁸ and *b.* Total pp. (not numbered), 80+604+150+208+68=1110 pp.

16.

1689=90. Y Bibl | Cyssegr-lan, | . . . | Printiedig yn Llundain gan Charles Bill, a Thomas | Newcomb, Printwyr i Ardderchoccaf Fawrhydi y | Brenin ar Frenhines. 1689. |

Dy. 8° (16) ; small Roman type ; double columns, with marginal notes and references ; calf, with clasps ; 175×86 mm., 188×120 mm.
$$6\tfrac{7}{8}\times 3\tfrac{3}{8}\text{in.,} \qquad 7\tfrac{3}{8}\times 4\tfrac{3}{4} \text{ in.}$$

Reprint of No. 16, edited up to his death in 1688 by Stephen Hughes, and afterwards by David Jones, a clergyman who had been ejected from the living of Llandyssilio, Carmarthenshire, in 1662. The principal patron of this edition was Lord Wharton; but David Jones was patronised by other persons of quality and some ministers and citizens of London. 10,000 copies printed, soon distributed by the efforts of David Jones. (Calamy's *Ejected Ministers,* 1713, vol. II. p. 720).

DESCRIPTION.—Title, dated 1689 ; contents, *b ;* text (Gen.—Mal.), sigs. A²—Pp⁶ ; blank, *b ;* title of N.T., dated 1690; blank, *b ;* text (Matt.—Rev.), sigs. Pp.⁸—Eee⁶ and *b ;* title of Prys's Ps., dated 1690 ; index to first lines, *b ;* text, sigs. Eee⁸—Iii⁸ and *b.* Total pp. (not numbered), 604+208+68=880.

17.

1690. Y | Bibl | Cyssegr-lan, | . . . | Rhydychain, | Printiedig yn y Theatr yn y Flwyddyn MDCXC. |

La. f° (8) ; large Roman type, with marginal notes and references ; calf ;
$$324\times 179 \text{ mm.,} \qquad 386\times 244 \text{ mm.}$$
$$12\tfrac{3}{4}\times 7 \text{ in.,} \qquad 15\tfrac{3}{8}\times 9\tfrac{3}{8} \text{ in.}$$

Edition for use in churches. Generally known as *beibl yr Esgob Llwyd,* its publication having been chiefly promoted by William Lloyd, D.D., successively Bishop of St. Asaph and Worcester. The Mosaical dates appear for the first time in the margins of this edition.

DESCRIPTION.—Blank, *a ;* frontispiece, *b ;* title, with an engraving ; *Henuau . . Llyfrau,* etc., *b ;* text (Gen.—Apoc.), sigs. A—Lllll⁴ and *b ;* title of N.T., with an engraving ; blank, *b ;* text (Matt.—Rev.), sigs. A²—Fi³ and *b.* Total pp. (not numbered), 1058.

18.

1717-18. Y | Bibl | Cyssegr-lan, | . . . | Printiedig yn Llundain gan Brintwyr y Brenin, Ioan Basged, | ac Asseins Tomas Niwcwm a Harri Hils, a fuant feirw. M DCC XVII. |

Dy. 8° (16); small Roman type; double columns, with marginal notes and references; calf, with clasps; 182×90 mm., 196×123 mm.
7¼×3₁⁹₆ in., 7₁₃₆×7⅞ in.

First Welsh edition published by the S.P.C.K. (founded 1698), commonly known as *Beibl Moses Wiliams*, edited by Moses Williams, B.A., Vicar of Devynnock. It has contents preceding the chapters, and contains the Apocrypha; a Scripture Index or Chronology; two maps; and Prys's Ps., printed at Oxford. Copies were issued for Nonconformists without the Apocrypha and Scripture Index. The latter was, however, issued separately.

The Pr. Bk. so often found preceding this edition and the second issue of the O.T. in 1718, was not published until 1718 (see date on title), and was also issued separately.

The second issue, with the exception of the general title (bearing date 1718), and a portion of the O.T., and the addition of the Pr. Bk., was the same as the first. The Pr. Bk. (sigs. A—H⁶ and *b*) contains, for the first time in Welsh, *Gosodedigaethau a Chanonau Eglwysig* (=The Ecclesiastical Ordinances and Canons of 1603). Both issues numbered 10,000 copies, sold at 5s. 6d. per copy, bound.

DESCRIPTION.—A folded map of Palestine, *Llun Tir yr Addewid. . . . Rhodd J. Jones i'r Cymru;* title, dated 1717; contents, *b;* text (Gen.—Mal.), sigs. A²—Qq⁶ and *b;* text (Apocrypha), sigs. [a]—[k⁴]; blank, *b;* a folded map of the travels of the Apostles, *Teithiau yr Apostolion . . . . Rhodd Rhisiart Mostyn* [of Penbedw, Denbighshire] *i'r Cymru;* title of N.T., dated 1717, sig. Qq p. 13; blank, *b;* text (Matt.—Rev.), sigs. Qq²—Fff⁸; blank, *b;* Scripture Index, *Mynegai'r Bibl Cyssegrlan,* etc., sigs. A—B⁴; *Tabl Swyddau a Graddau Dynion,* sig. B⁴ and *b;* *Tabl Amser,* *b;* title of Prys's Ps., with imprint, *Printiedig yn Rhydychen, dros John Baskett, Printwr i Ardder- | choccaf Fawrhydi y Brenhin. 1717.;* index to first lines, *b;* text, in treble columns, sigs. A²—C² and *b;* Hymnau, sigs. C³—C⁴; *Gweddiau,* sig. C⁴ and *b;* *Tabl yr Hymnau, b.* Total pp. (not numbered, except last 4 pp.), 1172.

19.

1727. Y | Bibl | Cyssegr-lan, | . . . | Printiedig yn Llundain gan Brintwyr y Brenin, Joan Basged, | ac Asseins Harri Hils, a fu farw. 1727. |

Cr. 8° (8 and 16); small Roman type, double columns; calf;
160×88 mm., 165×104 mm.
6₁⁶₆×3½ in., 6½×4⅛ in.

Reprint of No. 19, omitting contents before chapters and references on margins. Published by the S.P.C.K., and issued in three forms, (1) Complete, with the Pr. Bk., Apocrypha, and Prys's Ps.; (2) Without the Pr. Bk. and Apocrypha; (3) N.T. only. The number of copies printed is not known. The price was 4s. per copy: ' *The Welsh Bible, with Apocrypha, Service, and Psalms, corrected by the Reverend Mr. Moses Williams. 4s.'—List of Books Printed and Sold by the Bible-Sellers of London, cyssylltiedig â'r ' Whole Duty of Man,' a argraffwya (yn Seisonaeg) yn 1737.* | Rowlands's *Llyfryddiaeth y Cymry,* p. 340.

DESCRIPTION.—Title of Pr. Bk., printed at Oxford, dated 1727; ? blank (all copies seen imperfect), *b;* text, sigs. A²—K⁴ and *b* (8 pp. to the sheet); general title, dated 1727; contents, *b;* text (Gen.—Mal.), sigs. A²—Tt⁸ and *b* (16 pp. to the sheet); text (Apocrypha), sigs. [a]—[l²]· (16 pp. to the sheet); blank, *b;* title of N.T., dated 1727; blank, *b;* text (Matt.—Rev.), sigs. Uu²—Kkk⁷ and *b* (16 pp. to the sheet); glossary of Hebrew names, etc. *(Arwyddocad rhai Enwau a Geirjau Hebraeg, . . . O gasgliad Moses Wiliams.),* sigs. Kkk⁸ and *b;* title of Prys's Ps., with the imprint, *Printiedig yn Rhydychen, dros Joan Basged, Printwr i | Ardderchoccaf Fawrhydi y Brenin. 1727.;* index to first lines, *b;* text, sigs. A²—H⁴ (8 pp. to the sheet).

20.

1741. Testament | Newydd. | ein | Harglwydd | a'n | Hiachawdwr | Jesu Grist. | Rhuf. I. xvi. | . . . Argraphwyd yn y Flwyddyn MDCCXLI. |

[Thomas Durston: Shrewsbury.]

Cr. 8° (16); double columns; calf; 152×88 mm., 169×106 mm.
6×3$\frac{7}{16}$ in., 6$\frac{11}{16}$×4$\frac{3}{16}$ in.

Without printer's name or place, probably to evade the rights of the King's printers, who had the sole privilege of printing the Scriptures. Type and devices identical with those generally used by Durston. Contents precede chapters.

DESCRIPTION.—Title, with an illustration of the Royal Arms ; blank, *b;* text, sigs. A²—H⁴ and *b.* Total pp. (not numbered), 488.

21.

1746. Y | Bibl | Cyssegr-lan, | . . . | Caer-Grawnt : | Printiedig gan Joseph Bentham, Printiwr i'r Brif-Ysgol. | M.DCC.XLVI. |

Dy. 8° (16) ; double columns, with marginal notes and references ; calf, sometimes with clasps ; 183×90 mm., 213×134 mm.
7$\frac{3}{16}$×3$\frac{9}{16}$ in., 8$\frac{3}{8}$×5$\frac{1}{4}$ in.

Third S.P.C.K. edition, known as *Beibl Rhisiart Morys.* Edited by Richard Morris, of the Navy Office. Copies occur with several variations. A full copy comprised the Pr. Bk., O.T., Apocrypha, N.T., Bible Index, Tables, Prys's Ps., Hymns, Prayers. A few copies have three maps, but most have only two. Many copies have been re-arranged for binding in two equal volumes. The maps were engraved by Nathaniel Hill. 15,000 copies were printed, and sold at 4s. 6d. each.

DESCRIPTION.—Blank, *a; Colect i'w arfer o flaen darllain yr | Ysgrythyr lân, | b;* title of Pr. Bk. ; blank, *b;* text, sigs. *A—*M⁸; blank, *b;* general title ; contents, *b;* text (Gen.—Num. xxxii. 22), sigs. A²—H⁵ and *b;* map, *Teithiau Plant | Israel yn yr | Anialwch | Rhodd Wm. Iones Esqr. FRS | J'r Cymru. |* [*Wm. Iones* was the father of Sir William Jones, the Orientalist] ; text (Num. xxxii. 22—Mal.), sigs. H⁶—Qq⁶ and *b;* text (Apocrypha), sigs. Qq⁷—Ccc²; blank, *b;* title of N.T.; blank, *b;* map, *Darluniad | Tir yr Addewid, Rhandiroedd | Plant Israel, y Llcocdd | hynodaf yn y Testament Newydd | a Theithiau Jesu Grist. | Anrheg Lewis Morys o Fôn | Mam-gymru, iw Gydwladwyr | yr Hen Frutaniaid; a | Diolch i Foneddigion | Lloegr am yrru i'n | Tlodion Lyfrau 'n | Rhodd ac yn Rhad | yn ein hiaith ein | Hunain.* | [the words, *Cyssegr-lan ac yn,* are crossed out in ink]; text (Matt.—Acts i. 5), sigs. Ccc⁴—Iii² and *b;* map, *Teithiau | yr | Apostolion. | Rhodd Wm. Iones Esqr. FRS. | J'r Cymru. | ;* text (Acts i. 6—Rev.), sigs. Iii³—Qqq⁴; blank, *b;* Mynegai'r Beibl Cyssegr-lan, sigs. Qqq⁵—Rrr⁸; *Tabl Swyddau a Graddau Dynion,* sig. Rrr⁸ and *b; Tabl Amser, | Tablau | Arian, Pwysau, a Mesurau,* sigs. Sss—Sss² and *b;* title of Prys's Ps.; *Llythyr yr | Arch-diacon Prys, b;* text, sigs. †A²—†D⁷ and *b; Emynau,* sigs. †D⁸—†E²; index to first lines, sig. †E² and *b;* Gweddiau, sigs. †E³—†E⁴; blank, *b.* Total pp. (not numbered), 1278.

22.

1752. Y | Bibl | Cyssegr-lan | . . . | Llundain : | Printiedig gan Tomas Basgett, Printiwr i Ardderchoccaf Fawrhydi'r | Brenhin ; a chan Wrthddrychiaid Rhobert Basgett. | M.DCC.LII. |

Dy. 8° (16) ; double columns, with marginal notes and references ; calf ;
196×98 mm., 209×134 mm.
7$\frac{3}{4}$×3$\frac{3}{4}$ in., 8$\frac{1}{16}$×5$\frac{1}{4}$ in.

A reprint, omitting the maps, of No. 22, by the same editor, publishers, and promoters. Copies occur with several variations. A full copy comprised the *Hyfforddiadau | i | Ymddygiad Defosiynol; Pr. Bk.* (without Ps.); O.T. and Apocrypha ; N.T.; Tables ; Prys's Ps. In some copies the titlepage to the *Hyfforddiadau* is dated MDCCLXII, printed by *Marc Bascett.* 15,000 copies were printed, and sold at 4s. 6d. per copy. 5,000 copies of the N.T. with Pr. Bk., and 5,000 of the Pr. Bk. only, were also issued separately.

NOTE.—The statement made in the preface of the 1903 re-issue of the 1885 edition of *Geiriadur Charles*, that there was an edition of the Welsh Bible in 1762, is an error, probably by taking the date of *Hyfforddiadau*, etc. (1762) preceding some copies of the 1752 Bible as the date of the Bible itself (see above.)

DESCRIPTION.—Blank, *a*; *Colect*, *b*; title of *Hyfforddiadau*; blank, *b*; text, sigs. A²—A⁴ and *b*, pp. 3-8; title of Pr. Bk.; blank, *b*; text, sigs. A²—K⁸; blank, *b*; general title; contents, *b*; text (Gen.—Mal.), sigs. A²—Qq⁶ and *b*; text (Apocrypha), sigs. Qq⁷—Ccc²; blank, *b*; 2 blank leaves; title of N.T.; blank, *b*; text (Matt.—Rev.), sigs. A²—O²; *Tabl Swyddau*, etc., *b*; *Tablau*, sigs. O³—O⁴ and *b*; title of Prys's Ps.; *Llythyr yr Arch-diacon Prys*, *b*; text, sigs. A²—E⁴; blank, *b*. Total pp. (not numbered, except *Hyfforddiadau*, etc.— 8 pp.), 1230.

23.

1756. Testament | Newydd | ein Harglwydd a'n Hiachawdwr Iesu Grist. | Argraphwyd yn y Flwyddyn MDCCLVI.

[? *John Eddowes: Shrewsbury.*]

Cr. 8° (16); double columns; calf; 155×90 mm., 174×110 mm.
6¼×3⁹⁄₁₆ in., 6¹³⁄₁₆×4⁴⁄₈ in.

Reprint of No. 21, omitting chapter contents. The title is copied from Rowlands's *Llyfryddiaeth y Cymry*, p. 444, which describes a copy containing on the inside of the cover an advertisement of the printing-office of J. Eddowes, *Gwerthwr Llyfrau, uc Argraphydd, yn yr Heol a elwir High Street, yn y Mwythig*. Two copies seen do not contain this advertisement. Dr. Llewelyn, *Historical Account*, 1768, p. 56, speaking of N.T. editions, says, *I believe it has been frequently publish-* | *ed by itself at Shrewsbury.*

DESCRIPTION.—Title; blank, *b*; text, sigs. A²—Hh⁸; blank, *b*. Total pp. (not numbered), 496.

24.

1769. Y | Bibl | Cyssegr-lan. | . . . | Llundain: | Printiedig gan Mark Baskett, Printiwr i Ardderchoccaf Fawrhydi'r Brenhin; a chan Wrthddrychiaid Robert Baskett. 1769. |

Dy. 8° (16); double columns, with notes and references in footnotes; calf;
197×113 mm., 220×138 mm.
7¾×₁₆⁷ in., 8¹¹⁄₁₆×5⅜ in.

The O.T. and N.T. only, edited by John Evans, M.A., of Portsmouth, known as *Ffeirad Plymouth*, who followed the orthography of No. 18, much to the annoyance of Richard Morris (see *Y Greal*, 1806, p. 282-3), and Evan Evans "Ieuan Brydydd Hir" (see his *Casgliad o Bregethau*, 1776, vol. II., pp. 323-326). Published by the S.P.C.K.

DESCRIPTION.—Title; contents, *b*; text (Gen.—Mal.), sigs. A²—5P⁴ and *b*; title of N.T.; blank, *b*; text (Matt.—Rev.), sigs. 5Q²—7G²; blank, *b*. Total pp. (not numbered), 2308.

25.

1770. Y | Bibl Sanctaidd: | sef, | Yr Hen Destament | a'r | Newydd, | gyd a | Nodau a Sylwiadau ar bob Pennod. | Neh. viii. 8. | A hwy a ddarllenasant yn eglur yn y Llyfr, yng Nghyfraith Duw; gan osod allan y synwyr, | fel y dyallent wrth ddarllain. | 2 Tim. iii. 16, 17. | . . . | Caerfyrddin, | Argraffwyd dros y Parchedig Mr. P. Williams, gan I. Ross. | M, DCC, LXX. |

4to (8); double columns, with marginal notes and references, and commentary at end of each chapter; calf; 225×155 mm., 257×211 mm.
8⅞×6¹⁄₁₆ in., 10½×8¼ in.

First edition of *Beibl Peter Williams*, and first Bible printed in Wales. Published by the editor, in shilling parts, the first appearing in 1767, and sold complete, with or without the Apocrypha, for £1. 8,600 copies printed.

DESCRIPTION.—Title; blank, *b*; *Llythyr y Cyhocddwr* | *at y* | *Darllenydd* |, sigs. A²—A³ and *b*, pp. iii.—vi.; *Swm yr holl Ysgrythurau*, sig. A⁴ and *b*, pp. vii.—viii.; *Erthyglau*, etc., sigs. b—b³ and *b*; *Rhai Holiadau ac Attebion*, sigs. b⁴ and *b*; *Mynegai'r Bibl*, sigs. c—c⁴ and *b*; *Llithiau*, etc., sig. d and *b*; *Y Calendar*, etc., sigs. d²—d³; *Tabl i gael y Pasg*, etc., *b*; *Tabl o'r Gwyliau Symmudol*, etc., sig. d⁴; *Enwau . . Llyfrau*, etc., *b*; text (Gen.—Num. xxxiii. 28), sigs. A—U² and *b*; map, *Teithiau Plant | Israel yn yr | Anialwch | Rhodd Rhist. Morys Esr. Ll.C.C. | i'r Cymry.* | ; text (Num. xxxiii. 29—Mal.), sigs. U³—5K⁴ and *b*; text (Apocrypha), sigs. A—X³ and *b*; blank leaf; title of N.T.; *Enwau . . Llyfrau*, etc., *b*; text (Matt.—Acts i. 15), sigs. A²—Q3 and *b*; map, *Teithiau | yr | Apostolion. | Rhodd Rhist. Morys Esr. Ll.C.C. | i'r Cymry.* | text (Acts i. 29—Rev.), sigs. Q⁴—Oo² and *b*; tables, etc., sigs. Oo³—Pp and *b*; title of Prys's Ps.; *Llythyr . . .* | *at y* | *Darllenydd Ystyriol.* |, *b*; text (Ps.), in treble columns, sigs. Pp³—*X and *b*; text (Hymns), sigs. *X²--*X³ and *b*; index to first lines, *b* and *X⁴*; *Gweddi dros holl Ystâd Eglwys Crist*, *b*. Total pp. (not numbered, except first 8 pp.), 1366.

EDITIONS.

1. 1770, Carmarthen (John Ross), 4°.
2. { a1779-81 / b1780-81 } Carmarthen (John Ross), 4°.
3. 1797-6, Carmarthen (John Ross), 4°.
4. 1805-4, Chester (W. C. Jones), f°.
5. 1807, Carmarthen (John Evans), 4°.
6. 1807, Merthyr (William Williams), 4°.
7. 1811, Carmarthen (John Evans), 4°.
8. 1815, Merthyr (William Williams), f°.
9. 1822-21-22, Carnarvon (Lewis Evan Jones), 4°.
10. 1822-21, Carmarthen (John Evans), 4°.
11. 1823-25, London (Henry Fisher, Son and Co.), f°.
12. 1824-23, Carmarthen (Jonathan Harris), 4°.
13. 1826-22, Carnarvon (Lewis Evan Jones), 4°.
14. 1827, London (Henry Fisher, Son, and Co.), f°.
15. 1828-30, Carmarthen (J. L. Brigstocke), 4°.
16. 1829, Carnarvon (Lewis Evan Jones), 4°.
17. 1830-29, Carmarthen (John Evans), 4°. Ps. Cân, 1825.
18. 1831, London (London Printing and Publishing Co., ltd.), f°.
19. 1835, London (H. Fisher, Son, and P. Jackson), f°.
20. 1835-32, Carmarthen (Jonathan Harris and Edward Morris), 4°.
21. 1836, London (Henry Fisher, Son, and Co.), f°.
22. 1837-40-36, Carnarvon (Lewis Evan Jones), 4°.
23. 1838, London (H. Fisher, R. Fisher, and P. Jackson), f°.
24. 1840, Swansea (E. Griffiths), 4°.
25. 1841, London (H. Fisher, R. Fisher, and P. Jackson), f°.
26. 1843, London (H. Fisher, R. Fisher, and P. Jackson), f°.
27. 1846, London (H. Fisher, R. Fisher, and P. Jackson), f°.
28. 1850, Carnarvon (Lewis Evan Jones), 4°.
29. 1858, Swansea (J. Rosser and D. Williams), 4°.
30. [1863], 4 issues—I.—III., London (London Printing and Publishing Co.); IV., Bradford (E. Slater), f°.
31. [1868], London—Glasgow (Blackie and Son), 4°.
32. 1873, London—Glasgow (William Mackenzie), 4°.

Owen Jones and Peter Williams.

1. [1871], London—Glasgow (Blackie and Son), la. 4°.
2. [1872], London—Glasgow (Blackie and Son), la. 4°.

Peter Williams and Matthew Henry.

1. [1874], Edinburgh (T. C. Jack), la. 4°.
2. [1876], Edinburgh (T. C. Jack), la. 4°.
3. 1878 (2 issues—2nd in 1895, from Porth (Jones & Jones), London (Murdoch), la. 4°.

Notes and Marginal References.

1811, N.T., Carmarthen (J. Evans), 8°.

1779. Testament | Newydd | ein Harglwydd | a'n | Hiachawdwr | Iesu Grist. | Ioan v. 39. | . . . | Rhuf. i. 16. | . . . | Argraphwyd yn y Flwyddyn ein Harglwydd | M,DCC,LXXIX. |

[*John Ross : Carmarthen.*]

12mo (24 and 12 alternately); calf, with clasps; 123×70 mm., 134×89 mm.
4$\frac{13}{16}$×2$\frac{3}{4}$ in., 5$\frac{1}{4}$×3$\frac{1}{2}$ in.

Edition brought out by Thomas Llewelyn, LL.D., of Hengoed.

DESCRIPTION.—Title; contents, *b*; text, sigs. A²—*T⁵ and *b*. Total pp. (not numbered), 682.

27.

1779. The | Holy Bible, | . . . | with | Arguments prefixed to the different Books ; | and | Moral and Theological Observations at the End of each Chapter : | composed by | The Pious and Reverend Mr. Ostervald, | Professor of Divinity, and one of the Ministers of the Reformed Church at Neuf- | chatel, in Swisserland. | Translated at the Desire of, and recommended by | The Society for propagating Religious Knowledge. | To which is prefixed, | A Preliminary Discourse concerning the Reading of the Holy Scriptures. | Carmarthen, | Printed by John Ross, M, DCC, LXXIX. |

La. f° (4); double columns, with marginal notes and references ; calf ;
370×212 mm., 409×256 mm.
14$\frac{9}{16}$×8$\frac{6}{16}$ in., 15$\frac{3}{8}$×10$\frac{1}{16}$ in.

An English Bible published in numbers by the S.P.C.K. and distributed from several centres in the United Kingdom, Southampton, Carlisle, Newcastle-upon-Tyne and Carmarthen. The titlepage bears the imprint of the local agent in each case. Re-issued with new general title in 1789 and 1807. Some copies contain the Apocrypha.

DESCRIPTION.—Title ; blank, *b*; *Subscribers names, a* and *b*; *The* | *Preliminary Discourse,* | etc., sigs. [b]—[c]²; *The Names . . . of all the Books,* etc., *b*; text (Gen.—Mal.), sigs. A—7X²; *Of the Time between the Captivity of Babylon, and the Coming of* | *Our Lord Jesus Christ.* | , *b*; text (Apocrypha), sigs. 9G—10K ; 2 blank leaves ; title of N.T., blank, *b*; text (Matt.—Rev.), sigs. 7Y²—10G and *b*; tables of kindred and affinity, etc., *a* and *b*. Total pp. (not numbered), 976.

28.

1779-81. Y | Bibl Sanctaidd : | . . . | gyd a | Nodau a Sylwiadau ar bob Pennod. | Yr ail argraphiad. | . . . | Caerfyrddin, | Argraffwyd dros y Parchedig Mr. P. Williams, gan I. Ross. | M, DCC, LXXIX. |

4° (8); 233×158 mm., 257×215 mm.
9$\frac{3}{16}$×6$\frac{1}{4}$ in., 10$\frac{1}{8}$×8$\frac{1}{2}$ in.

Reprint of No. 26, omitting the Apocrypha and a few of the tables at the end of N.T. 6,400 copies printed, issued in shilling parts.

DESCRIPTION.—Title ; blank, *b*; *Llythyr y Cyhoeddwr,* etc., sig. A²—A³ and *b*, pp. iii.—vi.; *Swm yr holl Ysgrythurau,* sig. A⁴ and *b*. pp. vii.—viii.; *Erthyglau Crefydd,* sigs. b—b³ and *b*; *Rhai Holiadau ac Attebion,* etc., sig. b⁴ and *b*; *Mynegai'r Bibl,* sigs. c—c⁴ and *b*; *Llithiau,* etc., sig. d and *b*; *Y Calendar,* etc., sigs. d²—d³; *Tabl i gael y Pasg,* etc., *b*; *Tabl o'r Gwyliau Symmudol,* etc., sig. d⁴; *Enwau . . . Llyfrau,* etc., *b*; text (Gen.—Mal.), sigs. A—5I²; blank, *b*; title of N.T., dated 1781 ; *Enwau . . . Llyfrau,* etc., *b*; text (Matt. i.—vi. 30), sigs. 5K²—5K⁴ and *b*; text (Matt. vi. 31—Rev.), sigs. B—2N³; *Tabl Swyddau,* etc., *b*; *Tablau Arian,* etc., sig. 2N⁴ and *b*; title of Prys's Ps., dated 1779 ; *Llythyr* | *at* | *y* | *Darllenydd Ystyriol,* *b*; text, in treble columns, sigs. Pp²—Uu⁴ and *b*; text (*Emynau*), sigs. Xx—Xx²; index to first lines, Xx² and *b*. Total pp. (not numbered, except first 8), 1176.

29(A).

1780-81-79. Y | Bibl Sanctaidd : | . . . | Yr ail argraphiad. | . . . | Caerfyrddin, | Argraffwyd dros y Parchedig Mr. P. Williams, gan I. Ross. | M, DCC,LXXX. |

Re-issue of No. 29 (A), with the title and all up to Lev. vii. 10, reprinted in 1780.

29(B).

1789-79. The | Holy Bible, | . . . | with | Arguments prefixed . . . | and | . . . Observations at the End of each Chapter : | . . . by | . . . Mr. Ostervald, | . . . | Carmarthen, | . . . John Ross, M, DCC,LXXXIX. |

La. f° (4); 370×212 mm., 408×256 mm.
14 9/16×8 5/16 in., 16 1/16 × 10 1/16 in.

Re-issue of No. 28, with date on general title altered, list of subscribers omitted, and Apocrypha inserted.

DESCRIPTION.—Title; blank, *b; The | Preliminary Discourse,* | etc., sigs. [b]—[c]²; *The Names . . . of all the Books,* etc., sigs. A—7X²; *Of the Time between the Captivity of Babylon, and the Coming of | Our Lord Jesus Christ.* |, *b;* text (Apocrypha), sigs. A--Hh² and *b;* title of N.T.; blank, *b;* text (Matt.—Rev.), sigs. 7Y²—10G and *b;* tables of kindred and affinity, etc., *a* and *b.* Total pp. (not numbered), 990.

30.

1789. Y | Bibl | Cyssegr-lan | . . . | Appwyntiedig i'w ddarllain mewn eglwysi. | Rhydychain : | Printiedig yn Argraphdy Clarendon, | Gan W. Jackson ac A. Hamilton, Printwyr i'r University. | Ac ar werth gan W. Dawson, yn Ystordy Biblau Rhydychain . . . 1789. | Cum Privilegio. |

La. f° (8); large Roman type, double columns ; calf ; 324×185 mm., 379×243 mm.
12 3/4 × 7 3/16 in., 14 15/16 × 9 9/16 in.

An edition for use in Churches, known as *Beibl Parri Llanasa,* having been seen through the press by Henry Parry, Vicar of Llanasa, Flintshire. Its errors are many, the most notorious being *Ail [sic] Epistol Paul yr Apostol at y Colossiaid.*

DESCRIPTION.—Title; blank, *b;* Latin dedication of No. 9, sig. a; Latin dedication of No. 6, *b* and sig. a², pp. ii.—iii.; names of promoters of No. 6, and contents, *b,* p.iv.; text (Gen.—Mal.), sigs. A—4O³ and *b;* text (Apocrypha), sigs. 4O⁴—5L³ and *b;* title of N.T.; blank, *b;* text (Matt.—Rev.), sigs. A—Ff² and *b.* Total pp. (not numbered, except 4 at beginning), 1058.

31.

1790. Y | Bibl Sanctaidd: | . . . | â | Nodau Ysgrythurol | ar ymyl y Ddalen, wrth y rhai y gwelir mai'r Ysgrythur | yw'r Deonglydd cywiraf o'r Ysgrythur. | . . . | Trefecca : | Argraphwyd, dros y Parchedig Gyhoeddwyr, | P. Williams, a D. Jones. | M,DCC,XC. |

Cr. 8° (12); very small Roman type, double columns, with marginal notes and references, and comments at foot ; calf ; 152×84 mm., 171×105 mm.
6×3 1/16 in., 6 3/4×4 1/8 in.

Known as *Beibl John Cann,* the editors and publishers (Peter Williams and David Jones, a Baptist minister, of Pontypool,) having adopted the marginal notes and references of John Canne's English edition of the Bible (1st ed'n, Amsterdam, 1647). The prospectus, with sample pages, was issued from *Trefecca : Medi 8, 1786.* 4,000 copies of the Bible were printed, issued in parts, and sold complete at 6s. each. The N.T. was also issued separately. This edition was reprinted in 1812 and 1823 (Carmarthen, Jonathan Harris, 12°), and the O.T. only in 1826 (same press). The same marginal references were used in No. 33, but with the notes of William Romaine.

DESCRIPTION.—Title ; blank, *b; Llythyr y Cyhoeddwyr at y Darllenydd, a; Enwau . . . Llyfrau,* etc., *b;* text (Gen.—Mal.), sigs. B—Aaa⁴; blank, *b;* title of N.T.; *Enwau . . . Llyfrau,* etc., *b;* text (Matt.—Rev.), sigs. Aaa[⁶]—Qqq⁶; blank, *b.* Total pp. (not numbered), 736.

NOTE.—William Rowlands " Gwilym Lleyn," seeing probably the first parts of this edition, dated 1788, assumed that the whole appeared in that year, and records it so, describing it as the third edition of No. 26 (see *Llyfryddiaeth y Cymry,* p. 632).

32.

1796. Y Bibl Cyssegr-lan, . . . gyda Nodau Cyfeiriol ar Ymyl y Dail, yn dangos mai'r Ysgrythur yw y Dehonglydd goreu o'r Ysgrythur. Gan John Canne. Caerfyrddin, Argraphwyd (ac ar werth yno) gan Ioan Daniel. M, DCC, XCVI. |

Dy. 8° (8); double columns, with marginal notes and references, and comments at foot ; boards and calf, sometimes with clasps; 196×112 mm., 215×135 mm.

7¾×4⅞ in., 8₇/₁₆×5⅜ in.

This edition is not a re-issue of No. 32, because although Canne's marginal references are adopted, Peter Williams's readings of certain verses are rejected, while the comments at foot are by William Romaine, M.A., of St. Dunstan's West, London. 4,000 copies printed, issued in 19 parts. N.T. also issued separately.

DESCRIPTION.—Title (not seen); contents, *b*; text (Gen.—Mal.), sigs. A—5G⁴ and *b*, pp. 1-800 ; title of N.T., *Testament Newydd* | . . . | *Yr Ysgrythurau Cyfeiriol ar Ymyl y Dail,* | *Gan y Parchedig John Canne;* | *A'r Sylwiadau ar Odreu'r Dail,* | *Gan y Parchedig William Romaine.* | . . . | *Caerfyrddin,* | . . . *Ioan Daniel.* | *M.DCC.XCVI.* | ; text (Matt.—Rev.), *b*—sigs. A²—2K⁴ and *b,* pp. 2-264; title of Prys's Ps.; text, in treble columns, *b*—sigs. A²—F and *b,* pp. 2-42; *Emynau,* sigs. F²—F³, pp. 43-45 ; index to first lines, sigs. F³—F⁴, pp. 45-47 ; *Gweddi dros holl Ystad Eglwys Crist,* sig. F⁴ and *b,* pp. 47-48; poem, *Rhagoriaeth y Bibl, b,* p. 48. Total pp., ii.+800+264+48=1,114.

33.

1797-6. Y | Bibl Sanctaidd : | . . . | Y trydydd argraphiad. | . . . | Caerfyrddin, | Argraffwyd dros y Parchedig Mr. P. Williams, gan I. Ross. | M, DCC, XCXVII. |

4° (8); 235×160 mm., 265×203 mm.

9⅛×6¼ in., 10₇/₁₆×8in.

Reprint of No. 26, omitting the Apocrypha and a few of the tables at the end of N.T. 4,000 copies printed, issued in shilling parts. The editor died (August 8, 1796,) while the edition was yet in the press, the remaining proofs being read by his son, John, who says at the foot of the last page, *N.B. Os gweli fai adgyweiria mewn cariad, gan gofio mai'r tro cyntaf yw i mi deithio trwy fath lafurus orchwyl.* | (*Cf.* note on p. vi. of the Bible.)

DESCRIPTION.—Title ; blank, *b; Llythyr y Cyhoeddwr,* etc., sigs. A²—A³ and *b,* pp. iii.—vi.; *Swm yr holl Ysgrythurau,* sig. A⁴ and *b,* pp. vii.—viii.; *Erthyglau,* sigs. b—b³ and *b; Rhai Holiadau ac Attebion,* etc., sig. b⁴ and *b; Mynegai'r Bibl,* sigs. c—c⁴ and *b; Llithiau,* etc., sig. d and *b; Y Calendar,* etc., sigs. d²—d³; *Tabl i gael y Pasg,* etc., *b; Tabl o'r Gwyliau Symmudol,* etc., sig. d⁴; *Enwau . . . Llyfrau,* etc., *b;* text (Gen.—Mal.), sigs. A—5I²; blank, *b;* title of N.T., dated 1796 ; *Enwau . . . Llyfrau,* etc., *b;* text (Matt.—Rev.), sigs. 5K²—2Y³; *Tabl Swyddau,* etc., *b; Tablau Arian,* etc., sig. 2Y⁴ and *b;* title of Prys's Ps., dated 1797 ; *Llythyr* | *at y* | *Darllenydd Ystyriol, b;* text, in treble columns, sigs. Pp²—Pp⁴ and *b,* and 7A—7F² and *b.* Total pp. (not numbered, except first 8), 1,176.

34.

1799.

NOTE.—Rowlands's *Llyfryddiaeth y Cymry,* p. 724, records a folio Welsh Bible under this date ; but no trace of a copy has been found. Rowlands :has more than probably wrongly described the 1799 8° ed'n (No. 36) as a f°. According to Rowlands, and also to Walter Davies "Gwallter Mechain" in *Y Gwyliedydd,* 1830, p. 263, this edition, the printing of which was commenced in 1798, and finished in 1799, was for use in Churches, published by the S.P.C.K., under the patronage of Richard Bagot, D.D., Bishop of Oxford, who instructed D. Davies, Vicar of Penegoes, Montgomeryshire, to adopt the orthography of No. 23, and to correct any errors occurring in it. Davies, however, appointed Evan Evans, of Llanfihangel, then at Jesus College, Oxford, to give in his corrections to the printers. The proofs of the Pentateuch were read by Robert Hughes, a Fellow of Jesus College, assisted by E. Hughes, of Caerwys; and the remainder by John Roberts, afterwards Vicar of Tremeirchion.

35.

1799.   Y | Bibl | Cyssegr-lan ; | . . . | Rhydychen : | Printiedig yn
Argraphdy Clarendon, | Gan W. Dawson, T. Bensley, a J. Cooke, |
Printwyr i'r Brif-Ysgol. | M DCC.XCIX. |

Dy. 8° (16); double columns, with marginal notes and references ; calf ;
178×91 mm., 212×137 mm.
7×3¹⁶⁄₁₆ in., 8⁷⁄₁₆×5⅜ in.

For patron, editors, and proof-readers, see note on No. 35. Published by the
S.P.C.K., at the instigation of Thomas Jones, Curate of Creaton. 10,000 copies were
printed, a number omitting the Pr. Bk. and Apocrypha. 2,000 of the N.T. were also
issued separately. " Mary Jones's Bible " is a copy of this edition.

DESCRIPTION.—Title of *Hyfforddiadau*, etc.; blank, *b;* text, sigs. A²—A⁴ and *b,*
pp. 3—8; title of Pr. Bk.; blank, *b;* text, sigs. A²—H³ and *b;* blank, *a; Colect, b;*
general title ; contents, *b;* text (Gen.—Mal.), sigs. A²—Qq⁶ and *b;* text
(Apocrypha), sigs. Qq⁷—Ccc²; blank, *b;* title of N.T.; blank, *b;* text (Matt.—Rev.),
sigs. A²—O²; *Tabl Swyddau,* etc., *b; Tablau . . . gan Risiart Morys,* sigs.
O³—O⁴ and *b;* title of Prys's Ps.; *Llythyr yr | Arch-diacon Prys, b;* text, sigs.
A²—D⁷ and *b; Emynau,* sigs. D⁸—E²; index to first lines, sig. E² and *b;*
Gweddiau, sigs. E³—E⁴; blank, *b.* Total pp. (not numbered, except first 8), 1188.

36.

1800.   Testament Newydd | . . . | Jesu Grist. | Rhydychen : |
Printiedig yn Argraphdy Clarendon, | gan Dawson, Bensley, a
Cooke, | Printwyr i'r Brif-Ysgol. | MDCCC. |

Cr. 8° (24); double columns; calf; 157×89 mm., 168×105 mm.
6³⁄₁₆×3½ in.,   6⅝×4⅛ in.

· An edition without chapter-contents and marginal references, but with the *Table
of Offices and Degrees* at the end, published by the Sunday School Society (founded
1785).

DESCRIPTION.—Title; contents, *b;* text, sigs. A²—K⁵ and *b;* table of offices, etc.,
sig. K⁶; blank, *b.* Total pp. (not numbered), 228.

37.

1800.   [Testament Newydd.]

[Shrewsbury.]

Mentioned in *Y Gwyddoniadur Cymreig,* 1856-79, vol. I., p. 639, as having been
issued in various sizes to the number of 10,000 copies. No authority for the statement
is cited ; and no copy is known. It may be the same as No. 40.

38.

1801.   Y Bibl Cyssegr-lan ; Sef yr Hen Destament a'r Newydd.
Rhydychen: Printiedig yn Argraphdy Clarendon, gan W. Dawson,
J. Bensley, a J. Cooke, Printwyr i'r Brif-ysgol. MDCCCI.

*Unplyg ; gyda'r Llyfr Gweddi Gyffredin, a Salmau Cân Edmund Prys,—y rhai
ydynt yn dwyn yr un amseriad—wedi eu cydrwymo ag ef.*

No copy found. Recorded as above in Charles Ashton's unpublished bibliography.

39.

1801.   Testament Newydd ein Harglwydd a'n Hiachawdwr Iesu
Grist. Yn y Mwythig : Printiedig ac ar werth gan J. a W.
Eddowes.

·   *12plyg ; heb rifnodi y tudalenau, ac heb amscriad. Nis gwyddom a gyhoeddwyd
hwn yn y ganrif bresennol ai peidio ; ond gwyddom fod yr argraffwyr yn argraffu,
o'r hyn lleiaf, rhwng 1790 a 1801.*

No copy found. Recorded as above in Charles Ashton's unpublished bibliography.

40.

1801. Testament Newydd | ein | Harglwydd | a'n | Iachawdwr | Iesu Grist. | . . . | Caerfyrddin : | Argraphwyd, dros Ioan Richards, ac ar werth gan· Ioan Evans. | M, DCCC, I. | Pris 3s. 6ch. heb ei rwymo, ynghyd a'r Mynegair, 4s. 6ch. |

Cr. 8° (8); double columns, with chapter-contents, and a short introduction to each book, to evade the rights of the King's printers ; calf ; 162×97 mm., 179×115 mm.
6⅜×3¹⅜ in., 7₇ᵣ×4¼ in.

DESCRIPTION.—Title; contents, *b;* text, sigs. B—3D²; blank, *b.* Total pp. (not numbered), 390. A number of copies was issued with a Bible Index (*Mynegair* [*sic* Mynegai]).

41.

1802. Y | Bibl Sanctaidd, | . . . | gyd ag | Ysgrythurau Cyfeiriol, a Sylwiadau ar ymyl y dail,·| Gan John Brown. | . . . | Caerfyrddin: | Argraffwyd (ac ar werth yno) gan Ioan Evans. | M, DCCC, II. |

Dy. 8° (8); double columns, with marginal notes and references ; calf, with clasps ; 195×91 mm., 212×131 mm.
7¹¹×3¹ᵣ in., 8⅜×5₁ᵣ in.

Issued in opposition to No. 33 in 13 sixpenny parts, the first in 1800, and the last early in 1802, price 10s. bound. Chapter-contents condensed. Marginal notes by John Brown, D.D., of Haddington. Contains also, for the first time in connection with the Welsh Bible, tables of the miracles and parables, and Dr. Isaac Watts's rhymed version of the Ps., translated by David Jones, of Caio. Copies occur without the Ps.

DESCRIPTION.—Title ; contents, *b;* text (Gen.—Mal.), sigs. A²—4N and *b;·*title of, N.T.; blank, *b;* text (Matt.—Rev.), sigs. 4N³—5Q⁴ and *b;* tables of miracles and parables, *b;* title of Watts's Ps.; text, *b*—sig. F; *Ffurf o ogoniant y Cristion, b;* index to first lines, *b*—sig. F² and *b.* Total pp. (not numbered), 908.

42.

1802. Testament Newydd | . . . | gᵧd a | Sylwiadau ar Odreu'r Dail. | A gyhoeddwyd gan | Titus Lewis, Gweinidog yr Efengyl. | . . . | Caerfyrddin : | Argraphwyd ac ar werth gan John Evans. | 1802. |

12° (12); double columns, without chapter-contents, but with a short comment at the foot of two of the pages to evade the rights of the King's printers ;
123×67 mm., 134×81 mm.
4⅜×2⅝ in., 5¼×5₁ᵣ in. ; 462 pp.

43.

1802. Pigion allan o Destament William Salesbury ; (yr hwn) oedd y cyntaf erioed a argraphwyd yn yr Jaith Gymraeg) ynghyd a sylwiadau cymhwysiadol at amryw o amgylchiadau ag sydd wedi cymmeryd lle yn ddiweddar yn Nghymru : neu, Bapuryn Achlysurol (Rhifyn y pedwarydd) yn cynnwys, ymmysg pethau eraill, ystyriaethau difrifol ar y gwahanol gyfieithiadau cymreig o'r ysgrythur, ac ar yr elyniaeth sydd wedi ymddangos yn erbyn y Cymreigiad diweddar o amryw fanau yn y Testament Newydd.— Mewn Llythyr at Dafydd Danes, o'r 'Scubor fawr, yn Llandyfriog, wrth Emlyn.

Penawd 16 tudalen 8plyg (Demy). Y mae y llythyr wedi ei arwyddo gan William Richards, ac yn ddyddiedig "Lynn, Mawrth 1, 1802." Diweddeb:— "Whittingham, Argraphydd. [Pris tair Ceiniog.]"

Recorded as above in Charles Ashton's unpublished bibliography.

43a.

1805-4.   Y | Bibl Sanctaidd : | . . . | Caerlleon, | Argraffwyd gan
W. C. Jones.—1805. |

La. f° (4); calf; 364×186 mm., 420×257 mm.
12$\frac{5}{16}$×7$\frac{3}{4}$ in.,   15$\frac{3}{8}$×10$\frac{1}{8}$ in.

First f° reprint of No. 26, omitting Apocrypha. Title of N.T. dated 1804; N.T.
also issued separately. Prys's Ps. also dated 1804. It was entirely a printer's venture,
issued in 34 parts at 1s. each, from 1803 to 1805, 12 nos. having appeared by Oct. 5,
1803. 1,200 copies printed, and sold at £1 14s. unbound, or £2 bound.

Sigs., A—G⁴ and b, and A—9M¹ and b. Total pp. (not numbered), 816.

44.

1806.   Testament | Newydd | . . . | Argraffiad Ystrydeb. | Caer
Grawnt : | Argraffedig gan Ioan Smith, Ystrydebiaethydd i'r
Brifathrofa, | oddi wrth ystrydebiaeth Andrew Wilson, o Lundain; |
tros | Gymdeithas Biblau Saesoneg ac Ieithoedd eraill. | Mai 6,
1806. |

Cr. 8° (24); double columns; chapter-contents; calf; 154×83 mm., 170×106 mm.
6$\frac{1}{16}$×3$\frac{1}{4}$ in.,   6$\frac{11}{16}$×4$\frac{1}{8}$ in.

First Welsh issue by the B. & F.B.S. Price 1s. Sigs., A—O¹⁰. Total pp., 332.

45.

1806.   Testament | Newydd | . . . | Argraffiad Ystrydeb. | Caer
Grawnt: | Argraffedig gan Richard Watts, Ystrydebiaethydd i'r
Brifathrofa, | oddi wrth ystrydebiaeth Andrew Wilson, o Lundain: |
tros | Gymdeithas Biblau Saesóneg ac Ieithoedd eraill. | Mai 6,
1806. |

Second issue of No. 45.

46.

1806.   Testament | Newydd | . . . | Caer   Grawnt : | . . . Richard
Watts, . . . | tros | Gymdeithas Biblau Saesoneg ac Ieithoedd
eraill. | Mai 6, 1806. |

Third issue of No. 45, with date in imprint on last page altered to May 7, thus
making three issues in two days, numbering 10,000 copies. (Canton's *History of the
British and Foreign Bible Society*, 1904 ; Vol. I., p. 101.)

47.

1807.   Y | Bibl | Cyssegr-Lan ; | . . . | Argraffiad Ystrydeb Caer
Grawnt. | Caer Grawnt : | Ystrydebwyd ac argraffwyd gan Richard
Watts, | . . . | tros | Gymdeithas Biblau Saesoneg ac Ieithoedd
eraill. | 1807. | Cum Privilegio. |

Cr. 8° (24); double columns ; chapter-contents ; calf ; 154×83 mm., 163×101 mm.
6$\frac{1}{16}$×3$\frac{1}{4}$ in.,   6$\frac{3}{8}$×4 in.

First Welsh Bible by the B. & F.B.S., dated in imprint on last page, *Mai 6, 1807.*
20,000 copies printed. N.T. also issued separately.

DESCRIPTION.—Title ; *Enwau . . . Llyfrau*, etc., b; text (Gen.—Cant.), sigs.
A²—U¹¹ and b, pp. 3—478; text (Isaiah—Mal.), sigs. U¹²—Dd¹² and b,
pp. (1)—(170); title of N.T.; blank, b; text (Matt.—Rev.), sigs. A—K² and b,
pp. 3—210 ; table of offices, etc., sig. K⁴ and b, pp. 211—212. Total pp., 860.

NOTE.—In some copies 4 pp., numbered 189, 190, 189*, 190*, are inserted after
Judges vi. 38. The type is thin-leaded, while the book, as a whole, is type-close.
These 4 pp. form a cancel sheet, owing to the omission of Judges viii. from the stereo
plates, the proof-reader, Dr. William Owen-Pughe, having passed the proof without
that chapter. This concerned 2,750 copies already sent out by the binder. The
remainder were remedied by abridging the chapter-contents in sheet H, thus getting
the omitted chapter into the same number of pp. ; *i.e.*, 2. A copy of this issue is in the
library of the Theological College, Bala. Verse 36 of Ps. cv. is omitted, and verse 33
repeated instead ; and a portion of verse 4 of Jer. xxxv. is omitted. Cancel sheets were
also issued for these. These omissions were detected by Thomas Charles of Bala.

48.

1806-08-13. Y | Bibl Sanctaidd; | gyd a | Sylwiadau Eglurhaol a Defnyddiol, | yn cynnwys | Esponiad Cyflawn | o'r | Hen Destament a'r Newydd. | Wedi eu cymmeryd allan o Esponiad | Thomas Coke, LL.D. | O Brif-Ysgol Rhydychen. | ... | Caerlleon: | Argraphwyd, ac ar werth, gan ɪ. Hemingway. | 1806.

4° (4); double columns, with marginal references and commentary at end of each chapter ; 228 × 185 mm., 260 × 217 mm. } O.T.;   223 × 171 mm., 287 × 229 mm. } N.T.
8⅛ × 7¼ in.,   10₁₆⅛ × 8₁₆⁷ in.   8₁₆⁵ × 6¾ in.,   11₁₆⁶ × 9 in.

The family Bible of the Wesleyan Methodists in Wales, sometimes called *Beibl Dr. Coke*, published in shilling parts comprising three books, viz.:—Book I., Gen.—II. Chron. (1806); Book II., Ezra—Mal. (1808) ; Book III., Matt.—Rev. (1813), part of the last being printed in London by Paris and Son, and part at Carmarthen by D. Rees, *for the Editor of the Carmarthen Journal* [*i.e.*, John Daniel], as stated at the bottom of the last page.

DESCRIPTION.—Title ; blank, *b ; Cynhwysiad y Llyfr Cyntaf*, sig. a²; *Enwau . . . Llyfrau*, etc., *b; Rhagymadrodd byr*, etc., by Thomas Roberts, of Bonwm, sigs. b—d, pp. v.—xiii.; blank, *b ;* text (Gen.—II. Chron.), sigs. A—10O and *b*, pp. 1—882; title of *Llyfr II.*, dated 1808; blank, *b; Cynhwysiad yr Ail Lyfr;* blank, *b ;* text (Ezra—Mal.), sigs. A—10D², pp. 1—861; blank, *b;* title of N.T., *Testament Newydd* | . . . | *Gyd a* | *Sylwadau eglurhaol a defnyddiol ar bob Pennod.* | *Wedi eu cymmerwyd* [*sic*] *allan o Esponiad* | *Thomas Coke, LL.D.* | . . . | *Caerfyrddin:* | *Argraphwyd gan D. Rees, yn Heol y Farchnad Issaf.* | *1813.* | ; *Enwau . . . Llyfrau'r Testament Newydd, b;* *Llithiau*, etc., sig. [a] and *b;* Y *Calendar*, etc., sigs. [a]²—[b] ; *Tabl i gael y Pasg, b; Tabl o'r Gwyliau Symmudol*, etc., sig. [b]²; *Enwau . . . Llyfrau'r Hen Destament, b;* text (Matt.—Rev.), sigs. B—9L and *b*, pp. 1—842 ; errata, *b*, p. 842. Total pp., xiv.+882+iv.+862+x.+842=2614.]

49.

1807. Y | Bibl Sanctaidd : | . . . | gyda | Nodau a Sylwadau | ar bob pennod. | . . . | Caerfyrddin : | Argraphwyd, dros Mr. David Humphreys, gan John Evans, yn Heol-y-Prior. | M,DCCC,VII. |

4° (8 and 4); 228 × 157 mm., 252 × 209 mm.
9 × 6₁₆³ in.,   9⅞ × 8₁₆³ in.

Reprint of No. 26, omitting the Apocrypha, issued in shilling parts, and sold bound in calf at £1 10s. The publisher, David Humphreys, was son-in-law to Peter Williams.

DESCRIPTION.—Title; blank, *b ; Llythyr y Cyhoeddwr*, sigs. A²—A³, pp. [iii—v]; *Gweddi*, etc., *b; Swm yr holl Ysgrythyrau*, sig. A⁴ and *b*, pp. [vii—viii]; *Erthyglau*, sigs. B—B³ and *b; Rhai Holiadau*, etc., sig. B⁴ and *b; Mynegai'r Bibl*, sigs. c—c⁴ and *b; Llithiau*, etc., sig. d and *b;* Y *Calendar*, etc., sigs. d²—e² (4 pp. to a sheet); *Enwau . . . Llyfrau*, etc., *b;* text (Gen.—Mal.), sigs. A—5K⁴ and *b;* title of N.T.; *Enwau . . . Llyfrau*, etc., *b;* text (Matt.—Rev.), sigs. A²—Oo² and *b;* tables, sigs. Oo³—Pp³ and *b;* title of Prys's Ps.; *Llythyr*, etc., *b;* text, in treble columns, sigs. Pp³—3A² (sigs. Ss—Zz, 4 pp. to a sheet); *Emynau*, *b;* index to first lines, 3A⁴ and *b*. Total pp. (not numbered except first 8), 1,200.

50.

1807. Y | Bibl Sanctaidd : | . . . | gyda | Nodau a Sylwadau ar bob pennod. | . . . | Merthyr Tydfil, | . . . William Williams, 1807. |

4° (4 and 2); 229 × 153 mm., 256 × 209 mm.
9 × 6 in.,   10₁₆⁵ × 8¼ in.

Reprint of No. 26, omitting Apocrypha. Sold bound in calf at £1 10s.

DESCRIPTION.—Title ; blank, *b ;* preliminary matter, 30 pp.; text (Gen.—Mal.), sigs. A—9D² and *b;* title of N.T.; contents, *b ;* text (Matt.—Rev.), sigs. A²—Ttt and *b;* tables, sigs. Ttt²—Uuu and *b;* title of Prys's Ps., dated 1807 ; text, in treble columns, *b*—Xxx, etc. (2 pp. to a sheet). Copy seen imperfect at end.

51.

1807. Holy Bible, | . . . | by . . . Mr. Ostervald, | . . . | The second edition, carefully revised and corrected. | Carmarthen, | Printed by John Ross, M,DCCC,VII, | For Hobday and Ryder, Albion-House, Birmingham. |

La. f° (4); 370×212 mm., 401×262 mm.
14$\frac{9}{16}$×8$\frac{6}{16}$ in., 16$\frac{8}{16}$×10$\frac{6}{16}$ in.

Re-issue of Nos. 28 and 30, same as No. 30, with the exception of general title.

51a.

1808. Y | Bibl | Cyssegr-Lan ; | . . . | Argraffiad Ystrydeb Caer Grawnt. | Caer Grawnt : | Ystrydebwyd ac argraffwyd gan Richard Watts, | Argraffydd i'r Brifathrofa ; | tros | Gymdeithas Biblau Saesoneg ac Ieithoedd eraill. | 1808. | Cum Privilegio. |

Cr. 8° (24); 154×83 mm., 173×103 mm.
6$\frac{1}{16}$×3$\frac{1}{4}$ in., 6$\frac{13}{16}$×4$\frac{6}{16}$ in.

Reprint of No. 48, dated in imprint on last page, *Mai 6, 1807.* N.T. also issued separately. " *20,000 Bibles and 30,000 Testaments were,*" according to Canton's *History of the British and Foreign Bible Society,* 1904, vol. I., p. 104, " *circulated* [in Wales] *at a loss to the Society of £1896.*"

52.

1808. Testament Newydd | . . . | gyd a | Sylwiadau ar odreu'r dail. | . . . | Merthyr Tydfil : | Argraphwyd ac ar werth gan W. Williams. | 1808. | [Pris 4s. wedi ei rwymo.] |

12° (12); double columns, without chapter-contents, but with a short comment at the foot of two of the pages to evade the rights of the King's printers ; calf ;
160×85 mm., 178×107 mm.
6$\frac{6}{16}$×3$\frac{6}{16}$ in., 7×4$\frac{1}{4}$ in.

DESCRIPTION.—Title ; contents, *b ;* text, sigs. A²—Ss⁷, pp. 3—493 ; advertisement, *Llyfrau Cymraeg,* etc., *b.* Total pp., 494.

53.

1809. Y | Bibl | Cyssegr-Lan ; | . . . | Argraphiad Cyfargraph. | Rhydychen : | Argraphedig yn Argraphdy Clarendon, | Gan Dawson, Bensley, a Cooke, | Argraphwyr i'r Brif-Ysgol ; | Ac a werthir gan W. Dawson yn Ystôr-dŷ Biblau Rhydychen, Pater noster Row, Llundain. | 1809. | Cum Privilegio. |

Dy. 8° (16) ; calf ; 190×122 mm., 225×149 mm.
7$\frac{1}{2}$×4$\frac{13}{16}$ in., 8$\frac{7}{8}$×5$\frac{7}{8}$ in.

Reprint of No. 36, *restoring the Orthography of proper Names after the Text published in the Year 1620.* (Preface, p.*6), under the sanction of the four Welsh bishops and the Bishop of Hereford. David Hughes, M.A., Rector of Llanfyllin, conducted the edition through the press for the S.P.C.K., with some assistance from Thomas Charles of Bala. Walter Davies, M.A. "Gwallter Mechain," says, *In this edition, the errors of 1799 are | avoided, as the edition of 1752 was followed. I was | one out of three deputed to read over the edition of | 1752, for the purpose of correcting inaccuracies in or- | thography and punctuation. I was an advocate for | uniformity in general ; but I was outvoted in almost | every instance.* | (*Gwaith ;* vol. III., p. 222.) N.T. also issued separately.

DESCRIPTION.—Title of *Hyfforddiadau ;* blank, *b ;* text, sigs. A²—A⁴ and *b,* pp. 3—8; preface (English), signed R. Llandaff, | W. Asaphens, | John. Bangor, | Thomas St. David's, | John Hereford. | May 25, 1809. |, pp. *5—*6 ; preface (Welsh), pp. *7—*8 ; blank, *a ;* Colect, *b ;* title of Pr. Bk.; blank, *b ;* text, sigs. A²—H⁴ and *b,* pp. 5—120 ; general title ; contents, *b ;* text (Gen.—Mal.), sigs. A²—Qq⁶ and *b,* pp. 3—620 ; text (Apocrypha), sigs. Qq⁷—Ccc² and *b,* pp. 621—772; title of N.T.; blank, *b;* text (Matt.—Rev.), sigs. A²—O², pp. 3—211; tables, *b*—O⁴ and *b,* pp. 212—216; title of Prys's Ps.; Llythyr, etc., *b;* text, sigs. A²—D⁷ and *b,* pp. 3—62; Emynau, sigs. D⁸—E², pp. 63—67; index to first lines, sigs. E² and *b,* pp. 67—68; Gweddiau, Sigs. E³—E⁴, pp. 69—71; blank, *b.* Total pp., 1,192.

54.

1811. Y | Bibl | Cyssegr-Lan; | . . . | Argraphiad Cyfargraph. | Rhydychen: | Argraphedig yn Argraphdy Clarendon, | Gan Bensley, Cooke, a Collingwood. | Argraphwyr i'r Brif-Ysgol ; | Ac a werthir gan E. Gardner, yn Ystôr-dŷ Beiblau Rhydychen, Pater noster Row, Llundain. | 1811. | Cum Privilegio. |

Dy. 8° (16); calf ; 190×122 mm., 213×143 mm.
7½×4¹³⁄₁₆ in.,   8¾ x 5⅝ in.

Reprint of No. 54.

55.

1811. Testament Newydd | . . . | Rhydychen. | Printiedig yn Argraphdy Clarendon. | Gan Bensley, Cooke, a Collingwood, | Printwyr i'r Brif-Ysgol. | MDCCCXI. |

Cr. 8° (24); 157×88 mm., 175×103 mm.
6³⁄₁₆×3⁷⁄₁₆ in.,   6⅞×4¹⁄₁₆ in.;

Reprint of No. 37. Copies occur with the date on title in Arabic figures, thus :—
1811 (Ashton's unpublished bibliography.)

56.

1811. Testament Newydd | . . . | gyda | Sylwadau ac Adnodau cyfeiriol ar Ymyl y Ddalen, | gan y diweddar | Barchedig Peter Williams. | . . . | Caerfyrddin : | Argraffwyd gan ɟ. Evans.—1811. |

Cr. 8° (12); large type, lines across the page, with marginal notes and references ; calf; 159×88 mm., 175×107 mm.
6¼×3½ in.,   6⅞×4¼ in.

No *Sylwadau* (=remarks) except a phrase here and there amongst the marginal references. Issued in 6 parts at 1s. each, sold bound for 5s. 6d.

DESCRIPTION.—Title ; Enwau . . . Llyfrau, etc., *b ;* text, sigs. A—3F⁶ and *b,* pp. 1-624. Total pp., ii.+624=626.

57.

1811. Y | Bibl Sanctaidd, | . . . | gyda | Nodau a Sylwadau | . . . | Peter Williams. | Y seithfed argraffiad. | Caerfyrddin : | Argraffwyd ac ar werth gan ɟ. Evans, yn Heol-y-Prior. | M, DCCC, XI. | ·

4° (8 and 4); 228×156 mm., 263×216 mm.
9×6⅛ in.,   10¾×8½ in.

Reprint of No. 26, omitting Apocrypha, issued in 32 parts at 1s. each.

Sigs., A-e² and *b ;* A—5K⁴ and *b ;* and A—3A⁴ and *b.* Total pp. (not numbered), 1,224.

58.

1812. Y | Bibl Sanctaidd : | . . . | Gydag Ysgrythyrau Cyfeiriol ar ymyl y dail, | Gan y Parchedig John Canne ; | ynghyd a | Sylwadau ar odreu y dail. | . . . | Caerfyrddin : | Argraphwyd, ac ar werth yno, gan Jonathan Harris. | M,DCCC,XII. |

Foolscap 8° (12); 139×77 mm., 154×92 mm.
5½×3¹⁄₁₆ in.,   6¹⁄₁₆×3⅝ in.

Reprint of No. 32, issued in 6 parts at 2s. each, sold bound for 9s. N.T. also issued separately.

DESCRIPTION.—Title ; contents, *b ;* text (Gen.—Mal.), sigs. B—3M and *b,* pp. [1]—[674]; title of N.T.; text (Matt.—Rev.), *b* of A—T⁵, pp. 2-221; table of offices, etc., *b.* Total pp., ii.+674+222=898.

59.

D

1 8 1 3. Y | Bibl Sanctaidd; | . . . | gyda nodau eglurhaol, a dosparth-
iadau ar | gynnwysiad y pennodau. | Gan y Parch. Samuel Clark,
M.A. | Hefyd, holl nodau cyfeiriol | Y Parch. John Brown, | ar
ymyl y ddalen. | Gwedi eu cyfieithu i'r Gymraeg, er budd i'r Cymry;
allan o'r argraffiad diweddaf | yn Saesoneg; | Gan John Humphreys.
| Llyfr I. | Gwrecsam : | Argraffwyd gan J. Painter, tros y
cyfieithydd. | M,DCCC,XIII. |

La. f° (4); double columns, with marginal notes and references, introduction to
the books, and a commentary; calf ; 360×167 mm., 419×260 mm.
15×6$\frac{9}{16}$ in.,   16$\frac{1}{4}$×10$\frac{5}{16}$ in.

A family Bible, sometimes called *Beibl Clark*, issued in 62 parts (the first 3
re-issued), comprising 2 books, published by John Humphreys, a Calvinistic Methodist
Minister, of Caerwys, Flintshire (died at·a great age 1829), and translated by him from
Clarke's *Old and New Testaments, with Annotations and Parallel Scriptures* (1690, f°;
reprinted 1760 and 1765). The 1760 English ed'n was published under the supervision
of Whitefield : hence his *Rhagymadrodd* in Humphreys's translation. The commentator
(born 1626, at Shotwick, near Chester ; died 1701, at High Wycombe) was an ancestor
of the late George Thomas Clark, of Talygarn, Glamorganshire. John Brown, whose
references are given on the margins, was the divine of Haddington.

DESCRIPTION.—Title of Book I.; blank, *b ;* title of Book II. ; blank, *b ;*
Rhagymadrodd | yr Awdwr | , sigs. a—a²; *Rhagymadrodd at y Darllenydd
difrifol,* signed *George Whitefield, b* of sig. a²—b ; *Llythyr y Cyhoeddwr at
ei gyd-wladwyr,* signed *J. Humphreys, | Caerwys, Mawrth 20fed, 1813.* |, sig. b ;
Cyfarwyddiadau, etc., and contents, *b ;* text (Gen.—Mal.), sigs. A—9I² and *b ;*
title of N.T.; blank, *b ;* text (Matt.—Rev.), sigs. 9K²—13L ; blank, *b.* Total pp.
(not numbered), 1,238.

NOTE.—Sigs. Aa—Zz are repeated.

60.

1 8 1 3. Y | Bibl | Cyssegr-Lan ; | . . . | Argraffiad Ystrydeb Caer
Grawnt. | Caer Grawnt : | . . . Ioan Smith, | Argraffydd i'r Brif-
athrofa : | tros | Gymdeithas Biblau Saesoneg ac Ieithoedd eraill. |
1813. | Cum Privilegio. |

Cr. 8° (24); 154×83 mm., 174×103 mm.
6$\frac{1}{16}$×3$\frac{4}{16}$ in.,   6$\frac{7}{8}$×4$\frac{1}{16}$ in.

Reprint of No. 48, dated in imprint on last page, *Mai 6, 1813.* N.T. also issued
separately.

61.

1 8 1 3. Y | Bibl | Cyssegr-Lan ; | . . . | Argraphiad Cyfargraph. |
Rhydychen : | . . . Argraphdy Clarendon, | Gan Bensley, Cooke, a
Collingwood, | Argraphwyr i'r Brif-Ysgol ; | . . . | 1813. | Cum
Privilegio. |

Dy. 8° (16); calf ; 190×122 mm., 223×144 mm.
7$\frac{1}{2}$×4$\frac{13}{16}$ in.,   8$\frac{13}{16}$×5$\frac{11}{16}$ in.

Reprint of No. 54.

62.

1 8 1 4. Y | Bibl Cyssegr-Lan, | . . . | Argraffiad Ystrydeb. | Llundain:
| . . . George Eyre ac Andrew Strahan, | . . . | Tros Gymdeithas y
Biblau Brutanaidd ac Ieithoedd eraill, | A Sefydliwyd yn Llundain
yn y Flwyddyn 1804. | Ac ar werth, i Gynnorthwywyr yn unig, gan
L. B. Seeley, | yn Ystordy y Gymdeithas, 169, Fleet Street. |
1814. |

Dy. 8° (16); double columns ; calf ; 198×111 mm., 223×139 mm.
7$\frac{11}{16}$×4$\frac{3}{8}$ in.,   8$\frac{3}{4}$×5$\frac{7}{16}$ in.

First London-printed Welsh edition (stereotyped) for the B. & F.B.S. N.T. also issued separately. Copy for press prepared by Thomas Charles. This edition was re-issued without date, and is often described as an 1804 edition, owing to the date of the founding of the B. & F.B.S. appearing in the imprint.

> DESCRIPTION.—Title ; contents, b; text (Gen.—Mal.), sigs. A²—3O⁷ and b; tables of weights, measures, money, and time, sig. 3O⁸; blank, b; title of N.T.; contents, b; text (Matt.—Rev.), sigs. A²—U⁸; table of offices, etc., b. Total pp., 960+320=1,280.

63.

1814. Testament | Newydd | . . . | Argraffiad Ystrydeb. | Llundain : | . . . George Eyre ac Andrew Strahan, | . . . | Ac ar werth gan Longman, Hurst, Rees, Orme, a Brown, | Paternoster-Row. | 1814. |

Re-issue of the N.T. of No. 63, with altered imprint.

64.

1815. Y | Bibl Sanctaidd : | . . . | gyd a | Nodau a Sylwadau | ar | Bob Pennod. | . . . | Merthyr Tydfil: | Argraphwyd gan William Williams. | 1815. |

La. f° (4) ; calf ; 333×157 mm., 374×232 mm.
13⁹⁄₁₆×6⅛ in., 14¾×9⅛ in.

Reprint of No. 26, omitting the Apocrypha and title of Prys's Ps. Issued in 24 parts.

Sigs., B—14S² and b, with 8 preliminary pp.

65.

1816-17. Y | Bibl Santaidd, | . . . | gydag | Ymyl-Nodau Cyfeiriol ac Eglurhaol, | a Chrynodeb o Gynnwysiad pob Llyfr a phob Pennod ; | hefyd, | Nodau | Hanesiol, Eglurhaol, ac Ymarferol, | ar odre y dail, | Gan y Parch. D. Davies, | Abertawe. | . . . | Deut. 6, 6, 7. | Caerfyrddin : | Argraffwyd gan J. Evans, yn Heol-y-Farchnad Isaf. | 1816. |

4° (8 and 4); double columns, with marginal notes and references, introductions to the books, and commentary at end of each chapter; calf; 238×183 mm., 267×211 mm.
9⅜×7³⁄₁₆ in., 10½×8⁶⁄₁₆ in.

A family Bible, commonly called *Beibl Dafis Abertawe*, issued in 40 parts at 1s. each. The editor died before the completion of the work. David Davies, Congregational Minister, of Pantteg, Carmarthenshire, wrote the notes to Revelations (see preface.)

> DESCRIPTION.—Title; contents, b; Y *Rhagymadrodd*, a and b; text (Gen.—Mal.), sigs. A—6H⁴ and b; *Cyfrifiad o rifedi* | *Llyfrau*, etc., b; title of N.T.; contents, b; text (Matt.—Rev.), sigs. 6I²—8B³ and b; *Rhai awgrymau*, etc., and glossary, 8B⁴ and b; title of Watts's Ps., trans. David Jones, of Caio, dated 1817; index to first lines, b; text, sigs. B—N² and b (4 pp. to a sheet). Total pp. (not numbered), 1358.

66.

1818. Y | Cyfammod Newydd, | yn cynnwys | Cyfieithiad Cyffredinol | Y Pedair Efengyl, | gwedi ci ddiwygiaw | Yn ol y Groeg | Gan John Jones, L.L.D. et J.C. | Llyndin : | Argraffwyd gan John Williams, Ship Place, Strand; | ac ar werth gan Lackington a Co., Finsbury- | Square; a phob gwerthwr llyfrau trwy | Gynmry. | Pris. 5s. | 1818. |

Cr. 8° (24); lines across the page, with chapter-contents ; short note at foot of few pages ; boards ; 150×80 mm., 189×116 mm.
5⅞×3⅛ in., 7⁷⁄₁₆×4⁹⁄₁₆ in.

A version of the four Gospels from the Greek, by John Jones, LL.D., a barrister-at-law, who went the Oxford and South Wales circuits; born 1772 at Derwydd, Llandybie, Carmarthenshire; died 1837 at Islington. He published in 1824 a *History of Wales*.

DESCRIPTION.—Title; blank, *b*; *Rhag-ysgrifen*, sig. A² and *b*; text, sigs. B—M and *b*. Total pp., iv.+250=254.

67.

1819. Y | Bibl | Cyssegr-Lan ; | . . . | Argraffiad Ystrydeb Caer Grawnt. | Caer Grawnt : | . . . Ioan Smith, | Argraffydd i'r Brifathrofa ; | tros | Gymdeithas Biblau Saesoneg ac Ieithoedd eraill. | 1819. | Cum Privilegio. |

Cr. 8° (24); 154×83 mm., 173×106 mm.
6⅟₁₆×3¼ in., 6¹³⁄₁₆×4⅜ in.

· Reprint of No. 48, dated in imprint on last page, *Mai 6, 1807*.

68.

1819. Testament | Newydd | . . . | Argraffiad Ystrydeb. | Caer Grawnt: | . . . I. Smith, Ystrydebiaethydd i'r Brifathrofa, | . . . | tros Gymdeithas Biblau Saesoneg ac Ieithoedd eraill. | 1819. | Cum Privilegio. |

Cr. 8° (24); type larger than in N.T. of No. 68, and no date in imprint on last page; calf; 151×83 mm., 172×104 mm.
5¹³⁄₁₆×3¼ in., 6¾×4½ in.

DESCRIPTION.—Title; blank, *b*; text, sigs. A²—O⁹ and *b*, pp. 3—330; table of offices, etc., sig. O¹⁰ and *b*, pp. 331—332.

69.

1819. Testament | Newydd | . . . | Argraffiad Ystrydeb. | Llundain : | . . . George Eyre ac Andrew Strahan, | . . . | tros Gymdeithas y Biblau Brutanaidd ac Ieithoedd eraill, | . . . | 1819. |

Dy. 8° (16); 198×111 mm., 224×144 mm.
7¹³⁄₁₆×4⅜ in., 8¹³⁄₁₆×5⅝ in.

Reprint of the N.T. of No. 63.

'0.

1819. Testament W. Salesbury. | Rhifyn I, | (Pris Chwe Cheiniog) | o'r | Testament Newydd, | yn ol | Y Cyfieithiad a Gyhoeddwyd | gan yr enwog | W. Salesbury, | gynt o'r | Cae Du, Llansannan, Sir Dinbych, | Yn y Flwyddyn 1567. | Hefyd, | Epistol Esgob Menyw at y Cembru, | A Llythyr yr Awdwr | At y Frenhines Elizabeth. | Bala : | Argraffedig gan R. Saunderson. | 1819. |

Foolscap 8° (8); lines across the page; marginal notes; wrapper;
130×80 mm., 158×102 mm.
5⅛×3⅛ in., 6¼×4 in.

. First part (all published) of a reprint of No. 5. Title on wrapper only.

Sigs., A—F, pp. 1—48.

71.

1820. Y | Bibl | Cyssegr-Lan; | . . . | Argraffiad Ystrydeb Caer Grawnt. | Caer Grawnt: | . . . Ioan Smith, | . . . | tros | Gymdeithas Biblau Saesoneg ac Ieithoedd eraill. | 1820. | Cum Privilegio. |

Cr. 8° (24); 154×83 mm., 174×107 mm.
6⅟₁₆×3¼ in., 6⅞×4⅛ in.

Reprint of No. 48, dated in imprint on last page, *Mai 6, 1807*.

72.

1820. Testament | Newydd | . . . | Argraffiad Ystrydeb. | Llundain : | . . . George Eyre ac Andrew Strahan, | . . . | tros Gymdeithas y Biblau Brutanaidd ac Ieithoedd eraill, | . . . | 1820. |

Dy. 8° (16); 198×111 mm., 220×144 mm.
$7\frac{13}{16} \times 4\frac{3}{8}$ in., $8\frac{11}{16} \times 5\frac{11}{16}$ in.

Reprint of the N.T. of No. 63.

73.

1821. Y | Bibl | Cyssegr-Lan; | . . . | Argraffiad Ystrydeb Caer Grawnt : | . . . Ioan Smith, | . . . | tros | Gymdeithas Biblau Saesoneg ac Ieithoedd eraill. | 1821. | Cum Privilegio. |

Cr. 8° (24); 154×83 mm., 173×106 mm.
$6\frac{1}{16} \times 3\frac{1}{4}$ in., $6\frac{13}{16} \times 4\frac{3}{16}$ in.

Reprint of No. 48, dated in imprint on last page, *Mai 6, 1807*.

74.

1821. Testament | Newydd | . . . | Argraffiad Ystrydeb. | Caer Grawnt: | . . . I. Smith, | . . . | tros Gymdeithas Biblau Saesoneg ac Ieithoedd eraill. | 1821. | Cum Privilegio. |

Cr. 8° (24); 151×83 mm., 172×104 mm.
$5\frac{15}{16} \times 3\frac{1}{4}$ in., $6\frac{3}{4} \times 4\frac{1}{8}$ in.

Reprint of No. 69.

75.

1821. Y | Bibl | Cyssegr-Lan; | . . . | Argraphiad Cyfargraph. | Rhydychen: | . . . Argraphdy Clarendon, | Gan Samuel Collingwood ac eraill, | Argraphwyr i'r Brif-Ysgol; | . . . | 1821. | Cum Privilegio. |

Dy. 8° (16); calf; 190×122 mm., 224×148 mm.
$7\frac{1}{2} \times 4\frac{13}{16}$ in., $8\frac{3}{16} \times 5\frac{13}{16}$ in. ; 1,188 pp.

Reprint of No. 54. Price, 15s. bound. N.T. also issued separately.

76.

1821. Y | Beibl | Cyssegr-Lan; | . . . | Y Cyfieithiad Cyntaf i'r Gymraeg, | Gan William Morgan, D.D. | A argraphwyd yn Llundain yn y flwyddyn 1588. | Dolgellau: | Ad-argraphwyd a Chyhoeddwyd, gan R. Jones. | 1821. |

4° (4); 2 founts of Roman type; double columns, with marginal notes, and short comments at foot of few pages; calf; 239×193 mm., 269×219 mm.
$9\frac{7}{16} \times 7\frac{5}{8}$ in., $10\frac{9}{16} \times 8\frac{5}{8}$ in.

Reprint of No. 6, omitting the Apocrypha. Issued in 22 parts at 1s. each, and sold bound at £1 7s.

Description.—Title; blank, *b;* Latin dedication to Queen Elizabeth, names of promoters, and contents, *a—b;* text (Gen.—Mal.), sigs. A—8M and *b*, pp. 1—686; title of N.T.; blank, *b;* text (Matt.—Rev.), sigs. A—3B² and *b*, pp. 3—204. Total pp., 894.

77.

1822-21-22. Y | Bibl Sanctaidd: | . . . | gyda | Nodau a Sylwadau | ar bob pennod. | Gan y diweddar Barchedig Peter Williams. | . . . | Yr Wythfed Argraffiad. | Caernarfon: | Argraffwyd a chyhoeddwyd gan L. E. Jones; ac ar werth gan E. Carnes, Tre-ffynnon. | M, DCCC, XXII. |

4° (4); 227×187 mm., 266×221 mm.
$8\frac{15}{16} \times 7\frac{3}{8}$ in., $10\frac{1}{2} \times 8\frac{3}{4}$ in.

Reprint of No. 26, issued in 32 parts at 1s. each, omitting the Apocrypha, but including, for the first time as part of *Bcibl Peter Williams*, a biography and portrait of the commentator from an engraving in *The Gospel Magazine* for 1777. The biography is an abridged reprint of the 1817 edition published and translated from the English of Peter Williams by Owen Williams ("Owain Gwyrfai"), of Waunfawr. Title of N.T. dated 1821, and Prys's Ps. 1822.

Sigs., a—h² and *b;* A—9T² and *b;* A—4D² and *b;* A—I [*sic* S] and *b.* Biography occupies last 10 pp. Total pp. (not numbered, except first 24), 1,206.

78.

1822-21. Y | Bibl Santaidd ; | . . . | gyda | Nodau a Sylwadau | ar bob pennod. | . . . | Caerfyrddin: | . . . J. Evans, . . . | M, DCCC, XXII. |

4° (8); 232 × 153 mm., 270 × 219 mm.
9⅛ × 6⅛ in., 10⅜ × 8⅝ in.

Reprint of No. 26, issued in 32 parts at 1s. each, omitting the Apocrypha, and substituting Watts's Ps. as in No. 66 for Prys's. Title of N.T. dated *M, DCCC, XXI.*

Sigs., A—5K⁴, A—Oo⁴, and A—N. Total pp. (not numbered, except first 8), 1,196.

79.

1822-21. Y | Bibl Santaidd, | . . . | gydag | Ysgrythyrau Cyfeiriol, | a | Sylwadau Eglurhaol, | y'nghanol y ddalen. | . . . | Caerfyrddin: | . . . J. Evans, . . . | M,DCCC,XXII. |

Dy. 8° (8); large type; double columns, with notes and references between; calf; 200 × 112 mm., 222 × 137 mm.
7⅞ × 4₁₆⁷ in., 8¾ × 5⅝ in.

With anonymous modern preface. Issued in 28 parts at 6d. each.

DESCRIPTION.—Title ; *Enwau . . . Llyfrau,* etc., *b; Rhagymadrodd, a—b,* pp. iii.—iv.; text (Gen.—Mal.), sigs. A—6O⁴ and *b,* pp. 1—1,018 ; title of N.T., dated 1821 ; *Enwau . . . Llyfrau,* etc., *b;* text (Matt.—Rev.), sigs. A²—2X² and *b,* pp. 1—348. Total pp., iv.+1,018+348=1,370.

80.

1822. Testament | Newydd | . . . | Argraffiad Ystrydeb. | Caer Grawnt: | . . . | Ioan Smith, | . . . | tros | Gymdeithas Biblau Saesoneg ac Ieithoedd eraill. | Cum Privilegio. | 1822. |

Cr. 8° (24); 151 × 83 mm., 175 × 102 mm.
5₁₆¹³ × 3¼ in., 6⅞ × 4 in.

Reprint of No. 69.

81.

1822. Testament Newydd | . . . | gyda | Sylwadau ar odre y Dail. | A Gyhoeddwyd y waith gyntaf | Gan y Parch. Titus Lewis, | . . . | Yr ail argraffiad. | . . . | Caerfyrddin: | Argraffwyd ac ar werth gan D. Evans, | yn Heol-Spilman, a J. Evans, yn Heol- | y-Farchnad Isaf. | 1822. |

12 (12); calf ; 119 × 68 mm., 127 × 78 mm.
4₁₆¹⁵ × 2₁₆¹³ in., 5 × 3⅛ in. ; 316 pp.

Reprint of No. 43, issued in 4 parts at 6d. each, sold bound for 1s. 6d.

DESCRIPTION.—Title; *Enwau a Threfn Llyfrau,* etc., *b;* text, pp. 3—416.

82.

1822. Testament Newydd | . . . | Gyda rhai | Sylwadau ar odreu'r dail, | Gan ʃ. Jenkins, | Gweinidog yr Efengyl yn Hengoed. | . . . | Merthyr Tydfil: | . . . ʃ. Jenkins, ar y Llan-dir : . . . | . . . | 1822. |

Foolscap 8° (8) ; double columns ; no chapter-contents ; note at foot of 2 pp., to evade the copyright of the King's printers ; calf; 127×79 mm., 144×96 mm.
5×3$\frac{1}{16}$ in., 5$\frac{11}{16}$×3$\frac{3}{4}$ in.

Known as *Testament Shôn Shincyn o'r Hengoed*, John Jenkins, D.D., Baptist minister, of Hengoed, Glamorganshire, having published and printed it at his own press.

DESCRIPTION.—Title ; contents, *b ;* text, sigs. A²—3I and *b*, pp. 3—434 ; Y *Graddau Carennydd a Chyfathrach*, sig. 3I² ; blank, *b*. Total pp., 436.

83.

1823. Y | Bibl | Cyssegr-Lan ; | . . . | Argraffiad Ystrydeb Caer Grawnt. | Caer Grawnt: | . . . Ioan Smith, | . . . | tros | Gymdeithas Biblau Saesoneg ac Ieithoedd eraill. | 1823. | Cum Privilegio. |

Cr. 8° (24); 154×83 mm., 174 X 107 mm.
6$\frac{1}{16}$×3$\frac{5}{16}$ in., 6$\frac{7}{8}$×4$\frac{3}{16}$ in.

Reprint of No. 48, dated in imprint on last page, *Mai 6, 1807.*

84.

1823. Testament Newydd | . . . | Yr Ysgrythyrau Cyfeiriol ar ymyl y dail, | Gan y Parch. John Canne; | ynghyd a | Sylwadau ar odreu y dail. | . . . | Caerfyrddin : | . . . Jonathan Harris. | M,DCCC,XXIII. |

Foolscap 8° (12); 139×77 mm., 150×89 mm.
5$\frac{1}{2}$×3$\frac{1}{16}$ in., 5$\frac{11}{16}$×3$\frac{7}{8}$ in.

Reprint of the N.T. of No. 32, price 2s.

DESCRIPTION.—Half title ; contents, *b ;* title; text, *b* of A—T⁵, pp. 2—221 ; table of offices, etc., *b*. Total pp., ii.+222=224.

85.

1823-25. Y | Bibl | Sanctaidd: | . . . | Gyd a | Nodau a Sylwiadau ar bob Pennod, | Gan y | Parch. Peter Williams. | . . . | Llundain: | Argraffwyd yn yr Argraff-Wasg Caxton, gan Henry Fisher. | (Argraffydd yn Gyffredin i'r Brenin.) | Cyhoeddedig yn 38, Heol Newgate, a chan holl Gwerthwyr Llyfrau yn y Deyrnas. | 1823. |

La. f° (4); 339×202 mm., 371×244 mm.
12$\frac{1}{4}$×7$\frac{7}{8}$ in., 15$\frac{11}{16}$×9$\frac{5}{8}$ in.

Reprint of No. 26, omitting Prys's Ps., but including a portrait of the editor (Peter Bailey Williams, Rector of Llanrug and Llanberis, son of Peter Williams), a large number of engravings, the biography as in No. 78, and the Apocrypha. Title of N.T. dated 1825. Imprint on last page, *Llundain: Argraphwyd yng Ngwasg Caxton, gan H. Fisher, Son, & Co.* This reprint was advertised by the publishers as being according to Peter Williams's original plan, and as having been first revised and corrected by Evan Evans (" Ieuan Brydydd Hir "). Issued in 138 parts at 6d. each, or in five-shilling sections. (See under No. 26 for reprints.)

DESCRIPTION.—Portrait of Peter Bailey Williams, dated 1825; *Tal-Eilun* ((frontispiece), dated *1823;* title; blank, *b; Llythyr y Cyhoeddwr*, etc., pp. 3—4 ;
Hanes . . . Peter Williams, sigs. [*a*]—[*b*]² and *b*, pp. 5—12; *Mynegai'r Bibl*,
sigs. [*c*]—[*d*] and *b*, pp. 13—18; *Swm yr holl Ysgrythurau, b* of sig. [*d*]—[*d*]²,
pp. 18—19; *Gweddi, b*, p. 20; *Erthyglau*, sigs. [*c*]—[*f*], pp. 21—25; *Llithiau, b*
of [*f*]—[*g*], pp. 26—29; *Tabl i gael allan y Pasg, b* of sig. [*g*], p. 30; *Tabl o'r
Gwyliau Symmudol*, sig. [*g*]², p. 31; *Enwau . . . Llyfrau*, etc., *b*, p. 32; text
(Gen.—Mal.), sigs. B—8 H²', pp. 5—675; tables, *b*, p. 676; text (Apocrypha),
sigs. 8 I—9 R² and *b*, pp. 677—804; *Talwyneb* (frontispiece); title of N.T., dated
1825; *Enwau . . . Llyfrau, b;* text (Matt.—Rev.), sigs. 9 S²—12 F, pp. 807—1033;
tables, *b*—12 F² add *b*, pp. 1034—1036; title of Prys's Ps.; index to first lines, *b;*
text, sigs. A²—H² and *b*, pp. 3—32; *Hymnau*, sigs. I—I², pp. 33—35; *Gweddiau*,
sig. I² and *b*, pp., 35—36. Total pp., 32+1032+36=1100.

86.

1823-27.   Y | Bibl Dwyieithog, | yn cynnwys yr | Ysgrythyrau
Santaidd, | yn ol y cyfieithad awdurdodedig, | Yn yr ieithoedd
Cymraeg a Saesoneg, | gyda | Darlleniadau a Chyfeiriadau Ymylenol
helaeth, | cyflenwedig a | Rhai Nodiadau Eglurhaol, | gan | Y
Parch. Joseph Harris. | Abertawy: | Argraffedig a Chyoeddedig gan
J. Harris a J. A. Williams, 25, Heol-Fawr. | MDCCCXXIII—
MDCCCXXVII. |

4to (4 and 8); double columns, with notes and references; calf;
240×182 mm., 265×216 mm.
9$\frac{7}{16}$×7$\frac{3}{16}$ in.,   10$\frac{7}{16}$×8$\frac{1}{2}$ in.

First Welsh-English Bible, edited and partly published by Joseph Harris " Gomer,"
who died (August, 1825,) while the work was in the press. Issued in 45 parts at
1s. each, or 9 sections at 5s. each, comprising 2 vols. (I., Gen.—Canticles ; II.,
Isaiah—Rev.) Vol. II. was published by J. A. Williams alone. The circulation
was very large, 1,500 copies being subscribed for in Glamorganshire and Monmouthshire only. Reprinted in 1839 and *circa* 1850.

DESCRIPTION.—Frontispiece, *Prodigal Son*, dated *1827;* title (Welsh), dated
MDCCCXXIII—MDCCCXXVII. ;   contents, *b;* title (English), dated
MDCCCXXIII—MDCCCXXVII.; contents, *b;* text (Gen.—Canticles, Vol. I.),
sigs. B—N⁶, pp. 1—785; *Terfyn y Gyfrol I.*, etc., *b;* title (Welsh) of Vol. II.,
dated *MDCCCXXV—MDCCCXXVII.*; blank, *b;* title (English) of Vol. II., dated
MDCCCXXV—MDCCCXXVII.; blank, *b;* text (Isaiah—Zech. vi. 5), sigs.
2N⁵—6Z⁴ and *b*, pp. 787—1056; text (Zech. vi. 5—Mal.), sigs. Æ—Œ², pp.
1057—1067; *Terfyn y Prophwydi*, etc., *b;* title (Welsh) of N.T., dated
MDCCCXXVII.; blank, *b;* title (English) of N.T., dated *MDCCCXXVII.*; blank,
b; text (Matt.—Rev.), sigs. B—2X², pp. 5—343; *Cyfres.—A Table, b.* Total pp.,
1,420.

87.

1824-23-24.   Y | Bibl Sanctaidd: | . . . | gyda | Nodau a Sylwadau
ar bob pennod. | Argraffiad Newydd. | . . . | Caerfyrddin : | . . .
Jonathan Harris, . . . | M,DCCC,XXIV. |

4° (4); calf; 244×155 mm., 268×213 mm.
9$\frac{3}{16}$×6$\frac{1}{8}$ in.,   10$\frac{9}{16}$×8$\frac{3}{8}$ in.

Reprint of No. 26, omitting the Apocrypha. Title of N.T. dated *M,DCCC,XXIII.*,
and Prys's Ps. *M,DCCC,XXIV.* Issued in 30 parts at 1s. each. Proposals for this
reprint appear in *Harris's Catalogue of Welsh Books* (1818), where it is requested that
subscribers should give their names to David Humphreys, Nant-y-llan, Llandefeiliog
(see under No. 50), or to printer.

Sigs., A—10E² and *b*, pp. 1—848; and A—4T² and *b*, pp. 1—352. Total pp., 1,200.

88.

1824. Y | Bibl | Cyssegr-Lan ; | . . . | Argraphiad Ystrydeb. | Rhydychain : | . . . Argraffdy Clarendon, | Gan Samuel Colling-wood ac ereill, | . . . | Tros y Bibl Gymdeithas Gartrefol a Thramor, | . . . | 1824. | Cum Privilegio. |

Dy. 8° (16); 190×99 mm., 221×149 mm.
7½×3⅞ in.,   8¾×5⅞ in.

Reprint of No. 63.

89.

1824. Y | Bibl | Cyssegr-Lan ; | . . . | Argraphiad Ystrydeb. | Rhydychain : | . . . Argraffdy Clarendon, | Gan Samuel Colling-wood ac ereill, | . . . | Tros y Gymdeithas er Taenu Gwbodaeth Gristionogol; | . . . | 1824. | Cum Privilegio. |

Dy. 8° (16); 190×122 mm., 225×148 mm.
7½×4¹³⁄₁₆ in.,   8⅞×5¹³⁄₁₆ in. ; 1,176 pp.

Reprint of No. 54, omitting prefaces, collect, etc.   N.T. also issued separately. |

90.

1824. Y | Bibl | Cyssegr-Lan; | . . . | Argraffiad Ystrydeb Caer-grawnt. | Caergrawnt: | . . . Ioan Smith, | . . . | tros | Gymdeithas Biblau Saesoneg ac Ieithoedd eraill. | 1824. | Cum Privilegio. |

Cr. 8° (24); calf ; 154×83 mm., 177×106 mm.
6¹⁄₁₆×3¼ in.,   6¹⁵⁄₁₆×4³⁄₁₆ in.

Reprint of No. 48.

90a.

1824. Testament | Newydd [. . . | Argraffiad Ystrydeb. | Llundain : | . . . George Eyre ac Andrew Strahan, | . . . | Tros Gymdeithas y Biblau Brutanaidd ac Ieithoedd eraill, | . . . | 1824. |

Dy. 8° (16); calf; 198×113 mm., 225×144 ·mm.
7¾×4⁷⁄₁₆ in.,   7⅞×5¹¹⁄₁₆ in. ; 320 pp.

Reprint of the N.T. of No. 63.

91.

1824. Y Testament Newydd | Dwyieithawg. | . . . | Gyda nodau cyfeiriol o bob adnod. | . . . | Clwyd-Wasg : | Dinbych, . . . | Thomas Gee : | . . . | 1824. | The Duoglott | New Testament. | . . . | With marginal notes to every verse. | . . . | Clwydian Press : | Denbigh, | . . . Thomas Gee : | . . . | 1824. |

Foolscap 8° (12); double columns, with references between;
141×79 mm., 162×99 mm.
5½×3⅛ in.,   6⅜×3¹³⁄₁₆ in.

First separate ed'n of N.T. in Welsh-English, issued in 6 parts at 1s. each·

DESCRIPTION.—Title; blank, *b;* contents (O.T.) *a;* contents (N.T.), *b;* text, sigs. A—2X⁴, pp. 1—547; table of offices, etc., *b.*   Total pp., iv.+548=552.

92.

E

1825. Y | Bibl Cyssegr-Lan, | . . . | Llundain : | . . . George Eyre ac Andrew Strahan, | . . . | Tros y Gymdeithas Biblau Brutanaidd a Thramor, | . . . | 1825. |

12° (24); double columns; leather; 115×62 mm., 133×81 mm.
4⁹⁄₁₆×2⁷⁄₁₆ in. ,5⁵⁄₁₆×3⁴⁄₁₆ in.

N.T. also issued separately.

DESCRIPTION.—Title ; contents, *b ;* text (Gen.—Mal.), sigs. A²—Gg⁷, pp. 3—709 ; blank, *b ;* title of N.T.; contents, *b ;* text (Matt.—Rev.), sigs. [A²]—K¹² and *b,* pp. [3]—[240]. Total pp., 710+240=950.

93.

1825. Testament | Newydd | . . . | Gyda | Sylwadau Eglurhaol ar bob Pennod. | Gan | Y Parchedig John Wesley, M.A. | . . . | Dolgellau, . . . Richard Jones, | 1825. |

4° (4); double columns, with references and commentary below text;
238 × 183 mm., 262 × 214 mm.
9⁶⁄₁₆×7³⁄₁₆ in., 10⁶⁄₁₆×8⁷⁄₁₆ in.

Translation of John Wesley's *Explanatory Notes upon the New Testament* (1st English ed'n, 1754), issued in 20 parts at 1s. each. Re-translated and published in 1850. (See 190a).

DESCRIPTION.—Title ; blank, *b ; Rhagymadrodd,* pp. v.—viii.; text, sigs. A—5N and *b.* Total pp. (not numbered, except first 6), vi.+418=424.

94.

1826. Y | Bibl Cyssegr-Lan, | . . . | Argraffiad Ystrydeb. | Llundain : | . . . George Eyre ac Andrew Strahan, | . . . | Tros y Gymdeithas Biblau Brutanaidd a Thramor, | . . . | 1826. |

Dy. 8° (16); 200×113 mm., 228×146 mm.
7⅞×4⁷⁄₁₆ in., 9×5¾ in.

Reprint of No. 63.

95.

1826. Y | Bibl | Cyssegr-Lan ; | . . . | Argraffiad Ystrydeb Caer Grawnt. | Caer Grawnt : | . . . Ioan Smith, | . . . | Cum Privilegio. | 1826. |

Cr. 8° (24); calf, stamped for the S.P.C.K.; 155×84 mm., 176×107 mm.
6⅛×3⁷⁄₁₆ in., 6¹⁸⁄₁₆×4⁷⁄₁₆ in.

Reprint of No. 48, dated in imprint on last page, *Mai 6, 1807.* Collect in English inside front cover.

96.

1826. Testament Newydd | . . . | Argraffiad Ystrydeb. | Caer Grawnt : | . . . Ioan Smith, | . . . | tros | Gymdeithas Biblau Saesoneg ac Ieithoedd eraill. | 1826. | Cum Privilegio. |

Cr. 8° (24); calf; 150×84 mm., 176×106 mm.
5⅞×3⁷⁄₁₆ in., 6¹⁸⁄₁₆×4⁷⁄₁₆ in.

Reprint of No. 69, with date in imprint of last page, *Mai 7, 1806.*

97.

1826. The | New Testament | in Welsh and English. | Testament Newydd, | . . . | Rhydychain : | . . . Argraffdy Clarendon, | Gan Samuel Collingwood ac eraill, | . . . | Tros y Bibl Gymdeithas Brutanaidd a Thramor, | . . . | 1826. |

Cr. 8° (24); parallel columns; 158×87 mm., 181×109 mm.
6¼×3¾ in., 7½×4⁵⁄₁₆ in.

First Welsh-English ed'n of N.T. for the B. & F.B.S., who *agreed to take 2,000 copies* of those worked off at the Clarendon Press for the S.P.C.K. The latter Society, however, refused to take any copies, because of the orthographical innovations of the editor, John Jones, M.A. (" Ioan Tegid "), who used the text of No. 54 to print from, and *read by that which was corrected by Mr. Charles, of Bala* [No. 63] (*Gwaith Gwallter Mechain;* 1866-68; vol. III., p. 219.)

DESCRIPTION.—Title; blank, *b ;* contents, *a ;* blank, *b ;* text, sigs. A—Gg⁵ and *b ;* table of offices, sig. Gg⁶ and *b.* Total pp. (not numbered), 712.

98.

1826. The Duoglott | New Testament, | with notes. | Testament Newydd | . . . | yn Gymraeg ac yn Saesoneg, | gyda | Sylwadau Eglurhaol. | . . . | Caerfyrddin: | . . . Jonathan Harris; | . . . |. 1826. |

Foolscap 8° (8); parallel columns; 136×77 mm., 147×93 mm,
5⅞×3 in., 5¹⅜×3¹⅜ in. ; 384 pp.

Issued in 9 parts.

DESCRIPTION.—Title; blank, *b ;* contents in Welsh and English, *a ;* blank, *b ;* text, sigs. A³—3B⁴, pp. (5)—(383); table of offices, etc., in Welsh and English, *a.* Total pp., 384.

99.

1826-22. Y | Bibl Sanctaidd: | . . . | gyda | Nodau a Sylwadau | ar bob pennod. | Gan y diweddar Barchedig Peter Williams. | . . . Y Nawfed Argraffiad. | Caernarfon: | Argraffwyd a Chyhoeddwyd gan L. E. Jones, yn Heol-y-Bont. | M,DCCC,XXII. |

4° (8); calf; 235×190 mm., 270×216 mm.
9¼×7½ in., 10⅝×8⁹⁄₁₆ in. ; 1,474 pp.

Reprint of No. 26, but the preliminary matter (including portrait and biography), and the tables and Prys's Ps. at the end, are the surplus sheets of No. 78. The general title-page, although dated like No. 78, is not the same (*Cf.*) Gen.—Mal. is of the same reprint as the N.T., called on title *Argraffiad Newydd,* and dated *M,DCCC,XXVI.* Issued in 46 parts, at 1s. each.

100.

1826-23. Y | Bibl Sanctaidd : | . . . | gydag | Ysgrythyrau Cyfeiriol ar ymyl y dail. | Gan y Parch. John Canne. | Ynghyd a | Sylwadau ar odreu y dail. | . . . | Caerfyrddin : | . . . J. Harris. | M, DCCC, XXVI. |

Foolscap 8° (12); 139×77 mm., 153×91 mm.
5½×3¹⁄₁₆ in., 6×3⁹⁄₁₆ in.

Reprint of the O.T. of No, 32, made up with the surplus sheets of the N.T. of No. 85, issued between 1825 and 1826 in 6 parts at 2s. each.

101.

1827. Y | Bibl | Cyssegr-Lan ; | . . . | Argraffiad Ystrydeb Caer Grawnt : | . . . Ioan Smith, | . . . | tros | Gymdeithas Biblau Saesoneg ac Ieithoedd eraill. | 1827. | Cum Privilegio. |

Cr. 8° (24); 154×84 mm., 179×108 mm.
6₁⁵₆×3₁⁵₆ in., 7₁⁵₆×4¼ in.

Reprint of No. 48.

102.

1827. Y Testament Newydd | Dwyieithawg. | . . . | Gyda nodau cyfeiriol o bob adnod. | . . . | Gomer-Wasg : | Dolgellau, | . . . R. Jones. | 1827. | The Duoglott | New Testament. | . . . | Gomerian Press: | . . . R. Jones. | 1827. |

Foolscap 8° (16); 137×74 mm., 149×95 mm.
5⅞×2¹⁵₆ in., 5½×3¾ in.

Reprint of No. 92, price 5s. in boards, and 6s. in calf.

DESCRIPTION.—Title; blank, *b;* text, sigs. A—XX³ and *b,* pp. 1—470; table of offices, etc., *b,* p. 470.

103.

1823-27. Y | Bibl | Sanctaidd : | . . . | Gyd a | Nodau a Sylwiadau ar bob Pennod, | Gan y | Parch. Peter. Williams. | . . . | Llundain: | . . . Argraff-wasg Caxton, gan Henry Fisher. | . . . | 1823. |

Re-issue of No. 86, omitting the Apocrypha. N. T. title-page dated *1827.*

104.

1827. Testament Newydd. | . . . | Argraffiad Ystrydeb. | Llundain : | George Eyre ac Andrew Strahan, . . . | Tros y Gymdeithas Biblau Brutanaidd a Thramor, | . . . | 1827. |

Dy. 8° (16); 200×111 mm., 224×141 mm.
7⅞×4⅞ in., 8¹³₆×5₁⁹₆ in. ; 320 pp.

Reprint of N.T. of No. 63, price 2s. 3d. and 3s.

105.

1828. Y | Bibl | Cyssegr-Lan ; | . . . | Argraphiad Ystrydeb. | Rhydychain: | . . . Argraffdy Clarendon, | Gan Samuel Collingwood ac ereill, | . . . | Tros y Gymdeithas er Taenu Gwbodaeth Gristionogol; | . . . | 1828. | Cum Privilegio. |

Dy. 8°(16); 190×122 mm., 226×150 mm.
7½×4¹⅜ in., 8¹³₆×5⅞ in. ; 1,184 pp.

Reprint of No. 54. N.T. also issued separately.

106.

1828. Y | Bibl | Cyssegr-Lan; | . . . | Argraffiad Ystrydeb Caer Grawnt. | Caer Grawnt: | . . . Ioan Smith, | . . . | Cum Privilegio. | 1828. |

Cr. 8° (24); 154×84 mm., 178×106 mm.
6₁⁵₆×3₁⁵₆ in., 7×4¹⁵₆ in.

Reprint of No. 48.

107.

1828-30. Y | Bibl | Sanctaidd; | sef yr | Hen Destament, | a'r | Newydd, | gyda | Nodau a Sylwadau ar bob Pennod, | gan y | Diweddar Barch. Peter Williams. | . . . | Caerfyrddin : | . . . J. L. Brigstocke, yn Heol-y-Bont. | M,DCCC,XXVIII. |

4° (4); 229×178 mm., 267×216 mm.
     9×7 in.; 10½×8½ in.

Reprint of No. 26, omitting the Apocrypha. Title of N.T. dated 1830. Issued in parts.

DESCRIPTION.—Frontispiece, *Tal-lun.* | *Duwioldeb, yn cael ei chynnorthwyo gan Ffydd a Gobaith, yn derbyn y Bibl Sanctaidd o ddwylaw Gwirionedd.* | *Piety, supported by Hope & Faith, receiving the Holy Bible from the hand of Truth.* | ; title and preliminaries, sigs. a—d² and b, and 1—2 and b; text (Gen.—Rev.), sigs. A—9U², pp. 5—1,007; tables, sigs. b of 9U²—9X² and b; Prys's Ps., sigs. A—L¹ and b. Total pp., 1,078.

108.

1828. Testament | Newydd, | . . . | Argraffiad Ystrydeb. | Rhyd-ychain: | . . . Argraffdy Clarendon, | Gan Samuel Collingwood ac eraill, | . . . | 1828. |

Cr. 8° (24); 157×84 mm., 193×117 mm.
     6³⁄₁₆×3⁶⁄₁₆ in., 7⁹⁄₁₆× 4⅝ in. ; iv.+356=360 pp.

Known as *Testament Tegid*, John Jones, M.A. (" Ioan Tegid ") having edited it for the S.P.C.K. He substituted his own system of orthography, as in No. 98, for that of No. 54 and its subsequent reprints. An order for 5,000 copies given by the B. & F.B.S. was rescinded in consequence of the alterations made in the orthography of which they had not been apprised.

109.

1829. Y | Bibl | Cyssegr-Lan ; | . . . | Caer Grawnt: | . . . Ioan Smith, | . . . | tros | Gymdeithas Biblau Saesoneg ac Ieithoedd eraill. | 1829. | Cum Privilegio. |

Cr. 8° (24); 154×84 mm., 182×109 mm.
     6¹⁄₁₆×3⁶⁄₁₆ in., 7¹⁄₁₆×4¼ in.

Reprint of No. 48, with rule border around titles of both O. and N.T.

110.

1829. Y | Bibl | Cyssegr-Lan ; | . . . | Argraffiad Ystrydeb. | Caer Grawnt: | . . . Ioan Smith, | . . . | tros Gymdeithas Biblau Saesoneg ac Ieithoedd eraill, | 1829. | Cum Privilegio. |

Cr. 8° (24); 154×84 mm., 179×108 mm.
     6¹⁄₁₆×3¹⁄₁₆ in., 7¹⁄₁₆×4¼ in.

Reprint of No. 48. N.T. also issued separately.

111.

1829. Y | Bibl | Cyssegr-Lan; | . . . | Argraffiad Ystrydeb. | Rhyd-ychain: | . . . Argraffdy Clarendon, | Gan Samuel Collingwood ac ereill, | . . . | Tros y Gymdeithas er Taenu Gwbodaeth Gristionogol ; |·. . . | 1829. | Cum Privilegio. |

Dy. 8° (16); 190×122 mm., 226×148 mm.
     7½×4¹³⁄₁₆ in., 8⅞×5¹³⁄₁₆ in.; 1,184 pp.

Reprint of No. 54.

112.

1829. Testament | Newydd | . . . | Argraffiad Ystrydeb. | Llundain: | . . . George Eyre ac Andrew Strahan, | . . . | Tros y Gymdeithas Biblau Brutanaidd a Thramor, | . . . | 1829. |

Dy. 8° on title [*Small-pica 8vo.*] (16); 200×111 mm., 227×143 mm.
$7\frac{7}{8}\times4\frac{3}{8}$ in., $8\frac{15}{16}\times5\frac{5}{8}$ in.; 320 pp.

Reprint of the N.T. of No. 63.

113.

1829. Testament | Newydd, | . . . | Argraffiad Ystrydeb. | Rhydychain: | . . . Argraffdy Clarendon, | Gan Samuel Collingwood ac eraill, | . . . | Tros y Gymdeithas er Taenu Gwybodaeth Gristionogol, | . . . | 1829. |

Cr. 8° (24); 157×84 mm., 193×115 mm.
$6\frac{3}{16}\times3\frac{5}{16}$ in., $7\frac{5}{8}\times4\frac{9}{16}$ in.; iv.+356=360 pp.

Reprint of No. 109.

114.

1829. [Y | Bibl Sanctaidd: | . . . | gyda | Nodau a Sylwadau | ar bob pennod. | Gan y diweddar Barchedig Peter Williams. | . . . | Caernarfon: | . . . L. E. Jones, . . . | M,DCCC,XXIX. |]

4° (8); 236×179 mm., 261×216 mm.
$9\frac{1}{4}\times7\frac{1}{16}$ in., $10\frac{1}{4}\times8\frac{1}{2}$ in.

No perfect copy seen. Title copied from No. 100. Reprint of No. 26, omitting the Apocrypha. Issued in parts.

115.

1830-29. Y | Bibl | Santaidd: | . . . | yn nghyd a | Sylwadau helaeth ar bob Pennod, | a | Nodau Cyfeiriol | ar ymyl y ddalen. | . . . | Caerfyrddin: | . . . J. Evans, . . . | M, DCCC, XXX. |

4° (8 and 4); 240×156 mm., 268×219 mm.
$9\frac{7}{16}\times6\frac{1}{8}$ in., $10\frac{1}{2}\times8\frac{5}{8}$ in.

Reprint of No. 26, omitting the Apocrypha. Issued in 30 parts at 1s. each.

DESCRIPTION.—Title; blank, *b*; *Llythyr y Cyhoeddwr*, sig. A^2 and *b*; *Gweddi dros holl ystad Eglwys Crist*, sig. A^3; *Tablau o Oesoedd y Byd*, *b*; *Swm yr holl Ysgrythyrau*, sig. A^4 and *b*, pp. [vii]—[viii]; *Erthyglau*, sigs. B—B^3 and *b*; *Rhai Holiadau*, etc., sig. B^4 and *b*; *Myncgai y Bibl*, sigs. C—C^4 and *b*; *Llithiau*, sig. D and *b*; *Y Calendar*, sigs. D^2—D^3; *Tabl i gael y Pasc*, *b*; *Tabl o'r Gwyliau Symudol*, sig. D^4; *Enwau . . . Llyfrau*, *b;* text (Gen.—Mal.), sigs. A—$5K^4$ and *b;* title of N.T., dated *M,DCCC,XXIX.*; *Enwau . . . Llyfrau*, *b;* text (Matt.—Rev.), sigs. A^2—Oo^2 and *b;* tables, sigs. Oo^3—Oo^4 and *b;* title of Watts's Ps. (translated by David Jones), called *Y Pedwarydd Argraffiad*, and dated *1825;* index to first lines, *b;* text, in treble columns, sigs. B—N^2 and *b*. Total pp. (not numbered), 1,194.

116.

1830. Y | Bibl | Cyssegr-Lan, | . . . | Argraffiad Ystrydeb. | Llundain: | . . . George Eyre ac Andrew Strahan, | . . . | Tros y Gymdeithas Biblau Brutanaidd a Thramor, | . . . | 1830. |

Dy. 8°, on title [*Small-pica 8vo.*], (16); 200×111 mm., 230×141 mm.
$7\frac{7}{8}\times4\frac{3}{8}$ in., $9\frac{1}{16}\times5\frac{9}{16}$ in.; 1,278 pp.

Reprint of No. 63, omitting tables.

117.

1830. Testament Newydd | . . . | Argraffiad Ystrydeb. | Rhydychain: | . . . Argraffdy Clarendon, | Gan Samuel Collingwood ac eraill, | Argraffwyr i'r Brifysgol; | tros y BiblGymdeithas Brutanaidd a Thramor, | . . . | 1830. |

Cr. 8° (24) ; 156×83 mm., 181×108 mm.
6⅛×3₁₆⁶ in., 7⅛×4¼ in. ; iv.+354=358 pp.

Price, to societies, 1s. 5d. and 2s. 2d.; to subscribers, 1s. 1d. and 1s. 9d.

118.

1831. Y | Bibl | Cyssegr-Lan ; | . . . | Caer Grawnt: | . . . Ioan Smith, | . . . | tros | Gymdeithas Biblau Saesoneg ac Ieithoedd eraill. | Cum Privilegio. | M.DCCC.XXXI. |

Cr. 8° (24); 154×84 mm., 177×106 mm.
6₁₆¹×3₁₆⁶ in., 6¹⁰₁₆×4⅜ in.

Reprint of No. 48.

119.

1831. The | New Testament, | in Welsh and English. | Testament Newydd, | . . . | Rhydychain: | . . . Argraffdy y Brifysgol, | Gan Samuel Collingwood ac eraill, | . . . | Tros y Gymdeithas er Taenu Gwybodaeth Gristionogol. | . . . | 1831. |

Cr. 8° (24); 159×85 mm., 195×116 mm.
6¼×3₁₆⁶ in., 7⅞×4₁₆⁹ in.

Reprint of No. 98.

Sigs., A—Gg⁵. Total pp. (not numbered), 730.

120.

1831. Y | Bibl | Sanctaidd: | . . . | gyd a | Nodau a Sylwadau ar bob pennod, | gan y | Parch. Peter Williams. | . . . | Llundain : | . . . H. Fisher, Son, & Co. . . . |

Reprint of No. 86. Title of N.T. dated *1831*. A wrapper of one of the parts is dated *1830*.

121.

1831. Testament | Newydd | . . . | Llundain: | . . . George Eyre ac Andrew Strahan, | . . . | Tros y Gymdeithas Biblau Brutanaidd a Thramor, | . . . | 1831. |

12° (24); 115×62 mm., 131×81 mm.
4₁₆⁹×2₁₆⁷ in., 5⅛×3⅛ in.; 240 pp.

Reprint of the N.T. of No. 93.

122.

1832. Y | Bibl | Cyssegr-Lan; | . . . | Caer Grawnt: | . . . Ioan Smith, | . . . | tros | Gymdeithas Biblau Saesoneg ac Ieithoedd eraill. | Cum Privilegio. | M.DCCC.XXXII. |

Cr. 8° (24); 154×84 mm., 179×108 mm.
6₁₆¹×3₁₆⁶ in., 7₁₆¹×4¼ in.

Reprint of No. 48, with rule border around titles of both O. and N.T.

123.

1832. Y | Bibl | Cyssegr-Lan, | . . . | Llundain: | . . . George Eyre ac Andrew Spottiswoode, | . . . | Tros · y Bibl Gymdeithas Frytanaidd a Thramor, | . . . | 1832. |

12° (24); 115×62 mm., 131×81 mm.
$4\frac{9}{16}×2\frac{7}{16}$ in., $5\frac{1}{16}×3\frac{3}{16}$ in.

Reprint of No. 93.

124.

1833. Y | Bibl | Cyssegr-Lan; | . . . | Caer Grawnt: | . . . Ioan Smith, | . . . | M.DCCC.XXXIII. |

Cr. 8° (24); 154×84 mm., 177×107 mm.
$6\frac{1}{16}×3\frac{5}{16}$ in., $7×4\frac{3}{16}$ in.

Reprint, for the S.P.C.K., of No. 48. Collect inside front cover.

124a.

1833. Y Bibl Cyssegr-Lan; | . . . | Rhydychain: | . . . | 1833. |

Dy. 8vo.

Recorded in the Salesbury Library shelf-list. No copy found.

125.

1833. Y | Bibl Teuluaidd, | . . . | gyd ag | Adfyfyriadau helaeth ar bob pennod, | gan | Y Parch. John Brown, | o Haddington, | a holl nodau cyfeiriol yr un gwr ar ymyl y ddalen: | hefyd, | Pigion o'r pethau mwyaf nodedig a rhagorol yn Esponiad | y | Parch. Matthew Henry, | gyd a hynny, | Nodiadau Achlysurol ar Fannau Neillduol, | allan | o waith amryw o'r awdwyr mwyaf enwog a dysgedig ; y'nghyd a'r teithwyr goreu eu gair, | yn gystal hen a diweddarach. | . . . | Bala: | . . . R. Saunderson. | 1833. |

4° (8); 223×186 mm., 288×235 mm.
$7\frac{3}{16}×7\frac{5}{1}$ in., $11\frac{5}{16}×9\frac{1}{4}$ in.

Family Bible, edited by John Humphreys, of Caerwys. Issued in shilling parts, comprising three books, viz.:—I., Gen.—Ps.; II., Prov.—Mal.; III., Matt.—Rev.

126.

1833. Testament Newydd. | . . . | Caer Grawnt. | . . . Ioan Smith, | Argraffydd i'r Brifathrofa. | Cum Privilegio. | M.DCCC.XXXIII. |

Cr. 8° (24); 154×84 mm., 174×106 mm.
$6\frac{1}{16}×3\frac{5}{16}$ in., $6\frac{13}{16}×4\frac{3}{16}$ in. ; 332 pp.

Reprint of N.T. of No. 48.

DESCRIPTION.—Title; blank, b; Enwau . . . Llfrau [sic], etc., sig. A²; blank, b; text, sigs. A³—O¹⁰ and b, pp. 5—332.

127.

1833. Testament | Newydd | . . . | Llundain: | . . . George Eyre ac Andrew Spottiswoode, | . . . | Tros y Bibl Gymdeithas Frytanaidd a Thramor, | . . . | 1833. |

12°, on title *Pearl 24mo.* (24); 115×62 mm., 131×81 mm.
$4\frac{9}{16}×2\frac{7}{16}$ in., $5\frac{1}{16}×3\frac{3}{16}$ in.

Reprint of N.T. of No. 93.

128.

1834. Y | Bibl Cyssegr-Lan; | . . . | Rhydychen : | Argraphdy y Brifysgol, | Gan Samuel Collingwood ac ereill, | . . . | Tros y Gymdeithas er Taenu Gwybodaeth Gristionogol. | . . . | M.DCCC.XXXIV. | Cum Privilegio. |

Dy. 8° (16); double columns, with marginal notes and references; calf;

205 × 103 mm., 231 × 154 mm.
8₁⁄₁₆ × 4 in., 9⅛ × 6₁⁄₁₆ in.

N.T. also issued separately.

DESCRIPTION.—Blank, *a · Colect, b;* title, *a;* blank, *b; Enwau . . . Llyfrau,* etc., *a;* blank, *b;* Bishops preface (in English and Welsh), *a;* blank, *b;* text (Gen.—Mal.), sigs. A—3K⁶ and *b;* text (Apoc.), sigs. 3K⁷—4A²; blank, *b;* title of N.T.; blank, *b;* text (Matt.—Rev.), sigs. 4A⁴—4T⁷ and *b;* 3 maps (folded). Total pp. (not numbered), 1,414.

129.

1834. Y | Bibl | Cyssegr-Lan ; | . . . | Caer Grawnt: | . . . Ioan Smith, | . . . | Cum Privilegio. | M.DCCC.XXXIV. |

Cr. 8° (24); 150×85 mm., 178×105 mm.

5⅞ × 5₁⁄₁₆ in., 7 × 4⅛ in.

Reprint of No. 48 for the S.P.C.K.

130.

1835-32. Y | Bibl Sanctaidd: | . . . | gyda | Nodau a Sylwadau ar bob pennod. | Argraffiad Newydd. | . . . | Caerfyrddin: | . . . Edward Morris, Heol-Awst. | 1835. |

4° (4); 241×181 mm., 256×207 mm.

9₁⁄₁₆ × 7¼ in., 10₁⁄₁₆ × 8¼ in.

Reprint of No. 26, omitting the Apocrypha. Title of N.T. dated *1832.* Issued in 30 parts at 1s. each. This reprint was commenced by Jonathan Harris, of Dark Gate, Carmarthen, and finished by the printer whose name appears in the imprint of the general title. (See p. 3 of wrapper of *Seren Gomer,* Feb., 1836.)

131.

1835. Y | Bibl | Sanctaidd : | . . . | Gyd a | Nodau a Sylwiadau ar bob Pennod, | Gan y | Parch. Peter Williams. | . . . | Llundain : | . . . | H. Fisher, Son, a P. Jackson, 38, Newgate-Street. | . . . | 1835. |

Reprint of No. 86, omitting the Apocrypha.

131a.

1835. Y | Bibl Cyssegr-Lan; | . . . | Argraffiad Ystrydeb. | Llundain : | . . . George Eyre ac Andrew Spottiswoode, | . . . | Tros y Bibl Gymdeithas Frytanaidd a Thramor, | . . . | 1835. |

Dy. 8°, on title [*Smallpica 8vo.*] (16); 200×111 mm., 230×144 mm.

7⅞ × 4⅜ in., 9₁⁄₁₆ × 5⅝ in.;

Reprint of No. 63, omitting tables.

132.

1835. Y | Bibl Cyssegr-Lan; . . . | | Argraffiad Ystrydeb. | Caer Grawnt: | . . . Ioan Smith, | . . . | tros | Gymdeithas Biblau Saesoneg ac Ieithoedd Eraill. | Cum Privilegio. | M.DCCC.XXXV. |

Cr. 8 (24); 154×84 mm., 179×108 mm.

6₁⁄₁₆ × 3₁⁄₁₆ in., 7₁⁄₁₆ × 4¼ in.

Reprint of No. 48.

133.

F

1835. Testament | Newydd | . . . | Caer Grawnt: | . . . Ioan Smith, | . . . | tros | Gymdeithas Biblau Saesoneg ac Ieithoedd Eraill. | Cum Privilegio. | M.DCCC.XXXV. |

Cr. 8° (24); cloth; 151×83 mm., 179×108 mm.
$5\frac{15}{16}\times3\frac{1}{4}$ in., $7\frac{1}{16}\times4\frac{1}{4}$ in.

Reprint of No. 69, omitting table of offices, etc., at end. The words, *For use in* | *Sunday Schools* | *exclusively.* | appear on front of cover.

DESCRIPTION.—Title; blank *b; Enwau . . . Llyfrau,* etc., sig. A^2; blank, *b;* text, sigs. A^3—O^{10} and *b*, pp. 5—332.

134.

1835. Testament | Newydd | . . . | Llundain: | . . . George Eyre ac Andrew Spottiswoode, | . . . | Tros y Bibl Gymdeithas Frytanaidd a Thramor, | . . . | 1835. |

12°, on title *Pearl 24mo.* (24); 115×62 mm., 131×81 mm.
$4\frac{9}{16}\times2\frac{7}{16}$ in., $5\frac{3}{16}\times3\frac{3}{16}$ in.; 240 pp.

Reprint of the N.T. of No. 93.

135.

1835. Y | Testament | Cyfeirnodawl: | Sef y | Cyfieithiad Arferedig | o'r | Testament Newydd, | y'nghyd a chyfeiriadau, | ac | Agoriad a Holiadau | Daearyddol, Hanesyddol, Athrawiaethol, | Ymarferol, a Phrofiadol; | . . . | At yr hyn y chwanegir | Amrywiol Dablau Buddiol. | Wyddgrug: | Argraffwyd gan y cyhoeddwr, J. Lloyd. | 1835. |

32° (16); morocco, gilt edges; no chapter-contents; 80×44 mm., 86×54 mm.
$3\frac{1}{8}\times1\frac{3}{4}$ in., $3\frac{3}{8}\times2\frac{1}{8}$ in.

Issued in parts, and sold for 3s. (unbound) and 4s. (bound). Seventh thousand issued in 1840.

DESCRIPTION.—Title; blank, *b; Nodiadau Rhagarweiniol*, sigs. A^2—A^3 (not given) and *b; Agoriad i'r Testament*, sig. A^4 (not given) and *b;* text, sigs. B—$2C^5$; *Llyfrau y Testament*, etc., *b; Tablen | O'r pethau hynotaf*, etc., sig. $2C^6$; *Cyssondeb Cryno o'r Efengylau, a*—$2C^7$; *Cyfres o enwau*, etc., *b*—$2D^3$; *Mynegai daëaryddol*, etc., sigs. $2D^3$—$2D^6$ and *b; Tablen o gyfeiriadau*, sig. $2D^7$ and *b; Cyfarwyddiadau i'r Dospeirth | Biblaidd*, sig. $2D^8$; imprint, *b*. Total pp. (not numbered), 440.

136.

1836. Y | Bibl | Cyssegr-Lan; | . . . | Caer Grawnt: | . . . Ioan Smith, | . . . | tros | Gymdeithas Biblau Saesoneg ac Ieithoedd Eraill. | Cum Privilegio. | M.DCCC.XXXVI. |

Cr. 8° (24); 154×83 mm., 179×108 mm.
$6\frac{1}{16}\times3\frac{1}{4}$ in., $7\frac{1}{16}\times4\frac{1}{4}$ in.

Reprint of No. 48.

137.

1836. Y | Bibl | Cyssegr-Lan; | . . . | Caer Grawnt: | . . . Ioan Smith, | . . . | Cum Privilegio. | M.DCCC.XXXVI. |

Cr. 8° (24); 154×83 mm., 175×108 mm.
$6\frac{1}{16}\times3\frac{1}{4}$ in., $6\frac{7}{8}\times4\frac{1}{4}$ in.

Reprint of No. 48 for the S.P.C.K.

138.

1836. Y | Bibl | Cyssegr-Lan; | . . . | Rhydychen: | . . . Argraphdy y Brifysgol, | Gan Samuel Collingwood ac Ereill, | . . . | Tros y Gymdeithas er Taenu Gwybodaeth Gristionogol. | . . . | M.DCCC.XXXVI. | Cum Privilegio. |

Dy. 8° (16); 190×122 mm., 227×148 mm.
$7\frac{1}{2}\times4\frac{13}{16}$ in., $8\frac{15}{16}\times5\frac{13}{16}$ in.; 1,180 pp.

Reprint of No. 54.

139.

1836. Y | Bibl | Sanctaidd: | . . . | Gyd a | Nodau a Sylwiadau ar bob Pennod, | Gan y | Parch. Peter Williams. | . . . | Llundain: | . . . H. Fisher, Son, a P. Jackson, . . . | 1836. |

Reprint of No. 86, omitting the Apocrypha.

140.

1836. Testament | Newydd. | . . . | Caer Grawnt. | . . . Ioan Smith, | . . . | tros | Gymdeithas Biblau Saesoneg ac Ieithoedd Eraill. | Cum Privilegio. | M.DCCC.XXXVI. |

Cr. 8° (24); 151×83 mm., 178×107 mm.
$5\frac{6}{16}\times3\frac{1}{4}$ in., $7\times4\frac{3}{16}$ in.; 332 pp.

Reprint of No. 69, omitting table of offices, etc., at end, and including *Enwau . . . Llyfrau*, etc., as in No. 134.

141.

1837. Y | Bibl Cyssegr-Lan; | . . . | Argraffiad Ystrydeb. | Llundain: | . . . George Eyre ac Andrew Spottiswoode, | . . . | Tros y Bibl Gymdeithas Frytanaidd a Thramor, | . . . | 1837. |

Dy. 8°, on title *Small Pica 8vo.* (16); 203×114 mm., 228×146 in.
$8\times4\frac{1}{2}$ in., $9\times5\frac{3}{4}$ mm.

Reprint of No. 63, omitting tables.

142.

1837. Y | Bibl Cyssegr-Lan; | . . . | Llundain: | . . . George Eyre ac Andrew Spottiswoode, | . . . | Tros y Bibl Gymdeithas Frytanaidd a Thramor, | . . . | 1837. |

12° (24); 115×62 mm., 131×81 mm.
$4\frac{9}{16}\times2\frac{7}{16}$ in., $5\frac{3}{16}\times3\frac{3}{16}$ in.

Reprint of No. 93. N.T. also issued separately.

143.

1837-40-36. Y | Bibl | Sanctaidd: | . . . | gyda | Nodau a Sylwadau | ar bob pennod. | Gan y diweddar Barchedig Peter Williams. | . . . | Y Degfed Argraffiad. | Caernarfon: | . . . Lewis Evan Jones; Heol-y-Bont. | M,DCCC,XXXVII. |

4° (4); 236×157 mm., 269×214 mm.
$9\frac{5}{16}\times6\frac{1}{8}$ in., $10\frac{5}{8}\times8\frac{3}{8}$ in.; 1,268 pp.

Reprint of No. 26, omitting the Apocrypha. Title of N.T. dated *M,DCCC,XL*, and title of Prys's Ps. *1836*. Issued in parts at 1s. each. Described on title of N.T. as *Argraffiad Newydd.*

144.

1838. [Y Bibl, etc.]

[*London.*]

8vo.

Recorded by Mr. J. Glyn Davies, librarian, University College, Aberystwyth. Fuller details unobtainable.

145.

1838. Y | Bibl | Sanctaidd: | . . . | Gyd a | Nodau a Sylwiadau ar bob pennod, | gan y | Parch. Peter Williams. | . . . | Llundain: | . . . | H. Fisher, R. Fisher, a P. Jackson. |

Reprint of No. 86, omitting the Apocrypha. Title of N.T. only dated.

146.

1838. Testament | Newydd | . . . Caer Grawnt: | . . . | Ioan W. Parker, | . . . | Cum Privilegio. | M.DCCC.XXXVIII. |

Small 4° (24); 157×88 mm., 216×172 mm.
$6\frac{3}{16}\times3\frac{7}{16}$ in., $8\frac{1}{2}\times6\frac{3}{4}$ in.; 354 pp.

An edition for the S.P.C.K., with wide margins.

147.

1839. Y | Bibl Cyssegr-Lan; | . . . | Rhydychen: | . . . Argraphdy y Brifysgol, | Samuel Collingwood ac Ereill, | . . . | Tros y Gymdeithas er Taenu Gwybodaeth Gristionogol. | . . . | M.DCCC.XXXIX. | Cum Privilegio. |

Dy. 8° (16); 190×122 mm., 230×148 mm.
$7\frac{1}{2}\times4\frac{13}{16}$ in., $9\frac{1}{16}\times5\frac{13}{16}$ in.; 1,032 pp.

Reprint of No. 54, omitting the Apocrypha.

148.

1839. Y | Bibl Cyssegr-Lan, | . . . | Argraffiad Ystrydeb. | Llundain: | . . . George Eyre ac Andrew Spottiswoode, | . . . | Tros y Bibl Gymdeithas Frytanaidd a Thramor, | . . . | 1839. |

Dy. 8°, on title *Smallpica 8vo.* (16); 198×111 mm., 230×145 mm.
$7\frac{13}{16}\times4\frac{3}{8}$ in., $9\frac{1}{16}\times5\frac{11}{16}$ in.

Reprint of No. 63, omitting tables. N.T. also issued separately.

149.

1839. Y | Bibl Dwyieithog, | . . . | Gan | Y Parch. Joseph Harris. | . . . | Abertawy: | Argraffwyd a chyhoeddwyd gan B. Hull, Heol Oroyd. | 1839. | The | Duoglott | Bible, | . . . | By | The Rev. Joseph Harris. | . . . | Swansea: | Printed and published by B. Hull, Orange Street. | 1839. |

4° (4); 237×172 mm., 272×213 mm.
$9\frac{5}{16}\times6\frac{3}{4}$ in., $10\frac{11}{16}\times8\frac{3}{8}$ in.; 1,416 pp.

Reprint of No. 87.

150.

1840. Y | Bibl Cyssegr-Lan | . . . | Argraffiad Ystrydeb. | Llundain: | . . . George Eyre ac Andrew Spottiswoode, | . . . | Tros y Bibl Gymdeithas Frytanaidd a Thramor, | . . . | 1840. |

Dy. 8°, on title *Smallpica 8vo.* (16); 198×111 mm., 229×144 mm.
$7\frac{13}{16}\times4\frac{3}{8}$ in., $9\times5\frac{11}{16}$ in.

Reprint of No. 63, omitting tables. N.T. also issued separately.

152.

1840. Y | Bibl | Santaidd: | . . . | ynghyd a | Sylwadau helaeth ar bob Pennod, | a | Nodau Cyfeiriol ar ymyl y ddalen. | . . . | Abertawy: | Argraffedig a Chyhoeddedig gan E. Griffiths, Heol Fawr. | M, DCCC, XL. |

4° (4); 236×191 mm., 270×211 mm.
$9\frac{5}{16}\times7\frac{1}{2}$ in., $10\frac{5}{8}\times8\frac{5}{16}$ in.; 1,350 pp. (not numbered).

Reprint of No. 26, omitting the Apocrypha.

153.

1840. The | New Testament, | in Welsh and English. | Testament Newydd, | . . . | Rhydychen : | . . . Argraphdy y Brifysgol, | Gan Samuel Collingwood ac Ereill, | . . . | Tros y Gymdeithas er Taenu Gwybodaeth Gristionogol. | . . . | 1840. |

Cr. 8° (24); 158×83 mm., 179×108 mm.
$6\frac{1}{4}\times3\frac{1}{4}$ in., $7\frac{1}{16}\times4\frac{1}{4}$ in.

Reprint for the S.P.C.K. of No. 98, omitting table of offices, etc.

Description.—Title; blank, *b*; contents, *a*; blank, *b*; text, sigs. A—Gg[6] and *b*, pp. 1—706. Total pp., 710.

154.

1840. Testament | Newydd | . . . | Caer Grawnt: | . . . Ioan W. Parker, | . . . | tros | Gymdeithas Biblau Saesoneg ac Ieithoedd Eraill. | Cum Privilegio. | M.DCCC.XL. |

Cr. 8° (24); calf, with clasp; 155×87 mm., 179×112 mm.
$6\frac{1}{8}\times3\frac{7}{16}$ in., $7\frac{1}{16}\times4\frac{3}{8}$ in.

Reprint for the Naval and Military Bible Society, of No. 69, omitting table of offices, etc., and including *Enwau . . . Llyfrau*, etc., as in Nos. 134 and 141.

Description.—Title; blank, *b*; *Enwau . . . Llyfrau*, etc., sig. A[2]; blank, *b*; text, sigs. A—P[6] and *b*, pp. 1—348. Total pp., iv.+348=352.

155.

1840. Testament | Newydd | . . . | Llundain : | . . . George Eyre ac Andrew Spottiswoode, | . . . | Tros y Bibl Gymdeithas Frytanaidd a Thramor, | . . . | 1840. |

12°, on title [*Pearl 24mo.*] (24); 116×60 mm., 129×77 mm.
$4\frac{9}{16}\times2\frac{3}{8}$ in., $5\frac{1}{16}\times3\frac{1}{16}$ in.; 240 pp.

Reprint of the N.T. of No. 93.

156.

1840. Testament | Newydd, | . . . | Rhydychen : | . . . Argraphdy y Brifysgol, | Gan Samuel Collingwood ac ereill, | . . . | Tros y Gymdeithas er Taenu Gwybodaeth Gristionogol, | . . . | M.DCCC.XL. | Cum Privilegio. |

Cr. 8° (24); 157×84 mm., 177×108 mm.
$6\frac{3}{16}\times3\frac{5}{16}$ in., $6\frac{15}{16}\times4\frac{1}{4}$ in.

Reprint of No. 37.

156a.

1840. The | Christian's. New Evangelical and Self-Interpreting | Family Bible, | . . . | with a suitable | Introduction to each book, | and | Practical Observations at the end of every chapter: | also are annexed, all the | Marginal Readings and References placed parallel with the Text; in which every | obscure and important passage is fully explained, | and the Text quoted, and evfry [sic] period of time placed at the head of its respective column. | The whole carefully Collated, and Selected from the Most Esteemed Authors. | Swansea : | Printed and Published by Bishop Hull, Orange Street. | 1840. |

4° (4); calf; double columns; 243×181 mm., 274×216 mm, 9$\frac{2}{8}$×7$\frac{1}{2}$ in., 10$\frac{12}{16}$×8$\frac{1}{2}$ in.

DESCRIPTION.—Frontispiece, *The Holy Family;* title ; *The Names . . . of the Books,* etc., *b ; Introduction,* sigs. *a—c²* and *b ;* text (Gen.—Mal.), sigs. B—6Y² ; blank, *b ;* text (Apocrypha), sigs. B—3B², pp. 1—187; blank, *b ;* title of N.T., dated *1840; The Names . . . of the Books,* etc., *b ;* text (Matt.—Rev.), sigs. 6Z—8T² ; *A Table of Offices, b.* Total pp. (not numbered, except Apocrypha), 920.

157.

1841. Y | Bibl Cyssegr-Lan, | . . . | Llundain: | . . . George E. Eyre ac Andrew Spottiswoode, | . . . | Tros y Bibl Gymdeithas Frytanaidd a Thramor, | . . . | 1841. |

4° (8); double columns, with marginal notes and references; leather, gilt edges stamped on front side, *Y Fibl Gymdeithas | Frytanaidd a Thramor | Blwyddyn y Jubili | 1853.* | ; 245×189 mm., 284×229 mm. 9$\frac{5}{8}$×7$\frac{7}{16}$ in., 11$\frac{3}{16}$×9 in.

First 4° Welsh Bible by the B. & F.B.S. This or a reprint of it is the Bible generally used on pulpits.

DESCRIPTION.—Title; blank, *b; Enwau . . . Llyfrau,* etc., sig. A² ; blank, *b;* text (Gen.—Mal.), sigs. A³—5Q⁴, pp. [5]—[863]; blank, *b;* title of N.T.; blank, *b;* text (Matt.—Rev.), sigs. 5R²—7G² and *b,* pp. [867]—[1156].

158.

1841. Y | Bibl Cyssegr-Lan, | . . . | Llundain: | . . . George E. Eyre ac Andrew Spottiswoode, | . . . | Tros y Bibl Gymdeithas Frytanaidd a Thramor, | . . . | 1841. |

Cr. 8°, on title [*Nonpareil Reference 12mo.*] (24); leather, gilt edges; double columns, with marginal notes and references; 158×93 mm., 172×111 mm. 6$\frac{1}{4}$×3$\frac{11}{16}$ in., 6$\frac{3}{4}$×4$\frac{3}{8}$ in.

DESCRIPTION.—Title; blank, *b; Enwau . . . Llyfrau,* etc., sig. A² ; blank, *b;* text (Gen.—Mal.), sigs. A³—2G⁸, pp. [5]—[711]; blank, *b;* title of N.T.; blank, *b;* text (Matt.—Rev.), sigs. 2G¹⁰—2R⁸ and *b,* pp. [715]—[952].

159.

1841. Y | Bibl | Cyssegr-Lan; | . . . | Caer Grawnt: | . . . Ioan W. Parker, | . . . Cum Privilegio. | M.DCCC.XLI. |

Cr. 8° (24); leather, gilt edges; 151×86 mm., 175×109 mm. 5$\frac{15}{16}$×3$\frac{3}{8}$ in., 6$\frac{7}{8}$×4$\frac{5}{16}$ in.; 784 pp.

Reprint for the S.P.C.K. of No. 48. N.T. also issued separately.

160.

1841. Y | Bibl | Sanctaidd : | . . . | Gyd a | Nodau a Sylwiadau ar bob pennod, | Gan y | Parch. Peter Williams. | . . . | Llundain: H. Fisher, R. Fisher, a P. Jackson. |

Reprint of No. 86, omitting the Apocrypha. Title of N.T. dated *1841,* and frontispiece dated *1840.*

160a.

1842. Y | Bibl Cyssegr-Lan, ... | Llundain : | ... George E. Eyre
ac Andrew Spottiswoode, | . . . | Tros y Bibl Gymdeithas
Frytanaidd a Thramor, | . . . | 1842. |

12°, on title [*Pearl 24mo.*] (24); 116×60 mm., 127×80 mm.
$4\frac{9}{16}×2\frac{3}{8}$ in., $5×3\frac{1}{8}$ in; 948 pp.

Reprint of No. 93.

161.

1842. Y | Bibl | Cyssegr-Lan ; | . . . | Caer Grawnt : | . . . Ioan
W. Parker, | . . . | Cum Privilegio. | M.DCCC.XLII. |

Cr. 8° (24); 151×83 mm., 170×102 mm.
$5\frac{15}{16}×3\frac{1}{4}$ in., $6\frac{11}{16}×4$ in.; 784 pp.

Reprint for the S.P.C.K. of No. 48. Collect inside front cover. N.T. also issued
separately.

162.

1842. Testament | Newydd | . . . Llundain: | . . . George E. Eyre
ac Andrew Spottiswoode, | . . . Tros y Bibl Gymdeithas
Frytanaidd a Thramor, | . . . 1842. |

Dy. 8°, on title [*Small Pica 8vo.*] (16); 198×111 mm., 223×140 mm.
$7\frac{13}{16}×4\frac{3}{8}$ in., $8\frac{3}{4}×5\frac{1}{2}$ in. ; 320 pp.

Reprint of N.T. of No. 63.

163.

1842. Yr Oraclau Bywiol, | neu | Ysgrifeniadau Cysegrlan | Apos-
tolion ac Efengylwyr | Ie. u Grist, | a elwir yn gyffredin | Y
Testament Newydd. | Wedi ci gyfieithu drwy gynnorthwy | y
beirniaid mwyaf dysgedig, | gan | John Williams, | gyda | Rhag-
lithiau ac | Attodiad, | gan | Alexander Campbell. | Llundain ; |
Simpkin, Marshall, and Co. | Llynlleifiad; D. Marples. | Gwrecsam;
Wm. Bayley. | 1842. |

Cr. 8° (16); lines across the page; 144×80 mm., 174×108 mm.
$5\frac{11}{16}×3\frac{1}{8}$ in., $6\frac{7}{8}×4\frac{1}{4}$ in.

A new translation from the Greek by the Rev. John Williams ("Philologus"), a
Baptist minister, of Rhosllanerchrugog, in which the words, *bedyddio* (=to baptize) and
bedyddiwr (=baptist), are rendered *trochi* (=to immerse) and *trochiedydd* (=immerser).
Imprint on colophon and on last page, *Llynlleifiad:* | *Argraffwyd gan D. Marples.*
Reprinted 1881 and 1887 (H. Humphreys, Carnarvon).

DESCRIPTION.—Half title; blank, *b;* title ; colophon, *b ; Nodiadau Rhaglithiol.,*
signed *J. Williams.*, sigs. *b—b⁵* and *b*, pp. iii.—xii.; *Rhaglith*, etc., signed
A. Campbell., sigs. *b⁸—e⁴* and *b*, pp. xiii.—lviii.; text, sigs. A—2F and *b*,
pp. 1—466; *Attodiad.*, signed *J. Williams.*, sigs. 2F²—2H⁸ and *b*, pp. 467—512.
Total pp., 572.

164.

1843. Y | Bibl | Sanctaidd : | . . . | gyd a | Nodau a Sylwiadau ar
bob pennod, | Gan y | Parch. Peter Williams. | . . . | Llundain: |
H. Fisher, R. Fisher, a P. Jackson. |

Reprint of No. 86, omitting the Apocrypha. Title of N.T. only dated.

165.

1843-2. Y | Bibl | Cyssegr-Lan; | . . . | Caer Grawnt : | . . . Ioan W. Parker, | . . . | Cum Privilegio. | M.DCCC.XLIII. |

Cr. 8° (24); 151×83 mm., 171×102 mm.
5⅛×3¼ in., 6⅞×4 in.; 784 pp.

Reprint for the S.P.C.K. of No. 48. N.T. title dated *1842*.

166.

1844. Y | Bibl Cyssegr-Lan, | . . . | Llundain: | . . . George E. Eyre ac Andrew Spottiswoode, | . . . Tros y Bibl Gymdeithas Frytanaidd a Thramor, | . . . | 1844. |

12°, on title [*Pearl 24mo.*] (24); 116×62 mm., 129×76 mm.
4⁹⁄₁₆×2⁷⁄₁₆ in., 5¹⁄₁₆×3 in.; 948 pp.

Reprint of No. 93. N.T. also issued separately.

167.

1844. Y | Bibl | Cyssegr-Lan ; | . . . | Caer Grawnt : | . . . Ioan W. Parker, | . . . | tros | Gymdeithas Biblau Saesoneg ac Ieithoedd Eraill. | Cum Privilegio. | M.DCCC.XLIV. |

Cr. 8°, on title [*Nonpareil 12mo.*] (24); 151×83 mm., 168×102 mm.
5¹⁵⁄₁₆×3¼in., 6⅝×4 in.; 784 pp.

Reprint of No. 48.

168.

1844. Testament | Newydd | . . . | Caer Grawnt : | . . . Ioan W. Parker, | . . . | M.DCCC.XLIV. |

Cr. 8° (24) ; 151×83 mm., 174×103 mm.
5¹⁵⁄₁₆×3¼in., 6⅞×4¹⁄₁₆ in. ; 232 pp.

Reprint for the S.P.C.K. of the N.T. of No. 48.

168a.

1845. Y | Bibl Cyssegr-Lan, | . . . | Llundain: | . . . George E. Eyre ac Andrew Spottiswoode, | . . . Tros y Bibl Gymdeithas Frytanaidd a Thramor, | . . . | 1845. |

12 (24); 116×62 mm., 126×76 mm.
4⁹⁄₁₆×2⁷⁄₁₆ in., 4¹⁸×3 in.; 948 pp.

Reprint of No. 93. Some copies bear a printed slip pasted inside front cover, worded, *Naval & Military Bible Society,* | *instituted in 1780.* | *Welsh Bible.* | *Reduced Price to Sailors . . . 8d.* | *Depository, 32, Sackville St., London.* | N.T. also issued separately.

169.

1845. Y | Bibl | Cyssegr-Lan ; | . . . | Caer Grawnt : | . . . Ioan W. Parker, | . . . | tros | Gymdeithas Biblau Saesoneg ac Ieithoedd Eraill. | Cum Privilegio. | M.DCCC.XLV. |

Cr. 8° (24); 151×83 mm., 175×108 mm.
5¹⁸×3¼ in., 6⅞× 4¹⁄₁₆ in. ; 784 pp.

Reprint of No. 48. N.T. also issued separately.

170.

1845. Testament | Newydd | . . . Llundain : | . . . George E. Eyre ac Andrew Spottiswoode, | . . . Tros y Bibl Gymdeithas Frytanaidd a Thramor, | . . . 1845. |

Dy. 8°, on title [*Smallpica 8vo.*] (16); 198×113 mm., 220×135 mm. 7¹³⁄₁₆×4¹⁄₁₆ in., 8⅝×5⁵⁄₁₆ in.; 320 pp.

Reprint of the N.T. of No. 63.

171.

1845. Y | Testament Newydd, | yn ol | Y Cyfieithiad Awdurdodedig, | ynghyd a | Nodiadau Eglurhaol. | Gwrecsam : | Argraffedig a chyhoeddedig gan W. Bayley. | 1845. |

32° (16); double columns; no chapter-contents or references; a few very brief notes at foot of pages; leather; 82×49 mm., 92×60 mm. 3¼×1¹⁵⁄₁₆ in., 3⅝×2⅜ in.

DESCRIPTON.—Title; contents, *b;* text, sigs. A²—2E⁶; blank, *b.* Total pp. (not numbered), 442.

171a.

1846. Y | Bibl Cyssegr-Lan, | . . . | Llundain: | . . . George E. Eyre ac Andrew Spottiswoode, | . . . | Tros y Bibl Gymdeithas Frytanaidd a Thramor, | . . . | 1846. |

Dy. 8°, on title [*Smallpica 8vo.*]; 198×112 mm., 221×138 mm. 7¹³⁄₁₆×4⅜ in., 8¹¹⁄₁₆×5⁷⁄₁₆ in.; 1,278 pp.

Reprint of No. 63.

172.

1846. Y | Bibl | Cyssegr-Lan; | . . . | Caer Grawnt: | . . . Ioan W. Parker, | ˙ . . . | tros | Gymdeithas Biblau Saesoneg ac Ieithoedd eraill. | Cum Privilegio. | M.DCCC.XLVI. |

Cr. 8°, on title [*Nonpareil 12mo.*] (24); 151×83 mm., 172×105 mm. 5¹⁵⁄₁₆×3¼ in., 6¾×4⅛ in.; 784 pp.

Reprint of No. 48. N.T. also issued separately.

173.

1846. Y | Bibl Cyssegr-Lan; | . . . | Rhydychen: | . . . Argraphdy y Brifysgol, | Tros y Gymdeithas er Taenu Gwybodaeth Gristion-ogol. | . . . | M.DCCC.XLVI. | Cum Privilegio. |

Dy. 8° (16); 193×122 mm., 220×142 mm. 7⁹⁄₁₆×4¹³⁄₁₆ in., 8⅝×5⁹⁄₁₆ in.; 984 pp.

Reprint of No. 54, omitting *Hyfforddiadau*, Pr. Bk., Prys's Ps., etc., but including the Apocrypha. Collect inside front cover. N.T. also issued separately.

174.

1846. Y | Bibl | Sanctaidd: | . . . | gyd a | Nodau a Sylwiadau ar bob pennod, | Gan y | Parch. Peter Williams. | . . . | Llundain: | H. Fisher, R. Fisher, a P. Jackson. |

Reprint of No. 86, omitting the Apocrypha. Title of N.T. only dated.

175.

G

1846. Y | Bibl Cyssegr-lan, | . . . | Llundain: | . . . George E. Eyre ac Andrew Spottiswoode, | . . . Tros y Bibl Gymdeithas Frytanaidd a Thramor, | . . . | 1846. |

12° (24); 116×62 mm., 126×76 mm.
4$\frac{9}{16}$×2$\frac{7}{16}$ in., 4$\frac{15}{16}$×3 in.; 948 pp.

Reprint of No. 93. N.T. also issued separately.

176.

1847. Y | Bibl Cyssegr-Lan, | . . . | Llundain: | . . . George E. Eyre ac William Spottiswoode, | . . . | Tros y Gymdeithas er Taenu Gwybodaeth Gristionogol. | . . . | 1847. |

4° (8); rough calf; 245×189 mm., 283×228 mm.
9$\frac{5}{8}$×7$\frac{7}{16}$ in., 11$\frac{1}{8}$×8$\frac{15}{16}$ in.

Reprint of No. 158, with the addition of the Apocrypha.

DESCRIPTION.—Title; blank, *b; Enwau . . . Llyfrau,* etc., sig. A²; blank, *b;* text (Gen.—Mal.), sigs. A³—5Q⁴, pp. [5]—[863]; blank, *b;* text (Apocrypha), sigs. A—Dd⁴; blank, *b;* title of N.T.; blank, *b;* text (Matt.—Rev.), sigs. 5R²—7G² and *b,* pp. [867]—[1156]. Total pp. (Apocrypha not numbered), 1,372.

177.

1847. Y | Bibl Cyssegr-Lan, | . . . | Llundain: | . . . George E. Eyre ac William Spottiswoode, | . . . Tros y Bibl Gymdeithas Frytanaidd a Thramor, | . . . | 1847. |

12°, on title [*Pearl 24mo.*] (24); 116×62 mm., 128×77 mm.
4$\frac{9}{16}$×2$\frac{7}{16}$ in., 5$\frac{1}{16}$×3$\frac{1}{16}$ in.; 948 pp.

Reprint of No. 93.

178.

1847. Y | Bibl | Cyssegr-Lan; | . . . | Caer Grawnt: | . . . Ioan W. Parker, | . . . | tros | Gymdeithas Biblau Saesoneg ac Ieithoedd eraill. | Cum Privilegio. | M.DCCC.XLVII. |

Cr. 8° (24) ; 151×83 mm., 171×106 mm.
5$\frac{15}{16}$×3$\frac{1}{4}$in., 6$\frac{3}{4}$×4$\frac{3}{16}$ in. ; 784 pp.

Reprint of No. 48.

179.

1848. Y | Bibl Cyssegr-Lan, | . . . | Llundain: | . . . G. E. Eyre ac W. Spottiswoode, | . . . | Tros y Bibl Gymdeithas Frytanaidd a Thramor, | . . . | 1848. |

Dy, 8°, on title [*Smallpica 8vo.*] (16); 198×111 mm., 222×139 mm.
7$\frac{13}{16}$×4$\frac{3}{8}$ in., 8$\frac{3}{4}$×5$\frac{1}{2}$ in.; 1,278 pp.

Reprint of No. 63.

180.

1848. Y | Bibl | Cyssegr-Lan; | . . . | Caer Grawnt: | . . . | Ioan W. Parker, | . . . | tros | Gymdeithas Biblau Saesoneg ac Ieithoedd eraill. | Cum Privilegio. | M.DCCC.XLVII. |

 Cr. 8°, on title [*Nonpareil 12mo.*] (24); 151×83 mm., 175×108 mm.

        5$\frac{14}{16}$×3$\frac{1}{4}$ in., 6$\frac{7}{8}$×4$\frac{1}{4}$ in.; 784 pp.

Reprint of No. 48.

181.

1849. Testament yr Athraw; | yn cynnwys, | Y Testament Seis-Gymreig; | yn nghyda | Gramadeg byr o elfenau y Gymreig ; a | thraethawd ar ddysgu darllen Saesonaeg; | . . . | Hefyd, | Esboniad byr ar holl anhawsderau | y Testament Newydd. | Gan John Jones, Merthyr-Tydvil, | (Gynt o Langollen). | Merthyr-Tydvil : — | . . . J. Jones, | . .. | MDCCCXLIX. |

 Cr. 8° (4, 8, 12, 16 and 24); cloth, gilt edges; 154×83 mm., 175×107 mm.

        6$\frac{1}{16}$×3$\frac{1}{4}$ in., 6$\frac{7}{8}$×4$\frac{3}{16}$ in.

Re-issue of No. 98, omitting its title, but with extra matter by *Jones Llangollen*, printed and published at his own press.

 DESCRIPTION.—Map, *Palestine* | . . . | *By W. Hughes;* general title; blank, *b ; Rhagymadrodd.*, signed *John Jones*, sigs. A²—Â³, pp. 3—5; *Gramadeg Byr* | *o elfenau . . . Cymraeg.*, *b*—sig. c⁶, pp. 6—27; *Geiriau Ansathredig.*, from *Trysorfa yr Athrawon:* . . . *gan Arfonwyson* [John William Thomas]. . . *1837.*, sigs. c⁶—c⁸, pp. 27—31; *Dwnediad.*, signed *Arfonwyson.*, sigs. c⁸—D³, pp. 31—37; *Cyfarwyddiadau i ddarllen Saesonaeg.*, *b*—sig E³, pp. 38—49; *Cyfarwyddiadau i ddarllen rhyddiaith a* | *phlethiaith.* | [*Allan o Lyfr* R. J. Prys, gyda gwelliadau.*], sigs. E³—E⁴ and *b*, pp. 49—52; *Geiriadur Personol a Lleol.*, sigs. A—E² and *b*, pp. i—xl; *Geiriadur Defnyddiau*, sigs. E³—F⁴, pp. xli—li; *Y Misoedd Iuddewig.*, *b*—sig. G, pp. lii—liii, *Sectau a Swyddau*, *b*—sig. G², pp. liv—lv; *Pwysau, Mesurau*, etc., sig. G² and *b*, pp. lv—lvi; *Hen Gyfieithiadau*, sigs. G³—G⁶, pp. lvii—lxi; *Rhagarweiniad*, *b*—sig. I² and *b*, pp. lxii—lxxii; *Henafion y Beibl.*, sigs. K—Q and *b*, pp. lxxiii—xcviii; *Gwyrthiau*, sig. Q²; *Damegion*, sig. Q² and *b*; *Ychydig o Ymresymiadau . . . Crist*, *b*; *Gwelliadau*, sigs. R—R⁵, pp. xc\i—cv; *Darlleniadau neilldlol yr Hen Syriaeg*, sig. R⁶ and *b*, pp. cv—cvi; poem, *Y Llwyddiant Apostolaidd*, sig. R⁶ and *b*; *Esboniad*, sigs. R—T⁴ and *b*, pp. 355—386; *Byr-Hanes o Gristionogaeth*, sigs. U—U⁴, pp. 387—393; *Uchder Mynyddoedd*, *b*, p. 394; *Tymhorau Canaan*, *b*, p. 394. Total pp. (text not numbered), 944.

182.

1850. Y | Bibl Cyssegr-Lan; | . . . | Llundain: | . . . George E. Eyre ac William Spottiswoode, | . . . Tros y Bibl Gymdeithas Frytanaidd a Thramor, | . . . | M.DCCC.L. |

 12°, on title [*Pearl 24mo.*] (24); 116×62 mm., 124×75 mm.

        4$\frac{9}{16}$×2$\frac{7}{16}$ in., 4$\frac{7}{8}$×2$\frac{15}{16}$ in.; 948 pp.

Reprint of No. 93.

183.

1850. Y | Bibl Cyssegr-Lan, | . . . | Llundain: | . . . George E. Eyre ac William Spottiswoode, | . . . | Tros y Gymdeithas er Taenu Gwybodaeth Gristionogol. | . . . | M.DCCC.L. |

 12°, on title [*Pearl 24mo.*] (24); 116×62 mm., 128×77 mm.

        4$\frac{9}{16}$×2$\frac{7}{16}$ in., 5$\frac{1}{16}$×3$\frac{1}{16}$ in.; 948 pp.

Reprint for the S.P.C.K. of No. 93.

184.

*Cyfarwyddyd i Gymmro ; by Robert John Pryse (Gweirydd ap Rhys); Denbigh, T. Gee, 1849.

1850. Y | Bibl | Sanctaidd : | . . . | gyda | Nodau a Sylwadau | ar bob pennod. | Gan y diweddar Barchedig Peter Williams. | . . . | Y Deuddegfed Argraffiad. | Caernarfon: | . . . Lewis Evan Jones ; Heol-y-Bont. | M,DCCCL. |

4° (4); 236×153 mm., 265×213 mm.
9⁴₁₆×6 in.,   10⁷₁₆×8⅜ in.; 1,270 pp.

Reprint of No. 26, omitting the Apocrypha, but containing a map, *Teithiau | yr | Apostolion.* | *Engraved by I. J. Morgan, Liverpool.* | , between the Old and the New Testaments. The N.T. in the copy seen is that of No. 144. Title of Prys's Ps. is dated *1850,.* |

185.

[*Circa* **1850**]. Y | Bibl Dwyieithawg, | . . . | Gyda Nodiadau Eglurhaol, a Darlleniadau a Chyfeiriadau Ymylenol, | . . . | Gan y diweddar Barch. Joseph Harris. | The | Duoglott Bible, | . . . | With Explanatory Notes, Marginal Readings and References, | arranged by | The Late Rev. Joseph Harris. | Peter Jackson, Late Fisher, Son, and Co. | The Caxton Press, . . . London; | . . . |

4° (8); 237×168 mm., 275×215 mm.
9⁴₁₆×6⅝ in.,   10¹³₁₆×8½ in. ; 1,416 pp.

Reprint of No. 87, in 2 vols., without date. Engraved titles to both vols. bear the imprint, *Llundain: Argraffwyd gan Fisher a'i Gyf.* There are numerous plates. Re-issued with new title, bearing the imprint, *Published by the London Printing and Publishing Company, Limited*, etc., and on engraved titles the imprint, *Hamilton and Adams | Paternoster Row, London.* | The lists of illustrations and some of the sheets of the N.T. were also re-set for the re-issue. Both issues undated.

186.

1850. Testament | Newydd | . . . | Caer Grawnt: | . . . Ioan W. Parker, | . . . | tros | Gymdeithas Biblau Saesoneg ac Ieithoedd Eraill. | Cum Privilegio. | M.DCCC.L. |

Cr. 8° (24); 153×83 mm., 170×105 mm.
6×3¼ in.,   6¹¹₁₆×4⅛ in.; 332 pp.

Reprint of No. 69, price 4d.

187.

1850. Testament Newydd | . . . | gwedy ei dynnu, | yd y gadei yr ancyfiaith 'air yn ci gylydd | or | Groec a'r Llatin, | . . . | Cyfieithiad | William Salesbury. | Argraffiad Newydd. | Caernarfon : | . . . Robert Griffith, . . . | 1850. |

Cr. 8° (16); lines across the page; boards, cloth back; 170×103 mm., 287×139 mm.
6¹¹₁₆×4₁₆ in.,   8⅛×5½ in.

Reprint of No. 5, edited by the Rev. Isaac Jones, sometime of Aberystwyth. Issued in parts, the first in 1849 (see *Y Bedyddiwr*, 1849, p. 114). Imprint on last page :—*Caernarfon: argraffwyd gan James Rees, Heol y Castell.*

DESCRIPTION.—Title; blank, *b;* Dr. Richard Davies's address, etc., sigs. A—A⁷ and *b*, pp. iii.—xiv.; William Salesbury's address, etc., sigs. A⁸, p. xv.; contents, *b*, p. xvi.; text, sigs. B—2I¹⁰ and *b*, pp. 1—500. Total pp., 16+500=516.

188.

1850. Y | Testament Daearyddol; | . . . | a | Geiriadur . . . | hefyd | pump o ddarlun-leni . . . | a | Thraithawd ar iaith ffigyrol y Bibl. | Gan y Parch. T. Roberts, Llanuwchllyn. | Bala: | . . . Griffith Jones. | 1850. |

12° (16); double columns; explanatory notes; leather, gilt edges;

110×62 mm., 119×75 mm.
4⁴⁄₁₆×2⁷⁄₁₆ in., 4¹¹⁄₁₆×2¹⁵⁄₁₆ in.

First ed'n of *Y Testament Daearyddol.* The literary cognomen of the editor was *Scorpion.*

Sigs., A—X⁸, with 4 preliminary pp. Total pp. (not numbered), 356.

189.

1850. The | New Testament, | in Welsh and English. | Testament Newydd, | . . . | Rhydychen : | . . . Argraphdy y Brifysgol, | Tros y Gymdeithas er Taenu Gwybodaeth Gristionogol. | . . . | 1850. |

Cr. 8° (16); 157×84 mm., 178×107 mm.
6³⁄₁₆×3⁷⁄₁₆ in., 7×4³⁄₁₆ in.; ii.+706=708 pp.

Reprint of No. 98, omitting table of offices, etc.

190.

1850. Esboniad | ar | Y Testament Newydd; | Gan y | Parch. John Wesley, M.A. | Gynt Cymrawd o Goleg Lincoln, Rhydychain. | Wedi ci gyfieithu | Gan Rowland Hughes. | Caernarfon : | Cyhoeddedig ac argraffedig gan H. Humphreys, | Castle Square. | 1850. |

Cr. 8° (16); double columns, with references between text and commentary ; cloth; 145×84 mm., 163×105 mm.
5¹¹⁄₁₆×3⁶⁄₁₆ in., 6⁷⁄₁₆×4⅛ in.

New translation of No. 94, price 7s. 6d.

DESCRIPTION.—Portrait, *Y Parch. John Wesley.;* title; blank, *b ; Rhagymadrodd.,* sigs. A²—A³ and *b*, pp. 3—6; text, sigs. A⁴—2X³ and *b*, pp. 7—646.

191.

1851. Y | Bibl Cyssegr-Lan, | . . . | Llundain: | . . . G. E. Eyre a W. Spottiswoode, | . . . | Tros y Bibl Gymdeithas Frytanaidd a Thramor, | . . . | M.DCCCLI. |

Dy. 8°, on title *Smallpica 8vo.* (16); 198×111 mm., 219×137 mm.
7¹⁄₁₆×4⅜ in., 8⅝×5⅜ in.; 1,278 pp.

Reprint of No. 63.

192.

1851. Y | Bibl Cyssegr-Lan, | . . . | Llundain : | . . . George E. Eyre a William Spottiswoode, | . . . | Tros y Bibl Gymdeithas Frytanaidd a Thramor, | . . . | M.DCCC.LI. |

12°, on title [*Pearl 24mo.*] (24); 116×62 mm., 127×75 mm.
4⁹⁄₁₆×2⁷⁄₁₆ in., 5×2¹¹⁄₁₆ in; 948 pp.

Reprint of No. 93.

193.

1851. Testament | Newydd | . . . | Caer Grawnt: | . . . Ioan W. Parker, | . . . | tros | Gymdeithas Biblau Saesoneg ac Ieithoedd Eraill. | Cum Privilegio. | M.DCCC.LI. |

Cr. 8° (24); 153×83 mm., 172×103 mm.
6×3¼ in., 6⅘×4₁⁶/₁₆ in. ; 332 pp.

Reprint of No. 69, price 4d.

194.

1852. Y | Bibl Cyssegr-Lan, | . . . | Llundain: | . . . G. E. Eyre a W. Spottiswoode, | . . . | Tros y Bibl Gymdeithas Frytanaidd a Thramor, | . . . | M.DCCC.LII. |

Dy. 8°, on title [*Smallpica 8vo.*] (16); 198×111 mm., 219×137 mm.
7¾×4⅜ in., 8⅝×5⅜ in. ; 1,278 pp.

Reprint of No. 63, with leather cover stamped on front, *Y Fibl Gymdeithas Frytanaidd a Thramor | Blwyddyn y Jubili | 1853 |* .

195.

1852. Y | Bibl | Cyssegr-Lan ; | . . . | Caer Grawnt : | . . . Ioan W. Parker, | . . . | tros | Gymdeithas Biblau Saesoneg ac Ieithoedd Eraill. | Cum Privilegio. | M.DCCC.LII.

Cr. 8°, on title [*Nonpareil 12mo.*] (24); 151×83 mm., 171×105 mm.
5₁₁/₁₆×3¼ in., 6¾×4⅓ in.; 784 pp.

Reprint of No. 48, price 10d.

196.

1852. Testament | Newydd | . . . | Caer Grawnt: | . . . Ioan W. Parker, | . . . | tros | Gymdeithas Biblau Saesoneg ac Ieithoedd Eraill. | Cum Privilegio. | M.DCCC.LII. |

Cr. 8° (24); 153×83 mm., 168×103 mm.
6×3¼ in., 6⅝×4₁/₁₆ in.; 332 pp.

Reprint of No. 69, price 4d.

197.

1852. Y Bibl Cyssegr-Lan | . . . | Llundain: | . . . George E. Eyre ac William Spottiswoode, | . . . | Tros y Gymdeithas er Taenu Gwybodaeth Gristionogol. | . . . | 1852. |

Cr. 8° (24); 151×83 mm., 171×105 mm.
5₁₁/₁₆×3¼ in., 6¾×4½ in.; 784 pp.

Reprint for the S.P.C.K. of No. 48. 15,000 copies of Bible printed, and 5,000 of N.T. separately.

198.

1852. Y | Bibl Cyssegr-Lan; | . . . | Rhydychen: | . . . Argraphdy y Brifysgol, | Tros y Gymdeithas er Taenu Gwybodaeth Gristionogol. | . . . | 1852. | Cum Privilegio. |

La. f° (4); 343×197 mm., 381×266 mm.
13½×7¾ in., 15×10½ in.

Pulpit ed'n for the Welsh Churches, issued under the sanction of the four Welsh bishops, whose preface is printed in English and Welsh after the general title, signed *C. Bangor, C. St. David's, Thos. Vowler St. Asaph, A. Llandaff. Hydref 10, 1852.* The stereotype plates prepared for this edition are still used when reprints are made.

DESCRIPTION.—Title; blank, *b*; Bishops' preface, *a*; contents, *b*; text, sigs. A—11E. Total pp. (not numbered), iv.+938=942.

199.

1852. Testament | Newydd | . . . | Llundain: | . . . G. E. Eyre a W. Spottiswoode, | . . . | Tros y Bibl Gymdeithas Frytanaidd a Thramor, | . . . | M.DCCC.LII. |

12°, on title [*Ruby 32mo.*] (32); 112×61 mm., 121×74 mm.
$4\frac{3}{8} \times 2\frac{3}{8}$ in., $4\frac{3}{4} \times 2\frac{15}{16}$ in.

Sigs., A—K^{11} and *b*. Total pp. (not numbered), 310.

200.

1853-52. Y | Bibl Cyssegr-lan, | . . . | Llundain: | . . . George E. Eyre a William Spottiswoode, | . . . | Tros y Bibl Gymdeithas Frytanaidd a Thramor, | . . . | M.DCCC.LIII. |

12°, on title *Pearl 24mo.* (24); 116×62 mm., 125×76 mm.
$4\frac{9}{16} \times 2\frac{7}{16}$ in., $4\frac{15}{16} \times 3$ in.; 948 pp.

Reprint of No. 93. Title of N.T. dated *M.DCCC.LII.*

201.

1853. Testament | Newydd | . . . | Caer Grawnt: | Ioan W. Parker, | . . . | Tros | Gymdeithas Biblau Saesoneg ac Ieithoedd Eraill. | Cum Privilegio. | M.DCCC.LIII. |

Cr. 8° (24); 153×83 mm., 169×102 mm.
$6 \times 3\frac{1}{4}$ in., $6\frac{5}{8} \times 4$ in.; 332 pp.

Reprint of No. 69, price 4d.

202.

1853. The | New Testament, | in Welsh and English. | Testament Newydd, | . . . | Llundain: | . . . G. E. Eyre a W. Spottiswoode, | . . . | Tros y Bibl Gymdeithas Frytanaidd a Thramor, | M.DCCC.LIII. |

12°, on title *Ruby 32mo.* (32); parallel columns; leather, gilt edges;
112×61 mm., 120×73 mm.
$4\frac{3}{8} \times 2\frac{3}{8}$ in., $4\frac{3}{4} \times 2\frac{7}{8}$ in.

Front of cover stamped, *The Year of Jubilee 1853.*

Sigs., A—U^{3}. Total pp. (not numbered), 614.

202a.

1853. The | New Testament, | in Welsh and English. | Testament Newydd, | yn cynwys mil o nodiadau byrion, ac y'nghylch ugain | mil o gyfeiriadau ysgrythyrol y Parch. T. Scott. | Llangollen: | . . . H. Jones. | MDCCCLIII. |

12° (16 and 12); parallel columns; calf; 117×68 mm., 141×95 mm.
$4\frac{5}{8} \times 2\frac{11}{16}$ in., $5\frac{9}{16} \times 3\frac{3}{4}$ in.

Issued in 9 parts at 6d. each, the first in 1852.

DESCRIPTION.—*Map of Canaan*, etc.; another map, *The Countries travelled by the Apostles*, etc.; title; blank, *b;* contents, *a;* blank, *b;* text, sigs, A—GGG^{2}, pp. 5—733; table of offices, etc. (in Welsh and English), *b*—GGG^{3}, pp. 734—735; chronological tables, *b*—GGG^{5}; errata, *b*. Total pp., 740.

203.

1853. Testament | Newydd | . . . | Llundain : | . . . G. E. Eyre a W. Spottiswoode, | . . . | Tros y Bibl Gymdeithas Frytanaidd a Thramor | . . . | M.DCCC.LIII. |

12°, on title [*Ruby 32mo.*] (32); 112×61 mm., 121×74 mm.
4⅞×2⅜ in.,   4¾×2¹⅜ in.; 310 pp.

Reprint of No. 200.

204.

1853. Llyfr | y Prophwyd Eshaiah | wedi ei gyfieithu o newydd | a'i drefnu | (cyn agosed ag y dichon) | yn ol yr Hebraeg | Gan | Y Parchedig Thomas Briscoe, S. T. B. | . . . | Holywell, | W. Morris, | . . . | 1853. |

Dy. 8° (8); lines across the page, in verse, with marginal notes; cloth;
160×99 mm., 221×140 mm.
6¼×3⅞ in.,   8¹¹⁄₁₆×5½ in.

New version from Hebrew of Isaiah.   Price 3s. 6d.

DESCRIPTION.—Half title; blank, *b*; title; colophon, *Baxter, Printer, Oxford.*, *b*; preface, sigs. b—b², pp. i—iii ; blank, *b*; *Disgrifiad o'r Prophwyd Eshaiah | Gan yr Esgob Lowth.* | , sigs. b³—b⁴, pp. v—vii; blank, *b*; errata slip; text, sigs. B—U¹ (last sig. not given), pp. 1—145; blank, *b*.   Total pp., xii.+146=158.

205.

1853. The | Gospel of St. Matthew | in Welsh and English, | for the use of | Children, Tourists, Visitors, etc., etc. | Llangollen : | . . . H. Jones. | 1853. | Price Sixpence. |

12° (16); wrapper; 117×68 mm., 141×95 mm.
4⅞×2¹¹⁄₁₆ in.,   5⁹⁄₁₆×3¾ in.; 96 pp.

Re-issue of part I. of No. 203.

206.

1854. Y | Bibl Cyssegr-Lan, | . . . | Llundain: | . . . George E. Eyre a William Spottiswoode, | . . . | Tros y Bibl Gymdeithas Frytanaidd a Thramor, | . . . | M.DCCC.LIV. |

4°, on title [*Pica 4to.*] (8); 245×189 mm., 285×230 mm.
9⅝×7⁷⁄₁₆ in.,   11¼×9¹⁄₁₆ in.; 1,156 pp.

Reprint of No. 158.

207.

1854. Y | Bibl Cyssegr-Lan | . . . | Llundain: | . . . George E. Eyre a William Spottiswoode, | . . . | Tros y Bibl Gymdeithas Frytanaidd a Thramor, | . . . | M.DCCC.LIV. |

Cr. 8°, on title *Nonpareil Ref. 12mo.* (32); 160×93 mm., 174×113 mm.
6¹⁄₁₆×3¹¹⁄₁₆ in.,   6⅞×4¹⁄₁₆ in.; 952 pp.

Reprint of No. 159, with front of cover stamped *Blwyddyn | y Jubili, | 1853.* |

208.

1854. Y | Bibl | Cyssegr-Lan; | . . . | Caer Grawnt: | . . . Ioan
W. Parker, | . . . | Tros Gymdeithas Biblau Saesoneg ac Ieithoedd
Eraill. | Cum Privilegio. | M.DCCC.LIV. |

Cr. 8° (24); 151×83 mm., 171×105 mm.
5$\frac{15}{16}$×3$\frac{1}{4}$ in., 6$\frac{3}{4}$×4$\frac{1}{8}$ in.; 784 pp.

Reprint of No. 48.

209.

1854. Testament | Newydd | . . . | Llundain : | . . . G. E. Eyre
a W. Spottiswoode, | . . . | Tros y Bibl Gymdeithas Frytanaidd
a Thramor, | . . . | M.DCCC.LIV. |

12°, on title [*Ruby 32mo.*] (32); 112×61 mm., 120×72 mm.
4$\frac{3}{8}$×2$\frac{3}{8}$ in., 4$\frac{3}{4}$×2$\frac{15}{16}$ in.; 310 pp.

Reprint of No. 200.

210.

1854. Testament Newydd, | . . . | Bibl Gymdeithas Americanaidd, |
Caerefrog Newydd: | sefydlwyd yn y flwyddyn MDCCCXVI. |
1854. | The New Testament | . . . | New York: | American Bible
Society, | instituted in the year MDCCCXVI. | 1854. |

Cr. 8° (32); parallel columns; no chapter contents;
161×90 mm., 173×107 mm.
6$\frac{5}{16}$×3$\frac{9}{16}$ in., 6$\frac{13}{16}$×4$\frac{1}{4}$ in.; 698 pp.

Welsh-English. First recorded American-printed Scriptures in Welsh.

210a.

1854. The | New Testament, | in Welsh and English. | Testament
Newydd, | . . . | Llundain: | . . . G. E. Eyre a W. Spottiswoode,
| . . . Tros y Bibl Gymdeithas Frytanaidd a Thramor, | . . . |
M.DCCC.LIV. |

12°, on title *Ruby 32mo.* (32); 112×61 mm., 120×73 mm.
4$\frac{3}{8}$×2$\frac{3}{8}$ in., 4$\frac{3}{4}$×2$\frac{7}{8}$ in.; 614 pp.

Reprint of No. 202a. Price 1s. and 1s. 6d.

211.

1854. The | New Testament, | in Welsh and English. | Testament
Newydd, | . . . | Rhydychen: | . . . Argraphdy y Brifysgol, | Tros
y Gymdeithas er Taenu Gwybodaeth Gristionogol. | . . . | 1854. |

Cr. 8° (16); 157×84 mm., 171×193 mm.
6$\frac{3}{16}$×3$\frac{5}{16}$ in., 6$\frac{11}{16}$×4$\frac{1}{16}$ in.; ii.+706=708 pp.

Reprint of No. 98, omitting table of offices, etc.

212.

1854. Llyfr | Y Patriarch Iôb | wedi ei gyfieithu o newydd | a'i
drefnu | . . . | yn ol yr Hebraeg | Gan | Y Parchedig Thomas
Briscoe, S.T.B. | . . . | Holywell, | W. Morris. | . . . | 1854. |

Dy. 8° (8); lines across the page, in verse, with marginal notes; cloth;
160×99 mm., 221×138 mm.
6$\frac{5}{16}$×3$\frac{7}{8}$ in., 8$\frac{11}{16}$×5$\frac{7}{16}$ in.

New version from the Hebrew. Price 2s.

DESCRIPTION.—Half title; blank, *b*; title; colophon, *Baxter, Printer, Oxford.* |, *b*;
preface, *a*; blank, *b*; contents, *a*; blank, *b*; text, sigs. B—L³, pp. 1—77;
blank, *b*. Total pp., viii.+78=86.

213.

H

1855. Y | Bibl Cyssegr-Lan, | . . . | Llundain: | . . . George E. Eyre a William Spottiswoode, | . . . Tros y Bibl Gymdeithas Frytanaidd a Thramor, | . . . | M.DCCC.LV. |

12°, on title [*Pearl 24mo.*] (24); 116×62 mm., 127×76 mm.
4$\frac{9}{16}$×2$\frac{7}{16}$ in.,   5×3 in.; 948 pp.
Reprint of No. 93.

214.

1855. Y | Bibl Cyssegr-lan, | . . . | Llundain: | . . . G. E. Eyre a W. Spottiswoode, | . . . | Tros y Gymdeithas er Taenu Gwybodaeth Gristionogol. | . . . | M.DCCC.LV. |

Dy. 8°, on title *Smallpica 8vo.* (16); 198×111 mm., 222×135 mm.
7$\frac{7}{16}$×4$\frac{3}{8}$ in.,   8$\frac{3}{4}$×5$\frac{5}{16}$ in.; 1,278 pp.

Reprint of No. 63, with Collect pasted on leaf facing title.

215.

1855. Y | Bibl Cyssegr-lan, | . . . | Llundain: | . . . George E. Eyre a William Spottiswoode, | . . . | Tros y Bibl Gymdeithas Frytanaidd a Thramor, | . . . | M.DCCC.LV. |

Cr. 8°, on title *Nonparcil Ref. 12mo.* (32); 160×93 mm., 175×112 mm.
6$\frac{4}{16}$×3$\frac{11}{16}$ in.,   6$\frac{7}{8}$×4$\frac{3}{8}$ in.; 952 pp.
Reprint of No. 159.

216.

1855. Testament | Newydd | . . . | Llundain : | . . . G. E. Eyre a W. Spottiswoode, | . . . Tros y Bibl Gymdeithas Frytanaidd a Thramor, | . . . | M.DCCC.LV. |

Dy. 8°, on title *Smallpica 8vo.* (16); 198×111 mm., 221×138 mm.
7$\frac{11}{16}$×4$\frac{3}{8}$ in.,   8$\frac{11}{16}$×5$\frac{7}{16}$ in.; 320 pp.

Reprint of the N.T. of No. 63.

217.

1855. Testament | Newydd | . . . | Caer Grawnt : | Argraffwyd yn Ngwasg y Brifathrofa. | Tros | Gymdeithas Biblau Saesoneg aç Ieithoedd eraill. | Cum Privilegio. | M.DCCC.LV. |

Cr. 8° (32); double columns; calf; 157×88 mm., 172×104 mm.
6$\frac{3}{16}$×3$\frac{7}{16}$ in.,   6$\frac{3}{4}$×4$\frac{1}{8}$ in.; iv.+348=352 pp.
Price 4d.

217a.

1855. Testament Newydd, | . . . | Bibl Gymdeithas Americanaidd, | Gaerefrog Newydd: | . . . | 1855. |

Cr. 8° (32); 161×90 mm., 173×107 mm.
6$\frac{5}{16}$×3$\frac{9}{16}$ in.,   6$\frac{13}{16}$×4$\frac{1}{4}$ in.; 698 pp.

Welsh-English. Reprint of No. 210a, 2nd *edition* on back of title.

218.

1855. Llyfr y Diarhebion | a | Llyfr y Psalmau | Wedi eu cyfieithu o newydd | a'u trefnu | . . . | yn ol yr Hebraeg | Gan | Y Parchedig Thomas Briscoe, S.T.B. | . . . | Holywell, | W. Morris, . . . | . . . | 1855. |

Dy. 8° (8); lines across the page, in verse, with marginal notes; cloth;. 158×103 mm., 222×138 mm.
6$\frac{3}{16}$×4$\frac{1}{8}$ in.,   8$\frac{3}{4}$×5$\frac{7}{16}$ in.

New version from the Hebrew.

DESCRIPTION.—Title; colophon, *Rhydychain:* | *Argraphedig gan 1. Wright, Argraphydd i'r Brif-Athrofa,* | *ar draul y cyficithydd.* |, *b;* preface, *a;* blank, *b;* contents (Prov.), *a;* errata, *b;* text (Prov.), sigs. B—I² and *b,* pp. 1—60; contents (Ps.), sig. I³; blank, *b;* text (Ps.), sigs. I⁴—Ll, pp. 63—257; advertisement, *b.* Total pp., vi.+258=264.

219.

1856. Y | Bibl Cyssegr-Lan, | . . . | Llundain : | . . . George E. Eyre a William Spottiswoode, | . . . | Tros y Bibl Gymdeithas Frytanaidd a Thramor, | . . . | M.DCCC.LVI. |

Cr. 8°, on title *Nonpareil Ref. 12mo.* (32); 160×93 mm., 175×113 mm.
6$\frac{13}{16}$×3$\frac{11}{16}$ in.,   6$\frac{7}{8}$×4$\frac{7}{16}$ in.; 952 pp.
Reprint of No. 159.

220.

1856. Y | Bibl Cyssegr-lan; | . . . | Rhydychen : | . . . Argraphdy y Brifysgol, | Tros y Gymdeithas er Taenu Gwybodaeth Gristionogol. | . . . | 1856. | Cum Privilegio. |

Cr. 8° (16); calf; 143×87 mm., 160×105 mm.
5$\frac{5}{8}$×3$\frac{7}{16}$ in.,   6$\frac{5}{16}$×4$\frac{1}{8}$ in.; 612 pp. (not numbered).

Title of N.T. not dated. Collect pasted on leaf facing title.

221.

1856. Y | Bibl | Cyssegr-Lan; | . . . | Caer Grawnt: | Argraffwyd yn Ngwasg y Brifathrofa | tros | Gymdeithas Biblau Saesoneg ac Ieithoedd eraill. | Cum Privilegio. | M.DCCC.LVI. |

Cr. 8° (24) ; 151×83 mm., 171×105 mm.
5$\frac{11}{16}$×3$\frac{1}{4}$ in.,   6$\frac{3}{4}$×4$\frac{1}{8}$ in. ; 784 pp.

Reprint of No. 48, price 10d.

222.

1856. Testament | Newydd | . . . | Llundain: | . . . G. E. Eyre a W. Spottiswoode, | . . . | Tros y Bibl Gymdeithas Frytanaidd a Thramor, | . . . | M.DCCC.LVI. |

Dy. 8°, on title *Small Pica 8vo.* (16); 198×111 mm., 221×138 mm.
7$\frac{13}{16}$×4$\frac{3}{8}$ in.,   8$\frac{11}{16}$×5$\frac{7}{16}$ in.; 320 pp.
Reprint of the N.T. of No. 63.

223.

1856. Testament Newydd, | . . . | Bibl Gymdeithas Americanaidd, | Caerefrog Newydd : | . . . | 1856. |

Cr. 8° (32); 161×90 mm., 173×107 mm.
6$\frac{6}{16}$×3$\frac{9}{16}$ in.,   6$\frac{13}{16}$×4$\frac{1}{4}$ in.; 698 pp.

Welsh-English. Reprint of No. 210a, *3rd edition* on back of title.

224.

1856. Testament Newydd | . . . | Llundain: | . . . G. E. Eyre a W. Spottiswoode, | . . . | Tros y Bibl Gymdeithas Frytanaidd a Thramor, | . . . | M.DCCC.LVI. |

12°, on title [*Ruby 32mo.*] (32); 112×61 mm., 120×72 mm.
$4\frac{3}{8}\times2\frac{3}{8}$ in., $4\frac{3}{4}\times2\frac{13}{16}$ in.; 310 pp.

Reprint of No. 200.

225.

1857. Y | Bibl Cyssegr-Lan, | . . . | Llundain: | . . . G. E. Eyre a W. Spottiswoode, | . . . | Tros y Bibl Gymdeithas Frytanaidd a Thramor, | . . . | M.DCCC.LVII. |

Dy. 8°, on title *Smallpica 8vo.* (16); 198×111 mm., 220×136 mm.
$7\frac{13}{16}\times4\frac{3}{8}$ in., $8\frac{5}{8}\times5\frac{3}{8}$ in.; 1,278 pp.

Reprint of No. 63.

226.

1857. Y | Bibl Cyssegr-Lan, | . . . | Llundain: | . . . G. E. Eyre a W. Spottiswoode, | . . . | Tros y Bibl Gymdeithas Frytanaidd a Thramor, | . . . | 1857. |

Cr. 8° (24); 151×83 mm., 171×105 mm.
$5\frac{15}{16}\times3\frac{1}{4}$ in., $6\frac{3}{4}\times4\frac{1}{8}$ in.; 784 pp.

Reprint of No. 48, price 10d. N.T. also issued separately.

227.

1857. Y | Bibl Cyssegr-Lan, | . . . | Llundain: | . . . George E. Eyre a William Spottiswoode, | . . . | Tros y Gymdeithas er Taenu Gwybodaeth Gristionogol, | . . . | M.DCCC.LVII. |

4° (8); 245×189 mm., 279×200 mm.
$9\frac{5}{8}\times7\frac{7}{16}$ in., $11\times7\frac{7}{8}$ in.; 1,156 pp.

Reprint of No. 158.

228.

1857. Testament Newydd | . . . | Rhydychen: | . . . Argraphdy y Brifysgol, | Tros y Bibl Gymdeithas Frytanaidd a Thramor, | . . . | 1857. | Cum Privilegio. |

Sm. 4° (16); large type, double columns, with references; calf;
162×119 mm., 176×140 mm.
$6\frac{3}{8}\times4\frac{11}{16}$ in., $6\frac{15}{16}\times5\frac{1}{2}$ in.

Sigs., A—Pp⁸. Total pp. (not numbered), 608.

229.

1858. Y | Bibl Santaidd, | . . . | Gyda | Nodau a Sylwadau ar bob pennod. | Gan y | Parch. Peter Williams. | . . . | Abertawy: | . . . J. Rosser a D. Williams, Heol Fawr. | M,DCCC,LVIII. |

4° (4); 240×182 mm., 278×216 mm.
$9\frac{7}{16}\times7\frac{3}{16}$ in., $10\frac{15}{16}\times8\frac{1}{2}$ in.

Reprint of No. 26, omitting the Apocrypha. Issued in 24 parts.

Sigs., 1—228, with 4 preliminary pp. Total pp. (not numbered), 916.

230.

1 8 5 8. Y | Bibl Cyssegr-Lan, | . . . | Llundain : | . . . G. E. Eyre a W. Spottiswoode, | . . . Tros y Bibl Gymdeithas Frytanaidd a Thramor, | . . . | M.DCCC.LVIII. |

12°. N.T. also issued separately. Reported. Fuller details unobtainable.

231.

1 8 5 8. Y | Bibl Cyssegr-Lan, | . . . | Bibl Gymdeithas Americanaidd, | Caerefrog Newydd: | . . . | 1858. |

Cr. 8°, on title *Welsh Nonpareil Ref.*, 12mo. (16); 163×97 mm., 187×118 mm.
$6\frac{7}{16}×3\frac{13}{16}$ in., $7\frac{7}{8}×4\frac{5}{8}$ in.
First American ed'n of the whole Bible.

Sigs., 1—59⁶, pp. [1]—[939].

232.

1 8 5 8. The | New Testament, | in Welsh and English. | Testament Newydd, | . . . | Llundain: | . . . G. E. Eyre a W. Spottiswoode, | . . . | Tros y Bibl Gymdeithas Frytanaidd a Thramor, | M.DCCC.LVIII. |

12°, on title *Ruby 24mo.* (32); 112×61 mm., 121×75 mm.
$4\frac{3}{8}×2\frac{3}{8}$ in., $4\frac{11}{16}×2\frac{7}{16}$ in.; 614 pp.
Reprint of No. 202a.

233.

1 8 5 9. Y | Bibl Cyssegr-Lan, | . . . | Llundain: | . . . George E. Eyre a William Spottiswoode, | . . . | Tros y Gymdeithas er Taenu Gwybodaeth Gristionogol, | . . . | M.DCCC.LIX. |

4°, on title *Pica Medium 4to Ref.* (8); 248×189 mm., 283×227 mm.
$9\frac{13}{16}×7\frac{7}{16}$ in., $11\frac{1}{8}×8\frac{15}{16}$ in.; 1,156 pp.
Reprint of No. 158.

233a.

1 8 5 9. Y | Bibl Cyssegr-Lan, | . . . | Llundain : | . . . George E. Eyre a William Spottiswoode, | . . . | Tros y Bibl Gymdeithas Frytanaidd a Thramor, | . . . | M.DCCC.LIX. |

12°, on title *Pearl 24mo.* (32); 115×62 mm., 127×77 mm.
$4\frac{1}{2}×2\frac{7}{16}$ in., 5×3 in.; 948 pp.
Reprint of No. 93. N.T. also issued separately.

234.

1 8 5 9. Y | Bibl Cyssegr-Lan, | . . . | Bibl Gymdeithas Americanaidd, | Caerefrog Newydd: | . . . | 1891. |

Cr. 8°, on title *Welsh Nonpareil Ref.*, 12mo. (16); 163×97 mm., 187×118 mm.
$6\frac{7}{16}×3\frac{13}{16}$ in.; $7\frac{7}{8}×4\frac{5}{8}$ in.; 940 pp.
Reprint of No. 232, *2nd edition* on p. 3.

234a.

1 8 5 9. Testament | Newydd | . . . | Llundain: | . . . | George E. Eyre a William Spottiswoode, | . . . | Tros y Bibl Gymdeithas Frytanaidd a Thramor, | . . . | M.DCCC.LIX. |

Royal 16°, on title *Brevier 16mo.* (32); leather;
132×93 mm., 144×108 mm.
$5\frac{3}{16}×3\frac{11}{16}$ in., $5\frac{11}{16}×4\frac{1}{4}$ in.; 396 pp. (not numbered).

First recorded of the fourpenny N.T. generally in use at present in Sunday Schools.

235.

1859. Y | Testament Daearyddol; | . . . | Gan y Parch. T. Roberts. | Trydydd Argraffiad. | Bala : | . . . Griffith Jones. | M.DCCC.LIX. |

12° (16); leather; 110×62 mm., 119×75 mm.
$4\frac{5}{16}\times2\frac{7}{16}$ in., $4\frac{11}{16}\times2\frac{15}{16}$ in.

Third ed'n, augmented, of No. 189, with 4 maps. Price 3s. 6d.

Sigs., A—2D[6] and *b*, with 4 preliminary pp., and 4 pp. of advertisements at end. Total pp. (not numbered), iv.+428=432.

236.

1859. Testament | Newydd | . . . | Bibl Gymdeithas Americanaidd, | Caerefrog Newydd: | . . . | 1859. |

12°, on title [*Welsh Nonpareil 32mo.*] (16); double columns; cloth;
106×59 mm., 114×73 mm.
$4\frac{3}{16}\times2\frac{5}{16}$ in., $4\frac{1}{2}\times2\frac{7}{8}$ in.

First American ed'n of N.T. (Welsh only).

Sigs., 1—26[8] and *b*, pp. 1—412.

237.

1860. Y | Bibl Cyssegrlan, | . . . | Llundain : | . . . G. E. Eyre a W. Spottiswoode, | . . . | Tros y Bibl Gymdeithas Frytanaidd a Thramor, | . . . | M.DCCC.LX. |

Dy. 8°, on title *Smallpica 8vo.* (32); 200×113 mm., 217×135 mm.
$7\frac{7}{8}\times4\frac{7}{16}$ in., $8\frac{1}{2}\times5\frac{5}{16}$ in.; 1,278 pp.

Reprint of No. 63.

237a.

1860. Y Bibl | Cyssegr-Lan; | . . . | Caer Grawnt: | Argraffwyd yn Ngwasg y Brif-Athrofa; | Tros y | Gymdeithas er Taenu Gwybodaeth Gristionogol, | . . . | Cum Privilegio. | M.DCCC.LX. |

Cr. 8°, on title [*Nonp. 12mo.*] (24); 151×86 mm., 174×106 mm.
$5\frac{15}{16}\times3\frac{3}{8}$ in., $6\frac{7}{8}\times4\frac{3}{16}$ in.; 784 pp.

Reprint of No. 48.

238.

1860. Y | Bibl Cyssegr-Lan, | . . . | Llundain: | . . . George E. Eyre a William Spottiswoode, | . . . | Tros y Gymdeithas er Taenu Gwybodaeth Gristionogol. | . . . | M.DCCC.LX. |

12° on title [*Pearl 24mo.*] (32); 115×62 mm., 127×75 mm.
$4\frac{1}{2}\times2\frac{7}{16}$ in., $5\times2\frac{7}{8}$ in.; 948 pp.

Reprint of No. 93.

239.

1860. Y | Bibl Cyssegr-Lan, | . . . | Llundain : | . . . George E. Eyre a William Spottiswoode, | . . . | M.DCCC.LX. |

4°. Reported. Fuller details unobtainable.

240.

1860. Testament | Newydd | . . . | Llundain: | . . . G. E. Eyre a W. Spottiswoode, | . . . | Tros y Bibl Gymdeithas Frytanaidd a Thramor, | . . . | M.DCCC.LX. |

12°, on title *Ruby 24mo.* (32); 112×61 mm., 122×73 mm.
$4\frac{3}{8}\times2\frac{3}{8}$ in., $4\frac{13}{16}\times2\frac{7}{8}$ in.; 310 pp.

Reprint of No. 200.

241.

1860. Testament | Newydd | . . . | Llundain: | . . . G. E. Eyre a W. Spottiswoode, | . . . | Tros y Bibl Gymdeithas Frytanaidd a Thramor, | . . . | M.DCCC.LX. |

Royal 16°, on title *Brevier 16mo.* (32); 132×93 mm., 144×108 mm.
5⅞×3¹¹⁄₁₆ in., 5¹¹⁄₁₆×4¼ in.; 396 pp.
Reprint of No. 235.

242.

1860. Testament Newydd, | . . . | Rhydychen: | . . . Argraphdy y Brifysgol, | Tros y Gymdeithas er Taenu Gwybodaeth Gristionogol. | . . . [1860. | Cum Privilegio. |

Cr. 8°. Reported. Fuller details unobtainable.

243.

1860. The | New Testament, | In Welsh and English. | Testament Newydd . . . | Llundain: | . . . G. E. Eyre a W. Spottiswoode, | . . . | Tros y Gymdeithas er Taenu Gwybodaeth Gristionogol | . . . M.DCCC.LX. |

12°, on title *Ruby 24mo.* (32); 112×61 mm., 123×74 mm.
4⅜×2⅜ in., 4¹⁄₁₆×2⁷⁄₁₆ in.; 614 pp.
Reprint of No. 202a.

244.

1861. Y | Bibl Cyssegr-Lan, | . . . | Llundain: | . . . George E. Eyre a William Spottiswoode, | . . . | Tros y Bibl Gymdeithas Frytanaidd a Thramor, | . . . | M.DCCC.LXI. |

4° (16); 248×187 mm., 281×228 mm.
9¹³⁄₁₆×7⅜ in., 11¹⁄₁₆×8⅛; 1,156 pp.

Reprint of No. 158.

244a.

1861. Y | Bibl Cyssegr-Lan, | . . . | Llundain : | . . . George E. Eyre a William Spottiswoode, | . . . | Tros y Gymdeithas er Taenu Gwybodaeth Gristionogol. | . . . | M.DCCC.LXI. |

4°, on title *Pica Medium 4to Reference* (8); 248×187 mm., 281×227 mm.
9¹³⁄₁₆×7⅜ in., 11¹⁄₁₆×8⅛ in.; 1,156 pp.
Reprint of No. 158.

245.

1861. Y | Bibl Cyssegr-Lan, | . . . | Llundain : | . . . George E. Eyre a William Spottiswoode, | . . . | Tros y Bibl Gymdeithas Frytanaidd a Thramor, | . . . | M.DCCC.LXI. |

Cr. 8°, on title *Nonpareil Ref. 12mo.* (32); 160×93 mm., 175×115 mm.
6¹⁄₁₆×3¹¹⁄₁₆ in., 6⅞×4½ in.; 952 pp.

Reprint of No. 159. N.T. also issued separately.

246.

1861. Y | Bibl Cyssegr-Lan, | . . . | Llundain: | . . . George E. Eyre a William Spottiswoode, | . . . | M.DCCC.LXI. |

16°. Reported. Fuller details unobtainable.

247.

1861. Testament | Newydd | . . . | Llundain: | . . . George E. Eyre a William Spottiswoode, | . . . | Tros y Bibl Gymdeithas Frytanaidd a Thramor | . . . | M.DCCC.LXI. |

Royal 16°, on title *Brevier 16mo.* (32); 132×93 mm., 144×108 mm.
$5\frac{3}{16}\times3\frac{11}{16}$ in., $5\frac{11}{16}\times4\frac{1}{4}$ in.; 396 pp.

Reprint of No. 235.

248.

1861. Testament | Newydd | . . . | Bibl Gymdeithas Americanaidd, | Caerefrog Newydd: | . . . | 1861. |

12°, on title [*Welsh Nonpareil 32mo.*] (16); 106×59 mm., 114×73 mm.
$4\frac{3}{16}\times2\frac{5}{16}$ in., $4\frac{1}{2}\times2\frac{7}{8}$ in.; 412 pp.

Reprint of No. 237, *2nd Edition* on back of title.

248a.

1861. The | New Testament, | In Welsh and English. | Testament Newydd, | . . . | Llundain: | . . . G. E. Eyre a W. Spottiswoode, | . . . | Tros y Bibl Gymdeithas Frytanaidd a Thramor, | . . . | M.DCCC.LXI. |

12°, on title *Ruby 24mo.* (32); 112×61 mm., 123×73 mm.
$4\frac{3}{8}\times2\frac{3}{8}$ in., $4\frac{3}{4}\times2\frac{7}{8}$ in.; 614 pp.

Reprint of No. 202*a*.

249.

1862-61. Y | Bibl Cyssegr-Lan, . . .| | Llundain: | . . . G. E. Eyre a W. Spottiswoode, | . . . | Tros y Gymdeithas er Taenu Gwybodaeth Gristionogol. | . . . | M.DCCC.LXII. |

Dy. 8°, on title *Smallpica 8vo.* (32); leather, gilt edges;
200×113 mm., 217×138 mm.
$7\frac{7}{8}\times4\frac{7}{16}$ in., $8\frac{1}{2}\times5\frac{7}{16}$ in.; 1,278 pp.

Reprint of No. 63. Title of N.T. dated *M.DCCC.LXI.*

249a.

1862. Y | Bibl Cyssegr-Lan, | . . . Llundain: | . . . G. E. Eyre a W. Spottiswoode, | . . | Tros y Bibl Gymdeithas Frytanaidd a Thramor, | . . . | M.DCCC.LXII. |

Dy. 8°, on title *Smallpica 8vo.* (32); 200×113 mm., 218×138 mm.
$7\frac{7}{8}\times4\frac{7}{16}$ in., $8\frac{5}{8}\times5\frac{7}{16}$ in.; 1,278 pp.

Reprint of No. 63. N.T. also issued separately.

250.

1862. Y | Bibl Cyssegr-Lan, | . . . | Llundain: | . . . George E. Eyre a William Spottiswoode, | . . . Tros y Bibl Gymdeithas Frytanaidd a Thramor, | . . . M.DCCC.LXII. |

12°, on title *Pearl 24mo.* (32); 115×62 mm., 126×76 mm.
$4\frac{1}{2}\times2\frac{7}{16}$ in., $4\frac{15}{16}\times3$ in; 948 pp.

Reprint of No. 93.

251

1862. Y | Bibl Cyssegr-Lan, | . . . | Rhydychen: | . . . Argraphdy y Brifysgol, | Tros y Bibl Gymdeithas Frytanaidd a Thramor, | . . . | M.DCCC.LXII. |

24mo. Reported. Fuller details unobtainable.

252.

1862. Testament Newydd | . . . | Rhydychen: | Argraphdy y Brif-
ysgol, | Tros y Bibl Gymdeithas Frytanaidd a Thramor, | . . . |
1862. | Cum Privilegio. |

Sm. 4° (16); 162×119 mm., 181×42 mm.
6⅜×4¹¹⁄₁₆ in., 7½×5¹⁹⁄₁₆ in.; 608 pp.

Reprint of No. 229.

253.

1862. Y | Testament Daearyddol; | . . . | Gan y Parch T. Roberts. |
Trydydd Argraffiad. | Bala: | . . . Griffith Jones. | M.DCCC.LXII. |

12° (16); 110×62 mm., 122×73 mm.
4⁵⁄₁₆×2⁷⁄₁₆ in., 4¹³⁄₁₆×2⅞ in.; 432 pp. (not numbered).

Fourth ed'n, augmented (called third on title), of No. 189, with 4 maps.

254.

1862. Yr Efengyl | yn ol | Sant Ioan. | Rhydychen: | . . . Argraphdy
y Brifysgol, | Tros y Bibl Gymdeithas Frytanaidd a Thramor. |
. . . | M.DCCC.LXII. | Cum Privilegio. |

32°, on title *Brevier* 6*mo.*; double columns; cloth; 101×57 mm., 113×72 mm.
4×2¼ in., 4⁷⁄₁₆×2¹⁄₁₆ in.
Sig. A⁸. Total pp. (not numbered), 88.

255.

[1863.] Bibl | yr | Addoliad Teuluaidd. | Gyda | Nodau a Sylwadau
ar bob pennod | . . . | gan y | Parch. Peter Williams. | Wedi ci
addurno a darluniau heirdd oddiar ddur. | . . . | London Printing
and Publishing Company, Limited | . . . |

La. f° (4); 356×216 mm., 386×263 mm.
14×8½ in., 15³⁄₁₆×10⁷⁄₁₆ in.; 1,102 pp.

Reprint of No. 26, with engraved title in black and red, and numerous steel
engravings. Not dated. Re-issued at least three times, the third with coloured plates
and new title in red and blue, bearing imprint, *Argraffwyd a chyhoeddwyd gan | E.
Slater, | . . . | 24, Chapel St., Bradford |*. Issued in parts, and bound in various
leathers, gilt edges, sometimes with brass clasps.

256.

1863. Testament | Newydd | . . . | Llundain: | . . . | George E. Eyre
a William Spottiswoode, | . . . | Tros y Bibl Gymdeithas Frytanaidd
a Thramor, | . . . | M.DCCC.LXIII. |

Royal 16°, on title *Brevier* 16*mo.* (32); 132×93 mm., 146×109 mm.
5³⁄₁₆×3¹¹⁄₁₆ in., 5⅝×4⁶⁄₁₆ in.; 396 pp.
Reprint of No. 235. Price 4d.

257.

1863. Testament | Newydd | . . . | Bibl Gymdeithas Americanaidd,
| Caerefrog Newydd: | . . . | 1863. |

12°, on title [*Welsh Nonpareil 32mo.*] (16); 106×59 mm., 115×71 mm.
4⁹⁄₁₆×2⁷⁄₁₆ in., 4⁹⁄₁₆×2¹³⁄₁₆ in.; 412 pp.

Reprint of No. 237, *3rd Edition* on back of title.

258.

1863. The | New Testament, | in Welsh and English. | Testament Newydd, | . . . | Llundain: | . . . George E. Eyre a William Spottiswoode, | . . . Tros y Bibl Gymdeithas Frytanaidd a Thramor, | . . . | M.DCCC.LXIII. |

12°, on title *Ruby 24mo.* (32); 112×61 mm., 123×74 mm.
$4\frac{3}{8}\times2\frac{3}{8}$ in., $4\frac{3}{4}\times2\frac{15}{16}$ in.; 614 pp.

Reprint of No. 202*a*.

259.

1864. Y | Bibl Cyssegr-Lan, | . . . | Llundain: | . . . George E. Eyre a William Spottiswoode, | . . . | Tros y Bibl Gymdeithas Frytanaidd a Thramor, | . . . | M.DCCC.LXIV. |

Dy. 8°, on title *Smallpica 8vo.* (32); 200×113 mm., 218×138 mm.
$7\frac{7}{8}\times4\frac{7}{16}$ in., $8\frac{5}{8}\times5\frac{7}{16}$ in.; 1,278 pp.

Reprint of No. 63. Price 3s., 3s. 9d., 4s. 6d., and 6s. 6d.

260.

1864. Y | Bibl Cyssegr-Lan, | . . . | Llundain: | . . . George E. Eyre a William Spottiswoode, | . . . | Tros y Bibl Gymdeithas Frytanaidd a Thramor, | . . . | M.DCCC.LXIV. |

Dy. 16°, on title *Pearl 16mo.* (32); double columns, leather;
126×84 mm., 137×98 mm.
$4\frac{15}{16}\times3\frac{5}{16}$ in., $5\frac{3}{8}\times3\frac{7}{8}$ in.

DESCRIPTION.—Title; blank, *b;* contents, *a;* blank, *b;* text (Gen.—Mal.), sigs. A^4—R^7 and *b;* title of N.T., not dated; blank, *b;* text (Matt.—Rev.), sigs. R^8—Y^{15}, blank, *b.* Total pp. (not numbered), 700.

261.

1864. Testament | Newydd | . . . | Llundain: | . . . George E. Eyre a William Spottiswoode, | . . . | Tros y Bibl Gymdeithas Frytanaidd a Thramor, | . . . | M.DCCC.LXIV. |

Royal 16°, on title *Brevier 16mo.* (32); 132×93 mm., 146×110 mm.
$5\frac{3}{16}\times3\frac{11}{16}$ in., $5\frac{3}{4}\times4\frac{5}{16}$ in.; 396 pp.

Reprint of No. 235. Price 4d.

262.

1864. The | New Testament, | in Welsh and English. | Testament Newydd, | . . . | Llundain: | . . . George E. Eyre a William Spottiswoode, | . . . | Tros y Bibl Gymdeithas Frytanaidd a Thramor, | . . . | M.DCCC.LXIV. |

12°, on title *Ruby 24mo.* (32); leather, with brass rims and clasp;
112×61 mm., 122×74 mm.
$4\frac{3}{8}\times2\frac{3}{8}$ in., $4\frac{13}{16}\times2\frac{15}{16}$ in.; 614 pp.

Reprint of No. 202*a*.

263.

1864. Testament Newydd, | . . . | Bibl Gymdeithas Americanaidd, | Caerefrog Newydd : | . . . | 1864. |

Cr. 8° (32); 161×90 mm., 173×107 mm.
$6\frac{5}{16}\times3\frac{9}{16}$ in., $6\frac{13}{16}\times4\frac{1}{4}$ in.; 698 pp.

Welsh-English. Reprint of No. 210*a*, *4th edition* on back of title.

263a.

1865. Y | Bibl Cyssegr-lan, | . . . | Llundain : | . . . George E. Eyre
a William Spottiswoode, | . . . | Tros y Bibl Gymdeithas
Frytanaidd a Thramor, | . . . | M.DCCC.LXV. |

4°, on title *Pica Medium 4to. Marg. Ref.* (16); 250×188 mm., 284×228 mm.
9⅛×7¾ in., 11₁⁵⁄₁₆×9 in.; 1,156 pp.

Reprint of No. 158.

264.

1865. Y | Bibl Cyssegr-lan, | . . . | Rhydychen: | . . . Argraphdy y
Brifysgol, | . . . | Tros y Bibl Gymdeithas Frytanaidd a Thramor,
| . . . | M.DCCC.LXV. |

4°. Reported. Fuller details unobtainable.

265.

1865. Y | Bibl Cyssegr-lan, | . . . | Llundain : | . . . George E.
Eyre a William Spottiswoode, | . . . | Tros y Bibl Gymdeithas
Frytanaidd a Thramor, | . . . | M.DCCC.LXV. |

Cr. 8°, on title *Noupareil 16mo.* (32); double columns; calf and cloth; price 10d.;
146×89 mm., 157×106 mm.
5¾×3½ in., 6₃⁄₁₆×4₁⁄₁₆ in.

Sigs., A—Cc¹¹ and *b*. Total pp. (not numbered), 822.

266.

1865. Y | Bibl Cyssegr-lan, | . . . | Rhydychen : | . . . Argraphdy
y Brifysgol, | Tros y Bibl Gymdeithas Frytanaidd a Thramor, |
. . . | M.DCCC.LXV. |

32mo. Reported. Fuller details unobtainable.

267.

1865. Y | Bibl | Cyssegr-lan; | . . . | Caer Grawnt: | Argraffwyd yng
Ngwasg y Brif-Athrofa; | tros y | Gymdeithas er Taenu Gwy-
bodaeth Gristionogol, | . . . | Cum Privilegio. | M.DCCC.LXV. |

Cr. 8°, on title [*Nonpareil 12mo.*] (24); 151×86 mm., 171×105 mm.
5₁³⁄₁₆×3⅜ in., 6¾×4⅛ in.; 784 pp.

Reprint of No. 48.

268.

1865. Testament | Newydd | . . . | Llundain: | . . . George E. Eyre
a William Spottiswoode, | . . . | Tros y Bibl Gymdeithas Frytanaidd
a Thramor, | . . . | M.DCCC.LXV. |

Royal 16°, on title *Brevier 16mo.* (32); 132×93 mm., 145×109 mm.
5₁³⁄₁₆×3₁₃⁄₁₆ in., 5₁₁⁄₁₆×4₃⁄₁₆ in.; 396 pp.

Reprint of No. 235. Price 4d.

269.

1865. Testament | Newydd | . . . | Caer Grawnt: | . . . C. J. Clay,
. . . | Tros y Bibl Gymdeithas Frytanaidd a Thramor, | . . . |
1865. |

32° (32); double columns; cloth; 88×55 mm., 96×65 mm.
3₇⁄₁₆×2₇⁄₁₆ in., 3₁⁵⁄₁₆×2₉⁄₁₆ in.

Sigs., A—P⁶. Total pp., iv.+460=464.

270.

1865. Testament | Newydd | . . . | Bibl Gymdeithas Americanaidd, |
Caerefrog Newydd: | . . . | 1865. |

32°, on title [*Welsh Nonpareil 32mo.*] (16); double columns; cloth;
106×59 mm., 114×73 mm.
4¹⁄₁₆×2¹⁄₁₆ in., 4½×2⅞ in.; 412 pp.

Reprint of No. 237, *4th Edition* on back of title.

270a.

1866. Y | Bibl Cyssegr-lan, | . . . | Llundain: | . . . G. E. Eyre a
W. Spottiswoode, | . . . | Tros y Bibl Gymdeithas Frytanaidd a
Thramor, | . . . | M.DCCC.LXVI.

Dy. 8°, on title *Smallpica 8vo.* (32); 200×113 mm., 222×140 mm.
7¾×4¹⁄₁₆ in., 8¾×5½ in.; 1,278 pp.

Reprint of No. 63. Price 3s.

271.

1866. Y | Bibl Cyssegr-lan, | . . . Llundain: | . . . G. E. Eyre a
W. Spottiswoode, | . . | Tros y Gymdeithas er Taenu Gwybodaeth
Gristionogol. | . . . |

Dy. 8°, on title *Smallpica 8vo.* (32); 203×114 mm., 220×139 mm.
8×4½ in., 8¹¹⁄₁₆×5¹⁄₁₆ in.

Reprint of No. 63. N.T. only dated *M.DCCC.LXVI.* Price 3s.

Sigs., A—Rr¹⁶. Total pp., 1,280 (not numbered).

272.

1866. Y | Bibl | Cyssegr-lan, | . . . | Llundain: | . . . George E. Eyre
a William Spottiswoode, | . . . | Tros y Bibl Gymdeithas Frytanaidd
a Thramor, | . . . | M.DCCC.LXVI. |

Cr. 8°, on title *Nonpareil 16mo.* (32); 146×89 mm., 155×105 mm.
5¾×3½ in., 6⅛×4¼ in.; 822 pp.

Reprint of No. 266. Price 10d.

273.

1866. Testament | Newydd | . . . | Llundain: | . . . George E. Eyre
a William Spottiswoode, | . . . | Tros y Gymdeithas er Taenu
Gwybodaeth Gristionogol. | . . . | M.DCCC.LXVI. |

Royal 16°, on title [*Brevier 16mo.*] (32); 132×93 mm., 145×109 mm.
5¹⁄₁₆×3¹¹⁄₁₆ in., 5¹¹⁄₁₆×4¼ in.; 396 pp.

Reprint of No. 235. Price 4d.

274.

1866. Testament | Newydd | . . . | Caer Grawnt: | . . . C. J. Clay,
. . . | Tros y Bibl Gymdeithas Frytanaidd a Thramor, | . . . |
1866. |

32° (32); 88×55 mm., 99×70 mm.
3¹⁄₁₆×2¹⁄₁₆ in., 3⅞×2¾ in.; iv.+460=464 pp.

Reprint of No. 270.

275.

1866. Y Septuagint, neu y Beibl Sanctaidd, yn ol Cyfieithad y LXX. Gyda sylwadau, gan E. Andrews, B.A. Rhifyn I. Caerfyrddin, W. Spurrell.

Title copied from the wrappers of the May no. of *Yr Haul*, 1868, where it is advertised as having been issued in 1866, with a commentary and brief English footnotes. Its price was 7d. A specimen of the work had been issued in 1865. The translator had prepared for the press a complete translation, to be issued in three volumes (see *Crockford's Clerical Directory, 1868*, p. 13); but owing to the lack of subscribers, no more than part I. was printed. The translator was the Rev. Evan Andrews, vicar of Llandefeiliog, Kidwelly.

277.

1867. Y | Bibl Cyssegr-lan, | . . . | Llundain: | . . . George E. Eyre a William Spottiswoode, | . . . Tros y Bibl Gymdeithas Frytanaidd a Thramor, | . . . M.DCCC.LXVII. |

Dy. 16°, on title *Pearl 16mo.* (32); 126×84 mm., 138×97 mm.

4¼×3 in., 5⅞×3 in.; 700 pp.

Reprint of No. 261.

278.

1867. Y | Bibl Cyssegr-lan, | . . . | Llundain: | . . . George E. Eyre a William Spottiswoode, | . . . | Tros y Bibl Gymdeithas Frytanaidd a Thramor, | . . . | M.DCCC.LXVII.

4°, on title *Pica Medium 4to. Marg. Ref.* (16); 249×189 mm., 282×228 mm.

9×7 in., 11¼×9 in.; 1,156 pp.

Reprint of No. 158.

279.

1867-66. Y | Bibl Cyssegr-lan, | . . . | Rhydychen: | . . . Argraphdy y Brifysgol, | Tros y Bibl Gymdeithas Frytanaidd a Thramor, | . . . | M.DCCC.LXVII. |

La. 8°, on title *Small Pica 8vo. Refs.* (12); double columns, with references;

233×145 mm., 256×170 mm.

9×5⅛ in., 10×6¼ in.; price 9s.

DESCRIPTION.—Title ; blank, *b;* *Enwau . . . Llyfrau*, etc., *a;* blank, *b;* text (Gen.—Mal.), sigs. A—4E² and *b;* title of N,T., dated *1866.;* blank, *b;* text (Matt.—Rev.), 4E⁴—*5F⁶ and *b.* Total pp. (not numbered), iv.+1,180=1,184.

280.

1867. Y | Bibl Cyssegr-lan, | . . . | Llundain: | . . . George E. Eyre a William Spottiswoode, | . . . | 1867. |

8°. Reported. Fuller details unobtainable.

281.

1867. Y | Bibl Cyssegr-lan; | . . . | Rhydychen: | . . . Argraphdy y Brifysgol, | Tros y Gymdeithas er Taenu Gwybodaeth Gristionogol. . . . | | 1867. | Cum Privilegio. |

12° (32); leather; 120×68 mm., 132×82 mm.

4¾×2 in., 5×3¼ in.

Collect inside front cover.

Sigs., A—Dd¹² and *b.* Total pp. (not numbered), 860 pp.

282.

1867. Testament | Newydd | . . . | Bibl Gymdeithas Americanaidd, | Caerefrog Newydd: | . . . | 1867. |

12°, on title [*Welsh Nonpareil 32mo.*] (16); 106×59 mm., 114×73 mm.
$4\frac{3}{16}\times2\frac{5}{16}$ in., $4\frac{1}{2}\times2\frac{7}{8}$ in.; 412 pp.

Reprint of No. 237, *5th Edition* on back of title.

282a.

1867. Yr Efengyl | yn ol | Sant Ioan. | Rhydychen: | . . . Argraphdy y Brifysgol, | Tros y Bibl Gymdeithas Frytanaidd a Thramor, | . . . | 1867. | Cum Privilegio. |

32°, on title *Brevier 32mo.*, limp cloth; 101×57 mm., 113×72 mm.
$4\times2\frac{1}{4}$ in., $4\frac{7}{16}\times2\frac{13}{16}$ in.; 88 pp.

Reprint of No. 255.

283.

1868. Y | Bibl | Cyssegr-lan | Gyda Nodau Esponiadol. | . . . | Gan y | Parch. Peter Williams. | Dan olygiaeth y | Parch. J. R. Kilsby Jones. | . . . | William Mackenzie. | Llundain, Llynlleifiad, Caerodor, ac Abertawy. |

La. 4° (8); double columns, with notes and references between, and commentary at end of each chapter; 283×209 mm., 340×248 mm.
$11\frac{1}{8}\times8\frac{1}{4}$ in., $13\frac{3}{8}\times9\frac{3}{4}$ in.

Reprint of No. 26, omitting all prefatory matter, but containing numerous steel engravings. Printed at Glasgow.

DESCRIPTION.—Frontispiece, *Moses;* title; contents, *b;* text (Gen.—Mal.), sigs. 1^2—108 and *b*, pp. 1—864; title of N.T., dated *MDCCCLXVIII.;* blank, *b;* text (Matt.—Rev.), sigs. 109—146 and *b*, pp. 865—1,166; title of Prys's Ps.; tables of Ps. and Hymns, *b;* text, in treble columns, sigs. 1^2—6, pp. 3—42. Total pp., ii.+1,166+42=1,210.

284.

1868. Y | Bibl Cyssegr-lan, | . . . | Bibl Gymdeithas Americanaidd, Caerefrog Newydd: | . . . | 1891. |

Cr. 8°, on title *Welsh Nonpareil Ref.*, *12mo.* (16);
163×97 mm., 187×118 mm.
$6\frac{7}{16}\times3\frac{13}{16}$ in., $7\frac{3}{8}\times4\frac{5}{8}$ in.; 940 pp.

Reprint of No. 232, *3rd Edition* on p. 3.

285.

1868. Testament Newydd, | . . . | Bibl Gymdeithas Americanaidd, | Caerefrog Newydd: | . . . | 1868. |

Cr. 8° (32); 161×90 mm., 173×107 mm.
$6\frac{5}{16}\times3\frac{9}{16}$ in., $6\frac{13}{16}\times4\frac{1}{4}$ in.; 698 pp.

Welsh-English. Reprint of No. 210*a*, *5th edition* on back of title.

285a.

1868. Testament | Newydd | . . . | Caer Grawnt: | . . . C. J. Clay, . . . | Tros y Bibl Gymdeithas Frytanaidd a Thramor, | . . . | 1868. |

32° (32); 88×55 mm., 96×64 mm.
$3\frac{7}{16}\times2\frac{3}{16}$ in., $3\frac{13}{16}\times2\frac{1}{2}$ in.; iv.+460=464 pp.

Reprint of No. 270. Price, 2d., 3d., 6d., and 9d.

286.

1 8 6 9.   Y | Bibl Cyssegr-lan, | . . . | Llundain: | . . . George E. Eyre
a William Spottiswoode, | Tros y Bibl Gymdeithas Frytanaidd a
Thramor, | . . . | M.DCCC.LXIX. |

Cr. 8°, on title *Nonpareil 16mo.* (32); 146×89 mm., 155×105 mm.
5⅜×3½ in.,   6⅛×4⅛ in.; 822 pp.
Reprint of No. 266.   Price 10d.

287.

1 8 6 9.   Testament | Newydd | . . . | Bibl Gymdeithas Americanaidd,
Caerefrog Newydd: | . . . | 1869. |

12°, on title [*Welsh Nonpareil 32mo.*] (16); 166×59 mm., 114×73 mm.
4⅜×2⅞ in.,   4½×2⅞ in.; 412 pp.

Reprint of No. 237, *6th Edition* on back of title.

287a.

1 8 7 0.   Y | Bibl Cyssegr-lan, | . . . | Llundain: | . . . G. E. Eyre a
W. Spottiswoode, | Tros y Bibl Gymdeithas Frytanaidd a Thramor,
| . . . | M.DCCC.LXX. |

Dy. 8°, on title *Smallpica 8vo·* (32); 203×114 mm., 222×140 mm.
8×4½ in.,   8¾×5½ in.; 1,280 pp. (not
numbered).
Reprint of No. 63.   Price 3s.

288.

1 8 7 0.   Testament | Newydd | . . . | Llundain: | . . . George E. Eyre
a William Spottiswoode, | . . . | Tros y Bibl Gymdeithas Frytanaidd
a Thramor, | . . . | M.DCCC.LXX. |

Royal 16°, on title *Brevier 16mo.* (32); 132×93 mm., 145×109 mm.
5⁵⁄₁₆×3¹¹⁄₁₆ in.,   5¹¹⁄₁₆×4¼ in.; 396 pp. (not
numbered).

Reprint of No. 235.   Price 4d.

289.

1 8 7 0.   The | New Testament, | in Welsh and English. | Testament
Newydd, | . . . | . . . George E. Eyre a William Spottiswoode,
| . . . | Tros y Bibl Gymdeithas Frytanaidd a Thramor, |
. . . | M,DCCC,LXX. |

12°, on title *Ruby 24mo.* (32); 112×61 mm., 122×73 mm.
4⅜×2⅜ in.,   4¹⁵⁄₁₆×2¾ in.; 614 pp.

Reprint of No. 202a.

290.

1 8 7 0.   Llyfr y Psalmau. | . . . | Rhydychen: | . . . Argraphdy y
Brifysgol, | Tros y Bibl Gymdeithas Frytanaidd a Thramor, | . . .
| 1870. | Cum Privilegio. |

Sm. 4° (32); large type, double columns, with references between verses; limp
cloth; 161×117 mm., 182×142 mm.
6¹⁄₁₆×4⅝ in.,   7¹⁄₁₆×5⁹⁄₁₆ in.

Sigs., A—E¹⁰ and *b*.   Total pp. (not numbered), 148.

291.

1870. Can y Caniadau: | neu | Gyfieithad Llythyrenol | o | Ganiadau Solomon | o'r Hebraeg, | yn nghyd a | Nodiadau Byrion, | . . . | Gan A. Rhys Thomas, | . . . | Llanelli: | . . . B. R. Rees, . . . | 1870. | Pris Chwe Cheiniog. |

Dy. 8° (8); lines across the page in verse, with notes after chapters;
171 × 102 mm., 212 × 137 mm.
6¾ × 4 in.,   8⅜ × 5¾ in.; 20 pp.

292.

[**1871.**] Y | Beibl Teuluaidd | Cynnwysfawr | . . . | yn nghyd a lluaws o | nodiadau . . . , cyfeiriadau ysgrythyrol | a gwahanol ddarlleniadau. | Y cyfan wedi ci ddethol a'i olygu gan y | Parch. Owen Jones, | . . . | At yr hyn y chwanegwyd, | Sylwadau ymarferol ac efengylaidd . . . | . . . Peter Williams. | . . . | Addurnedig a chyfres o gerfluniau detholedig. | . . . | Llundain : | Blackie a'i Fab, . . . | Glasgow, ac Edinburgh. |

La. 4° (8); double columns, with marginal notes and references between, and commentary at foot of page; morocco, gilt edges, brass clasps;
309 × 218 mm., 370 × 264 mm.
12³⁄₁₆ × 8⁹⁄₁₆ in.,   14⁹⁄₁₆ × 10⅜ in.

Family Bible, edited by the Rev. Owen Jones ("Meudwy Môn"), who included the commentary of Peter Williams. Contains numerous steel engravings. Issued between 1866 and 1870 in 32 parts, at 2s. 6d. each. Not dated.

DESCRIPTION.—Half title; blank, *b;* frontispiece, *The Fall of Man;* engraved title, *The Giving of the Law;* blank, *b;* title; imprint (at foot), *Glasgow:* | *W. G. Blackie and Co., Printers,* | *Villafield.* |, *b;* Y *Rhagymadrodd.,* p. (v); *Enwau . . . Llyfrau,* etc., *b,* p. (vi); *Rhestr o'r Cerf-luniau,* pp. (vii)—(viii); *Rhag-arweiniad.,* pp. (ix)—(xvi); publishers' notices, etc., referring to Bible, in Welsh and English, pp. 1—4; testimonials, pp. 5—7; blank, *b;* text (Gen.—Mal.), sigs. 1—130⁴, pp. (1)—(1039); *Golwg gryno ar brif ddygwyddiadau,* etc., sig. 130⁴ and *b,* pp. (1039)—(1040); family register; frontispiece, *Daughters of Jerusalem, weep not for me;* engraved title, *The Annunciation to the Shepherds;* blank, *b;* title of N.T.; blank, *b;* text (Matt.—Rev.), sigs. 131²—183, pp. (1043)—(1057); blank, *b;* *Mynegai Amseryddol,* etc., sigs. 183²—184⁴ and *b,* pp. (1459)—(1472). Total pp., xvi.+8+1,472=1,496.

293.

1871. Y | Bibl Cyssegr-lan, | . . . | Llundain: | . . . George E. Eyre a William Spottiswoode.

4°, on title *Pica Medium 4to. Marg. Ref.* (16); brass clasp and rims;
250 × 188 mm., 277 × 228 mm.
9⅞ × 7⅜ in.,   10⅞ × 9 in.; 1,156 pp.

Reprint of No. 158, with a number of coloured plates, 4 maps, and a family register. N.T. only dated *M.DCCC.LXXI.*

294.

1871. Y | Bibl Cyssegr-lan, | . . . | Llundain: | . . . George E. Eyre a William Spottiswoode, | M.DCCC.LXXI. |

4°, on title *Pica Medium 4to. Marg. Ref.* (16); leather;
246 × 186 mm., 285 × 223 mm.
9¹¹⁄₁₆ × 7⁶⁄₁₆ in.,   11³⁄₁₆ × 8¹³⁄₁₆ in.; 1,156 pp.

Reprint of No. 158.

294a.

1 8 7 1. Y | Bibl Cyssegr-lan, | . . . | Llundain: | . . . George E. Eyre
a William Spottiswoode, | Tros y Bibl Gymdeithas Frytanaidd a
Thramor, | . . . | M.DCCC.LXXI. |

Dy. 16°, on title *Pearl 16mo*. (32); 126×84 mm., 137×97 mm.
4⅛×3⁵⁄₁₆ in., 5⅝×3¹³⁄₁₆ in.; 700 pp. (not
numbered).

Reprint of No. 261.

295.

1 8 7 1. Testament | Newydd | . . . | Llundain : | . . . G. E. Eyre
a W. Spottiswoode, | . . . | Tros y Bibl Gymdeithas Frytanaidd
a Thramor, | . . . | M.DCCC.LXXI. |

Dy. 8°, on title *Smallpica 8vo*. (32); 203×114 mm., 221×141 mm.
8×4½ in., 8¹¹⁄₁₆×5⁹⁄₁₆ in.; 320 pp. (not
numbered).

Reprint of the N.T. of No. 66.

296.

1 8 7 1. Testament | Newydd | . . . | Bibl Gymdeithas Americanaidd,
| Caerefrog Newydd: | . . . | 1871. |

32°, on title [*Welsh Nonpareil 32mo.*] (16); 106×59 mm., 114×73 mm.
4⁵⁄₁₆×2⁷⁄₁₆ in., 4½×2⅞ in.; 412 pp.

Reprint of No. 237, *7th Edition* on back of title.

297.

1 8 7 1. Testament | Newydd | . . . | Bibl Gymdeithas Americanaidd,
| Caerefrog Newydd: | . . . | 1871. |

32°, on title [*Welsh Nonpareil 32mo.*] (16); 106×59 mm., 114×73 mm.
4⁵⁄₁₆×2⁷⁄₁₆ in., 4½×2⅞ in.; 412 pp.

Reprint of No. 237, *8th Edition* on back of title.

297a.

1 8 7 1. Testament Newydd | . . . | Bibl Gymdelthas Americanaidd,
| Caerefrog Newydd : | . . . | 1871. |

Cr. 8° (32); 161×90 mm., 173×107 mm.
6⁵⁄₁₆×3⁷⁄₁₆ in., 6⅛×4¼ in.; 698 pp.

Welsh-English. Reprint of No. 210a, *6th edition* on back of title.

297b.

1 8 7 2. Y | Bibl Cyssegr-lan, | . . . | Rhydychen: | . . . Argraphdy y
Brifysgol, | Tros y Fibl Gymdeithas Frytanaidd a Thramor, | . . .
| M.DCCC.LXXII. | Cum Privilegio. |

La. 8°, on title *Sm. Pica 8vo. Gydâ Chyfeir*. (24); 233×145 mm., 255×172 mm.
9⁵⁄₁₆×5⅛ in., 10¹⁄₁₆×6¾ in.;
iv.+1,180=1,184 pp

Reprint of No. 289. N.T. dated 1872.

298.

K

1872. Y | Bibl Cyssegr-lan; | . . . | Llundain: | Y Gymdeithas er Taenu Gwybodaeth Gristionogol; | . . . |

La. 8° (16); double columns, with marginal notes and references; cloth;
230 × 142 mm., 260 × 166 mm.
9 1/8 × 5 9/16 in.,   10 1/4 × 6 9/16 in.

Pr. Bk. only dated *1872.* Imprint on back of title, *Argraphedig gan John Childs a'i Fab.*

Description.—Title, *Llyfr | Gweddi Gyffredin,* | . . . | *ynghyd a'r | Psallwyr* . . . | . . . *Llundain:* | *Y Gymdeithas er taenu Gwybodaeth Gristionogol;* | . . . | *1872.* | ; imprint, *b;* text, sigs. *a²—c* and *b,* and sigs. 1—13⁴ and *b;* title of Bible; blank, *b; Enwau . . . Llyfrau,* etc., *a;* blank, *b;* text (Gen.—Mal.), sigs. 1—55⁶; blank, *b;* text (Apoc.), sigs. 55⁷—67³ and *b;* title of N.T.; blank, *b;* text (Matt.—Rev.), sigs. 1*—20; imprint, *b.* Total pp. (not numbered), 1,620.

299.

[1872.] Y | Beibl Teuluaidd | Cynnwysfawr, | . . . | yn nghyd a lluaws o | Nodiadau Beirniadol ac Eglurhaol, Cyfeiriadau Ysgrythyrol, | a gwahanol Ddarlleniadau. | Y cyfan wedi ei ddethol a'i olygu gan y | Parch. Owen Jones, | . . . | At yr hyn y chwanegwyd, | Sylwadau Ymarferol ac Efengylaidd, y | Diweddar Barch. Peter Williams. | Yn addurnedig gan gyfres ddetholedig o ddarluniau hanesyddol. | Llundain: | Blackie a'i Fab, . . . | Glasgow ac Edinburgh. |

La. 4° (8); morocco, gilt edges, brass clasps; 303 × 212 mm., 340 × 248 mm.
11 6/16 × 8 6/16 in.,   13 3/8 × 9 3/4 in.

Reprint of No. 293, omitting publishers' notices, etc., and slightly re-arranged. Issued in parts between 1870 and 1872. Not dated.

Description.—Half title; blank, *b;* frontispiece, *Moses | restoring the tables of the Law* | ; engraved title; blank, *b;* title; blank, *b; Y Rhagymadrodd.,* sig. *a³,* p. (v); *Enwau . . . Llyfrau,* etc., *b,* p. (vi); *Rhestr o'r Cerf-lunitu,* sig. *a⁴,* p. vii; blank, *b; Rhagarweiniad.,* sigs. *b—b⁴* and *b,* pp. (ix)—(xvi); *Cofrhestr Deuluaidd,* etc., 4 plates (coloured); text (Gen.—Mal.), sigs. 1—130⁴, pp. (1)—(1039); *Golwg gryno ar brif ddygwyddiadau,* etc., sig. 130⁴ and *b,* pp. (1039)—(1040); title of N.T.; blank, *b;* text (Matt.—Rev.), sigs. 131²—183, pp. (1043)—(1457); blank, *b; Mynegai Amseryddol,* etc., sigs. 183²—184⁴ and *b,* pp. (1459)—(1472). Total pp., xvi.+1,472=1,488.

300.

1872. Y | Bibl Cyssegr-lan, | . . . | Bibl Gymdeithas Americanaidd, | Caerefrog Newydd: | . . . | 1872. |

Cr. 8°, on title *Welsh Nonpareil Ref., 12mo.* (16); 163 × 97 mm., 187 × 118 mm.
6 7/16 × 3 13/16 in.,   7 3/8 × 4 5/8 in.; 940 pp.

Reprint of No. 232, *4th Edition* on p. 3.

300a.

1872. The | New Testament, | in Welsh and English. | Testament Newydd, | . . . | Llundain: | . . . George E. Eyre a William Spottiswoode, | . . . | Tros y Bibl Gymdeithas Frytanaidd a Thramor, | . . . | M.DCCC.LXXII. |

12°, on title *Ruby 24mo.* (32); leather, with brass rims and clasp;
112 × 61 mm., 122 × 74 mm.
4 3/8 × 2 3/8 in.,   4 13/16 × 2 13/16 in.; 614 pp.

Reprint of No. 202a.

301.

1873-1. Y | Bibl Cyssegr-lan, | . . . | Llundain: | . . . G. E. Eyre a W. Spottiswoode, | . . . Tros y Bibl Gymdeithas Frytanaidd a Thramor, | . . . | M.DCCC.LXXIII. |

Dy. 8°, on title *Smallpica 8vo.* (32); 203 × 114 mm., 220 × 138 mm.
8 × 4½ in.,   8⅝ × 5⅞₁₆ in.; 1,280 pp. (not numbered, except pp. 33—40).

Reprint of No. 63. Price 3s. Title of N.T. dated *M.DCCC.LXXI.*

301a.

1873. Testament | Newydd | . . . | Llundain: | . . . George E. Eyre a W. Spottiswoode, | . . . | Tros y Bibl Gymdeithas Frytanaidd a Thramor, | . . . | M.DCCC.LXXIII. |

Royal 16°, on title *Brevier 16mo.* (32); 132 × 93 mm., 145 × 109 mm.
5⅜₁₆ × 3⅛₁₆ in., 5⅛₁₆ × 4¼ in.; 396 pp. (not numbered).

Reprint of No. 235. Price 4d.

302.

1873. Y | Bibl Sanctaidd, | . . . | Gyd a | Nodau a Sylwadau ar bob pennod, | Gan y Parch. Peter Williams. | . . . | Llundain : | Cyhoeddwyd gan William Mackenzie, . . . | . . . | MDCCCLXXIII. |

La. 4° (8); double columns, with notes and references between, and commentary at end of chapters ; morocco, gilt edges ; 291 × 211 mm., 334 × 254 mm.
11⁷₁₆ × 8⅝₁₆ in., 13⅛ × 10 in.

Reprint of No. 26, omitting preliminary matter, biography, tables, Apocrypha, Prys's Ps., etc., and including numerous steel engravings and coloured plates. Re-issue of No. 284. Edited by the Rev. James Rhys Kilsby Jones.

DESCRIPTION.—Frontispiece, *Moses;* engraved title; blank, *b;* title; colophon, *Ystrydebwyd ac argraphwyd gan William.Mackenzie, 45 a 47 Heol Howard, Glasgow.,* b; *Enwau . . . Llyfrau,* a; blank, *b; Cofiyfr Teuluaidd,* 2 plates; map, *Canaan;* text (Gen.—Mal.), sigs. 1—108 and *b,* pp. 1—864; map, *Canaan;* title of N.T., dated MDCCCLXXIII.; blank, *b;* frontispiece, *Yr Jachawdwr.;* text (Matt.—Rev.), sigs. 109²—146³ and *b,* pp. 867—1166. Total pp., 1,172.

303.

1873. Testament Newydd, | . . . | Bibl Gymdeithas Americanaidd | Caerefrog Newydd: | . . . | 1873. |

Cr. 8° (32); 161 × 90 mm., 173 × 107 mm.
6⅝₁₆ × 3⁹₁₆ in., 6⅛₁₆ × 4¾ in.; 698 pp.

Welsh-English. Reprint of No. 210a.

304.

1873. Y | Bibl Cyssegr-lan, | . . . | Llundain : | . . . George E. Eyre a William Spottiswoode, | . . . Tros y Bibl Gymdeithas Frytanaidd a Thramor, | . . . | M.DCCC.LXXIII. |

Cr. 8°, on title *Nonpareil 12mo. Marg. Ref.* (32); leather;
160 × 93 mm., 178 × 114 mm.
6⅝₁₆ × 3₁₁ in., 7 × 4½ in.; 952 pp.

Reprint of No. 159.

305.

1873. Y | Bibl Cyssegr-lan, | . . . | Llundain: | . . . George E. Eyre a William Spottiswoode, | . . . Tros y Bibl Gymdeithas Frytanaidd a Thramor, | . . . | M.DCCC.LXXIII. |

Dy. 16°, on title *Pearl 16mo.* (32); 126×84 mm., 137×97 mm.
4¹⁸⁄₁₆×3¹⁶⁄₁₆ in., 5⅜×3¹³⁄₁₆ in; 700 pp.

Reprint of No. 261.

306.

1873. Testament Newydd, | . . . | Bibl Gymdeithas Americanaidd, | Caerefrog Newydd: | . . . | 1873. |

Cr. 8° (32); 161×90 mm., 173×107 mm.
6⁷⁄₁₀×3⁹⁄₁₀ in., 6¹³⁄₁₀×4¼ in.; 698 pp.

Welsh-English. Reprint of No. 210a, *7th Edition* on back of title.

306a.

[1873-6.] Y | Bibl Cyssegr-lan | . . . | Gyda sylwadau eglurhaol ac ymarferol ar bob pennod | gan y | Parch. Thomas Rees, D.D. | Wedi ei addurno a llawer o ddarluniau ar ddur. | Llundain : | Virtue & Co., . . . |

4° (8); double columns, with notes and references between, and commentary at end of chapters and at foot of pages; 255×193 mm., 314×249 mm.
10×7⁹⁄₁₆ in., 12⁶⁄₁₆×9¹³⁄₁₆ in.

Family ed'n, issued between 1873 and 1876, in 10 pts.—9 at 5s., and 1 at 3s. Contains numerous steel engravings.

DESCRIPTION.—Engraved title ; blank, *b;* title, not dated; *Enwau . . . Llyfrau,* etc., *b; At y Darllenydd., a* and *b,* dated *Abertawy, Chwefror 22, 1876; Cyflyfr Teuluol,* etc., 2 plates; text (Gen.—Mal.), sigs. B—7C³ and *b,* pp. 1—1118; title of N.T.; *Enwau . . . Llyfrau,* etc., *b;* text (Matt.—Rev.), sigs. 7C⁴—9I², pp. 1119—1531; *Taflen,* etc., *b.* Total pp., 1,540.

307.

1874. Y | Bibl Cyssegr-lan ; | . . . | Llundain : | Y Gymdeithas er Taenu Gwybodaeth Gristionogol; | . . . |

La. 8° (16); 230×142 mm., 257×163 mm.
9⁷⁄₁₀×5⁷⁄₁₀ in., 10⅛×6⁷⁄₁₆ in.; 1,620 pp.

Reprint of No. 299. Pr. Bk. only dated *1874.*

308.

[1874.] Y Bibl Cysegr-lan, | . . . | gyda | Nodiadau Eglurhaol, | Gan y Parch. Peter Williams, | a'r Parch. Matthew Henry; | a | Sylwadau Arweiniol i bob llyfr, | Gan y Parch. R. T. Howell, | Abertawe. | . . . | Edinburgh: | Cyhoeddwyd gan Thomas C. Jack. | Abertawe: | E. Slater. |

La. 4° (8); double columns, with notes and references between, and commentary at foot of pages; morocco, gilt edges, brass rims and clasps;
290×212 mm., 317×245 mm.
11⁷⁄₁₆×8⅜ in., 12½×9⅝ in.

Family Bible, with numerous coloured plates. Imprint on back of title, *Argraffwyd gan Ballantyne and Co., Llundain ac Edinburgh.* Some copies bear the following imprint on general title ; *Edinburgh: | Cyhoeddwyd gan Thomas C. Jack. | Caerdydd: | N. Berry & Co.* | (See *Y Drysorfa,* 1874, p. 179.)

DESCRIPTION.—Frontispiece, *Moses viewing the Promised Land* ; engraved title; blank, *b;* title; imprint, *b; At y Darllenydd,* signed *Capel yr Arglwyddes Huntingdon, | Abertawe, Mawrth 1669, 1874.* | *R. Thomas Howell.* |, sig. *a;* blank, *b; Llythyr y Parch. Peter Williams at y Darllenydd.,* sig. *a²—b,* pp. iii—iv; *Hanes Bywyd Peter Williams.,* sigs. *a³—b¹* and *b,* pp. v—x; *Hanes Bywyd Matthew Henry.,* sigs. *b²—b⁴,* pp. xi—xv; *Cynnwysiad., b;* text (Gen.— Mal.), sigs. 1—110³ and *b,* pp. 1—878; *Cofrestr y Teulu.,* 2 plates; title of N.T.; blank, *b; Family Portrait Gallery,* 2 plates; text (Matt.—Rev.), sigs. 111—148⁴, pp. 881—1183; blank, *b.* Total pp., 1,202.

309.

1874. Y | Bibl Cyssegr-lan, | . . . | Llundain : | . . . George E. Eyre a W. Spottiswoode, | . . . | M.DCCC.LXXIV. |

16°. Reported. Fuller details unobtainable.

310.

1874. Testament | Newydd | . . . | Llundain: | . . . George E. Eyre a William Spottiswoode, | . . . | Tros y Bibl Gymdeithas Frytanaidd a Thramor, | . . , | M.DCCC.LXXIV. |

Royal 16°, on title *Brevier 16mo.* (32); 132×93 mm., 145×109 mm.
5$\frac{3}{16}$×3$\frac{11}{16}$ in., 5$\frac{11}{16}$×4$\frac{1}{4}$ in.; 396 pp.

Reprint of No. 235. Price 4d.

311.

1874. Testament | Newydd | . . . | Bibl Gymdeithas Americanaidd, | Caerefrog Newydd: | . . . | 1874. |

32°, on title [*Welsh Nonpareil 32mo.*] (16); 106×59 mm., 114×73 mm.
4$\frac{3}{16}$×2$\frac{5}{16}$ in., 4$\frac{1}{2}$×2$\frac{7}{8}$ in.; 412 pp.

Reprint of No. 237, *9th Edition* on back of title.

311a.

1874. The | New Testament, | in Welsh and English. | Testament Newydd, | . . . | Llundain: | . . . George E. Eyre a William Spottiswoode, | . . . | Tros y Bibl Gymdeithas Frytanaidd a Thramor, | . . . | M.DCCC.LXXIV. |

12°, on title *Ruby 24mo.* (32); 112×61 mm., 124×76 mm.
4$\frac{5}{8}$×2$\frac{3}{8}$ in., 4$\frac{5}{8}$×3$\frac{7}{16}$ in.; 614 pp.

Reprint of No. 202a.

312.

1875. Y | Bibl Cyssegr-lan, | . . . | Llundain : | . . . G. E. Eyre a W. Spottiswoode, | . . . | Tros y Bibl Gymdeithas Frytanaidd a Thramor, | . . . | M.DCCC.LXXV. |

Dy. 8°, on title *Smallpica 8vo.* (32); 203×114 mm., 220×138 mm.
8×4$\frac{1}{2}$ in., 8$\frac{5}{8}$×5$\frac{7}{16}$ in.; 1,280 pp.

Reprint of No. 63. Price 3s.

313.

1875. Testament | Newydd | . . . | Llundain: | . . . G. E. Eyre a W. Spottiswoode, | . . . | Tros y Bibl Gymdeithas Frytanaidd a Thramor, | . . . | M.DCCC.LXXV. |

Sm. 4° (16); 162×119 mm., 183×143 mm.
6$\frac{3}{8}$×4$\frac{11}{16}$ in., 7$\frac{3}{16}$×5$\frac{5}{8}$ in.; 608 pp.

Reprint of No. 229, with a copy of No. 291 bound at end.

314.

1875. Testament | Newydd | . . . | Caer Grawnt: | . . . C. J. Clay, . . . | Tros y Bibl Gymdeithas Frytanaidd a Thramor, | . . . | 1875. |

32° (32); 88×55 mm., 100×69 mm.
3$\frac{7}{16}$×2$\frac{3}{16}$ in., 3$\frac{15}{16}$×2$\frac{11}{16}$ in.; iv.+460=464 pp.

Reprint of No. 270.

315.

1875. Testament | Newydd | . . . | Bibl Gymdeithas Americanaidd, Caerefrog Newydd: | . . . | 1875. |

32°, on title [*Welsh Nonpareil 32mo.*] (16); 106×59 mm., 114×73 mm. 4$\frac{3}{16}$×2$\frac{6}{16}$ in., 4$\frac{1}{2}$×2$\frac{7}{8}$ in.; 412 pp.

Reprint of No. 237, 10th Edition on back of title.

315a.

[1876.] Y Bibl Cysegr-lan, | . . . | gyda | Nodiadau Eglurhaol, | Gan y Parch. Peter Williams, | a'r | Parch. Matthew Henry; | a | Sylwadau Arweiniol i bob llyfr, | Gan y Parch. R. T. Howell, | Abertawe. | . . . | Edinburgh : | Thomas C. Jack, | Grange Publishing Works. |

La. 4° (8); mottled calf; 290×212 mm., 320×247 mm. 11$\frac{7}{16}$×8$\frac{3}{8}$ in., 12$\frac{9}{16}$×9$\frac{3}{4}$ in.; xvi.+1,184=1,200 pp.

Reprint of No. 309, omitting editor's preface.

816.

1876. Y | Bibl Cyssegr-lan, | . . . | Rhydychen : | . . . Argraphdy y Brifysgol, | Tros y Fibl Gymdeithas Frytanaidd a Thramor, | . . . | M.DCCC.LXXVI. | Cum Privilegio. |

La. 8°, on title *Sm. Pica 8vo. Gyda Chyfeir.*

Reprint of No. 280. N.T. dated *1876*. Price 7s. 6d. Copy seen wanting title and all to Gen. iv. 25.

817.

1876. Y | Bibl Cyssegr-lan, | . . . | Llundain: | . . . George E. Eyre a William Spottiswoode, | . . . | Tros y Bibl Gymdeithas Frytanaidd a Thramor, | . . . | M.DCCC.LXXVI. |

16mo. Reported. Fuller details unobtainable.

818.

1876. Y | Bibl Cyssegr-lan : | . . . | Llundain : | . . . G. E. Eyre a W. Spottiswoode, | . . . | 1876. |

12mo. Reported. Fuller details unobtainable.

819.

1876. Testament | Newydd | . . . | Llundain : | . . . G. E. Eyre a W. Spottiswoode, | . . . | Tros y Bibl Gymdeithas Frytanaidd a Thramor, | . . . | M.DCCC.LXXVI. |

La 8°. Reported. Fuller details unobtainable.

820.

1876. Testament | Newydd | . . . | Llundain: | . . . George E. Eyre a William Spottiswoode, | . . . | Tros y Bibl Gymdeithas Frytanaidd a Thramor, | . . . M.DCCC.LXXVI. |

12mo. Reported. Fuller details unobtainable.

821.

1876. The | New Testament | in Welsh and English. | Testament Newydd, | . . . | Llundain : | . . . George E. Eyre a William Spottiswoode, | . . . | Tros y Bibl Gymdeithas Frytanaidd a Thramor, | . . . M.DCCC.LXXVI. |

12°, on title *Ruby 24mo*. (32); 112×61 mm., 123×74 mm.
4⅜×2⅝ in., 4¹¹⁄₁₆×2⅞ in.; 614 pp.

Reprint of No. 202a.

322.

[*Circa* **1876.**] Y | Testament Newydd, | gyda chyfeiriadau, | Cyssondeb yr Efengylau, | Mynegai Daearyddol, | ynghydag amrywiol dablau. | . . . | Wrexham: | . . . R. Hughes a'i Fab. |

32° (32); cloth and leather, with clasp; 84×46 mm., 95×57 mm.
3⁶⁄₁₆×1¹⅜ in., 3¾×2¼ in.

Not dated. Reprint of No. 136, called *Y Testament Bach Cyfeiriadol.*

Sigs., A—Pp¹⁶. Total pp. (not numbered), 480.

323.

1876. Llyfr | y | Diarhebion. | Llundain: | . . . G. E. Eyre a W. Spottiswoode, | . . . | Tros y Bibl Gymdeithas Frytanaidd a Thramor, | . . .M.DCCC.LXXVI. |

32°, on title *Brevier 32mo*. (64); 100×58 mm., 114×75 mm.
3¹⅜×2¼ in., 4½×2¹¹⁄₁₆ in.; 64 pp.

324.

1877. Y | Bibl Cyssegr-lan, | . . . | Llundain: | . . . George E. Eyre a William Spottiswoode, | . . . | Tros y Bibl Gymdeithas Frytanaidd a Thramor, | . . . | M.DCCC.LXXVII. |

4°, on title *Pica Medium 4to. Marg. Ref.* (16); 250×188 mm., 285×232 mm.
9⅞×7¾ in., 11¼×9¼ in.; 1,156 pp.

Reprint of No. 158.

326.

1877. Y | Bibl Cyssegr-lan, | . . . | Llundain: | . . . G. E. Eyre a W. Spottiswoode, | Tros y Bibl Gymdeithas Frytanaidd a Thramor, | . . . | M.DCCC.LXXVII. |

Dy. 8°, on title *Smallpica 8vo.* (32); 203×114 mm., 222×140 mm.
8×4½ in., 8¾×5½ in.; 1,280 pp.

Reprint of No. 63. Price 3s. N.T. also issued separately.

327.

1877. Y | Bibl Cyssegr-lan, | . . . | Llundain: | . . . George E. Eyre a William Spottiswoode, | . . . | Tros y Bibl Gymdeithas Frytanaidd a Thramor, | . . . | M.DCCC.LXXVII. |

Cr. 8°, on title *Nonpareil Demy 12mo. Marg. Refs.* (32); leather, with brass rims and clasp; 160×93 mm., 176×114 mm.
6⁶⁄₁₆×3¹¹⁄₁₆ in., 6¹³⁄₁₆×4½ in.; 952 pp.

Reprint of No. 159.

328.

1877. Bibl yr Athraw, | . . . | gyda | Chyfeiriadau a Mynegair: | . . . | Cyhoeddedig gan | Hughes a'i Fab, | . . . Wrexham. | Argraphedig gan George E. Eyre a William Spottiswoode, | . . . | M.DCCC.LXXVII. |

Cr. 8° (32); leather, with brass clasp; 160×93 mm., 176×114 mm.
$6\frac{5}{16}\times3\frac{11}{16}$ in., $6\frac{15}{16}\times4\frac{1}{2}$ in.

Re-issue of No. 328, with Peter Williams's concordance, other extra matter, and 12 coloured maps. Imprint on last page of extra matter, *Llundain: argraffwyd gan G. E. Eyre a W. Spottiswoode.*

DESCRIPTION.—General title; blank; text (Gen.—Mal.), sigs. A^3—Z^4, pp. 5—711; blank, *b;* title of N.T. (not dated); blank, *b;* text (Matt.—Rev.), sigs. Z^6—Gg^{12} and *b*, pp. 713—952; title (same as general title); blank, *b; Rhagdraith i'r Attodiad.*, signed *Y Golygydd.*, dated *Rhagfyr, 1876., a; Cynnwysiad., b; Mynegair Ysgrythyrol.*, sigs. A—H^{12} and *b*, pp. 1—248; *Dangoseg . . . o enwau priodol*, etc., *b*—I^6, pp. 248—267; other extra matter, sigs. I^6—K^3 and *b*, pp. 267—294; 12 coloured maps. Total pp., 952+iv.+294=1,250.

329.

1877. Testament | Newydd | . . . | Llundain: | . . . George E. Eyre a William Spottiswoode, | . . . | Tros y Bibl Gymdeithas Frytanaidd a Thramor, | . . . | M.DCCC.LXXVII. |

Royal 16°, on title *Brevier square 16mo.* (32); 132×93 mm., 146×111 mm.
$5\frac{3}{16}\times3\frac{11}{16}$ in., $5\frac{3}{4}\times4\frac{5}{16}$ in.; 396 pp.

Reprint of No. 235. Price 4d.

330.

[1878.] Bibl | yr | Addoliad Teuluaidd; | . . . Gyd a | Sylwadau eglurhaol | y | Parch. Peter Williams | . . . | Nodiadau ac Eglur-iadau gan y | Parch. Matthew Henry, y Parch. Albert Barnes, ac eraill; | . . . | Arweiniad i bob un o'r Llyfrau Sanctaidd; a chyfeir-iadau Ysgrythyrol. | . . . | Dan olygiad Gweirydd ap Rhys. | . . . | London: | John G. Murdoch, | 41, Castle Street, Holborn. |

4° (8); double columns, with notes and references between, and commentary at foot; 278×201 mm., 330×247 mm.
$10\frac{15}{16}\times7\frac{15}{16}$ in., $13\times9\frac{11}{16}$ in.

Family Bible, with coloured illustrations. Edited by Robert John Pryse ("*Gweirydd ap Rhys*"). Not dated.

DESCRIPTION.—Frontispiece, the Lord's Prayer in fourteen languages; engraved title (coloured); blank, *b;* title; blank, *b; Annerchiad y Detholydd at ei Gydwladwyr., a;* blank, *b; Llythyr y Cyhoeddwr at y Darllenydd.*, pp. v—vi; *Hanes Bywyd . . . Peter Williams.*, pp. 7—xii; *Hanes Bywyd Matthew Henry.*, pp. 13—xvii; *Enwau . . . Llyfrau*, etc., *b; Cynhwysiad*, pp. xix—xxxi; *Crynhodeb*, etc., *b; Family Register*, etc., 4 plates; text (Gen.—Mal.), sigs. A—3K and *b*, pp. 1—882; title of N.T.; blank, *b;* text (Matt.—Rev.), sigs. $3K^3$—$4F^4$ and *b;* pp. 885—1192. Total pp., xxxii.+1,192=1,224.

331.

1879. Y | Bibl Cyssegr-lan, | . . . | Rhydychen: | . . . Argraphdy y Brifysgol, | Tros y Bibl Gymdeithas Frytanaidd a Thramor, | . . . | M.DCCC.LXXIX. |

12mo. Reported. Fuller details unobtainable.

332.

1880. Y | Bibl Cyssegr-lan, | . . . | Llundain: George E. Eyre a William Spottiswoode, | . . . | Tros y Bibl Gymdeithas Frytanaidd a Thramor, | . . . | M.DCCC.LXXX. |

Cr. 8°, on title *Nonpareil 16mo.* (32); 146×89 mm., 158×105 mm.
5⅞×3½ in., 6¼×4⅛ in.; 822 pp.
Reprint of No. 266. Price 10d.

332a.

[*Circa* **1880.**] Y | Bibl Cyssegr-lan; | . . . | Llundain: | . . . Y Gymdeithas er Taenu Gwybodaeth Gristionogol; | . . . |

Foolscap 8° (16); double columns, with notes and references on margins; cloth;
141×87 mm., 158×102 mm.
5⁹⁄₁₆×3⁷⁄₁₆ in., 6⁵⁄₁₆×4 in.

Not dated. Imprint on back of title, *Argraphedig gan John Childs a'i Fab.* Collect inside front cover.

DESCRIPTION.—Title; imprint, *b; Enwau . . . Llyfrau*, etc., *a;* blank, *b;* text (Gen.—Mal.), sigs. 1—51⁷ and *b;* title of N.T.; blank, *b;* text (Matt.—Rev.), sigs. 52—68⁸; imprint, *b.* Total pp. (not numbered), 1,088.

333.

1880. Bibl Cyssegr-lan, | . . . | Rhydychen: | . . . Argraphdy y Brifysgol, | Tros y Bibl Gymdeithas Frytanaidd a Thramor, | . . . | M.DCCC.LXXX. |

Cr. 8°, on title *Nonp. 12mo. Refs.* (32); double columns; leather;
162×96 mm., 179×113 mm.
6⅜×3¾ in., 7×4⁷⁄₁₆ in.; 918 pp.

333a.

1880. Testament Newydd | . . . | Rhydychen: | . . . Argraphdy y Brifysgol, | Tros y Gymdeithas er Taenu Gwybodaeth Gristionogol. | . . . | 1880. | Cum Privilegio. |

Sm. 4° (16); 162×119 mm., 183×142 mm.
6⅜×4¹¹⁄₁₆ in., 7⁷⁄₁₆×5⁷⁄₁₆ in.; 608 pp. (not numbered).
Reprint of No. 229.

334.

[**1880.**] Y | Testament Daearyddol; | . . . | Gan y Parch. T. Roberts. | Trydydd Argraffiad. | Wrexham: | . . . Hughes a'i Fab. |

12° (16); 111×63 mm., 119×75 mm.
4⅜×2½ in., 4¹¹⁄₁₆×2¹⁵⁄₁₆ in.; 432 pp, (not numbered).

Not dated. Fifth ed'n, augmented, called third on title, of No. 189. 4 maps.

335.

[**1880.**] Yr Efengyl | yn ol | Sant Marc | Gyd ag Esboniad Ymarferol | gan y | . . . W. Walsham How, D.D. | . . . | Cyfieithwyd gan y | Parch. Ellis Roberts, | Periglor Llangwm, Sir Ddinbych. | Cyhoeddwyd dan gyfarwyddid Pwyllgor y Traethodau. | Llundain: Cymdeithas er Lledaenu Gwybodaeth Gristionogol: | . . . | ·

Cr. 8° (16); lines across the page, with marginal references, and commentary at foot; 162×90 mm., 180×120 mm.
6⅜×3⁹⁄₁₆ in., 7¹⁄₁₆×4¾ in.

Translator better known to Welshmen as *Elis Wyn o Wyrfai.*

DESCRIPTION.—Title; blank, *b;* introduction, pp. 3—4 (not numbered); text, pp. 5—114 (not numbered).

336.

1881. Y | Bibl Cyssegr-lan | . . . | Llundain: | . . . George E. Eyre a William Spottiswoode, | . . . | Tros y Bibl Gymdeithas Frytanaidd a Thramor, | . . . | M.DCCC.LXXXI. |

12°, on title *Diamond 24mo. Marg. Ref.* (32); double columns; leather;
125×85 mm., 139×103 mm.
$4\frac{7}{8}\times3\frac{6}{16}$ in., $5\frac{7}{16}\times4\frac{1}{16}$ in.; 1,010 pp.

N.T. also issued separately.

337.

1881. Testament | Newydd | . . . | Llundain: | . . . George E. Eyre a William Spottiswoode, | . . . | Tros y Bibl Gymdeithas Frytanaidd a Thramor, | . . . | M.DCCC.LXXXI. |

Royal 16°, on title *Brevier square 16mo.* (32); 133×95 mm., 146×111 mm.
$5\frac{1}{4}\times3\frac{3}{4}$ in., $5\frac{3}{4}\times4\frac{5}{16}$ in.; 396 pp.

Reprint of No. 235. Price 4d.

337a.

[1881.] Yr Oraclau Bywiol: | . . . | Gan John Williams, | Gyda Rhaglithiau ac Attodiad, gan | Alexander Campbell. | Ail Argraffiad, | Dan olygiad Owen Davies, Caernarvon, | gyda rhagarweiniad. | Caernarvon: | . . . H. Humphreys, | . . . |

Cr. 8° (16); lines across the page; cloth; 144×80 mm., 168×106 mm.
$5\frac{11}{16}\times3\frac{1}{8}$ in., $6\frac{5}{8}\times4\frac{3}{16}$ in.

Reprint of No. 164, edited, with an introduction, by the Rev. Owen Davies, D.D., Carnarvon. Price 5s.

DESCRIPTION.—Portrait, *Parch. J. Williams,* | *o'r Drefnewydd.* | ; title, not dated; blank, *b*; *Rhagarweiniad i'r ail argraffiad.* | *Braslun o hanes bywyd y Parch. J. Williams.* | , signed *Caernarfon, Hydref 29, 1881, Owen Davies.* | , sigs. A^2—A^4 and *b*, pp. 3—8; *Nodiadau Rhaglithiol.*, sigs. A^5—B and *b*, pp. 9—18; *Rhaglith,* etc., sigs. B^2—D^8 and *b*, pp. 19—64; text, sigs. E—2I and *b*, pp. 65—530; *Attodiad.*, sigs. $2I^2$—$2M^3$ and *b*, pp. 531—582; *Dangoseg i'r geiriau ansathredig,* etc., sigs. $2M^4$ and *b*, pp. 583—584; *Dangoseg i gynnwysiad y gwaith.*, sigs. $2M^5$ and *b*, pp. 585—586; advertisements, 6 pp. Total pp., 586.

338.

1881. Testament Newydd, | . . . | Bibl Gymdeithas Americanaidd, | Caerefrog Newydd: | . . . | 1881. |

Cr. 8° (32); 161×90 mm., 173×107 mm.
$6\frac{5}{16}\times3\frac{9}{16}$ in., $6\frac{13}{16}\times4\frac{1}{4}$ in.; 698 pp.

Welsh-English. Reprint of No. 210a, *8th edition* on back of title.

338a.

1881. Y | Proffwydi Byrion, | mewn | Alleiriad, | gyda | Sylwadau ar y testun, | ynghyd ag | Amryw ddarlleniadau ar ymyl y ddalen o'r tri hen gyfieithad, y LXX, y Syriaeg, a'r Vulgate, | Gan John Davies, | Ietwen. | Llandilo: | . . . D. W. a G. Jones, . . . | 1881. |

La. 8° (8); lines across the page in verse, with readings on margin, and commentary at foot in double columns; cloth; 202×128 mm., 238×161 mm.
$7\frac{15}{16}\times5\frac{1}{16}$ in., $9\frac{3}{8}\times6\frac{5}{16}$ in.

New version from Hebrew of Minor Prophets.

DESCRIPTION.—Title; blank, *b*; *At y Darllenydd.*, sigs. A^2—A^3 and *b*, pp. iv—vi; text (Hos.—Mal.), sigs. B—DD^3 and *b*, pp. 1—206; *Taflen Amseryddol.*, sigs. DD^4—FF^2, pp. 207—219; blank, *b*. Total pp., vi+220=226.

339.

1882. Y | Bibl Cyssegr-lan, | . . . | Rhydychen: | . . . Argraphdy y
Brifysgol, | . . . | Tros y Bibl Gymdeithas Frytanaidd a Thramor,
| . . . | M.DCCC.LXXXII. |

8°. Reported. Fuller details unobtainable.

340.

1882. Y | Bibl Cyssegr-lan, | . . . | Bibl Gymdeithas Americanaidd,
Caerefrog Newydd : | . . . | 1882. |

Cr. 8°, on title *Welsh Nonpareil Ref.*, 12mo. (16); 163×97 mm., 187×118 mm.
6⁷⁄₁₆×3¹⁸⁄₁₆ in., 7⅜×4⅝ in.; 940 pp.

Reprint of No. 232, *5th Edition* on p. 3.

340a.

1882. Testament | Newydd | . . . | Llundain: | . . . | G. E. Eyre
a W. Spottiswoode, | . . . | Tros y Bibl Gymdeithas Frytanaidd
a Thramor, | . . . | M.DCCC.LXXXII. |

Sm. 4° (16); 162×119 mm., 181×143 mm.
6⅜×4¹⁄₁₆ in., 7⅛×5⅝ in.; 698 pp. (not numbered).

Reprint of No. 229.

341.

1882. Testament | Newydd | . . . | Caer Grawnt: | . . . C. J. Clay,
| Tros y Bibl Gymdeithas Frytanaidd a Thramor, | . . . | 1882. |

32° (32); 88×55 mm., 100×70 mm.
3⁷⁄₁₆×2³⁄₁₆ in., 3¹⁶⁄₁₆×2¾ in.; iv.+460=464 pp.

Reprint of No. 270.

342.

1882. Y | Testament Newydd | Diwygiedig: | neu, | y cyfnewidiadau
a gynnwysir yn yr adolygiad | o'r Testament Newydd Saesneg, |
yr hwn a gyhoeddwyd yn 1881. | Wedi ei gyfieithu i'r Gymraeg, |
gan | Y Parch. John Ogwen Jones, B.A., | Rhyl. | Dinbych : | . . .
Thomas Gee. | MDCCCLXXXII. |

Cr. 8° (8 and 16); double columns, with readings between verses; cloth;
155×91 mm., 173×113 mm.
6⅛×3¹⁄₁₆ in., 6¹³⁄₁₆×4⁷⁄₁₆ in.

Translation of the new readings in the English Revised Version.

DESCRIPTION.—Title; blank, b; *Rhagymadrodd.*, sigs. A²—A⁴, pp. 3—7; *Eglurhad.*,
b; text, sigs. B—L⁶ and b, pp. 9—162.

343.

1882. Testament | Newydd | . . . | Bibl Gymdeithas Americanaidd,
Caerefrog Newydd: | . . . | 1882. |

32°, on title [*Welsh Nonpareil 32mo.*] (16); 106×59 mm., 114×73 mm.
4³⁄₁₆×2⁴⁄₁₆ in., 4½×2⅞ in.; 412 pp.

Reprint of No. 237, *11th Edition* on back of title.

343a.

1883. Y | Bibl Cyssegr-lan, | . . . | Rhydychen: | . . . Argraphdy y Brifysgol, | . . . | Tros y Bibl Gymdeithas Frytanaidd a Thramor, | . . . M.DCCC.LXXXIII. |

Cr. 8°, on title *Nonp. 12mo. Refs.* (32); double columns; leather;
162×96 mm., 179×115 mm.
6⅝×3¹¹⁄₁₆ in., 7×4½ in.; 918 pp.

344.

1883. Testament | Newydd | . . . | Caer Grawnt: | . . . C. J. Clay, | . . . | Tros y Bibl Gymdeithas Frytanaidd a Thramor, | . . . | 1883. |

32° (32); 88×55 mm., 99×70 mm.
3¹⁄₁₆×2⁷⁄₁₆ in., 3⅞×2¾ in.; iv.+460=464 pp.

Reprint of No. 270.

344a.

1884. Y | Bibl Cyssegr-lan, | . . . | Llundain : | . . . Eyre a Spottiswoode, | . . . | Tros y Bibl Gymdeithas Frytanaidd a Thramor. | . . . | M.DCCC.LXXXIV. |

Dy. 8°, on title *Smallpica 8vo.* (32); 203×114 mm., 222×140 mm.
8×4½ in., 8¾×5½ in.; 1,280 pp.

Reprint of No. 63. Price 2s. 6d.

345.

1885. Testament | Newydd | . . . | Llundain: | . . . George E. Eyre a William Spottiswoode, | . . . | Tros y Bibl Gymdeithas Frytanaidd a Thramor, | . . . | M.DCCC.LXXXV. |

12°, on title *Ruby 24mo.* (32); double columns; limp cloth;
125×73 mm., 138×88 mm.
4¹¹⁄₁₆×2⅞ in., 5⁷⁄₁₆×3⅞ in.; 256 pp.; price 1d.

345a.

1885. Testament | Newydd | . . . | Rhydychen: | . . . Argraphdy y Brifysgol. | Tros y Bibl Gymdeithas Frytanaidd a Thramor, | . . . | M.DCCC.LXXXV. |

24°. Reported. Fuller details unobtainable.

346.

1885. Testament Newydd, | . . . | Bibl Gymdeithas Americanaidd, | Caerefrog Newydd: | . . . | 1885. |

Cr. 8° (32); 161×90 mm., 173×107 mm.
6¹⁄₁₆×3¹⁄₁₆ in., 6¹³⁄₁₆×4¼ in.; 698 pp.

Welsh-English. Reprint of No. 210a, *9th edition* on back of title.

346a.

1887. Testament | Newydd | . . . | Llundain: | . . . George E. Eyre a William Spottiswoode, | . . . | Tros y Bibl Gymdeithas Frytanaidd a Thramor, | . . . | M.DCCC.LXXXVII. |

24°. Reported. Fuller details unobtainable.

347.

1887. Testament Newydd | . . . | Llundain: | Y Feibl Gymdeithas Frytanaidd a Thramor, | . . . | Argraphedig yn Argraphdy y Brifysgol, Rhydychen. | Pris Un Geiniog. | 1887. | Cum Privilegio. |

12°, on title *Ruby 24mo.* (32); 125 × 73 mm., 137 × 86 mm.
$4\frac{15}{16}$ × $2\frac{7}{8}$ in., $5\frac{3}{8}$ × $3\frac{3}{8}$ in.; 256 pp., price 1d.

Reprint of No. 345*a*.

348.

[1887.] Y | Testament Daearyddol: | . . . | Gan y Parch. T. Roberts. | Wedi ei olygu a'i helaethu | Gan y Parch. John Peter (Ioan Pedr), | Bala. | Argraffiad Newydd a Diwygiedig. | Wrexham: | . . . Hughes and Son. |

Foolscap 8° (16); cloth and leather; 133 × 77 mm., 160 × 101 mm.
$5\frac{1}{4}$ × $3\frac{1}{16}$ in., $6\frac{5}{16}$ × 4 in.

Sixth ed'n, revised and enlarged, of No. 189, with 4 maps. Price, 3s. 6d. and 5s.

DESCRIPTION.—Map; title, not dated; blank, *b*; *Rhagymadrodd.*, etc., dated *Mai, 1887.*, *a*—*b*, pp. iii.—iv.; text, sigs. A—PP[8] and *b*, pp. 5—612. Total pp., iv.+612=616.

349.

[1887.] Yr Oraclau Bywiol: | . . . | Gan John Williams, | Gyda Rhaglithiau ac Attodiad, gan | Alexander Campbell. | Ail Argraffiad, | Dan olygiad Owen Davies, Caernarfon, | gyda rhagarweiniad. | Trydydd argraffiad. | Caernarfon: | . . . H. Humphreys, | . . . |

Cr. 8° (16); 144 × 80 mm., 163 × 106 mm.
$5\frac{11}{16}$ × $3\frac{1}{8}$ in., $6\frac{7}{16}$ × $4\frac{3}{16}$ in.; 686 pp.

Re-issue of No. 338, and reprint of No. 164. Price 3s. 6d.

350.

1888–7. Y | Bibl Cyssegr-lan, | . . . | Rhydychen: | . . . Argraphdy y Brifysgol, | Tros y Bibl Gymdeithas Frytanaidd a Thramor, | . . . | M.DCCC.LXXXVIII. |

Cr. 8°, on title *Nonp. 12mo. Refs.* (32); leather, with brass rims and clasp;
162 × 96 mm., 179 × 115 mm.
$6\frac{3}{8}$ × $3\frac{11}{16}$ in., 7 × $4\frac{1}{2}$ in.; 918 pp.

Reprint of No. 344. N.T. title dated *1887*.

351.

1888. Y | Bibl Cyssegr-lan, | . . . | Rhydychen: | . . . Argraphdy y Brifysgol, | Tros y Bibl Gymdeithas Frytanaidd a Thramor, | . . . | M.DCCC.LXXXVIII. |

8°. Reported. Fuller details unobtainable.

352.

1888. Testament Newydd | . . . | Llundain: | Y Feibl Gymdeithas Frytanaidd a Thramor, | . . . Argraphdy y Brifysgol, Rhydychen. | Pris Un Geiniog. | 1888. | Cum Privilegio. |

12°, on title *Ruby 24mo.* (32); 125 × 73 mm., 137 × 86 mm.
$4\frac{15}{16}$ × $2\frac{7}{8}$ in., $5\frac{3}{8}$ × $3\frac{3}{8}$ in.; 256 pp.; price 1d.

Reprint of No. 345*a*.

353.

[1888.] Testament yr Efrydydd: | . . . | Yn cynwys | y Cyfnewidiadau, mewn darlleniadau a chyfieithiadau, a fab- | wysiadwyd yn y Cyfieithiad Diwygiedig i'r Saesonaeg, | wedi eu corphori yn y testyn, | ac hefyd | y cyfieithiadau ar ymyl y dalenau: | yn nghyd a | Chasgliad helaeth o gyfieithiadau ereill ar destynau pwysig | gan y prif feirniaid, a nodiadau beirniadol er | rhoddi rheswm am y cyfnewidiadau. | At yr hyn yr ychwanegwyd | Rhag-Draethawd, yn cynwys Hanes y Prif Ysgriflyfrau, a'r Argraffiadau o'r Testyn | Gwreiddiol, yn nghyda'r Cyfieithiadau i'r Gymraeg, &c. | Wedi eu casglu a'u cyfieithu gan | Y Parch. Owen Williams, | Gweinidog yr Efengyl. | Caernarfon: | . . . H. Humphreys, | . . . |

Cr. 8° (16); half persian; 151×92 mm., 193×129 mm.
$5\frac{15}{16}\times3\frac{5}{8}$ in., $7\frac{5}{8}\times5\frac{1}{8}$ in.; 24+344=368 pp.

Ed'n of N.T. embodying the readings of the English Revised Version and others. Title not dated. Preface signed, *Pant-teg,* | *Tregarth, ger Bangor,* | *Tachwedd 3ydd, 1888.* |

354.

1888. The Book of Job | Translated by | William Morgan, D.D. | Oxford | J. G. Evans, . . . | London | Henry Frowde, . . . | 1888 |

Foolscap 8° (16); lines across the page; vellum; 105×57 mm., 173×113 mm.
$4\frac{1}{8}\times2\frac{1}{4}$ in., $6\frac{13}{16}\times4\frac{7}{16}$ in.

Reprint of the Book of Job as in No. 6. Edited by John Gwenogvryn Evans, M.A., Litt. D.

DESCRIPTION.—Half title, *Welsh Classics for the People* | *Edited by* | *J. Gwenogvryn Evans, M.A.* | *Llyvyr Iob* | *Cyfieithad Dr. Morgan* | *1588* | ; colophon, *b;* title; colophon, *b;* facsimile page; blank, *b;* text, sigs. B—H², pp. 1—99; *Editor's note.*, *b;* advertisements, 10 pp. Total pp., 106.

355.

1889. Y | Bibl Cyssegr-lan, | . . . | Y Gymdeithas er Taenu Gwybodaeth Gristionogol, | M.DCCC.LXXXIX. |

12°. Reported. Fuller details unobtainable.

356.

1889. Testament | Newydd | . . . | Llundain : | . . . | M.DCCC.LXXXIX. |

Large 8°. Reported. Fuller details unobtainable.

357.

1889. Testament | Newydd | . . . | Bibl Gymdeithas Americanaidd, | Caerefrog Newydd, | . . . | 1889. |

32°, on title [*Welsh Nonparcil 32mo.*] (16); 106×59 mm., 120×78 mm.
$4\frac{3}{16}\times2\frac{5}{16}$ in., $4\frac{11}{16}\times3\frac{1}{16}$ in.; 412 pp.

Reprint of No. 237.

358.

1890. Testament | Newydd | . . . | Caer Grawnt: | . . . C. J. Clay, | Tros y Bibl Gymdeithas Frytanaidd a Thramor, | . . . | 1890. |

32° (32); 88×55 mm., 99×68 mm.

$3\frac{7}{16}×2\frac{3}{16}$ in., $3\frac{13}{16}×2\frac{11}{16}$ in.; iv.+460=464 pp.

Reprint of No. 270.

359.

1890. [N.T. Oxford.]

12°. Reported. Fuller details unobtainable.

359a.

1890. Llyfr Cyntaf Moses, | yr hwn a elwir | Genesis. | Rhydychen: | . . . Argraphdy y Brifysgol, | Tros y Bibl Gymdeithas Frytanaidd a Thramor. | . . . | M.DCCC.XC. | Cum Privilegio. |

32°, on title *Brevier 32mo.*; boards; 101×57 mm., 114×72 mm.

4×2¼ in., $4\frac{1}{2}×2\frac{13}{16}$ in.; 160 pp.

360.

1891. Y | Bibl Cyssegr-lan, | . . . | Bibl Gymdeithas Americanaidd, | Caerefrog Newydd: | . . . | 1891. |

Cr. 8°, on title *Welsh Nonpareil Ref., 12mo.* (16);

163×97 mm., 186×119 mm.

$6\frac{7}{16}×3\frac{13}{16}$ in., $7\frac{5}{16}×4\frac{11}{16}$ in.; 940 pp.

Reprint of No. 232, *7th Edition* on p. 3.

361.

1892. Ail Lyfr Moses, | yr hwn a elwir | Exodus. | Rhydychen: | . . . Argraphdy y Brifysgol, | Tros y Bibl Gymdeithas Frytanaidd a Thramor, | . . . | M.DCCC.XCII. | Cum Privilegio. |

32°, on title *Brevier 32mo.;* boards; 101×57 mm., 114×72 mm.

4×2¼ in., $4\frac{1}{2}×2\frac{13}{16}$ in.; 132 pp.

362.

1893. Yr | Efengyl | yn ol | Sant Luc. | Bibl Gymdeithas Americanaidd, | Caerefrog Newydd : | . . . | 1893. | (Welsh Luke.) 5,000 Printed.

12° (16); cloth; 106×59 mm., 120×79 mm.

$4\frac{3}{16}×2\frac{5}{16}$ in., $4\frac{3}{4}×3\frac{1}{8}$ in.; 60 pp.

Re-issue of pp. 88—144 of No. 237. Front cover stamped, *Columbian* | *Exposition* | *Holy* | *Scripture* | *Souvenir* | *Edition* | .

363.

1894-3. Y | Bibl Cyssegr-lan: | . . . | Rhydychen: | Argraphdy y Brifysgol, | Tros y Bibl Gymdeithas Frytanaidd a Thramor, | . . . | M.DCCC.XCIV.

12°. Title of N.T. dated *1893.* Reported. Fuller details unobtainable.

364.

1894. Y | Bibl Cyssegr-lan, | . . . | Rhydychen: | . . . Argraphdy y Brifysgol, | Tros y Fibl Gymdeithas Frytanaidd a Thramor, | . . . | M.DCCC.XCIV. | Cum Privilegio. |

La. 8°, on title *Sm. Pica 8vo. Gydâ Chyfeir.* (24);

233×145 mm., 256×173 mm.

$9\frac{3}{16}×5\frac{11}{16}$ in., $10\frac{1}{16}×6\frac{13}{16}$ in.; iv.+1,180=1,184 pp.

Reprint of No. 280.

365.

1894. Y | Testament Newydd | Newly Translated | from the readings adopted by the revisers of the | Authorized Version | By Thomas Briscoe, D.D. | . . . | Bangor | Jarvis & Foster, | MDCCCXCIV. |

Cr. 8° (16); lines across the page; no chapter-contents; cloth;
146×85 mm., 181×121 mm.
$5\frac{3}{4}\times3\frac{5}{16}$ in., $7\frac{1}{8}\times4\frac{3}{4}$ in.; x.+462=472 pp.

366.

1894. Testament | Newydd | . . . | Bibl Gymdeithas Americanaidd, | Caerefrog Newydd | . . . | 1894. |

32°, on title [*Welsh Nonpareil 32mo.*] (16); 106×59 mm., 120×78 mm.
$4\frac{3}{16}\times2\frac{5}{16}$ in., $4\frac{11}{16}\times3\frac{1}{16}$ in.; 412 pp.

Reprint of No. 237. *56,000 Printed* appears on p. 2.

367.

1894. Cyfieithiad Newydd | o'r | Testament Newydd; | wedi ei wneuthur o'r testyn mwyaf pur, yn ol y | beirniaid goreu, ac wedi ei gymharu yn ofalus | a'r cyfieithiad Cymraeg arferedig. | Ychwanegir y gwahanol ddarlleniadau ynghyd a'r | prif awdurdodau drostynt; hefyd, nodiadau | beirniadol ac esboniadol. Rhagflaenir | yr oll gan ddeg o bennodau | rhag-arweiniol. | Gan | Y Parch. W. Edwards, B.A., D.D., | . . . Caerdydd. | Cyfrol I. | . . . | Jenkyn Howell, Aberdâr, a Hughes a'i Fab, Pontypŵl. | MDCCCXCIV. |

Cr. 8° (16); lines across the page; cloth; 151×94 mm., 183×120 mm.
$5\frac{15}{16}\times3\frac{11}{16}$ in., $7\frac{3}{16}\times4\frac{3}{4}$ in.

New version from the Greek, etc.

DESCRIPTION.—Title; blank, *b; Gair at y Darllenydd.*, *a; Cynwysiad.*, *b;* ten preliminary chapters, sigs. A—E and *b*, pp. 1—50; *Talfyriadau*, etc., sig. E[2]; blank, *b;* text (Matt.—John), sigs. E[3]—H2[7], pp. 53—509. Total pp., iv.+510=514.

368.

[1895.] Bibl | yr | Addoliad Teuluaidd; | . . . | gyd a | Sylwadau Eglurhaol | y | Parch. Peter Williams | . . . | Dan olygiad Gweirydd ap Rhys. | Jones & Jones, | Hannah Street, Porth. |

4° (16); morocco, gilt, with brass corners and clasps; 285×207 mm., 317×244 mm.
$11\frac{3}{16}\times8\frac{1}{8}$ in., $12\frac{1}{2}\times9\frac{9}{16}$ in.

Re-issue, with new title, not dated, of No. 331. 8,000 copies sold in the colliery districts of South Wales up to 1904.

DESCRIPTION.—Frontispiece, *Christ blessing little Children.;* engraved title (coloured); blank, *b;* title; blank, *b; Llythyr y Cyhoeddwr at y Darllenydd.*, signed *Peter Williams.*, pp. v—vi; *Hanes Bywyd . . . Peter Williams.*, pp. vii—xii; *Hanes Bywyd Matthew Henry.*, pp. xiii—xvii; *Enwau . . . Llyfrau*, etc., *b; Cynhwysiad*, sigs. *b*—*b*[7], pp. xx—xxxi; *Grynhodeb*, etc., *b; Family Register*, etc., 4 plates; text (Gen.—Mal.), sigs. A—3K and *b*, pp. 1—882; coloured plate, *The Lord's Prayer in fourteen languages;* title of N.T.; blank, *b;* text (Matt.—Rev.), sigs. 3K[3]—4F[4] and *b*, pp. 885—1192. Total pp., xxxii+1,192=1,224.

369.

1895. Testament | Newydd | . . . | Caer Grawnt: | . . . J. & C. F. Clay, | Tros y Bibl Gymdeithas Frytanaidd a Thramor, | . . . | 1895. |

32° (32); 88×55 mm., 100×68 mm.
$3\frac{7}{16}\times2\frac{3}{16}$ in., $3\frac{15}{16}\times2\frac{11}{16}$ in.; iv.+460=464 pp.

Reprint of No. 270.

370.

1896. Psalmau Dafydd | O'r un cyfieithiad a'r Beibl Cyffredin. | The Psalms, | Translated into Welsh | By | William Morgan, D.D., | And originally printed in the year 1588; | Reproduced in photographic facsimile | for | Thomas Powel, M.A., | Professor of Celtic in the University College of South Wales and | Monmouthshire, | By | Charles J. Clark, | . . . London, W.C. | . . . | 1896. |

Sm. 4° (8 and 16); half persian, gilt top; 170×98 mm., 253×194 mm.
$6\frac{11}{16}\times3\frac{7}{8}$ in., $9\frac{15}{16}\times7\frac{5}{8}$ in.

4° (8 and 16); large paper copy; vellum, gilt top; 170×98 mm., 283×228 mm.
$6\frac{11}{16}\times3\frac{7}{8}$ in. $11\frac{1}{8}\times9$ in.

DESCRIPTION.—Frontispiece, *Ty Mawr*, *Wybrnant*, etc.; title; blank, *b;* dedication; Latin quotation, *b;* *Cynwysiad.*, pp. 5—6; 2 plates; *Rhagnodiadau.*, sigs. A^4—B and *b*, pp. 7—10; 2 plates; *Rhagnodiadau.* (continued), sig. B^2 and *b*, pp. 11—12; 3 plates; *Rhagnodiadau.* (continued), sigs. B^3—D^4, pp. 13—31; Welsh quotation, *b;* 2 plates, 2 pp. corrections in 1588 ed'n of Bible (facsimile); title of Psalms (facsimile); blank, *b;* text, in B.L. (facsimile), sigs. $A^{ii.}$—$L^{iv.}$; blank, *b;* *List of Subscribers.*, pp. 1—6. Imprint on last page, *Printed at the Bedford Press*, . . . *Strand, W.C.* Total pp., 32+178+6=216.

371.

[1897.] Y | Bibl Cyssegr-lan, | . . . | Llundain: | Y Bibl Gymdeithas Frytanaidd a Thramor, | . . . | . . . Eyre a Spottiswoode, | . . . |

Dy. 16°, on title *Pearl 16mo.* (32); 124×81 mm., 138×99 mm.
$5\times3\frac{3}{16}$ in., $5\frac{7}{16}\times3\frac{7}{16}$ in.; 702 pp.

Reprint of No. 261, with 8 maps. Special ed'n to commemorate Queen Victoria's Jubilee, 1897, stamped on cover, *Er Coffhad am Drigain Mlynedd o Deyrnasiad V.R. 1837—1897.* Price, without maps, 11d.; with maps, from 1s. to 3s.

372.

1897. Testament | Newydd | . . . | Llundain: | Y Feibl Gymdeithas Frytanaidd a Thramor, | . . . | M.DCCC.XCVII. | Cum Privilegio.

12°, on title *Ruby 24mo.* (32); 125×73 mm., 137×86 mm.
$4\frac{15}{16}\times2\frac{7}{8}$ in., $5\frac{3}{8}\times3\frac{3}{8}$ in.; 256 pp.; price 1d.

Reprint of No. 345*a*.

373.

1897. Llyfr Cyntaf ac Ail | Samuel, | . . . | Rhydychen: | . . . Argraphdy y Brifysgol, | Tros y Feibl-Gymdeithas Frytanaidd a Thramor, | . . . | M.DCCC.XCVII. | Cum Privilegio. |

32°, on title *Brevier 32mo.*; cloth; 101×57 mm., 114×75 mm.
$4\times2\frac{1}{4}$ in., $4\frac{1}{2}\times2\frac{15}{16}$ in.; 198 pp.

374.

1897. Llyfr y Psalmau. | . . . | Rhydychen: | . . . . Argraphdy y Brifysgol | Tros y Bibl Gymdeithas Frytanaidd a Thramor, | . . . | 1897. | Cum Privilegio. |

Sm. 4° (32); 161×117 mm., 178×140 mm.
$6\frac{5}{16}\times4\frac{5}{8}$ in., $7\times5\frac{1}{2}$ in.; 148 pp.

Reprint of No. 291.

375.

1898. Testament | Newydd | . . . | Caer Grawnt: |

24°. Reported. Fuller details unobtainable.

376.

1898. Cyfieithiad Newydd | o'r | Testament Newydd | . . . | Gan | Y Parch. W. Edwards, B.A., D.D. | . . . | Cyfrol II.: Actau Apostolion. | . . . | Evan Rees a'i Gwmni, . . . Caerdydd. | M.DCCCXCVIII. |

Cr. 8° (16); lines across the page; roan; 145×94 mm., 183×123 mm.
5¹⁵⁄₁₆×3¹⁵⁄₁₆ in., 7³⁄₁₆×4⅝ in.

Vol. II. of No. 368.

DESCRIPTION.—Title; blank, *b;* portrait (translator); blank, *b;* dedication, *a;* blank, *b; Gair at y Darllenydd.*, *a.; Talfyriadau*, etc., *b;* text (Acts), pp. 1—243 (not signatured); colophon, *b.* Total pp., viii.+244=252.

377.

1899. Yr Efengyl | yn ol | Sant Marc. | Rhydychen: | . . . Argraphdy y Brifysgol, | Tros y Feibl Gymdeithas Frytanaidd a Thramor, | . . . M.D.CCC.XCIX. | Cum Privilegio. |

32°, on title *Brevier 32mo.*; cloth; 101×57 mm., 114×74 mm.
4×2¼ in., 4½×2¹⁵⁄₁₆ in.; 72 pp.

378.

1900. Y | Bibl Cyssegr-lan, | . . . | Rhydychen: | . . . Argraphdy y Brifysgol, | Tros y Bibl Gymdeithas Frytanaidd a Thramor, | . . . | M.DCCC. | Cum Privilegio. |

La. 8°, on title *Sm. Pica 8vo. Gydâ Chyfeir.* (32);
233×145 mm., 256×173 mm.
9³⁄₁₆×5¹¹⁄₁₆ in., 10¹⁄₁₆×6¹³⁄₁₆ in.; iv.+1,180=1,184 pp.

Reprint of No. 280.

379.

1900. Y | Bibl Cyssegr-lan, | . . . | Bibl Gymdeithas Americanaidd, | Caerefrog Newydd: | . . . | 1900. |

Cr. 8°, on title *Welsh Nonpareil Ref.*, *12mo.* (16); 163×97 mm., 186×119 mm.
6¹⁄₁₆×3¹³⁄₁₆ in., 7¹⁄₁₆×4¹¹⁄₁₆ in.; 940 pp.

Reprint of No. 232. *24,000 Printed* appears on p. 3.

380.

1900. Testament Newydd | . . . | Llundain: | Y Feibl Gymdeithas Frytanaidd a Thramor, | . . . | . . . Argraphdy y Brifysgol, Rhydychen. | Pris Un Geiniog. | 1900. | Cum Privilegio. |

12°, on title *Ruby 24mo.* (32); 125×73 mm., 138×88 mm.
4¹³⁄₁₆×2⅔ in., 5¹⁄₁₆×3¹⁄₁₆ in.; 256 pp.; price 1d.

Reprint of No. 345*a.*

381.

1900. Yr Efengyl | yn ol | Sant Ioan. | Rhydychen: | . . . Argraphdy y Brifysgol, | Tros y Bibl Gymdeithas Frytanaidd a Thramor, | . . . | 1900. | Cum Privilegio. |

32°, on title *Brevier 32mo.*; 101×57 mm., 112×72 mm.
4×2¼ in., 4¾×2¹³⁄₁₆ in.; 88 pp.

382.

WELSH SCRIPTURES FOR THE BLIND.

EMBOSSED IN BRAILLE TYPE.

Colossians		B. & F. Blind Assoc.

MOON'S EMBOSSED TYPE.

Exodus (vol. I.)	1896	B. & F.B.S.
I. Samuel (2 vols.)	1897	..
II. Samuel (2 vols.)	1898	
I. Kings (2 vols.)	1900	
II. Kings (2 vols.)	1901	
Psalms (7 vols.)	1883	
Psalm xxiii., etc.	1882	
Isaiah (2 vols.)	1902	
Isaiah xl., etc.	1882	
The Sermon on the Mount	1882	
St. Mark	1893	
St. Luke xv.	1882	
St. John (2 vols.)	1882	
St. John xiv.	1882	
The Acts (2 vols.)	1891	
Romans	1883	
Corinthians	1894	
Galatians	1892	
Philippians	1890	
Colossians	1895	
Thessalonians	1895	
Timothy	1893	
Titus	1895	
Philemon	1895	
Hebrews	1888	
James	1882	
Peter	1887	"
John's Epistles	1895	
Jude	1895	
Revelation	1895	

LIST OF OWNERS.

The following list of owners is compiled from the schedules prepared as a preliminary to the Exhibition of Welsh Bibles in 1904, and from the lists of owners given in the late Charles Ashton's "Bywyd ac Amserau yr Esgob Morgan," 1891. Modifications must have occurred since; but the list is printed as containing the best information available as to the whereabouts of one or more copies of each issue. It does not pretend to be a complete census of owners of even the rare editions.

Aberffraw, Beulah Calvinistic Methodist Chapel, 240, 265, 352.
Aberystwyth University College, 5, 6 (3 copies—2 imperfect), 9 (4 copies—2 imperfect), 11 (5 copies), 13, 16 (4 copies), 17 (3 copies), 18 (3 copies), 19 (3 copies), 20 (4 copies), 21 (imperfect), 22 (7 copies), 23 (7 copies), 24 (imperfect), 25 (5 copies), 26 (3 copies), 27, 29A (2 copies), 31 (2 copies), 32 (3 copies), 33, 36 (3 copies), 37 (3 copies), 42, 43, 44, 45, 47 (imperfect), 48, 50, 54, 56, 59 (5 copies), 60 (N.T. only), 63, 66, 77, 80, 85, 92 (2 copies), 103, 106, 109, 128, 145, 154, 155, 161, 172, 181, 183, 186, 188 (2 copies), 189, 196, 203, 205, 213, 236, 255, 258, 288, 313, 315, 323, 335, 338 (2 copies), 343 (2 copies), 349, 355 (3 copies), 360, 362, 371.
American Bible Society, New York, 218, 237, 358, 361, 363, 367, 380.
Ancient Britons, Society of, London, 5, 6 (imperfect).
Anglesey, *Marquis of*, Plâs Newydd, Anglesey, 9.
Ashton, *Mrs.* Charles, Dinas Mawddwy, 16, 18, 22.
Bala-Bangor Congregational College, 9 (2 copies—imperfect).
Bala Theological College, 2 (imperfect), 5 (3 copies—1 imperfect), 6 (2 copies—1 imperfect), 9 (2 copies), 11, 13, 16, 17, 18, 19, 20, 22, 23, 25, 26, 27, 29A, 29B, 31, 32, 33, 36, 44, 45, 48, 49, 50, 52, 54, 55, 60, 63 (dateless), 66, 77, 88, 106, 143 (N.T. only), 147, 148, 149 (N.T. only), 165, 167, 199, 205 213, 219, 250, 355, 371.
Bangor Baptist College, 9, 10 (imperfect), 11, 12 (imperfect), 16, 17, 18, 22, 23, 25, 26, 32, 33, 36, 37, 44, 45, 49, 67, 98, 139, 164, 188.
Bangor University College Library, 5 (imperfect), 6 (imperfect), 8 (2 copies), 9 (2 copies), 10 (3 copies—imperfect), 11, 13, 16, 17, 18, 19, 20, 22, 23, 25, 26, 27 (imperfect), 29A, 31, 32, 33, 34, 35, 36, 37, 44, 49, 50, 57, 60, 77, 92.
Bangor Cathedral Library, 5 (imperfect), 6 (imperfect).
Bedford, *His Grace The Duke of*, Woburn, Bedfordshire, 16.
Blackie and Son, publishers, Glasgow, 300.
Bodedern Parish Church, Anglesey, 9.
Bodleian Library, Oxford, 5, 6, 9.
Bonnor, *Col.* R. B. Maurice-, Bryn-y-Gwalie, Llangedwyn, Oswestry, 5.
Bowen, *Rev.* T., Dowlais, 22.
Brecon Memorial College, 5 (wanting titlepage).
Briscoe, *The late Rev.* T., D.D., Holyhead, 6 (imperfect).
British and Foreign Bible Society, 5 (2 copies—1 imperfect), 6 (2 copies), 8 (4 copies—1 imperfect), 9 (2 copies), 11 (2 copies), 12 (2 copies), 13, 18 (2 copies), 19, 20, 22 (2 copies), 23, 24, 25 (3 copies), 32, 36 (3 copies), 45, 48, 52, 56, 61, 63 (2 copies—1 N.T. only), 87, 89, 92, 93 (N.T. only), 95, 97, 98, 105, 110, 111, 113, 118, 129, 147, 151, 153, 158, 159, 160, 174, 188, 205, 211, 213, 219, 220, 222, 225, 226, 227, 229, 232, 242, 260, 266, 277, 286, 294A, 309, 319, 327 (N.T. only), 333, 341, 352, 360, 372, 373, 375, 379, 381.
British Museum, 2 (imperfect), 3 (5 copies), 5, 6 (imperfect), 7 (2 copies), 8 (4 copies—2 imperfect), 9, 10, 11, 12, 13, 15, 16 (3 copies), 17, 18, 19, 20, 22, 23, 26, 30, 32, 43, 45, 50, 57, 59, 60, 61, 63 (2 copies—1 N.T. only), 66, 67, 72, 77, 84, 94, 96, 152, 164, 170, 174 (N.T. only), 188, 192, 230, 284, 293, 307, 309, 316, 331, 336.
Brown's University, U.S.A., 17, 19, 20, 32.
Cambridge University Library, 5, 9, 18, 22, 61, 67, 280.
Cambridge University Press, 284, 307, 325, 371.
Cardiff Public Libraries, 3, 5 (imperfect), 6 (2 copies—imperfect), 9 (3 copies—2 imperfect), 10 (imperfect), 11 (3 copies—imperfect), 12 (imperfect), 13 (imperfect), 15, 16 (3 copies), 17 (2 copies—1 imperfect), 19 (4 copies—imperfect), 20 (4 copies—2 imperfect), 21, 22 (7 copies—4 imperfect), 23 (4 copies—2 imperfect), 24 (imperfect), 25 (4 copies—1 imperfect), 26 (3 copies—1 imperfect), 27 (2

M

copies—1 imperfect), 28, 29A (2 copies—1 imperfect), 31 (2 copies—imperfect), 32 (4 copies), 33 (imperfect), 34 (imperfect), 36 (3 copies), 37, 42 (2 copies), 44, 46, 48, 49, 50, 51 (imperfect), 51a, 53, 54, 55, 56, 57, 59 (2 copies), 60 (2 copies), 61, 62, 63 (2 copies—1 dateless, 1 N.T. only), 64, 65 (imperfect), 66 (2 copies), 67 (2 copies), 69, 70, 72, 73, 77 (2 copies), 81, 83, 85, 86, 87 (2 copies), 90 (N.T. only), 91, 92 (2 copies), 93, 95, 96, 97, 98, 99, 103, 104, 106, 107, 110, 112, 113, 116 (2 copies), 117, 120, 123, 124a, 131 (imperfect), 132 (wanting titlepage), 134, 136, 137 (wanting titlepage), 138, 141, 182, 144 (imperfect), 154, 155, 156a, 158, 159, 162, 164, 167, 169, 171a, 173, 177, 178, 185, 187, 188, 191, 193, 194, 197, 201, 203, 205, 207, 208, 212, 213, 216, 217, 219, 222, 223, 234, 236, 241, 249a, 250 (N.T. only), 256 (3rd issue), 263, 266 (imperfect), 271, 287 (imperfect), 288, 289, 291, 292, 296, 299, 303, 306, 307, 308, 311, 317 (imperfect), 322, 323, 324, 334, 335, 337, 338, 339, 341, 343, 349, 350, 355, 358, 361 (2 copies), 363, 365, 366, 367 (2 copies), 368, 369, 371, 374, 377, 378, 379, 380 (2 copies), 381, 382.

Cardiff, Tabernacle Welsh Baptist Chapel, The Hayes, 244a.

Cardiff University College, 5, 6 (imperfect), 9 (2 copies—1 imperfect), 11, 12, 15, 18, 19, 20 (2 copies—1 N.T. only), 29A, 33, 34, 43, 49, 54, 57, 60, 63, 65, 70, 71, 72, 74, 75, 80, 84, 88, 96, 102, 106, 110, 113, 114, 118, 119, 125, 126 (Book I. only), 127, 135, 141, 149, 160 (N.T. only), 162 (N.T. only), 163, 167 (N.T. only), 168, 169, 170 (N.T. only), 171, 172, 173 (N.T. only), 174, 179, 180, 181, 186 (1st issue), 195, 196, 200, 204, 207, 215, 220, 230, 233, 234, 238, 246, 248, 251, 254.

Cardiff, Welsh Calvinistic Methodist Schoolroom, Pembroke Terrace, 160a.

Cartwright, Edward, printer, Dowlais, 76.

Casson, Randal, solicitor, Portmadoc, 5 (imperfect).

Davies, *Miss*, Penmaen Dovey, 5 (imperfect).

Davies, *Rev.* D. H., Newcastle Emlyn, 17, 19 (2 copies), 20, 22 (2 copies), 23, 26, 31, 33, 42, 44, 48, 50, 54, 87, 90, 108, 164, 174 (N.T. only), 188.

Davies, D. Tyssul, Llewelyn Street, Aberdare, 42, 106.

Davies, D. W., stationer, Carnarvon, 25.

Davies, David, grocer, Bridge Street, Dolgelly, 9 (imperfect).

Davies, David, 12, Stuart Street, Merthyr, 189.

Davies, Ebenezer, grocer, Royal Stores, Cathays, Cardiff, 214, 247.

Davies, *Rev.* J. E., Llangelynin, 5 (imperfect), 6 (imperfect).

Davies, J. Glyn, Aberystwyth, 54.

Davies, J. H., *M.A.*, Cwrt Mawr, 5 (3 copies—2 imperfect), 9, 11 (6 copies), 12 (2 copies—1 imperfect), 13, 15, 16 (4 copies), 17 (2 copies), 18, 19, 20, 22, 23, 25, 26, 27, 28, 29A, 32, 33, 37, 41, 42, 50, 56, 58, 59, 67, 68, 77, 82, 85, 87, 92, 93, 98, 103, 106, 113, 122, 130 (imperfect), 158, 160, 164, 188, 203 (Part I. only), 205, 206, 209, 213, 219, 224, 246, 257, 266, 272, 312, 337, 353, 360.

Davies, *The late Rev.* John, *M.A.*, South Hampstead, London, 9 (imperfect).

Davies, *Rev.* John, Bontddu, Dolgelly, 16, 26, 90, 137, 159, 237a, 250 (N.T. only), 277, 317, 355.

Davies, John, 34, Bridge Street, Lampeter, 19, 63.

Davies, Thomas " Tegwyn," tailor and draper, Dinas Mawddwy, 9 (imperfect).

Davies, *Mrs.* W. Cadwaladr, Glanafon, Menai Bridge, 17, 19, 22, 23, 26, 33.

Davies, W. L., Henfryn Mills, Llandysul, 256 (4th issue).

Edwardes, *Rev.* E., Caerdeon, Dolgelly, 9, 22, 23, 25.

Edwards, John, 12, Newport Road, Cardiff, 32, 78, 124, 165.

Edwards, *Rev.* Llewelyn, *M.A.*, Ardwyn, Aberystwyth, 5 (imperfect).

Edwards, P., Coedpoeth, Denbighshire, 6.

Ellis, *Rev.* Griffith, M.A., Bootle, 9 (imperfect), 25, 36, 101, 188, 208.

Evans, *Miss*, Pwllheli, 5 (imperfect).

Evans, D., Glan Conway, 23, 55, 72, 92, 133, 240.

Evans, E. W., " Y Goleuad " Office, Dolgelly, 9 (imperfect).

Evans, *Mrs.* Edward, Llanfihangel-yng-Ngwnfa, Llanfyllin, 4, 9.

Evans, *Rev.* Evan, Vicar of Aberayron, 6.

Evans, Evan, Parke, Pentrecwrt, Llandysul, 90, 115, 262.

Evans, Evan T., 20, Vale View, Nantymoel, 293.

Evans, *Rev.* Geo. Eyre, Tanybryn, Aberystwyth, 178, 226.

Evans, J. H. Silvan, *M.A.*, Whitland, 4 (imperfect), 9 (imperfect), 18.

Evans, Jenkin, Tudor Road, Cardiff, 280.

Evans, Owen, 25, Chapel Street, Denbigh, 198, 246 (N.T. only), 264, 337.

Evans, T. C. " Cadrawd," Llangynwyd, 23, 26, 31, 50, 58, 75, 129, 193, 231 (N.T. only), 261, 317, 339, 345, 371.

Fisher, *Rev.* J., Cefn Rectory, St. Asaph, 16, 22, 54, 58, 77.

Goodwin, D. G., Uffington, 94, 221, 249, 298.

Gough, *Mrs.* Alan, Gelliwig, Pwllheli, 8.

Griffith, Edward, J.P., Springfield, Dolgelly, 9, 32, 36, 44, 54, 59, 63 (dateless), 73, 139, 147, 152, 172, 202, 326, 329, 342.

Griffith, John, Vronheulog, Bangor, 9 (imperfect).

Griffith, W. J., Upper Bangor, 16.
Griffiths, *The Misses*, The Poplars, Aberdare, 22, 23, 25, 78 (imperfect), 158, 167, 253.
Griffiths, *Mrs.*, Pantglâs, Aberdare, 112, 245, 264.
Griffiths, R. P., Llangynnidr National School, Crickhowell, 16.
Hengoed (Glam.), Baptist Chapel Vestry, 150 (imperfect).
Herbert, *The Hon. Mrs.*, Llanover, 6.
Hereford, All Saints Church Library, 13 (chained).
Hereford Cathedral Library, 5 (chained).
Hughes, David, shoemaker, Tanygrisiau, Blaenau Ffestiniog, 9.
Hyslop, *Rev.* A. E. H., All Saints' Vicarage, Cardiff, 11 (imperfect).
Jacob, H. Morgan, 58, Plymouth Road, Penarth, 22.
James, *Rev.* A. O., *M.A.*, Long Buckby Vicarage, near Rugby, 9.
James, *Rev.* H. A., *M.A.*, School House, Rugby, 6.
James, John Lloyd " Clwydwenfro," March, Cambs., 6 (incomplete), 13 (imperfect), 17, 20, 26, 293, 339.
James, *Rev.* R., Llanwrtyd, 273, 275, 279, 290, 305, 352.
Jenkins, Daniel, Pantrhiw, Llangeler, 327.
Jenkins, James, 110, Railway Street, Splott, Cardiff, 131*a*.
Jenkins, John Austin, *B.A.*, Cardiff, 106 (N.T. only), 166, 256 (1st issue), 259, 302.
Jesus College, Oxford, 5, 6.
John, E. T. " Ieuan Dyfed," Merthyr, 32.
John Rylands Library, Manchester, 5, 6, 16, 18, 22, 63 (dateless).
Jones and Jones, Hannah Street, Porth, 369.
Jones, *Miss*, 12, Constantine Terrace, Carnarvon, 278.
Jones, *Mr.*, tailor, Carnarvon, 5 (imperfect).
Jones, *Mrs.*, 31, Kincraig Street, Cardiff, 104 (imperfect).
Jones, *Mrs.*, Parkswadog, Llangeler, 88.
Jones, *Rev.* D., Laugharne Vicarage, 16.
Jones, D., Roe Wen, Talycafn, R.S.O., 62.
Jones, D., Ty'nyclawdd, Swyddffynnon, 54, 80, 108, 205, 213, 219.
Jones, Evan Parry, *J.P.*, Cefnfaes, Blaenau Ffestiniog, 9.
Jones, *Councillor* Henry, Liverpool, 9.
Jones, N., 16, Berthwin Street, Cardiff, 270, 309, 330.
Jones, J., Menai Bridge, 100.
Jones, J. Davies, Brynhyfryd, Menai Bridge, 100.
Jones, John " Myrddin Fardd," Chwilog, 6 (imperfect).
Jones, John, Caegwernog, Llanelltyd, near Dolgelly, 9 (imperfect).
Jones, L.D. " Llew Tegid," Garth, Bangor, 9, 26, 54, 159, 164, 205, 213, 235, 250 (N.T. only), 261, 288, 305, 327, 328, 355, 359, 370.
Jones, Maurice Lewis, Llanfyllin, 9.
Jones, *The late Rev.* Michael D., of Bala, Library of, 6 (imperfect), 20.
Jones, Morris, *J.P.*, Plas Uchaf, Dolgelly, 9.
Jones, *Rev.* R. J., *M.A.*, Broniestyn, Aberdare, 23, 43, 77, 261.
Jones, R. Prys, Pontypridd, 9.
Jones, Richard, Drysiog, Aber Bargoed, 289, 294, 303, 337*a*, 344, 344*a*, 351.
Jones, Robert, Cymmunod, Bryngwran, 6.
Jones, *Miss* Sarah, Glenview, Pentrecwrt, Llandysul, 220, 316.
Jones, Thomas, postmaster, North Shields, 108, 228, 251, 261, 320, 345*a*, 347, 357.
Jones, Thomas, saddler, 38, Rhosmaen Street, Llandilo, 9 (imperfect).
Jones, William, Cilfodau Terrace, Bethesda, 6.
Jones, William, Wolseley Street, Newport, Mon., 80.
Lambeth Palace Library, 6, 7, 9.
Lewis, *Dr.*, Sunnyside, Pontypridd, 22.
Lewis, *Rev.* H. Elvet, 13, Highbury Grove, London, N., 16, 20, 22, 25, 32, 50, 57, 59, 99, 190.
Lewis, J.P., printer, Merthyr, 26, 59 (2 copies), 134.
Llanarth Parish Church, Cardiganshire, 9.
Llanfwrog Parish Church, Ruthin, 9.
Llanllwchhaiarn Parish Church, Newtown, Montgomeryshire, 9 (imperfect).
Matthews, T., *B.A.*, Llandebie, 22, 292 (imperfect).
Matthias, T., Pentrecwrt, Llandysul, 112.
Mee, Arthur, Llanishen, 157, 244, 301, 348.
Moon, *Miss*, Brighton, 383.
Morgan, Richard, painter, 11, Castle Street, Carnarvon, 9 (imperfect).
Morris, Abram, Gwynfa, Gold Tops, Newport, Mon., 186.
Morris, Edward, Pantysaer, Llanuwchllyn, 9.
Morris, John, *J.P.*, Lletty'r Eos, Llansannan, 5 (imperfect), 6, 9, 26.
Mostyn, *The Right Hon. Lord*, Mostyn, Flintshire, 5 (imperfect).
Nicholl, John Illtyd Dillwyn, *J.P.*, *D.L.*, Merthyr Mawr, Glamorganshire, 5.
Oxford University Press, 243, 252, 267, 283, 332, 346.

Owen, *Rev.* D. O'Brien, C.M. Bookroom, Carnarvon, 111, 142, 175, 210, 229, 256 (2nd issue), 269, 278, 314, 323 (imperfect).
Owen, E. H., *J.P.*, Ty Coch, near Carnarvon, 5 (imperfect), 6, 9.
Owen, Henry, *D.C.L.*, Poyston, Pembrokeshire, 9.
Pamplin, William, Llandderfel, Corwen, 5 (imperfect), 9 (imperfect).
Pentrevoelas Parish Church, 9.
Perkins, *Mrs.*, 28, Clive Street, Grangetown, Cardiff, 150 (wanting original titlepage).
Phillimore, Egerton G., *M.A.*, Ty'nrhos, Cemmaes Road, Mont., 9 (imperfect), 11 (2 copies).
Powell, T., *M.A.*, Hafodwen, Penarth, 7, 9 (2 copies), 11, 18, 351.
Prichard, R., Dyfnian Fawr, Llanfair P.G., 6 (imperfect).
Pugh, Robert, Hafod-y-morfa, Llanelltyd, Dolgelly, 9 (imperfect). •
Quaritch, Bernard, 15, Piccadilly, London, 5 (2 copies—imperfect), 6 (4 copies—imperfect), 9 (3 copies—2 imperfect), 13.
Rees, D. J., 14, Elm Street, Cardiff, 156, 176, 179, 184, 282.
Rees, *Mrs.* Margaret, Llwyncelyn Cottage, Aberdare, 95, 137, 337 (N.T. only), 345.
Reynolds, Llywarch, solicitor, Merthyr, 9, 54, 59, 86, 87.
Richards, *The late Mrs.*, Vronheulog, Llandderfel, Corwen, 9 (imperfect).
Richards, D. M., Y Wenallt, Aberdare, 295, 339.
Roberts, *Mrs.*, Commercial Street, Newtown, Mont., 6 (imperfect).
Roberts, *The late Rev.* R., Dolgelly, 6 (imperfect).
Roberts, *Rev.* R. J., Pool Quay, Welshpool, 6 (imperfect), 9.
Roberts, *The late* W. J. "Gwilym Cowlyd," Llanrwst, 5 (imperfect).
Rogers, John, Avenue Villa, Bury Port, Pembrey, 112.
Rowland, Edward, Brynoffa, Wrexham, 5 (imperfect).
Royle, *Mrs.*, Brynygroes, Bala, 9.
St. Asaph Cathedral Library, 5 (imperfect), 6, 9 (3 copies), 11, 16, 17, 18 (2 copies), 19 22 (2 copies), 23.
St. David's Cathedral Library, 9, 158, 188.
St. David's College, Lampeter, 9 (imperfect), 42, 98, 188.
Salesbury, P. H. B., 3, Little George Street, Westminster, London, 6.
Shankland, *Rev.* T., Bangor, 11, 16, 17, 18, 19, 20, 22, 23, 25, 26, 29B, 31, 32, 33, 34, 35, 36, 37, 44, 45, 82, 83, 198.
Society for the Promotion of Christian Knowledge, 36.
Stanley, *The Right Hon.* Lord, Penrhos, Holyhead, 9.
Stepney-Gulston, Alan, *J.P.*, *D.L.*, Derwydd, Carmarthenshire, 16, 25.
Stevens, *Mr.*, 11, Strathnairn Street, Roath, Cardiff, 137.
Swansea Public Library, 4, 5 (imperfect), 6 (imperfect), 9 (3 copies—2 imperfect), 16, 17, 18, 19, 22, 23, 25, 26, 28, 32, 33, 36, 42, 49, 56, 67, 72, 79, 87, 90 (N.T. only), 93, 112, 120, 129 (2 copies—1 N.T. and Apoc. only), 144, 173 (N.T. only), 174 (N.T. only), 186, 188, 199, 205, 211, 213, 228, 239, 253, 268, 274, 284.
Thomas, *Ven. Archdeacon*, Llandrinio Rectory, 5 (3 copies—2 imperfect), 6, 11 (imperfect), 16, 22, 23, 93 (2 copies), 188, 205, 213, 219.
Thomas, Evan, coal merchant, Dolgelly, 9 (imperfect).
Thomas, H. P., chemist, Aberffraw, 88 (2 copies), 340, 344.
Thomas, John, Post Office, Llanwrtyd, 26.
Thomas, *Mrs.* Sarah, Llwynygrug, Dolgelly, 6 (imperfect).
Thomas, T. H. "Arlunydd Penygarn," 46, The Walk, Cardiff, 20, 87.
Thomas, *Rev.* Thomas, *J.P.*, Green Park, Pantdefaid, Llandysul, 9, 22, 25, 42, 54, 188.
Thomas, William, Cynrig Cottage, Aberdare, 158.
Treharne, *Mrs.* Jacob "Tiberog," Trecynon, Aberdare, 50, 307.
Trevecca Calvinistic Methodist College, 6 (2 copies), 9, 11, 16, 23, 25 (3 copies), 26 (3 copies), 31, 33, 36, 49, 54, 59, 60, 77, 88, 146, 153, 186 (2nd issue), 293.
Ty'nygroes Calvinistic Methodist Chapel, 222, 250 (N.T. only), 281, 310, 373.
Vaughan, John, *J.P.*, Nannau, Merionethshire, 9.
Verney, *Sir* Edmund Hope, *Bart.*, Claydon, Bucks., 5 (imperfect), 6, 9.
Welsh Museum, Cardiff, 9, 19.
Westminster Abbey Library, 6, 22.
Wilkins, Charles, *F.G.S.*, Merthyr, 9 (2 copies—1 imperfect).
Williams, *Mrs.*, Pembroke House, Conway Road, Cardiff, 88.
Williams, David, Old Curiosity Shop, King Street, Carmarthen, 116, 221, 266.
Williams, Ebenezer "Gwernyfed," 29, Tudor Terrace, Merthyr, 16, 20, 22.
Williams, George, 7, Moriah Terrace, Carnarvon, 9 (imperfect).
Williams, Hugh, *M.A.*, Bala, 16.
Williams, Hugh, Liverpool House, Dyffryn Ardudwy, 9.
Williams, *The late* J. Ignatius, Plasynllan, Whitchurch, 6.
Williams, *Sir* John, *Bart.*, *K.C.V.O.*, Plâs Llanstephan, Carmarthenshire, 1, 2, 4, 5, 6, 7 (2 copies), 8, 8a, 9, 10, 11 (imperfect), 12, 13 (imperfect), 16, 17 (2 copies), 19 (imperfect), 20, 22, 23 (imperfect), 25, 26 (2 copies), 27, 28, 29A, 29B, 30, 32, 36, 37, 44, 45, 47, 48, 50, 52, 56, 57, 58, 59 (2 copies), 66, 78, 82, 85, 90, 90a, 114, 149, 152, 156a, 168, 202a, 217a, 269.

LIST OF SUBSCRIBERS.

HIS ROYAL HIGHNESS THE PRINCE OF WALES, K.G.
Aberdare Free Library, per Arthur S. Morris, hon. sec.
Aberdeen Public Library, per G. M. Fraser, librarian.
Aberystwyth Welsh Library, University College of Wales, per J. Glyn Davies, Welsh librarian (2 copies).
E. G. Allen and Son, ltd., 28, Henrietta Street, Covent Garden, London.
American Bible Society, Bible House, Astor Place, New York, per the Rev. W. I. Haven, D.D., corresponding secretary.
F. E. Andrews, 49, Newport Road, Cardiff.
Prof. E. Anwyl, *M.A.*, 62, Marine Terrace, Aberystwyth.
Asher and Co., 13, Bedford Street, Covent Garden, London, W.C. (2 copies).
Robert William Atkinson, Angleham, Penarth, Glamorgan.
Bala Theological College, per the Rev. Alun Jones, registrar.
The Lord Bishop of Bangor (The Right Rev. W. H. Williams, D.D.), Glyngarth Palace, Menai Bridge.
Bangor University College, per *Prof.* W. Lewis Jones, *M.A.*, librarian.
J. M. Barry, auctioneer, Merthyr.
Barry Public Library, per John Roch, librarian.
The Ven. W. L. Bevan, *M.A., Archdeacon of Brecon.*
The Rev. Llewellyn J. M. Bebb, *M.A., Principal of St David's College*, Lampeter.
C. Biddle, *High Constable*, Garthnewydd, Merthyr Tydfil.
Birkenhead Central Library, per John Shepherd, librarian.
Birmingham Central Free Library, per A. Capel Shaw, librarian.
Henry Blackwell, University Place, and 10th Street, New York (2 copies).
Bootle Central Library, per Charles H. Hunt, librarian.
Boston Public Library, per Horace G. Wadlin, librarian.
The Rev. Oliver Bowen, *B.A.*, Longcross Street Baptist Church, Cardiff.
Bradford Free Library and Art Museum, per Butler Wood, librarian.
Col. Joseph A. Bradney, *F.S.A., B.A.*, Talycoed, Monmouth.
Bristol City Library, per E. R. Norris Matthews, *F.R.Hist.S.*, librarian.
British and Foreign Bible Society, per *The Rev.* T. H. Darlow, *M.A.*, literary superintendent.
Briton Ferry Urban District Council Public Library, per librarian.
Brooklyn Public Library, Mass., U.S.A., per Frank P. Hill, librarian.
John Davies-Brown, *M.A.*, 77, Column Road, Cardiff.
The Honourable Mrs. Bulkeley-Owen, Tedsmore Hall, Oswestry.
The Most Honourable The Marquis of Bute, Cardiff Castle (2 copies).
Cambridge, Trinity College Library, per *Dr.* Sinker, librarian.
Cardiff, University College of South Wales and Monmouthshire, per J. Austin Jenkins, *B.A.*, registrar.
E. Cartwright, printer, Dowlais.
The Right Honourable The Earl of Cawdor, Stackpole Court, Pembroke (2 copies).
W. H. Cheetham, manager, British and Foreign Bible Society, 135, Deansgate, Manchester.
Cilfynydd Workmen's Hall and Institute, per John Evans, librarian.
"The Connoisseur," 97, Temple Chambers, Temple Avenue, London, E.C.
Copenhagen, Royal Library (N. O. Lange, librarian), per Francis Edwards, 83, High Street, Marylebone, W.
Cwmcarn and Abercarn Institute, per Jack Games, secretary, Fairview, Abercarn, Mon.
Cwmparc Workmen's Institute, per Howell Price, sec.
The Honourable Society of Cymmrodorion, per E. Vincent Evans, secretary, 64, Chancery Lane, London, E.C.
Arthur Daniel, Victoria Buildings, Troedyrhiw.
The Very Rev. W. H. Davey, *M.A., The Dean of Llandaff*, The Deanery, Llandaff.
The late W. Cadwalader Davies, Glanafon, Menai Bridge (2 copies).
The Rev. Charles Davies, *Baptist minister*, 6, The Walk, Cardiff.
Charles Morgan Davies, architect, Merthyr.
The Rev. David Davies, *M.A. (Cantab.)*, Canton Rectory, Cardiff.

The Rev. David Henry Davies, Ffinnant House, Newcastle-Emlyn.
E. Davies, 29, Commercial Street, Newport, Mon.
The Rev. E. O. Davies, *B.Sc.*, Theological College, Bala.
The Rev. E. T. Davies, *B.A.*, *Canon of Bangor*, The Vicarage, Pwllheli.
Eleazar Davies, *L.R.C.P.*, *L.R.C.S.*, Ifor House, Fochriw (2 copies).
The Rev. Gwynoro Davies, Barmouth.
The Rev. J. Davies, *Rector*, Llaniestyn Rectory, Pwllheli.
J. H. Davies, *M.A.*, Cwrtmawr, Llangeitho, Llanio Road.
Jacob Davies, 17, Sincroft Street, Moss Side, Manchester.
James Davies, solicitor, Gwynfa, Broomy Hill, Hereford.
The Rev. John Davies, *Calvinistic Methodist minister*, Bontddu, Dolgelly.
The Rev. John Davies, Pandy, Abergavenny.
John Davies, Hafan Dawel, 7, Plasturton Place, Cardiff (4 copies).
John Davies, 34, Bridge Street, Lampeter.
John Davies, 75, Heald Place, Manchester.
John Davies, solicitor, 3, Church Street, Merthyr.
The Rev. Ll. Lloyd Davies, *M.A.*, The Vicarage, Whitchurch, Cardiff.
The Rev. Owen Davies, *D.D.*, Cefnfaes, Carnarvon.
Samuel Davies, 20, The Avenue, Merthyr.
William Davies, *Bursary Clerk*, St. David's College, Lampeter.
Deighton, Bell and Co., booksellers and publishers, Cambridge (2 copies).
The late R. J. Derfel, 6, Store Street, Ardwick, Manchester.
E. S. Dodgson, *c/o Dr.* H. Krebs, The Taylorian Library, Oxford.
Dublin Public Library, per Henry Campbell, town clerk.
John Duncan, *J.P.*, *F.I.J.*, " South Wales Daily News " Office, Cardiff.
G. W. Eccles, 1, Rugby Chambers, Chapel Street, Bedford Row, London, W.C. (4 copies).
Edinburgh Public Library, per Hew Morrison, *LL.D.*, principal, librarian.
The Ven. Frederic W. Edmondes, *M.A.*, *Archdeacon of Llandaff.*
E. Bromley Edmunds, Penrhos House, Groeswen, near Pontypridd.
The Rev. E. Edwardes, *M.A.*, Caerdeon Vicarage, Dolgelly.
The Rev. D. Charles Edwards, *M.A.*, Hafodybryn, Llanbedr, R.S.O., Merionethshire.
The Rev. Ellis Edwards, *M.A.*, *Vice-Principal*, Theological College, Bala.
Frank Edwards, *M.P.*, The Cottage, Knighton, Radnorshire (2 copies).
Isaac Edwards, auctioneer and accountant, Dowlais.
John Edwards, Coed Cymmer, Dolgelly.
O. M. Edwards, *M.A.*, Lincoln College, Oxford.
The Rev. Thomas John Edwards, 4, Cambrian Terrace, Merthyr.
The Rev. W. Edwards, *B.A.*, *D.D.*, *Principal*, Baptist College, Cardiff.
The Rev. W. A. Edwards, *M.A.*, Llangan Rectory.
The Rev. Griffith Ellis, *M.A.*, 10, Pembroke Road, Bootle.
Mrs. Thomas E. Ellis, Llwyn, Llanbadarn Road, Aberystwyth.
The Rev. A. Owen Evans, *B.A.*, Diocesan Inspector of Schools, Bangor.
D. Emlyn Evans, Cemmaes, Mont.
Evans Bros., printers, stationers, etc., 17, Pier Street, Aberystwyth.
The Rev. E. Evans, Llansadwrn Rectory, Menai Bridge, Anglesey.
E. Vincent Evans, secretary to the Honourable Society of Cymmrodorion, 64, Chancery Lane, London.
E. W. Evans, printer and publisher, Dolgelly.
The Rev. George Eyre Evans, Tan-y-bryn, Aberystwyth.
H. Tobit Evans, *J.P.*, Traeth Saeth, Aberporth.
Hugh Evans, printer and publisher, 444, Stanley Road, Kirkdale, Liverpool.
Isaac Evans, 38, High Street, Menai Bridge.
The Rev. J. Evans, *Calvinistic Methodist minister*, 9, High Street, Llanidloes.
J. Daniel Evans, Clarendon Road, Garston.
J. Gwenogvryn Evans, *M.A.*, *D.Litt.*, Tremvan, Llanbedrog, Pwllheli.
John Evans, Minhafren, Llandinam, Mont.
The Rev. John Evans, *B.A.*, 2, Rosedale Villas, Cheltenham.
John Henry Westyr Evans, solicitor, 17, Quay Street, Cardiff.
Owen Evans, 25, Chapel Street, Denbigh.
The Rev. Owen Evans, Olive Mount, Kingsley Road, Liverpool.
Samuel J. Evans, *M.A.*, headmaster, The County School, Llangefni.
The Rev. T. Eli Evans, *Congregational minister*, Saweldy, Lampeter.
T. J. Evans, 13, Canonbury Park, South London, N.
Thomas Evans, Harford Square, Lampeter.
The Rev. W. Evans, *M.A.*, 35, Laws Street South, Pembroke Dock.
The Rev. William John Evans, *B.A.*, Dulas Villa, Lampeter.
The Rev. J. Fisher, *B.D.*, Cefn Rectory, St. Asaph.
The Rev. W. Ll. Footman, *M.A.* (*Oxon.*), headmaster, St. David's College School, Lampeter.

W. A. Foster, Glyn Menai, Bangor.
Edward Foulkes, Erw Fair, Llanberis.
Jack Games, Fairview, Abercarn, Mon.
Frederick J. Gibbins, Gilfach House, Neath.
The Rev. Stephen Gladstone, *M.A.*, Hawarden Rectory, Chester.
Charles Henry Glascodine, 3, Elm Court, Temple, London.
Glasgow, Mitchell Library, per F. T. Barrett, librarian.
Glasgow University Library, per James Maclehose and Son.
D. G. Goodwin, Uffington, Shrewsbury.
The Rev. C. A. H. Green, *M.A.*, The Vicarage, Aberdare.
Edward Griffith, *J.P.*, Springfield, Dolgelly.
The Rev. G. Penar Griffiths, Pentre, Swansea.
The late Edwin Grove, *J.P., D.L.*, Brendin View, Newport, Mon.
J. E. Moore-Gwyn, *J.P., D.L.*, Duffryn, Neath.
W. Haines, Y Bryn, Penpergwm, Abergavenny.
W. Harpur, *M.Inst. C.E., F.S.I., F.R.M.S.*, Town Hall, Cardiff.
The Rev. W. Harries, *Baptist minister*, 56, Taff Embankment, Cardiff.
Harvard University Library, Cambridge, Mass., U.S.A.
The Rev. Gilbert Heaton, *M.A.*, St. Mary's, Cardiff.
The Rev. W. Hobley, South Road, Carnarvon.
Evan Howells, Cardiff Street, Abercanaid.
Arthur Hughes, *M.D.*, Barmouth, Merionethshire.
Arthur Hughes, 8, Station Terrace, Lampeter.
Gabriel Hughes, 28, Vale Road, Rhyl.
J. Meredith Hughes, *F.R.Hist.S.*, Bryn-y-Maen Vicarage, Colwyn Bay.
Richard Hughes, Ty Hen Isaf, Llanerchymedd, Anglesey.
W. Gwynne Hughes, *J.P., D.L.*, Glancothi, Nantgaredig.
The Rev. W. W. Poole-Hughes, *M.A.*, Llandovery. College (2 copies).
The Rev. Andrew E. H. Hyslop, All Saints' Vicarage, Cardiff.
Ireland, National Library of, Dublin, per T. W. Lyster, *M.A.*, librarian.
Sir Henry Mather Mather-Jackson, *Bart.*, Llantilio Court, Abergavenny.
C. H. James, *J.P.*, 64, Park Place, Cardiff.
The Rev. H. A. James, *D.D.*, School House, Rugby.
F. T. James, Penydarren House, Merthyr.
H. E. H. James, *B.A.*, Springfield, Haverfordwest.
Ivor James, 47, Coveny Street, Moors, Cardiff.
The Rev. R. James, Belmont House, Llanwrtyd.
W. P. James, The Lindens, Romilly Crescent, Cardiff.
Jarvis and Foster, publishers, Lorne House, Bangor.
Edward Jenkins, Gwalia Hotel, Llandrindod.
J. Austin Jenkins, *B.A.*, 274, Newport Road, Cardiff.
The Rev. John Jenkins ("Gwili"), Jesus College, Oxford.
Rees Jenkins, Bronyderi, Glyncorrwg, Port Talbot.
Thomas Jenkins, civil engineer, Tyla Morris, Briton Ferry.
L. Lloyd John, solicitor, Corwen (2 copies).
A. Emrys-Jones, *M.D., M.R.C.S., J.P.*, 10, St. John Street, Manchester.
D. W. Jones, Galon Uchaf, Merthyr.
David Jones, Ty'nyclawdd, Swyddffynnon, Ystradmeurig, R.S.O.
The Rev. David Jones, *B.A.*, 21, Ivy Street, Penarth (2 copies).
The Rev. David Jones, *B.A.*, The Vicarage, Penmaenmawr.
E. Parry Jones, *J.P.*, Blaenyddol, Ffestiniog.
Edmund James Jones, *C.E.*, Fforest Legionis, Pontneathvaughan.
The Rev. Edmund O. Jones, *M.A.* (*Oxon.*), The Vicarage, Llanidloes.
The Rev. Evan Jones, 27, Segontium Terrace, Carnarvon.
The Rev. Griffith Jones, *M.A.*, The County School for Boys, Penarth.
Henry Jones, Gwynedd, 131, Boughton, Chester.
The Rev. J. D. Jones, *Congregational minister*, Abercanaid, Merthyr.
Prof. J. Morris Jones, *M.A.*, Llanfair Pwll Gwyngyll, Anglesey.
The Rev. James Jones, *Congregational minister*, Fochriw.
John G. Jones, Rhiwlas Board School, Llansilin, Oswestry.
The Rev. John Morgan Jones, 6, Wordsworth Avenue, Cardiff.
The Rev. John Morgan Jones, *B.A.*, 7, The Avenue, Merthyr.
L. D. Jones ("Llew Tegid"), 3, Edge Hill, Garth, Bangor.
Lewis Jones, "Journal" Office, Rhyl.
The Rev. M. H. Jones, *B.A.*, 13, Morley Street, Carmarthen.
Owen Wyn Jones, 20 and 22, Falcon Road, Battersea.
The Rev. R. J. Jones, *M.A.*, Broniestyn, Aberdare.
Rhys D. Jones, *B.A.* (*Oxon.*), Clyncae, Llanwrtyd.
T. D. Jones, solicitor, Leighton House, Fleet Street, London, E.C.
The Rev. T. W. Jones, Devil's Bridge, R.S.O., Cardiganshire.

Thomas Jones, Anwylfan, East Kilbride.
Thomas Jones, Five Elms, Garston Old Road, Grassendale, Liverpool.
Thomas Jones, postmaster, North Shields.
Tom Jones, Ystrad House, Lampeter.
T. Llechid Jones, *B.A.*, Talysarn, Carnarvon.
T. Rhys Jones, 7, Park Street, Park Square, Newport, Mon.
The Rev. W. Jones, *M.A.*, Fourcrosses, Chwilog, R.S.O., Carnarvonshire.
William Jones, *M.P.*, 24, Gordon Street, Gordon Square, London, W.
William Jones, Pencae, Abercanaid.
William Jones, Cefn Bodig, Bala.
William Jones, 83, Park Road, Colwyn Bay.
John Jordan, *County Alderman*, Parcyderi, Llansamlet.
J. A. Kidd, 288, Newport Road, Cardiff.
Lambeth Palace Library, per S. W. Kershaw, M.A.
Lampeter, St. David's College Library.
E. Laws, *F.S.A.*, Brython, Tenby.
Thomas J. Lean, Middleton House, Moira Terrace, Cardiff.
Leeds Public Free Library, per Thomas W. Hand, librarian.
The Rev. D. Morgan Lewis, *M.A.*, University College of Wales, Aberystwyth.
Gething Lewis, Cathedral Road, Cardiff (2 copies).
The Rev. H. Elvet Lewis, 13, Highbury Grove, London, N.
Henry Lewis, *J.P.*, Belmont, Bangor.
J. Rice Lewis, 42, Shrewsbury Road, Oxton, Birkenhead.
John D. Lewis, Gomerian Press, Llandyssul.
John P. Lewis (" Melltenydd "), 46, High Street, Merthyr.
W. A. Jones, *M.A.*, The County School, Rhyl.
Sir William Thomas Lewis, *Bart.*, The Mardy, Aberdare (3 copies).
Llanelly Public Library, per J. Boulton, librarian.
Sir John T. D. Llewellyn, *Bart.*, Penlle'rgaer, Swansea (2 copies).
R. W. Llewellyn, *J.P.*, *D.L.*, Baglan, Briton Ferry.
H. Meuric Lloyd, *J.P.*, barrister-at-law, Delfryn, Llanwrda, R.S.O.
Isaac T. Lloyd, *M.P.S.*, 267, King's Road, Chelsea, London, S.W.
Prof. John Edward Lloyd, *M.A.*, Gwnen Deg, Bangor.
John R. Lloyd, North and South Wales Bank, 138, London Road, Liverpool.
London, British Museum, per G. K. Fortescue, keeper of printed books.
London, Dr. Williams Library, Gordon Square, W.C., per the Rev. Francis Henry
    Jones, *B.A.*, librarian.
London, Guildhall Library, per Chas. Welch, *F.S.A.*, librarian.
London, Memorial Hall Library, Farringdon Street, per the Rev. T. J. Crippen.
London, St. Martin's Public Library.
London, Shoreditch Public Library, per W. C. Plant, librarian.
London, Sion College Library, Victoria Embankment, E.C., per *The Rev.* W. H. Milman,
    M.A., librarian.
London, Tate Public Library, Lambeth, per Frank J. Burgoyne, librarian.
Manchester, John Rylands Library, per H. Guppy, *M.A.*, librarian.
Manchester Public Free Library, per Chas. W. Sutton, M.A., librarian.
Mardy Library and Reading Room, per D. V. Lewis, sec.
Edward P. Martin, *J.P.*, The Hill, Abergavenny.
James Matthews, librarian, 42, Harrow Road, Maindee, Newport, Mon.
T. Matthews, *B.A.*, Gwynfa, Fishguard, Pem.
Merthyr Tydfil, Town Hall Library.
Charles Morgan, *B.A.*, Pupil Teachers' School, Cardiff.
D. T. Morgan, Fairfield House, Merthyr.
Miss G. E. F. Morgan, Buckingham Place, Brecon.
Rhys Morgan, *M.A.*, Intermediate School, Pontypridd.
Lieut.-Col. W. Ll. Morgan, Bryn Briallu, Swansea.
Abram Morris, *F.R.Hist.S.*, Gwynfa, Gold Tops, Newport, Mon.
Lieut.-Col. D. Morris, Brynffin, Ammanford.
John Morris, *J.P.*, Lletty'r Eos, Llansannan, near Abergele.
R. Jones-Morris, *J.P.*, Ty Cerrig, Talsarnau, R.S.O., Merionethshire.
The Rev. Silas Morris, *M.A.*, *Principal*, Baptist College, Bangor.
T. E. Morris, *LL.M.*, *B.A.*, 8, Fig Tree Court, Temple, London, E.C.
J. J. Neale, Park Road, Penarth.
Newcastle-on-Tyne Public Library, per Basil Anderson, *B.A.* (*Lond.*), librarian.
Newport Free Library, per J. C. Brook, sec.
New Tredegar Workmen's Hall and Reading Room, per Isaac Jones, sec.
Nottingham Public Library, per J. Potter Briscoe, *F.R.S.L.*, librarian.
The late A. C. Humphreys-Owen, *M.P.*, Glansevern, Berriew, R.S.O., Mont.
The Rev. David Owen, Alltmawr, Builth.
David Owen, North and South Wales Bank, 138, London Road, Liverpool.

N

The Rev. David O'Brien-Owen, Calvinistic Methodist bookroom, Carnarvon (2 copies).
Evan Owen, *J.P.*, 30, Ruthin Gardens, Cardiff.
Henry Owen, *D.C.L. (Oxon), F.S.A.*, Poyston, Haverfordwest (2 copies).
Sir Isambard Owen, *M.A., M.D.*, Durham College of Science, Newcastle-upon-Tyne.
The Rev. O. G. Owen (" Alafon "), Ysgoldy, Cwmyglo, R.S.O., North Wales.
Owen Owen, Aelybryn, Pwllheli.
Owen Owen, 2, Uplands Crescent, Swansea.
The Rev. Canon R. Trevor Owen, *M.A., F.S.A.*, The Vicarage, Bodelwyddan, Rhuddlan, R.S.O.
W. J. Owen, Kimberley House, Bangor.
His Honour Judge Owen, Ty Gwyn, Abergavenny.
Oxford, Meyrick Library, Jesus College, per E. E. Gunner, *M.A.*, librarian.
Gwilym Parry, Chapel Place, Denbigh.
Morris Parry, 21, Victoria Road, Chester.
William Parry, Talybryn, Bwlch, R.S.O., Breconshire (3 copies).
Penmount Chapel Library, per John Williams, 4, Salem Terrace, Pwllheli.
The Rev. T. A. Penry, *Congregational minister*, The Manse, Aberystwyth.
Philadelphia Free Library, per John Thomson, librarian.
J. Allanson Picton, *M.A., J.P.*, Caerlŷr, Penmaenmawr.
Ellis Pierce (" Elis o'r Nant ") Dolyddelen.
H. T. Poland, 73, Crawford Street, Roxbury, Mass., U.S.A.
Prof. Thomas Powel, *M.A. (Oxon.)*, University College, Cardiff.
Ferdinando Hamlyn Price, Erbistock, Ruabon.
The Rev. James Price, 24, Wright Street, Greenhays, Manchester.
D. P. Pritchard, Crumlin Hall, near Newport, Mon.
D. Rhys Phillips, Public Library, Swansea.
L. J. Pritchard, Menai Lodge, Chiswick, W.
Walter Pritchard, 33, Friars' Road, Bangor.
The Rev. Owen Prys, *M.A., Principal*, Trevecca College.
Bernard Quaritch, 15, Piccadilly, London.
Queensland Public Library, per J. L. Woolcock, *B.A.*, hon. sec. to the trustees.
Lady Reade, Carreglwyd, Anglesey.
Alfred Rees, *L.R.C.P. (Lond.), M.R.C.S. (Eng.)*, 29, Cathedral Road, Cardiff.
Evan J. Rees, 46, N. Court Street, Memphis, Tenn., U.S.A.
Howell Rees, *J.P.*, 15, Richmond Road, Cardiff.
Li. S. Rees, *Lec. Divinity*, 1, Newton Street, Abercanaid (3 copies).
Rees Rees, *J.P.*, Ynyslwyd Cottage, Aberdare.
R. P. Rees, chemist, Dowlais.
Walter Rees, 3, Prince's Street, Cardiff.
Mrs William Rees, St. Paul, Minn., U.S.A.
William J. Rees, Emporia, Kansas, U.S.A.
H. R. Reichel, *M.A., LL.D., Principal*, University College, Bangor.
Llywarch Reynolds, *B.A.*, Old Church Place, Merthyr.
D. M. Richards, *M.J.I.*, Wenallt, Aberdare.
Edwin Richards, *J.P.*, Heathfield, Nantyderry.
Robert Rickards, *J.P.*, The Priory, Usk.
A. Rhys Roberts, solicitor, 63, Queen Victoria Street, London, E.C.
David Roberts, bookseller, Ffestiniog.
D. P. Roberts, 120, North End, Croydon, Surrey.
Edward Roberts, *H.M. Inspector of Schools*, Plas Maesmila, Carnarvon (2 copies).
The Rev. E. L. Roberts, Saltney Ferry, Chester.
The Very Rev. Griffith Roberts, *M.A., The Dean of Bangor*, The Deanery, Bangor.
John Roberts, *M.D.*, Chester.
Robert Roberts, 21, High Street, Sheffield.
T. F. Roberts, *M.A., LL.D., Principal*, University College of Wales, Aberystwyth.
W. Ll. Roberts, Penyceunant, Penybontfawr, Oswestry.
William Owen Roberts, Plasdulyn, Llanbedr-y-Cennin, Talycafn, North Wales.
Professor F. N. Robinson, Harvard University, Cambridge, Mass., U.S.A.
Sidney Robinson, *M.P.*, Fairwater Croft, near Cardiff.
Michael Rowed, 22, The Promenade, Swansea.
Charles Jenkins Ryland, Clifton House, Southerndown, Glam.
St. Andrew's University Library, per J. M. Anderson, librarian.
The Lord Bishop of St. Asaph (The Right Rev. A. G. Edwards, *D.D.*), The Palace, St. Asaph (2 copies).
Salford Free Library, per Ben H. Mullen, *M.A.*, curator.
David Salmon, *Principal*, Training College, Swansea.
E. W. Shackell, *J.P.*, 191, Newport Road, Cardiff.
The Rev. Thomas Shankland, librarian, University College, Bangor.
The Very Rev. J. Allan Smith, *M.A., The Dean of St David's*, The Deanery, St. David's.
H. Sotheran & Co., 140, The Strand, London, W.C. (2 copies).

John E. Southall, 5, Woodland Road, Newport, Mon.
Alan Stepney-Gulston, *J.P.*, *D.L.*, Derwydd, Llandebie, Carm.
B. F. Stevens & Brown, American Library and Literary Agency, 4, Trafalgar Square,
London, W.C. (2 copies).
Sunderland Public Library.
Swansea Public Library, per S. E. Thompson, librarian.
Thomas Teague, *J.P.*, 44, Greenway Road, Neath.
Abraham Thomas, *J.P.*, Llansamlet.
D. A. Thomas, *M.P.*, Llanwern, Newport.
D. Christmas Thomas, 2, Brecon Road, Merthyr.
The late D. Lewis Thomas, 15, Ninian Road, Cardiff.
D. Lleufer Thomas, *M.A.*, barrister-at-law, Swansea.
Dan Thomas, Wellington Street, Merthyr.
David Thomas, Secretary's Office, L. & N.W. Railway, Euston, London.
Alderman Edward Thomas, *J.P.*, 3, Windsor Place, Cardiff.
Prof. The Rev. E. Lorimer Thomas, *M.A.*, St. David's College, Lampeter.
Gomer Ll. Thomas, 5, Courtland Terrace, Merthyr.
Sir Griffith Thomas, 1, Gloucester Place, Swansea.
The Rev. J. Ll. Thomas, *M.A.*, The Vicarage, Aberpergwm, Glyn Neath.
J. Lyn Thomas, *C.B.*, *L.R.C.P. (Lond.)*, *F.R.C.S. (Eng.)*, Greenlawn, Penylan, Cardiff.
The Rev. John Thomas, *Congregational minister*, Merthyr.
John Thomas, Whitchurch Road, Cardiff.
John E. Thomas, 17, The Avenue, Treharris.
The late Miss L. M. Thomas, Blunsdon Abbey, Highworth, Wiltshire.
Morgan Thomas, 13, Court Ucha Terrace, Port Talbot.
Owen Thomas, plumber, Menai Bridge.
T. W. Thomas, *M.O.H.*, *M.R.C.S.*, etc., Bryn Derwen, Caerphilly.
Samuel Thomas, 5, The Green, Abertyswg, Cardiff.
T. H. Thomas, *R.C.A.*, 45, The Walk, Cardiff.
Thomas Thomas, Bryn Gafel, Trecynon, Aberdare (2 copies).
The Right Honourable Viscount Tredegar, Tredegar Park, Newport (2 copies).
Tredegar Workmen's Hall and Institute, per Geo. Hopkins, sec.
Treharris Workmen and Tradesmen's Library.
Colonel J. P.-Turberville, *J.P.*, *D.L.*, Ewenny Priory, Bridgend.
The Honourable Lord Henry Vane-Tempest, *M.V.O.*, Plas Machynlleth, North Wales.
Gwilym Vaughan, printer, Ammanford.
James Venmore, Parkside, Anfield Road, Liverpool.
Sir Edmund Verney, *Bart.*, Claydon House, Winslow, Bucks.
Thomas Wallace, *M.D.*, Howard Lodge, Newport Road, Cardiff.
Mathew Warlow, Warlow Street, Merthyr.
Mrs. J. J. Watkins, Greenhill, Crickhowell.
T. E. Watson, *J.P.*, St. Mary's Lodge, Newport, Mon.
Thomas Webster, 241, High Street, Bangor.
The Rev. H. J. Whitty, Emporia, Kansas, U.S.A.
C. Wilkins, *F.G.S.*, Springfield, Merthyr.
Aneurin Williams, Menai View, North Road, Carnarvon.
Alderman C. M. Williams, Pier Street, Aberystwyth.
The Rev. Canon Camber Williams, *M.A.*, The Parade, Carmarthen.
The Rev. D. D. Williams, Ivy House, Oswestry.
The late David Williams, 110, Brecknock Road, London, N.
David Thomas Williams, 8, Harford Square, Lampeter.
Evan Williams, Ystrad Caron, Tregaron.
G. J. Williams, *F.G.S.*, *H.M. Inspector of Mines*, Bangor.
Prof. The Rev. Hugh Williams, *M.A.*, Theological College, Bala.
Hugh Williams, Shop Goch, Pwllheli.
Hugh Williams, 2, Victoria Avenue, Upper Bangor.
The late J. Ignatius Williams, Plasynllan, Whitchurch, Cardiff.
The Rev. J. V. Williams, Llanrhyddlad, Valley, Anglesey.
Sir John Williams, *Bart.*, *K.C.V.O.*, Plâs Llanstephan, Carm.
The Rev. John Williams, *M.A.*, Llanwddyn Vicarage, Oswestry.
The Rev. John Williams, 179, Kingsley Road, Princes Road, Liverpool.
John H. Williams, *J.P.*, Devonshire Place, Aberavon.
Morgan S. Williams, *J.P.*, *D.L.*, St. Donat's Castle, Llantwit Major.
The Rev. R. Peris Williams, Bron Haul, Wrexham.
The late Richard Williams, *F.R.H.S.*, Celynog, Newtown.
The Rev. Robert Williams, *M.A.*, The Vicarage, Llandilo.
The Rev. T. Meredith Williams, *B.A.*, The Vicarage, Llanarth, Cardiganshire.
William Williams, Bryn Bugail, Mynytho, Pwllheli.
William J. Williams, *M.D.*, Grange Road, W. Middlesborough (2 copies).
W. Llewelyn Williams, *M.P.*, Lamb Building, Temple, E.C.